Grand Prix
Showdown!

How Lewis Hamilton joined the greats – the full drama
of every championship-deciding Grand Prix since 1950

Christopher Hilton

Haynes Publishing

© Christopher Hilton, 2009

First edition, titled *Grand Prix Showdown! The full drama of the races which decided the World Championship 1950-1992*, published in 1992 This second edition, reformatted, fully updated and re-titled *Grand Prix Showdown! How Lewis Hamilton joined the greats – the full drama of every championship-deciding Grand Prix since 1950*, published in June 2009

A catalogue record for this book is available from the British Library

ISBN 978 1 84425 709 6

Library of Congress catalog card no 2009923197

All photographs courtesy LAT

Published by Haynes Publishing,
Sparkford, Yeovil, Somerset BA22 7JJ, UK
Tel: 01963 442030 Fax: 01963 440001
Int.tel: +44 1963 442030 Int.fax: +44 1963 440001
E-mail: sales@haynes.co.uk
Website: www.haynes.co.uk

Haynes North America Inc.,
861 Lawrence Drive, Newbury Park, California 91320, USA

Designed and typeset by Dominic Stickland
Printed and bound in the UK

CONTENTS

PREFACE

As the clocks moved towards 4.45 and the folds of cloud suddenly darkened over Interlagos, a lone red Ferrari crossed the line to begin the final lap of the 2008 Brazilian Grand Prix. The man driving it, Felipe Massa, came from Sao Paulo and was slightly under a minute and a half from becoming World Champion. He carried with him the 100,000 people at Interlagos – Sao Paulo's circuit – and a whole country of 160 million beyond.

Exactly 14.9 seconds later a white, yellow and orange Renault crossed the line. The man driving it, Fernando Alonso, had been World Champion twice and knew all about last laps but, this late November afternoon, he wasn't a player. That he was running second didn't matter because it hadn't been his season.

Rain fell more heavily from the darkened cloud.

Exactly 0.7 of a second after Alonso, the other Ferrari crossed the line. The man driving it, Kimi Räikkönen, was defending champion but he, too, wasn't a player. That he was running third didn't matter because it hadn't been his season, either.

Exactly 11.7 seconds after that, a red and white Toyota crossed the line. The man driving it, Timo Glock, was in the process of establishing himself in Formula 1. The three cars in front – and the two behind – were all on intermediate tyres for wet weather but he'd risked dries and they were working well enough to take him safely towards fourth place. No other cars threatened him. That he was running fourth did matter because the points would consolidate his position in mid-table, something important for his career.

Exactly 12.4 seconds after that, a blue and red Toro Rosso crossed the line. The man driving it, Sebastian Vettel, had already won the

Italian Grand Prix – the youngest to achieve such a thing – and was establishing a career at racing speed. That he was running fifth did matter because the points would consolidate his position in the top half of the table, something very important for his career.

He'd moved into the fifth place four laps before. The move, overtaking Lewis Hamilton, was ordinary and orthodox in its execution, the kind racers do all the time. It was in no sense ordinary in its consequences. Hamilton needed fifth to be champion even if Massa won the race. When Vettel sailed by, all unknowing he made Massa champion – if it stayed like that.

Exactly 0.8 of a second after Vettel crossed the line Hamilton followed him in his silver and red McLaren, but it looked as if it would stay like that: Massa masterful and with a protective gap, Alonso and Räikkönen just running to the end, Glock with his own protective gap to Vettel, Hamilton unable to find the speed to challenge Vettel.

Hamilton had been building a big career for most of his 23 years: karting at eight, telling Ron Dennis, the man running McLaren, that he wanted to drive for him at ten, winning junior formulae and, in 2007, creating the most accomplished debut season in a McLaren that the World Championship had known. But now, with only 2.6 miles to go and the rain falling harder, he was in the wrong place at the wrong time. From the beginning in 1950, championship-deciding races had always been potentially brutal for those yet to win. You might never get the chance again and down the years many hadn't.

Vettel and Hamilton moved in tandem through the first contorting corner, the Senna S. The track curved left and as they accelerated up past 150 miles an hour the on-board camera captured Hamilton's gloved hand adjusting the steering wheel as if the McLaren had become a thoroughbred horse straining to break free.

The 2.6 miles were divided into three timing sectors which revealed, to three decimal points, how long each car took to cover them and, because you could look at the previous lap for direct comparison, whether a car was going faster or slower.

Glock ran along the straight towards the left-handed Descida do Lago at the end of the back straight, and, just before he reached it, completed the first sector. The previous lap he'd done it in 20.1 seconds, now he'd done 24.8 – not just 4.7 slower but so slow it might even open the championship.

Vettel did 21.8, which was 0.5 of a second slower than before.

Hamilton did 21.6, which was 0.3 of a second slower than before.

The rain, of course, would explain that, just as it would explain what was happening to Glock.

Vettel and Hamilton braked from 190 miles an hour for Descida do Lago and Hamilton's hands were adjusting again, making deft and intuitive corrections. Vettel already seemed in the middle distance, still uncatchable and taking the championship away from Hamilton with him. They rounded the long, looping right known only as Turn 7 holding 200 miles an hour to the tightening right-hander, Laranja. After a spoon curve they were at Turn 10, another right-hander, hauling their speeds down to 50 miles an hour. They could see moving shapes in the semi-darkness up ahead, clearly a couple of back-markers.

The entry to Turn 10 proved deceptive. Hamilton's McLaren suddenly twitched but Vettel got the angle so wrong that he had both wheels on the kerbing. Hamilton's wasn't close enough to exploit that and they began the long climb for home. A graceful left-hander curve, Mergulho, would bring them to the second timing point.

The previous lap Glock had done 46.0 seconds, now he'd done 54.7 – not just 8.7 seconds slower but, adding the 4.7 from the first sector, the whole of his lead over Vettel and Hamilton had perished. In this rain Glock was struggling simply to keep the Toyota on the track. The dry tyres found the wet surface like sheet ice.

Vettel did 45.1, which was the same as the lap before.

Hamilton did 45.2, which was 0.3 of a second faster.

They travelled towards Junção, a sharp left and almost the shape of a V, which was down an undulation. Suddenly four cars were together: the two back-markers, Vettel, Hamilton. The first of them was Robert Kubica in a BMW, lapped and minding his own business. The second of them was a red and white car hugging the kerbing on the outside – and not a back-marker at all...

It was Glock.

Vettel was already abreast, Hamilton directly behind. He nosed the

McLaren out and followed Vettel through. The moves were ordinary and orthodox in their execution, the kind racers do all the time. The consequences were historic. The track resembled a crooked elbow on the climb towards the finish, and Vettel and Hamilton went through that as comfortably as they had done the seventy laps before. They flowed round the long curve to the final straight which dipped then rose to the line. The computers on their exactness had recorded it all.

MAS

13.2 seconds later
ALO

16.2 seconds later
RAI

38.0 seconds later
VET

38.9 seconds later
HAM

Formula 1 had its youngest and only mixed race champion. It was, and will always be, an extraordinary moment.

The Ferrari pit miscounted it and were into devilish dances of delight while Massa's father Luiz Antonio's face swelled into volcanic happiness. Then, as the computers spoke so silently, they all fell into a cavern of silence.

The McLaren pit didn't miscount it and, released from all their agonies, the Hamilton clan – father, brother and girlfriend prominent – were suddenly doing their own devilish dances, bringing them out into the pit lane. If they weren't on the way up to the folds of cloud which had threatened so much and brought so much, they certainly seemed poised to levitate.

Before the race there'd been racist noises from Spain (a product of Hamilton's previous season with Alonso, a Spanish hero, of course), a strange episode when he was presented with a black cat and the jeers of the 100,000 Massa-lovers at Interlagos. In one hour 34 minutes and 50.3 seconds Hamilton had scattered the racists, the cat lovers and the cat callers.

He was tremendously English about it, polite and understated, which only added to the destruction.

He was not alone in the quietness. Jimmy Clark from the Scottish Borders had been like that, and Black Jack Brabham from Hurstville, Sydney, who, in the only other finish to really rival what Hamilton had just done, got out, pushed his car to the finishing line in Florida in 1959 and collapsed. There'd been Juan Manuel Fangio from Balcarce, Argentina, who, like Hamilton, proved that gentlemen are born, not made. There'd been Phil Hill, the quiet Californian, who had seen great tragedy with his own eyes and never lost his perspective. There'd been Jackie Stewart – now happily Sir Jackie – from the heart of Scotland who won three championships and barely ever raised his voice. There'd been Niki Lauda from Vienna, who was amused by the notion that he was genuinely superhuman, and made major speeches lasting two or three sentences, nothing omitted. There'd been Mario Andretti, the other quiet American. There'd been Alain Prost from an anonymous little town in the middle of France, four times champion, who disliked fuss. There'd been Mika Häkkinen from Finland who whispered when he spoke and won two championships by incisive driving, a wry smile and a waspish sense of humour. There'd been Emerson Fittipaldi from this same Sao Paulo who'd behave with dignity, nearly die in a plane crash and find God.

You could have put all these champions on a grid and it would have been a highly competitive but gentlemanly place. The others would have seen something of Lewis Hamilton in themselves and he'd have seen something of himself in them.

You could have populated a third grid with quite different champions: Mike Hawthorn from Farnham, who drove in a bow tie, liked a glass of beer and liked pretty girls even more. You could add James Hunt from genteel Surrey, who other people made into an English caricature but who always remained true to himself and won his championship in circumstances just like Hamilton – stormy weather, positions lost and gained, nobody sure of anything but a lot of high-octane swearing. There'd be Alan Jones from Melbourne who could handle himself and Graham Hill from London who could dance on tables and scale hotel pillars as recreation while he was winning two championships. This grid would have been noisier, edgier, a little bit more macho and by nature Hamilton would have been a stranger to it.

You could have populated a third grid with champions who somehow didn't fit the first two. There'd been Damon Hill, son of Graham, serious, intense and working it all out in his own way without dancing on tables. There'd beeen trenchant John Surtees from London who won championships on bikes and in a Ferrari and defied Enzo, Nelson Piquet from Rio who liked boats and the Mediterranean, Keke Rosberg from Finland who let the world know exactly what he thought, Jacques Villeneuve from Quebec, technologically literate who was always the son of Gilles and always, like Damon, himself too. There'd been Jody Scheckter from East London, South Africa, who won his championship and then taught the American military and police when to shoot and when not to shoot before farming in England. There'd been Denny Hulme from the South Island of New Zealand, who won his championship and found himself in a bullring as a prize. He felt sorry for the bulls, as you will see. There'd been Michael Schumacher, who ought to have been with the quiet table but somehow created too much sound and fury over too many championships for that. Hamilton would have been a stranger here, too.

Only five champions would populate the last grid: Giuseppe Farina from Turin, the first of all of them, wreathed in the mists of time and lost in them too, but with a reputation in an era of gentlemen on the track for being much less than a gentleman. There'd been Alberto Ascari from Milan, Farina's contemporary and a man tormented by terrible superstitions as his father had been. There'd been Jochen Rindt from the pleasant Austrian town of Graz, mysterious because in the mood he was arguably the fastest driver who ever lived and remains the only posthumous champion. There'd been Nigel Mansell from the British Midlands, who fought a strange career-long war of self-justification and at the same time raced as hard as any champion had ever done. There'd been Ayrton Senna from Sao Paulo, who didn't need a plane crash to find God and who was a hero to Lewis Hamilton. This grid would have shadows reaching across it and, although in one sense Hamilton had joined his hero, in another he was a stranger to these people, too.

However richly talented, there was nothing mysterious and nothing inexplicable about him.

He had done more than join the extraordinary human dynasty of World Champions, stretching across six decades, who season-by-season contested sport's most glamorous, exhausting and dangerous title. In the three seconds it took Hamilton to overtake Glock you could argue that he changed the global perception of Grand Prix racing. He could cross all frontiers, especially the ones which hadn't been crossed before, and take Grand Prix racing there with him.

Perpetual motion is the key. A championship win is immortal because nothing can take it from you but it is already in the past as you cross the line. Some drivers find that harder to accept than others, but all have to. It's not just that by definition motor racing travels fast. It continues.

Hamilton seems to have found that easy and natural to accept. In mid-January, only ten weeks further on, the 2009 car is being launched at McLaren's headquarters near Woking in Surrey. Once upon a time, when it was down the road, you'd have called it a factory. This is a vast emporium curving round an artificial lake, a place of glass and broad spaces like a piece of futuristic Swedish furniture enlarged to make a building.

It takes your breath away.

It does something else, too: all this glass is a mirror to what Grand Prix racing has become and, quite unconsciously, it charts that, because when Farina won the first championship at Monza in 1950 everything about it was small, rudimentary, almost crude – including Monza itself. It had a lot of oily rags and no artificial lakes.

Now Hamilton and his team-mate Heikki Kovalainen unveil the car in what has become, for Formula 1 teams, careful choreography – literally an unveiling, a cloak drawn back to show the car underneath

15

– and then Hamilton sits on a stool and answers questions. He is extremely accomplished at this.

Do you think about the past, like the last lap last year?

'You remember the chequered flag, then you try to move on. I have not really thought about the last year. I have not really thought about last season. I have put it behind me.'

And: 'I am World Champion and it's a great feeling but I will try to enjoy my life.'

And: 'When I went to America, no-one noticed me.'

And: 'I want to make fewer mistakes, avoid any mistakes.'

Here is a very modern man and this is how he crosses the frontiers on a very modern stage: a milestone in how Grand Prix racing grew, from Farina and the sheds to the emporium.

Hamilton was the thirtieth champion. This is the story of all of them, and each of their championships.

The book originally appeared in 1992, so sixteen races and seven champions have been added, embracing principally Michael Schumacher's extraordinary sequence as well as Hamilton's extraordinary arrival. I have taken the opportunity to update the original text and where necessary rework it.

In reconstructing the races (and I include the first edition as well as this one) I'm indebted to Sir Frank Williams, Ann Bradshaw, the late Teddy Mayer, Sir Jack Brabham, Stirling Moss, Jacky Ickx, John Watson, Bette Hill, Keke Rosberg, Sir Jackie Stewart, Jody Scheckter, John Surtees, Niki Lauda, Guy Edwards, Peter Windsor, Barry Griffin of Goodyear, Nigel Roebuck, Berdie Martin, Denny Hulme, Ron Dennis, the McLaren PR team of Matt Bishop, Steve Cooper, Beatrice Giusti; Mike Wilson. Phil Hill was kind enough to relive his championship race. He died in August 2008 and I have amended the chapter accordingly without, I hope, disturbing the essence of it.

I have trawled far and wide in the re-creation. I've drawn invaluable background from the magazines *Autocar*, *Motor Sport* and in particular *Autosport*. For permission to use extracts from the latter I'm deeply grateful to Simon Taylor, then Managing Director.

I've quoted from the following and I'm indebted to the publishers for permission: *Life In The Fast Lane* by Alain Prost, *Driving Ambition* by Alan Jones and Keith Botsford, *Keke* by Keke Rosberg and Keith Botsford, *To Hell And Back* by Niki Lauda, all published by Stanley Paul. *Life at the Limit* by Graham Hill, *All but my Life* by Stirling Moss, *Faster!* by Jackie Stewart and Peter Manso, *Jochen Rindt* by Heinz Pruller, *When the Flag Drops* by Sir Jack Brabham, *A Turn at the Wheel* by Stirling Moss, *Flying on the Ground* by Emerson Fittipaldi and Elizabeth Hayward, *Champion Year* and *Challenge me the Race* by Mike Hawthorn, all published by William Kimber but permission courtesy of Thorsons except the latter title courtesy of Harper Collins. *Against All Odds* by James Hunt and Eoin Young, *Mario Andretti World Champion* by Mario Andretti and Nigel Roebuck, both published by Paul Hamlyn. *Fangio: My Racing Life* by Juan Manuel Fangio and Roberto Carozzo, *Colin Chapman: The Man and his Cars* by Gerard 'Jabby' Crombac, *My Cars, My Career* by Stirling Moss and Doug Nye, all published by Patrick Stephens. *Jody: An Autobiography by Jody Scheckter*, published by Haynes. *Juan Manuel Fangio* by Gunther Molter, published by G. T. Foulis, *At The Wheel* by Jim Clark, published by Arthur Barker, *My Twenty Four Years of Racing* by Juan Manuel Fangio, published by Temple.

I've consulted *Graham* by Graham Hill and Neil Ewart, *Driven to Win* by Nigel Mansell and Derick Allsop (Stanley Paul), *Jim Clark: The Legend Lives On* by Graham Gauld and *Grand Prix Greats* by Nigel Roebuck (Patrick Stephens), *Grand Prix British Winners* by Maurice Hamilton (Guinness Publishing), *1988: Dans La Roue d'Alain Prost* by Johnny Rives (Calmann-Levy), *The Viking Drivers* by Fredrik Petersens (William Kimber), *The World Champions* by Anthony Pritchard (Leslie Frewin); *Jackie Stewart World Champion* by Jackie Stewart and Eric Dymock (Pelham Books). Kevin Desmond did a great deal of original research in his story of Alberto Ascari, *The Man with Two Shadows* (Proteus), and I have used it extensively, particularly the haunting statistics.

For reference I've leant heavily on *Marlboro's Grand Prix Guide*, the compendious four-volume set *Grand Prix!* by Mike Lang (G. T. Foulis), *Autocourse* (Hazleton, now CMG Publishing) and *History of the Grand Prix Car* by Doug Nye (Hazleton). Longines' timing service has been invaluable, while at the other extreme the Marlboro video collection (by

Quadrant) of seasonal highlights in the 1970s was vital in recapturing the moments. I pay particular tribute to the weekly *Autosport* magazine for its depth of coverage, while *Motor Sport* and *Autocar* were extremely useful in their coverage of the Showdown races.

The lines from *As Time Goes By* from the film *Casablanca* are reproduced with kind permission of Redwood Music Limited.

Formula One Management Ltd, and Dave Gillett, were swift and courteous in giving permission to use the FIA statistics for the Brazilian Grand Prix in 2008, enabling a much fuller reconstruction of Hamilton's triumph than would have been possible otherwise.

Incidentally the Indianapolis 500-mile race counted towards the World Championship from 1950 to 1960 in an attempt to make the Championship that of the world. Since virtually no Indy driver drove in any Grand Prix and vice versa the union had no meaning at all (except to clutter the record books with irrelevancies). I have decided in principle to ignore it. The Indy, wonderful as it may be, exercised no direct bearing on our championship. The United States Grand Prix, however, was first run in 1959 and paradoxically would exercise a very direct bearing on the championship, by deciding it...

1950

FARINA THE FIRST

Italian Grand Prix, Monza

The start was almost noiseless and that stands as a wonderful contradiction. In 1949 an Italian, Count Antonio Brivio, proposed to the General Assembly of the Fédération Internationale de l'Automobile that rather than having separate, self-contained Grand Prix races there should be a proper World Championship of which each Grand Prix was an integral part. The proposal was adopted.

World Championships were rare then. Of the major global sports, boxers had always competed for them and soccer's began in 1930. Interestingly, perhaps, motor bike racing launched its in 1949. The rest – tennis, golf, cricket, athletics, Rugby Union, ski racing – were grouped around their most notable individual events.

It was the way the world was and across living memory the way the world had always been, delightfully but literally amateurish. Wimbledon did not admit professionals and prize money until 1968. Athletics and Rugby wrestled with the concept of a World Championship into the 1980s. Rugby had no World Cup until 1989, and cricket's only started in 1975. By then a rich and full dynasty of Grand Prix World Champions spanned three complete generations.

The real moment was 2.30 on the warm and sunny afternoon of 13 May 1950, when in the presence of King George VI and Queen Elizabeth, 21 cars set off round Silverstone to contest the British Grand Prix – enhanced by the further title of Grand Prix de l'Europe – in the first of seven races to produce the first champion. Silverstone was won by an Italian doctor of political economy, Giuseppe Farina, driving an Italian car, an Alfa Romeo. As the car moved between the straw bales which marked out Silverstone's corners, Farina looking severe of countenance, nearly disdainful and yet somehow serene. No non-Italian car would win a race until 1954.

Alfa Romeo's 8-cylinder engine produced 350bhp and in style the car was true to its era, a stub nose, a long, straight rod-like body with a curve up to the cockpit, no roll-bar, no crash helmet for the driver who sat upright and peered through goggles over the tiny windshield. Three men drove this car; Farina, Juan Manuel Fangio from the ordinary, unremarkable town of Balcarce in the province of Buenos Aires, who was in Europe for only his second season, and a very experienced driver, Luigi Fagioli, who many people thought had actually retired.

After Silverstone, Fangio, a man with a priestly face full of inner strength, took Monaco, Farina took the Swiss at Bremgarten, Fangio took the Belgian at Spa and the French at Rhiems on 2 July. Italy at Monza, the last of the seven, was 3 September. The championship had poised itself perfectly, as it would so many times later, by arranging itself around arithmetic. A driver received eight points for a win then six, four, three, two down to fifth (the single point for sixth was not added for a decade, the nine points for a win not increased until 1961). Drivers did, however, get a point for fastest lap. The best four results counted out of the seven rounds. Fangio had 26 points and only three finishes, Farina 22 from three, Fagioli 24 but from four and all second places. Only victory and fastest lap could help him.

Alfa were supreme in a way it is hard to envisage now, but a middle-aged man working out of an ordinary, unremarkable town in the province of Romagna, Italy, had ideas about that. The town was Maranello, the man Enzo Ferrari. Five drivers competed in his cars in 1950, including a British privateer Peter Whitehead. Of the five, one was touched with an ability so rare and so combative that the full extent of it remains impossible to quantify. He was the son of a famous racer and none doubted that racing coursed through his blood. He was called Alberto Ascari and he was the only driver who might arguably take the fight to the Alfas. He knew Monza intimately.

On the morning of 3 September, Dr. Farina and his wife Else went to church in Monza to attend a special mass. It was an arbour of calm, a chance to seek strength, a place to compose himself for the afternoon. Of Farina, British author Anthony Pritchard wrote in The World Champions:

Very little of what Farina felt about racing ever became known, there was no explanation for his harsh, forceful driving that sometimes bordered on ruthlessness or for his moods that on occasion resulted in him giving up the race in the middle of a chase and made life so difficult for his team-manager.

Farina drove for Alfa Romeo immediately after the war, but left in 1946 when he thought that as number one driver he should have been allowed to win a race and wasn't. He had married late and his wife, who owned a famous fashion house, was as refined and elegant as he. In 1949, driving a Mascrati at Monza, Farina retired in disgust because his car couldn't catch the two in front of him. They were Ferraris. What might such a man do?

While Farina and Else prayed, 100,000 people were moving towards the town of Monza, a comfortable train ride from Milan, and the circuit set in pleasant royal parkland which spread round its fringe.

The temperature for the race had been heated weeks before during a non-championship race at Bari in the south of the country. Ferrari hadn't gone and Farina and Fangio were, in Fangio's words, the big favourites in the Alfas. They had an easy race taking and re-taking the lead until the second last lap. 'At that moment I had the annoying surprise of finding my tank running dry while Farina had enough petrol to continue. I had to stop at the pits, my engine coughing. I re-started and came in second. I was furious. It had been negligence on the part of the Alfa Romeo team when I stopped for refuelling on the twenty-eighth lap. I would rather not look for any other explanation of that little episode. I prefer to think that in the hurry of refuelling somebody thought my tank was full when it was only three-quarters or less.'

After the race Fangio examined his car and said to someone standing nearby, 'No, there is no leak in the tank' as if to pre-empt any suggestion that that was the explanation. Whatever, Alfa Romeo was Italian, Farina was Italian, Monza was the heartland of Italy and all of it a long, long way from Balcarce.

The Italian newspapers heated the temperature by stirring some rampant chauvinism of their own. They conceded that Fangio began as favourite but insisted it was 'morally just' for an Italian in an Italian team to have it instead. Nor had Fangio's peace of mind been improved by several mechanical failures in other races before Bari. He cursed them and tried to understand them but couldn't. He'd ask one mechanic, who would say it was trouble with the carburettor, ask another who would say the opposite.

Ferrari lurked. They had an inspired designer, Aurelio Lampredi, and he became convinced that an unsupercharged car was the future. It had teething troubles but ran strongly at a race at Geneva on 30 July, Ascari immediately taking the lead from Fangio before it broke down. Lampredi persisted. For Monza he had two new cars developing 330bhp at 7,000 revs and because they were unsupercharged they would need a single pit stop. The Alfas, drinking fuel down their thirsty throats – they were getting 2mpg and the Italian Grand Prix stretched across 80 laps and 312 miles (502km) – would need a couple of pit stops. Each might last more than half a minute. Alfa had squeezed 20bhp more from their engine.

Ferrari tested some days before and Ascari produced a time of 1m 59.0s. That became Alfa's target and they spent the two days of qualifying trying to beat it. Fangio did that, 1m 58.6s, to take pole position with Ascari, 1m 58.8s alongside him, then Farina, then another Alfa driver, Consalvo Sanesi.

And now it is the Sunday, now Farina is emerging from church, this man with a sombre, dignified face, this man who came from a wealthy family and who had begun competing as long ago as 1927 in a hill-climb when he broke his shoulder. Of him Enzo Ferrari would say, 'he was a great driver but I could never help feeling apprehensive about him, especially at the start of a race and one or two laps from the end. At the start he was not unlike a highly strung thoroughbred, liable to break through the starting tape in its eagerness. Nearing the finish he was capable of committing the most astonishing follies although it must be admitted in all justice that he risked only his own safety and never jeopardized that of others. As a consequence he was a regular inmate of hospital wards.'

What might such a man do? It was as simple for him as it was for Fagioli. He had to win the race. Fangio could afford to be second.

The afternoon was hot, almost sultry and when the crowd saw Farina they chanted, 'Viva Nino, Viva Nino!' Others bayed back, 'Viva Fangio!' In a crude radio box a commentator prepared to relay the race live to Argentina where already the newspapers had done some heating of their own by insisting that Fangio was 'the only possible champion'. They would be keeping an eye on any mechanical failure which affected Fangio but not Farina.

The basic configuration of Monza was as it remains and so were the echoing names of the corners: Curva Grande at the end of the straight, Curva di Lesmo before the run down to Curva del Vialone but the Parabolica, that magnificent horseshoe bringing the cars back to the straight was then a sharp right, a mini-straight and another sharp right. Its name, the Curva di Vedano, has melted into history. The savage and deeply dangerous bowls of concrete banking were not to be built for another five years and would be abandoned on police advice in 1962. Monza presented itself as rudimentary, as a track of the time. A low, open grandstand faced the grid and tapered away to one side, so many people in it they seemed to overhang the track.

The Italian Minister of Labour raised the flag and the engines from 27 cars rose and rose, burying the chants which echoed on. 'Viva Nino!' 'Viva Fangio!' The flag was lowered.

As the cars moved from the grid Lampredi, suddenly overwhelmed by a nightmarish vision of everything that could go wrong with his Ferraris, fainted in the pits. The three Alfas outpowered Ascari. Farina seized the lead from Fangio and Sanesi, but Ascari was combative. He was as Italian as Farina and many in that crowd worshipped him as they had worshipped his father. He overtook Sanesi, he overtook Fangio and as they crossed the line to complete the first lap he was attacking Farina. If he could get through, if he could hold the lead to the end, Fangio would be World Champion. Not that Ascari troubled himself about that. The championship had been far beyond his reach all season but he fully intended to win the race.

A question was born: Is Fangio biding his time, waiting, watching, pacing himself? The repertoire of a great driver contains many weapons and there are situations where patience can be the most powerful. He set fastest lap on lap 7 with exactly two minutes, safely locked up the single point for that, and then he played ... patience. Soft sunlight fell towards the track fashioning a carpet of shadows from the trees at its rim.

Through 13 laps Ascari attacked and Farina resisted. On lap 14 Ascari seemed momentarily and mysteriously in trouble because he was slow. We will never know why. He refound full speed and took Farina to a great roar. That done he taunted Farina, tried to coax Farina either to lose his temper – a shrewd tactic given Farina's temperament – or go so fast he blew his engine up. Farina did neither and retook Ascari to another great roar. Sanesi, meanwhile, had blown up.

Fangio ran comfortably third.

On lap 22 Ascari stopped out on the circuit, a problem with the back axle. As he walked towards the pits the crowd chanted his name. Alberto ought to have won, Alberto would have won. He'd been so close to Farina that another place, another time the length of that second pit stop by Farina would have left Alberto alone and too far in the lead. At the end of the same lap Fangio peeled off into the pits. A problem? A catastrophe? No. Mechanics pushed a jack under the rear of the car, raised it, and hammered the hubnuts off to change the rear wheels. During this flurry of movement the mechanics filled the tank. Fangio emerged to hunt Farina.

The hunt lasted across laps 23 and 24 and ended with almost shocking suddenness. Fangio's gearbox seized.

The car let me down in an inexplicable way. I could have wept with rage. The title of World Champion slipped through my fingers for no reason except bad luck.

Fangio knew that his disappointment was 'obvious, visible' and the team's management could not miss it or its possible implications. They made an immediate decision.

At this moment the mechanics were pushing Fangio's car into the park behind the pits. Piero Taruffi, a 46-year-old Italian making his Grand Prix debut, brought his Alfa in imagining he was making a routine stop for tyres and fuel. The management spoke quietly to him. He understood. He climbed out of the car and offered it to Fangio. The chivalry and generosity of this remained with Fangio ever after. He 'leapt into the cockpit once the mechanics had overhauled and refuelled it in great haste'. The hunt was on again. He was not alone.

Ascari had taken over the Ferrari of Dorino Serafini, an Italian driving his first and only Grand Prix. Ascari lay fully two minutes behind Farina but he was not a man to be deterred by anything so trivial as that, especially since Farina had to make his second fuel stop. Everything changed on lap 35. Fangio's engine dropped a valve and 'fate had spoken'. It is true that after the Alfas made their second pit stops Ascari moved up to second place, true that Farina could not be caught and won by 1m 18.6s, as big a margin then as it is now.

Fangio departed for Argentina feeling 'rather bitter. Some observers, in whispers, called attention to those repeated, too regular breakdowns saying they happened too often to be mere chance. I refused to listen to such guesswork. I understood only too well the joy of the Italian sports crowd and Italian newspapers about Farina, the first holder of the new title, World Champion. If I had paid attention to the rumours I would have felt as though I had marred my stablemate's victory. If a driver could no longer trust the firm for which he races that would be the end.'

Marcello Giambertone, Fangio's manager and friend, said:

As usual I was near the pits that day. I saw Fangio's eyes when he had to stop the first time. I saw them light up when he was given Taruffi's car. When he took off in it the mechanics who pushed the Alfa seemed very moved. Then Fangio stopped the second time and it was clear he could not fight against fate any longer. I heard some hard if ignorant remarks on what had happened. Some Fangio fans squarely said that public opinion had wanted an Italian winner so badly that first Fangio's and then Taruffi's cars were victims of sabotage. I refused to believe it and still refuse to credit such nonsense. The sabotage of Fangio would have sabotaged Alfa Romeo. If Farina had been put out of that race Fangio could still have brought Alfa Romeo the world title.

The historian is engaged in active combat against time itself. Too many are gone now who might have explained it, relived it – Farina, Fagioli, Fangio himself. The historian must face many silences, although those whispers find an equivalent which spans the years. Today drivers protest about not getting 'equal treatment' with their team-mate. Was it born at Monza on that September day?

The 1950s were more courteous than today and we see them wreathed in an aura of innocence and sportsmanship. In a very real sense they may not have been because human nature has surely not changed since 1950. And the whispers had begun. A World Championship inherently fashioned its own pressures, its own values and would in time become a valuable commodity in any currency on earth. Perhaps the tone had been set. Perhaps the first Showdown was the most important of all because it sired a lot of strange siblings – but it was the sire, they in its image.

1951

FANGIO'S FIRST BY AN INCH

Spanish Grand Prix, Barcelona

The calvalcade of 300,000 began coming at dawn that warm October Sunday, blocking every road. They'd travelled from all over Europe and as the sun rose over Barcelona they converged on the 3.9 mile (6.3km) circuit with its long, long straight named Avenida del Generalisimo Franco. Already Spaniards were taking their seats in temporary steel grandstands along this straight, settling for the wait. The flag would fall at 11 o'clock.

By perhaps 9.0, while dusky soldiers guarded the pits and mounted police moved by as a mobile deterrent to anyone and anything, the crowd continued to grow towards the 300,000. Men in uniform were not remarkable in Franco's fiefdom but crowds of this size were, and the fiefdom was based on absolute discipline. Spain knew all about anarchy. *Autosport's* reporter wrote:

Officials and police kept pushing people around trying to make some elbow-room in the paddock. The Press stand was filled to capacity and rarely have so many photographers attended a motor racing event. They clung to every conceivable part of the structure making it impossible for reporters to see anything of the circuit at all.

I decided the best view would be from the pits and persuaded Dave Francis and his Mintex men to allow us to squat in front of their temporary home. Alan Collinson of Ferodo also offered a view but his pit was not quite so well placed. No sooner had we arranged our lap charts and stop watches than an officious character in a Trilby hat told us in Spanish, French and atrocious English to get the heck out of it. No amount of argument prevailed and in the end Trilby hat brought along a great big policeman with a great big baton to support him. Needless to say Trilby hat won.

Two manufacturers dominated the season. Ferrari fielded four drivers led by the mystic and mystical Ascari, Alfa Romeo fielded five led by Fangio. The points were awarded as in 1950 and, headed towards Barcelona, it had come to the arithmetic again: Fangio with 27 points but he'd have to drop his five from France if he was second or won, Ascari with 25 but he'd have to drop his three from France if he came third, second or won. It was the perfect balance. Whoever won the race won the championship.

And still the cavalcade came, most on foot to search out a vantage point. By perhaps 10 o'clock they stood ten deep. Around large tracts of the circuit nothing lay between them and the cars but low cloth advertisement pennants.

The circuit was called Pedralbes. It had a hint of palm trees and ornate lamp-posts standing like sentries down the Avenida Franco. On some of the corners, vast straw bales had been stacked into waist-high walls. At one place the cars passed a plain back-garden fence and the crowd positioned themselves beside it, on the rim of the track close enough to touch the cars. A couple of policemen stood among them, watching too.

Qualifying spiced anticipation. Ascari and Fangio both beat the circuit record. The front row – four wide from left to right, slowest on the left – was Farina (Alfa Romeo), Froilan Gonzalez, a 30-year-old Argentinian (Ferrari), Fangio (Alfa Romeo), Ascari (Ferrari). Ascari's pole position conferred no immediate advantage because the first corner was all the way down at the other end of the Avenida.

Of Ascari, Fangio would write:

I deeply admired the graceful, pleasant style of Alberto's driving. He was a real champion and merited the title for his class, worthy in every way of his father Antonio. I felt it was a great honour to have him as a rival. Added to that was the technical superiority of the Ferraris in the last races. In such circumstances I was not sure of having much chance.

Something of deep significance happened quietly. Ferrari decided to use a smaller Pirelli tyre, 16 inches instead of 17. Ferrari's weakness was its rear axle layout, the circuit of Pedralbes was bumpy and smaller tyres might take some of the strain from the back of the car.

The Spanish Grand Prix could not be simply a race about one man against another. The context enlarged itself, the pride of Ferrari against the pride of Alfa Romeo. The two drivers stirred partisan emotions for different reasons, Ascari linked to the crowd because he was as Latin as they, Fangio who came to them from their own colonial history speaking the same language.

Lampredi fully understood the risk of the smaller tyres and his face was drawn. Gioacchino Colombo of Alfa Romeo appeared serene. His cars had covered several thousand kilometres in testing during the two weeks before the race and now they had modified superchargers to give more power.

Fangio would write:

You may imagine my state of mind as we lined up for the start. As in 1950 I might lose the title at the very last minute. In qualifying the Ferraris had given dazzling performances and Ascari was as dangerous as ever.

A cannon fired to signal five minutes. Farina was drinking water from a bottle over towards the pits and sprinted towards his Alfa Romeo. Nineteen cars formed the grid and they faced 70 laps (274.7 miles/442.0km). The red and yellow flag of Spain was hoisted, hovered, descended. The 19 set off along the Avenida, so broad that the cars were already spread out. Ascari thrust his Ferrari fractionally ahead of Gonzalez, Farina and Fangio following. The mechanics ran from the grid towards the pits dragging the starter trolleys. Lampredi and Colombo watched intently until the cars were out of sight and then they listened to the howl of their engines.

The cars swung right at the end of the Avenida on to the Carretera de Cornella a Fogas de Tordera, a straight road with a left kink leading to the hairpin which fed them on to the short Avenida de la Victoria, they braked for the left-hander on to the Paseo de Manuel Girona, went through the twin right-handers to the straight again. In its totality Pedralbes made a diagonal. On the straight the leaders reached 160mph (257kmh) and as they crossed the line Ascari led – just – from Farina, Fangio third, Gonzalez down to sixth.

On the third lap Fangio overtook Farina, Ascari, just ahead, was 'going like an arrow. I decided not to duel immediately but to hang on without pushing my car too hard. My main worry was refuelling. The Ferrari had extra tanks which meant a minimum number of stops while our Alfas would have to refill more often.' As each yard passed the weight of those tanks bore down on the smaller tyres.

Fangio understood how to hurry carefully. He rode out a lap and when he was ready he overtook Ascari, holding that to lap 6. The crowd shouted and pointed to the Ferrari of Taruffi as it came towards the pits. His nearside rear tyre was in ribbons, this same Taruffi who was known to be easy on tyres. The mechanics changed them in 24 seconds. On lap 7 Luigi Villoresi, an Italian in another Ferrari, pitted with the tread on his offside rear broken up.

Fangio forged on, wondering. While he'd been behind Ascari

a tiny piece of rubber flew off one of his tyres and hit me in the face, not harming me in the least. I was surprised. How could the tyres on his Ferrari wear out so fast?

Fangio noted what happened to Taruffi, had fleetingly seen Luigi Villoresi halting at the pits and felt the impact of Ascari's debris. He assembled the evidence in his mind and decided to launch his offensive now.

On lap 8 Ascari gesticulated towards his tyres as he passed the pits. On lap 9 he came in, the tyres virtually disintegrated. The tyre risk had been a disaster. Or had it? Lampredi would be tantalizing about that. 'Blowing up the tyres on a hoop leaning against a wall was without our knowing it pulling off those tyre treads. When we realized this it was too late.'

Ascari lost 32 seconds, pressing him back to sixth. This sort of challenge heated his blood and by lap 17 he'd reached third, a position vacated by Gonzalez who had a shredded tyre. On that lap Ascari pitted but only for a fleeting inspection of the car. He'd spun. He emerged sixth again behind Fangio, Farina, Italian Felice Bonetto in an Alfa, Villoresi, Gonzalez – and now Taruffi overtook him. Ascari's tyres were going off again already.

On lap 27 Johnny Claes in a much slower Lago-Talbot tried to scrabble out of Fangio's way at the mouth of the turn into Avenida, the brakes failed and the Belgian flew into the bales. The pit signalled Fangio in for fuel. He did not change tyres. The tanks were refilled in 24 seconds, the fuel slopping out of them as he accelerated away. Almost immediately Ascari came in again for more tyres.

Fangio maintained his pace until his signals told him he was a full minute and more ahead of Ascari, charging but fourth. Fangio eased off, lapped some ten seconds slower than his fastest lap and conserved his tyres. Through laps 42 to 49 the order remained constant – Fangio, Farina, Gonzalez, Ascari – but the Alfas would have to refuel again and the Ferraris wouldn't.

And Fangio had a moment. Andre Simon spun his Simca on the right-hander leading into the Avenida and as it spun Fangio arrived. He might have helplessly rammed it sideways. His strong, sure hands worked the big steering-wheel, correcting the drift, holding the car directly ahead as Simon churned across his front. The long, elegant Alfa passed safely by.

Fangio made that second stop for fuel on lap 53, away again in 34.5 seconds and still in the lead. Farina pitted next and it cost him second place to Gonzalez. On lap 55 Fangio lapped Ascari and each time he sped past the pits a tall, dark Italian mechanic held out a big board to give him the gap to Gonzalez. On lap 59 it was 34 seconds, the same on lap 60, it narrowed to 32, then 27, went back out to 28. Whatever Gonzalez did Fangio countered. Among the crowd Argentinians began to chant F-A-N-G-I-O and wave blue and white streamers. He crossed the line 54.3 seconds ahead of Gonzalez, Ascari fourth but two laps behind. Fangio remembers:

I had a habit of humming as well as chewing gum during a race. This time I spat out my gum and began to pray, silently. My prayer was answered.

The voices of 300,000 yelling fans accompanied me on the lap of honour. I was deeply thrilled at the sound of a crowd shouting in Spanish. It seemed as though I were in Buenos Aires. 'World Champion' was being shouted everywhere. The lap of honour seemed terribly long. Coming towards me from my pit I saw the engineering director of Alfa Romeo. He was emotional and it looked as though the mechanics had suddenly gone crazy. The engineering director embraced me and I, too, had a lump in my throat.

The crowd mobbed Fangio. Ascari finished almost overcome by fumes from the engine, his whole face covered in oil. He looked as if he'd come from a coal mine.

Many dignitaries made speeches during the party at the Ritz Hotel in Barcelona that evening, Fangio among them. He paid his tribute to Alfa Romeo and to his fellow drivers for the fine contests they'd had. Ascari, someone noted, 'smiles a little ruefully perhaps as he thinks of the past and the future.'

Ascari 'congratulated me like the sportsman he was,' Fangio said, 'although it was his tyres which had let him down. That is the way it goes in racing. Rarely does a driver make technical errors – his equipment often betrays him.'

1952
ASCARI, IN ABSENTIA

German Grand Prix, Nürburgring

Just before the season began Fangio gave an interview and the journalist doing it said he'd heard Alfa Romeo were withdrawing from Grand Prix racing to concentrate on sports cars. It was a curious feeling, Fangio would remember, being unemployed and hearing about it like this.

He journeyed to Europe to feel out the territory. He got an exploratory drive in a BRM but wondered if the car would stand up to racing. He got a drive in a Maserati in a non-championship race at Monza and on the second lap felt the car skidding. He heard the tyres scream and the car took off into a confused mass of trees and shadow.

I clung to the wheel but a jolt tore me from my seat and threw me forwards. At that instant I knew what it was like to die racing. The difference between life and death seemed banal, almost derisive.

He severely injured his neck and would take no part in any of the seven Grands Prix.

Alfa Romeo's withdrawal left Ferrari in a position of complete control, the withdrawal of Fangio left three Italians to take control: Farina who had joined Ferrari from Alfa, Taruffi and Ascari who were already there. Taruffi won the Swiss at Bremgarten, Ascari the next three – Belgium, France, Britain. In Belgium the son of a Farnham garage owner made his debut in a Cooper. Mike Hawthorn went to Spa in a Bedford van with the car in the back. The van kept breaking down but he made it and during the race learnt about Spa. Another driver went off into barbed-wire fencing but ducked. The wire tore the shirt off his back. Hawthorn finished fourth.

The matrix of the season was as it had been in 1951, the best four finishes to count. If Ascari won the fifth, the German Grand Prix at the Nürburgring, he was champion.

Each day for a week he drove round The Ring in his Fiat saloon learning. The circuit, lost in the Eifel Mountains towards the Luxembourg frontier, measured 14.1 miles (22.7km) of undulating countryside. It had hump-backs where cars were airborne, dips and unprotected ditches and ravines, corner after corner coming so fast that remembering it was a challenge. Brooding, darkening pine trees hemmed it. Often it rained, too, and rain was its final terror, cutting visibility so that drivers couldn't know if they'd be aquaplaning. No driver approached it with anything less than respect. Like the sea, you never forgot what it could do.

Ascari's reconnaissance paid an immediate dividend because in first qualifying he did 10m 8s, Farina 10m 25s. Farina responded the next day with a thunderous 10m 7s but Ascari countered: 10m 4.9s. These were innocent days, no qualifying times issued although we do know the 10m 4.9s got pole.

The meeting marked the circuit's twenty-fifth anniversary and part of the celebrations included a sports car race. A couple of supercharged Mercedes 300 SLs went quicker than all the Grand Prix cars except Ascari and Farina – because Alfa Romeo withdrew, Formula 1 had been left virtually empty in a competitive sense and the problem was partially solved by reducing all cars in the World Championship to Formula 2 specifications (2 litres unsupercharged or 500 cc supercharged).

On the afternoon of 3 August 30 cars lined up 4-3-4-3-4-3-4-2-3, seven Ferraris, the rest a bizarre admixture of the well-known (Maserati, BMW, Gordini) and the faintly remembered (Veritas, Aston-Butterworth, AFM). They faced 18 laps (254.7 miles/409.8km).

Ascari made a perfect start, Robert Manzon (Gordini) following, then Farina and Bonetto (Maserati) as they travelled down the start-finish straight to the first corner, a left to right loop called the Sudkehre. A crowd estimated at 260,000 camped all around the mighty circuit, some under the trees, some in stands, most sitting on the sloping hillsides trying to catch as much of the panorama as they could. They listened for the sound of approaching engines. Bonetto had already spun approaching Sudkehre, gathered the car up again, accelerated off hard.

The Ring tightened its embrace. On that first lap Paul Pietsch (Veritas) – who'd had to swerve violently to miss the spinning Bonetto – retired when the gearbox failed; Maurice Trintignant, a Frenchman in a Gordini, retired with brake and suspension problems. He had been a violent swerver to miss Bonetto, too. Bonetto himself screamed into the pits to have a rear tyre changed, screamed out again and plunged off bursting the tyre. Spectators gave him a shove and he was disqualified. Paul Frere, a Belgian in an HWM, retired, gearbox. Those first and second laps claimed nine cars.

By then Farina was past Manzon but already 6.5 seconds behind Ascari. By the third lap another couple of cars had gone and the remaining 19 were strung out like a strange necklace around the circuit but there was no doubt who led: Alberto Ascari. He sat upright in the car, his hands so firm and yet so sensitive on the steering-wheel, he watched very closely as the nuances and nightmares of the Ring ebbed past him and no doubt he remembered each of them from the Fiat.

Ascari was a great driver, his father Antonio a great driver. Antonio had been killed in a race in France in 1925. Alberto became maniacally, morbidly superstitious. Antonio was thirty-six when he died. Alberto was now thirty-three and dreaded becoming thirty-six himself. Alberto moved deeply into religion and took as his patron an obscure saint, Antonio, who had died when he was thirty-six.

In the art of driving a racing car Alberto was masterful. The superstition was not evident once Alberto sat in the car. He was cold and masterful there, and here was the mastery. By lap 4 he'd drawn the lead out to 59.6 seconds – Farina into the pits for fresh goggles – and by lap 5 to 69 seconds.

At half distance, he came in and changed his rear tyres. That lasted thirty-two seconds. He took no fuel on board. As he entered the pits he had been leading Farina by 45 seconds and as he pulled out Farina arrived. Farina's mechanics were one second quicker than Ascari's but twice he stalled the engine trying to get away, Ascari long gone.

Manzon was gone, too, but gone from the race. A wheel came off at a place called the Hatzenbach behind the pits, the Gordini churned but came to rest unscathed. The Ring had locked its embrace tighter and only 12 cars ran.

On lap 15 Ascari held a 48-second lead over Farina and the race became, as someone noted, 'monotonous'. There was always a chance of that around the length of the Ring, one superior car or driver drawing away not to be glimpsed again. The monotony compounded itself. The cars took more than ten minutes a lap, were gone past the spectators all in the moment and the 260,000 waited the ten minutes again. Nothing to do but have a look at your watch and measure the gaps.

A lot of people glanced at those watches. Ascari ought to have crossed the line to start lap 17 some 48 seconds before. The loudspeakers bayed Ascari coming into the pits. He slowed and stopped, and began calling 'oil, oil.' There had been a leak, the inside of the cockpit smeared with it. The mechanics grabbed a churn and began filling the tank. As they worked, Ascari tilted his head and gazed back down the straight waiting, waiting, waiting for Farina to appear. He did.

Farina swept by into the lead, Ascari still stationary. When he moved off the watches froze the lead at nine seconds. The hunt in the woods was on. It took Ascari the eight and a half miles (13.6km) to the Karusel – a tight, banked right loop – to cut Farina's lead by a single second; at the left kink called Wippermann a mile and a half further on he'd cut it by another. At Brunnchen, a right loop barely a mile beyond Wippermann, he'd cut it to six. At Schwalbenschwanz, an unfolding but sharp right-left-left-right, it was four; and the Schwalbenschwanz fed them out on to the long and complete majesty of the start-finish straight.

Ascari had driven one of the great laps at the Nürburgring.

Down the straight, more than two miles long, Ascari urged the Ferrari closer and closer to Farina. He overtook him as they passed the pits.

Farina was as enigmatic as Ascari was mystic but both were fast in racing cars. He responded immediately. Going in to the Sudkehre under braking he thrust his Ferrari level with Ascari's. Ascari held steady, let the car drift, emerged a length ahead. He set off again in a panorama of movement – sliding here, sliding there, taming each dip and rise – and Farina fell back.

Ascari won it by 14.1 seconds after a drive of 3h 6m 13.3s at an average speed of 82.2mph (132.2kmh). That was fast in 1952 and isn't exactly slow today round 14.1 miles of the Nürburgring.

1953

LIGHT AND DARKNESS

Swiss Grand Prix, Bremgarten

The statistic was so astonishing it had become almost absurd: 2m 34.5s. That was the time Bernd Rosemeyer, driving an Auto Union, lapped Bremgarten on the outskirts of Berne in 1936 during the Swiss Grand Prix. Year by year, while other circuits were doctored and tailored, Bremgarten stayed unaltered save for a bit of resurfacing. In August 1953, as twenty drivers gathered for the race, Rosemeyer's record still stood. Fangio had got closest with 2m 35.9s in 1951 – but in qualifying.

Ascari spearheaded Ferrari and, defending his championship, was partnered by Farina, Hawthorn and Villoresi. Fangio spearheaded Maserati supported by Gonzalez.

To beat Rosemeyer would be historically satisfying but the championship, a confused mass of possibilities, was also there for the taking at this seventh round of the season, only Monza to follow.

The four-best-finishes rule favoured Ascari who'd won in Argentina, Holland, Belgium and Britain for a working points total of 33.5 (the half for shared fastest lap at Silverstone.) Fangio finished only three times for 19. Whatever he got in Switzerland he kept. Farina had 20 from four rounds and would have to drop his lowest, two points in France. Hawthorn had 18 from five rounds and would have to drop his lowest, three points in Holland.

If, however, Ascari won he retained the championship. Not that the nine points – assuming he did fastest lap – added significantly to his total because he could only keep one of them. No: by winning he rationed any of his three rivals to six points for second. None could overhaul him even if they went on to win Monza.

Situated where the tram track from Berne ended, Bremgarten

was 4.5 miles (7.2km) and fringed by woodland. It offered no straight worthy of the name – the nearest a short, sharp rush past the pits. Bremgarten was essentially all curves and corners, with the slowest the hairpin near the start which forced cars down towards 50mph (80kmh).

Motor Sport reported:

Over the years the circuit has attained a reputation for being dangerous due to numerous fatalities, but this is not altogether justified because while it is not the safest it is certainly not the most dangerous. It is not, however, a circuit on which to learn, nor is it a circuit on which to make mistakes. In the past a number of accidents have occurred at the Eymatt corner, at a point where the circuit changes from very fast downhill swerves in bright sunlight to an uphill section under the shade of large trees and thick undergrowth and it is said that the sudden change of light is severe on the human eye and likely to cause faulty judgement.

This year the corner was lined with a wall of straw bales, painted black and white, and the road width reduced slightly in an endeavour to make the competitors more conscious of the corner's severity and visibility, on the old principle that the more dangerous a thing appears the more cautious people will be. Apart from this modification the circuit remains unchanged.

You could see the art of Ascari on an uphill left-hand bend during qualifying. The surface was bumpy but his grace and incision made him visibly faster than anyone else. Fangio was fast, too. In fact, in first qualifying Fangio was quickest (2m 40.1s), Ascari next (2m 40.7s). The second day it rained and the times stood.

As the flag fell to launch the 20 cars on the 65 laps (294.0 miles/473.1kmh), Fangio edged into the lead: Farina's Ferrari didn't fire properly and he was engulfed by half the grid before it did. Fangio led with Ascari tracking him and out there on lap 1 taking him. They crossed the line tight together with Hawthorn, Onofre Marimon, Villoresi, Bonetto and Farina in pursuit.

Ascari siphoned the lead out to a couple of seconds next time round and extended it by a second a lap. Hawthorn attacked Fangio, took him and they locked into a duel but Fangio lost third gear and drifted away. On lap 10 he eased into the pits and so did Bonetto in another Maserati. They swapped cars and Fangio set off again. Almost immediately he felt the left front tyre explode. On lap 11 he was back in the pits to have it changed. Then he flung himself into the race, as he would say, to try and make up a few places. He was tenth.

Ascari led Farina by 23.5 seconds, Farina mounted a magnificent charge and had already shaken his fist at Bonetto for making overtaking difficult. Farina's charge did not have enough momentum to disturb Ascari and the race settled into a procession, Ascari holding Farina comfortably at bay, keeping the gap constant. Of course Fangio mounted a charge of his own and reached fifth but each time the cars passed the pits the stopwatches showed he wasn't gaining on Ascari.

On lap 30 Fangio threaded through the hairpin but the vast crowd in the grandstand could hear the Maserati clattering. A piston had burnt out. As Fangio passed the grandstand a vast, dense ball of smoke burst from his exhaust pipe, so dense it blocked visibility full across the width of the track. Drivers behind braked violently while Fangio returned to the pits to wait for the end of the race so he could congratulate the winner.

Marimon harried Hawthorn for third place, passed him, and the duel became so intense that Marimon set fastest lap: 2m 45.7s. Ascari sailed on untroubled, easily in command, never seeming stretched. Farina followed keeping his own even pace. The thing had become a bore.

Ascari came through the hairpin and the crowd in the grandstand watched as he flowed towards them to begin another lap. They heard it then, that strident, false note which has such immediate implications for a racing car. As Ascari passed the pits they could hear it with absolute clarity.

Misfire.

Ascari inevitably slowed, a captive of what the engine would no longer do, but he'd travelled long past the pits. As he came past them Ferrari hoisted a signal to him. FASTER! Farina reacted instantly while Ascari had to tour the full length of the circuit. He reached the pits at a poignant instant, Farina in full flight towards him, and as he angled the Ferrari into the pits Farina went by into the lead.

Ascari's mechanics roved and roamed to locate the problem, and needed a long time. The engine fired on all four cylinders but seemed flat. Lampredi crouched and examined the underside searching in case anything obvious hung there. A minute ticked by and they found a choked carburettor jet. A mechanic gave it a felicitous tap with a mallet and the power flooded back. Ascari had lost 87 seconds, he was fourth and only 25 laps remained. The position: Farina in the lead, Marimon and Hawthorn still duelling but 45 seconds behind Farina, then Ascari.

Farina summoned himself and created a lap of 2m 43.1s, in its timing and ferocity the sort of gesture to settle any motor race. Mother Nature helped Farina, too. The sun was sinking, shining full and fierce into the drivers' faces on the short start-finish straight.

Autosport reported that 'it is useless to use tinted goggles because drivers would be unable to see in the dark, wooded sections of the circuit.' Hawthorn raised his left hand and cupped a shield to his eyes, shadow falling across his face. Ascari couldn't catch Farina blind.

Ascari charged as Fangio had done. On lap 45 Hawthorn finally edged past Marimon and two laps later Marimon did a complete spin when his transmission failed. The order: Farina, Hawthorn, Ascari but, of overriding importance to the team, Ferrari, Ferrari, Ferrari. Fangio had gone and Marimon had gone, taking with them the Maserati challenge. Bonetto in the third Maserati was a full lap behind the three Ferraris.

On lap 50 Farina led Hawthorn by 15.2 seconds, Hawthorn 10.3 seconds in front of Ascari. As the three cars passed the pits a light blue and yellow flag was brandished horizontally at them: HOLD STATION, don't race each other. The sun was far down now, shimmering in the drivers' eyes. Did Farina see the signal? Did Hawthorn? Did Ascari?

Farina did not slacken his pace and neither did Hawthorn or Ascari. On lap 51 Ascari drew up to Hawthorn and a lap later went past. He drew up to Farina and a lap after that went past. In catching and overtaking Farina, Ascari set the fastest lap of the race, 2m 41.3s.

Rosemeyer was safe.

Farina felt deeply enraged by what Ascari had done under the HOLD STATION. He sought Ascari out and heaped a torrent of abuse on him. Ascari shrugged and said he'd won his second World Championship – and become the first man to do it consecutively. Even the then staid *Autosport* wrote 'Farina is palpably annoyed and tells the winner so.'

Ferrari demanded to know why Ascari ignored the signal and he said that with the sun in his eyes he hadn't seen it.

One postscript.

It belongs to a man who was only 15 days old on 23 August 1953. More than half-way through the Portuguese Grand Prix in 1989 Nigel Mansell was black flagged three times for reversing in the pit lane during his stop for tyres. The black flag was held from the control point on the start-finish where you're doing 190mph (306kmh). Mansell did not stop. 'I would be prepared to swear on the Bible that I did not see the flag,' he said. The sun was low, fierce and full in his eyes. Have you ever, Mansell mused, tried driving blind at such a speed?

Mansell was driving a Ferrari.

1954

FANGIO, IN HIS SORROW

Swiss Grand Prix, Bremgarten

Fritz Nallinger was A professor and technical director of Daimler-Benz in Stuttgart. Early in 1953 he'd addressed the Board.

Gentlemen, after an interval of almost fourteen years Daimler-Benz AG will once more participate in Grand Prix racing and it has been decided to develop a new Formula 1 car which should be ready to start on 1 January 1954. I need not stress that there is little time at our disposal. Our future rivals started racing soon after the war. They have been able to test their cars in races and to improve them systematically. For us that was impossible. Our last Formula car was built before the war and between then and now there is a big gap. It is now up to us to decide whether we should build upon the achievements of our rivals or whether we should create something entirely new. I think you already know which direction we shall take.

The words launched an adventure to seize Formula 1. Instructions went out to the company's factories in West Germany to lend their expertise. Daimler would race under their more famous name, Mercedes.

The cars were not ready on 1 January 1954 and while work continued on them Fangio enjoyed a six-week break at Balcarce although he'd heard interesting whispers about the potential of the Mercedes. He made enquiries and Mercedes were extremely interested in him but he faced a problem because Mercedes did not anticipate being ready until the French Grand Prix at Rheims in July, third round of the season – and of the nine rounds a driver's five best results counted. Fangio reasoned that the wait would be worth it and in the meantime he'd be free to drive what he wanted. Thus he won the Argentinian and Belgian Grands Prix in a Maserati. Rheims was next.

Mercedes fielded three cars, one for Fangio, one for Karl Kling, one for Hans Herrmann, both Germans. The cars looked like an absolute revolution: wide, aerodynamically pure, very powerful and completely unlike anything else on the grid. The bodywork enclosed the wheels.

In qualifying Fangio adored the low centre of gravity, found the whole car frankly sensational and spoke of it to himself in terms of dreams but when reporters asked him he said only, 'it's not bad.' Fangio was astute enough never to forewarn the opposition. In the race he adored the power. He won, Kling a tenth of a second behind – the only cars on that lap. Fangio felt the World Championship within his grasp already and five rounds remained.

The next, the British at Silverstone, went wrong. Fangio had gearbox trouble and he finished only fourth, a lap behind the winner Gonzalez in a Ferrari, Kling seventh three laps behind Gonzalez.

Herrmann, who missed Silverstone because of an engine blow-out at Rheims, returned for the Nürburgring

A wet first qualifying session: the really fast times were set during the second. Towards the end and quite by chance Fangio found himself behind Marimon. Fangio would write:

At 31, Onofre was a lively young man, exuberant, loving a joke, laughing all the time. Beneath his merry exterior he held a great affection for me, I would almost say a veneration which intimidated me because I didn't know whether to behave like a father or a brother to him. He had come to Europe with me in 1951. I was proud when I read in newspapers that he belonged to the 'Argentinian school'.

Fangio watched the Maserati travelling down to Adenau on the far side of the circuit being driven in a clean style. 'It seemed to me I was sending him advice by telepathy and I smiled to myself with satisfaction when I saw Pinocho (his nickname) do exactly what I should have done at the wheel of his Maserati. I was approaching the wide, easy Adenau corner and thinking of accelerating to catch up with Marimon and greet him with a wave when I saw his machine suddenly go wild. Probably one of his wheels locked unexpectedly but what I could see confused me. Supple and obedient in his hands until that moment, the car seemed to take over, carrying him along in a terrible series of skids, slamming against everything in the way, brutally bouncing off objects. The car went off the track and I saw it disappear behind a grassy ridge. For a moment even then I did not suspect disaster.'

Marimon was dead.

Fangio returned and Marimon's chest was 'terribly crushed by the steering-wheel. He was surrounded by a group of German spectators who had extricated him from the wreckage and were now standing helplessly by while a priest was reciting a prayer in Latin. I remember now that his Latin with its strong German accent sounded strange to my ears because it was the same prayer I had learned as a choirboy in our little church at Balcarce. No death on the track, I think, has ever moved me as did this bitter loss. It was some moments before I was able to drag Froilan Gonzalez away – and it was a Froilan his friends had seldom seen, his powerful frame shaken by his suppressed emotion.'

Fangio, grieving, became deeply concerned about Gonzalez for the race. He was pale and obviously still shaken but assured Fangio he was all right. Then Fangio tried to concentrate on the race himself. He beat Hawthorn by 1m 37s but the victory brought him no pleasure. He had 36 points, Gonzalez second on 17.5, but that brought him no pleasure either.

Fangio did not want to take part in the Swiss Grand Prix at Bremgarten but Alfred Neubauer, the portly and patrician Mercedes team manager, insisted and perhaps that was the right decision.

Fangio went to the Swiss Grand Prix.

In qualifying another disaster threatened. Manzon was being given a trial by Ferrari, the circuit was wet and he crashed destroying the car completely but his injuries were diagnosed in hospital as no more than badly bruised ribs. As with every accident, and particularly when a car is out of control, survival is by chance.

A Briton, chirpy to the point of effervescence, medium build but strong, pondered other matters. He was in his fourth season of Grand Prix racing although it had been sporadic – one race in 1951, five for three teams in 1952, four races for two teams in 1953 and no point won at all until Belgium this season – but he was a master. His name:

Stirling Moss. He drove a Maserati. 'On the second practice day it rained and I set fastest time which not only boosted my confidence enormously but also impressed Neubauer on a circuit and in company which he respected. Still Fangio and Gonzalez had lapped quicker in the dry so I lined up third on the grid.'

Fangio was away fast, Kling out of form after a potential disaster of his own at the Nürburgring when his suspension collapsed. Fangio led over the line to complete lap 1, Gonzalez second, Moss third, Kling fourth, Hawthorn ('once again I made a poor start') eighth. There were sixty-five laps to run.

Autosport reported:

Next time round Fangio had increased his lead but Kling was not amongst those present. Trying to close up on Moss he overdid things at the hairpin and shot off backwards. He eventually turned up at the tail of the field getting an icy look from Neubauer as his car went past the pits.

Moss would write:

Early in the race I took second place from the Ferrari of Gonzalez but I noticed my car's oil pressure falling and eased back, letting Hawthorn by before finally retiring when the oil pressure vanished. Team manager Ugolino called Harry Schell (also Maserati) in for me to take over his car but when he stopped his engine had no oil pressure either.

The great days were coming: 22 August was not one of them. Hawthorn in the Ferrari started to:

catch up and I could see Gonzalez and Moss in front of me but going up to a nasty right-hand corner on a damp surface in the woods I braked, tried to turn and went straight on.

By now I suppose I was a bit jumpy and immediately concluded that the worst had happened, the steering had broken. In a split second I caught sight of one of the front wheels – an advantage of the conventional type of single-seater – and saw that it was locked. I released the brakes and scraped round.

It happened again several times and I dropped back but as the brake bedded down the trouble disappeared and I passed both Gonzalez and Moss to get into second place. I was gaining on Fangio, too, and I could see the agitation growing in the Mercedes pit. Then the engine started misfiring and I smelt petrol. I stopped at the pits and they found an unsecured union nut had come undone. Lampredi, normally an equable sort of person, flew into a towering rage to see the car stopped by such a trivial fault.

I re-started but soon afterwards the engine stopped and I managed to get the car to a standstill without any trouble. I took a look at the engine to make sure there was no escaping oil and no holes in the crankcase and then set off to walk back to the pits through the woods in the centre of the course. These woods are barred to the public during the race and the Swiss police use fierce Alsatian dogs to enforce the ban. One of them went for me, snarling and snapping, and it took the policeman in charge of it some time to calm it down. I got lost in the woods and it was about half an hour before I got back to the pits where I got a cool reception.

By then Moss had 'finally retired when the oil pressure vanished.' Another Maserati was called in for Moss to take over but when it stopped it had no oil pressure either.

On lap 30 Fangio was just over 17.5 seconds in front of Gonzalez and *Autosport* reported:

The difference between Fangio and his German team-mates was made even more apparent when he lapped Herrmann on the forty-second tour and Gonzalez also took the second Mercedes. The two leaders had then lapped everyone in the race.

Fangio became sublime those last few laps, quite alone in the race, quite alone out there on the long, wooded, difficult circuit; quite alone with his memories. He beat Gonzalez by 58 seconds.

One postscript.

This would be the last Grand Prix at Bremgarten, Gonzalez pole with 2m 39.5s, Fangio fastest lap with 2m 39.7s.

Rosemeyer was safe forever.

1955

BANK ON FANGIO

Italian Grand Prix, Monza

There was a very tragic reason why Bremgarten died, because the season of 1955 was itself tragic.

Fangio won Argentina in the Mercedes, Trintignant won Monaco in a Ferrari where Ascari (Lancia) lost control and went into the harbour. He returned to his home at Milan, taking all his superstitions with him. Four days after the race he went to Monza to watch some testing. He asked if he might drive a Ferrari 'to see how my back is.' He was wearing ordinary clothes and hadn't even his lucky crash helmet with him, the one he always wore against the superstitions. He started to make the Ferrari go fast but at the Curva Vialone – a left-hand corner – the car whipped out of control and he was thrown fatally from it.

It was 26 May.

His father Antonio had died in a racing car on the 26th day of the month, taking a left-hand corner. He had lived for 13,463 days. He left a widow and two children.

Alberto had been alive for 13,466 days. He left a widow and two children.

Fangio won Belgium from Moss, now with Mercedes and a week later all the leading drivers went to Le Mans to contest the 24-hour sportscar race. Here was starkest tragedy. At early evening Hawthorn in a Jaguar braked to make a pit stop, the Austin-Healey behind swerved to miss him and a Frenchman called Pierre Levegh – in a Mercdedes – rode up the Austin-Healey, was launched by banking and went in to the crowd. At least eighty people died and motor sport was fundamentally altered.

France, Germany, Spain and Switzerland cancelled their Grands

Prix – the end of Bremgarten – and the championship fell into turmoil, but a week after Le Mans the Dutch Grand Prix did take place. Fangio won from Moss. The British at Aintree did take place and Moss won from Fangio.

An Australian, Jack Brabham, made his debut in a Cooper-Bristol. He'd remember 'we rushed the car off, virtually half finished, to try to compete. Unfortunately on the morning of the race the clutch packed up and I had to start without a clutch.' He managed thirty-one laps.

If, as many believe, Fangio decided to pay his tribute to Moss by allowing him to win – Fangio would remain stoically and graciously enigmatic on the subject – the act of sportsmanship could have cost him the championship. Only Monza, as it seemed, remained. Had Fangio taken the eight points for a win and the point for fastest lap at Aintree it would scarcely have mattered if, after Monza, one of the four cancelled races (probably the French) was reinstated. He had 33 points, Moss only 22, the rest nowhere, but as the drivers reached Monza nobody knew about the French race. There were rumours that work was going on at Rheims, systems were being checked and the Grand Prix would be held on 9 October.

Monza posed the immediate problem. For months extensive work there had altered its whole nature, lengthening the circuit from 3.9 miles (6.2km) to 6.2 (10.0km) by adding two steeply banked concrete curves. These curves interlocked into the circuit. The first flowed away from half-way down the start-finish straight and looped over the old track before it reached the second curve, feeding the cars back on to the straight. Fangio described this as a 'sensational speed bowl'.

Ridges lay in the concrete, difficult to see but enough to shake the cars and make them dance. In this hypersensitive time the possible danger of the ridges, stoked by the Italian press, became a strong and emotive topic. The Press tracked the drivers, prising opinions from them. Fangio judged the ridges alone were not enough to cause 'an immediate catastrophe' but he wondered about the cumulative effect during a race. Fangio reasoned that a driver with sufficient skill to minimize the jarring could very well win.

Mercedes, famed for their attention to detail, had already tested at

Monza in August, a month before the Italian Grand Prix. They discovered that the altered track wore tyres quickly. They evaluated cars of three different lengths and decided on a streamlined medium wheelbase. Two of these cars were specially built for the race, an amazing step in 1955, but just to be sure Mercedes also took long and short wheelbased cars and a variation on the medium one. It is very, very easy to see why Mercedes were so difficult to beat.

As qualifying began Mercedes realized the ridges had been smoothed since the testing and the lone long chassis coped best although it still, as Moss remembers, 'bottomed out' over them.

Mercedes telephoned the factory at Stuttgart and said *build another overnight and get it down here*. Mercedes had a racing lorry for such emergencies and next morning, the car completed, it set off down the autobahn.

Moss likened qualifying to a game of 'musical chairs' on the banking. In first qualifying, while Mercedes were telephoning Stuttgart, cars were restricted to the banking to get used to it. Farina (Lancia-Ferrari) had a wheel throw a tread at between 160 and 170mph (257-273kmh), the car rotated several times and hammered a barrier. Farina escaped unhurt but extremely shaken.

Mercedes weren't the only ones 'bottoming'. Plenty did. On the second day – and now using the whole circuit – Farina lost another tread and, although this incident was less spectacular than his first, it persuaded the team to withdraw altogether. The Lancias, being run by Ferrari (Lancia had actually gone under in midsummer and the cars handed over to Enzo on 26 July) were contracted to a Belgian tyre company, Englebert, and clearly the Englebert tyres couldn't take it. Dunlop offered to help and so did Pirelli but Englebert began making legal noises. Lancia-Ferrari shook their heads, shrugged their shoulders and headed for home.

Hawthorn, who qualified on the sixth row, would remember:

I was driving a Super Squalo Ferrari and I didn't like the new track at all. When Lancia withdrew I told both Farina and Luigi Villoresi that they could have my car if they wanted a drive but there were no takers so I was stuck with it.

The front row lined up Fangio, Moss, Kling, all Mercedes.

On the afternoon of 11 September – warm and dry – Monza was entirely itself. A vast crowd had come and noisy squabbling broke out in the grandstand because the organizers had sold more tickets than there were seats. 'Standard bearers' escorted the drivers to their cars, they got themselves in and waiting for the flag not one of the twenty cars crept forward, something so unusual *Autosport* noted it.

Moss was away first, then Fangio, then Kling and now the complexity of the 'new' circuit revealed itself. The cars followed the old one all the way round and turned right on to the banking, followed that all the way round to the straight again to complete a lap. In other words they passed the pits twice each lap.

On the first 'half' of the first lap Moss led, but as they moved on to the banking Fangio got a tow from him. Moss selected a higher line on the banking, Fangio emerged from the tow and went 'under' him – inside. The Mercedes were clearly superior and Taruffi, who'd been on the fourth row in the fourth car, caught Fangio, Moss and Kling. Mercedes, Mercedes, Mercedes, Mercedes. A walk-over.

Hawthorn, going hard in his Ferrari, had a lot on his mind. 'Up to this time I had had no experience of throwing tyre treads and so I asked some of the Dunlop people what the symptoms were. They told me that I might feel no more than a slight vibration but that when it started I would have only a few seconds in which to slow the car before the tyre burst and things really started happening.' Hawthorn kept his senses alert to that. Le Mans had been only three months before.

Moss held the key to the championship, Moss tracking Fangio lap after lap, Moss right behind Fangio. If he won and Fangio didn't finish, if the French Grand Prix was on ... who knew? On lap 19 one of Fangio's rear wheels flung a stone which smashed Moss's windscreen. He made for the pits and to his 'astonishment' the mechanics had a replacement available, not something you'd expect then. Moss set off in a magnificent attempt to regain the ground he had lost and hammered out fastest lap – 2m 46.9s, 134.0 miles an hour. He unlapped himself by going past Fangio, Kling and Taruffi but Fangio, imperious, kept to the straightforward tactic of circulating evenly. He knew Moss had to regain the length of the circuit, the 6.2 miles. After 20 laps he led Kling by a couple of seconds.

Moss was poised to take sixth place on lap 27 when at the Vialone Curve a piston collapsed. Kling's transmission failed six laps later and he parked the car on the grass in front of the main stand where it stood like a spectre itself. This brought extreme anxiety to Neubauer. Two cars broken. What chance the remaining two?

Autosport:

The main interest now was whether or not Fangio and Taruffi could keep going without suffering the gearbox troubles which had knocked out their team-mates. Fangio made vague signs as he passed his pit but all appeared to be in order. Taruffi was putting on a magnificent show having taken over Moss's role of World Champion's shadow.

Neubauer need not have worried. Fangio won.

Three postscripts.

Fangio allowed Taruffi to catch him near the end and that was how they went across the line but in the pit lane Neubauer gesticulated desperately that the race was not over, that Fangio keep on and come all the way back again. Fangio did.

In the wake of Le Mans, Mercedes decided to leave Grand Prix racing. As Fangio took the chequered flag a second time the sound and sight of those magnificent cars – they'd won five of the six rounds – would be gone forever.

The French Grand Prix was not held at Rheims or anywhere else. Fangio had his third championship. 'The technical supremacy of the German cars was never in question so I won easily.'

1956
FOUR AND NO ESCAPE

Italian Grand Prix, Monza

The Mercedes withdrawal – Neubauer laid a white sheet like a shroud over one of them and burst into tears – left a vacuum which Lancia-Ferrari and Maserati hastened to fill. Enzo Ferrari signed Fangio and a young Englishman, Peter Collins, and in all fielded seven drivers. Maserati signed Moss to join a Frenchman, Jean Behra. Counting five privateers they'd field eight cars. Three British teams – Vanwall, BRM and Connaught – struggled with a variety of problems.

Connaught had briefly (and deceptively) raised all manner of expectations in late 1955. A student, Tony Brooks, won a non-championship Grand Prix at Syracuse much to his astonishment. He hadn't sat in a Grand Prix car before and only learnt the circuit midway through qualifying – the car hadn't yet arrived – by going round it on a scooter. In 1956 he partnered Hawthorn at BRM, and Hawthorn would write of his first test in the car:

I tried it on a wet day and found it very frightening indeed. It snaked at high speed and one had to hold it very firmly to keep it going in a straight line.

Fangio won Argentina, Moss won Monaco, Collins won Belgium and France, Fangio won Silverstone and the Nürburgring, but Moss had been consistent – third in Belgium, fifth in France, second at The Ring. They came back to Monza, the last of the eight races. Fangio had 30 points but from his full quota of five finishes. To score more he could afford to be no lower than second. Collins had 22 from four, Moss 19 from five. Moss could not take the championship. Even if he won Monza, set fastest lap and Fangio didn't finish Moss could total no more than 27 – but if Collins won, set fastest lap and Fangio didn't finish that was entirely different. Collins would get it. Fangio would write:

I have never been a spectacular racer, I never went into it as a form of escapism. I was always out to win if this was at all possible. If there was some crazy guy around I let him overtake and then tried to follow him, never letting him get out of sight. A lot of people would have beaten me if they had followed me. They lost because they overtook me.

This pragmatism was about to be applied to the Italian Grand Prix. He knew that the Lancia-Ferraris were fast (he was on pole) but anticipated tyre wear.

I saw that this problem could lose us a race which was potentially easy to win so I had a word with two of the other Lancia-Ferrari drivers, Eugenio Castellotti and Luigi Musso. 'Listen,' I said, 'you won't have to work too hard to win this race. At the start I'll set the rhythm. You follow me and you won't shred your tyres. Ten laps from the end I'll pull over and then you two, between you, can decide who wins. Even if I come third or fourth, I'm still World Champion [assuming Castellotti or Musso was winning the race, not Collins]. They went off to think it over, they came back and said 'No, we will all drive our own race.' I replied, 'Very well, it is up to you.'

They lined up three abreast, Musso, Castellotti and Fangio on the front row, Moss on the second, Collins on the third. The Lancia-Ferraris were fast. In qualifying all three had broken the lap record. Fangio's manager Giambertone noted that Fangio was perfectly calm, sure of himself as he took his seat behind the wheel. 'In this race I shall have to worry about tyres,' he said.

The starter dipped the flag and Fangio moved into the lead.

'I was just keeping up the right pace when, one on one side and one on the other, they overtook me on the main straight and they began to go faster than they should have done.' Musso led from

Castellotti, Fangio, Moss and Collins. On that opening lap Castellotti overtook Musso and their duel became so sharp that the Ferrari pit started to signal frantically CALM THIS DOWN, CALM THIS DOWN. Both drivers ignored the signals. Behind them Fangio, Moss, Harry Schell (Vanwall) and Collins jostled for positions, Schell overtaking Moss and then Fangio. This was only lap 3 of 50.

Fangio could and did discount Castellotti and Musso. 'I saw how smoke came from their tyres every time they braked. I guessed they would soon be out of the race.' Soon was very soon. In a sweep Moss overtook Schell and Fangio, and they began slipstreaming each other only yards apart. On the fifth lap Musso and Castellotti were in the pits for new tyres, their left rears virtually shredded. Moss led, Fangio had retaken Schell although he 'was having a bit of trouble' keeping the American behind him.

I was worried about my own car now because whenever I braked the right front wheel pulled outwards. This made me distinctly anxious because I thought the wheel must be loose. I touched the brake on one of the banked sections to see what would happen. Then I felt the car begin to go sideways into a spin. I took my foot off the accelerator and coasted into the pits.

This was on lap 19. Fangio had been nursing the tyres. Others, who hadn't, were lucky to be alive. Alfonso de Portago (also Lancia-Ferrari) survived a spin on the banking at 170mph (270kmh) when a whole tread came off. Castellotti had a tyre burst and that flung the car across the track spinning savagely on to the grass.

Collins reached fourth place before he lost a tread and the pit stop pressed him back to ninth.

Now Fangio was in the pits. The wheel had almost completely disengaged itself. A steering arm had broken. They'd drilled it out to lighten it and it had cracked on one side. With the stress of braking it snapped. The car could be repaired but that would take a long time. Fangio stood and watched as Musso, up to third, was signalled to come in and give his car to him. Musso declined by driving on at high speed.

Giambertone stood in the pits. 'Fangio's mechanic could not immediately find the indispensable spare part and had to take one from Portago's car. In addition the magneto had to be checked before Fangio's car took off again, driven by Castellotti and having lost four full laps.' There was of course no point in Fangio getting into it. He'd have to make up the four laps to win. Whether Castellotti made them up or not mattered little in the championship.

Fangio, without a car, fretted.

Giambertone 'went over to Sculati, Ferrari's technical director, to try and convince him that Fangio should get back in the race in another car. This led to a dispute which Sculati cut short by leaving the pit and going over to the Press stand.'

Musso came in for tyres and again declined to give his car to Fangio. No bitterness rose in Fangio. 'There was no reason for Musso to hand it over. The car I should have taken over if anything happened to mine was that of de Portago [the one damaged after the spin.] I spent more than 15 laps in the pits watching the race slipping away from me ...'

Giambertone said:

In the absence of Sculati, I virtually assumed responsibility for running the Ferrari pit. Minutes were passing and Moss's lead was growing all the time. When the moment was right I ordered a new wheel to be shown to Peter Collins, a categorical order to stop on the next lap for a tyre change, which his machine badly needed. As his tyres were being changed on all four wheels I went over to him. 'Peter,' I said, 'would you turn your car over to Fangio?' Without a second's hesitation the Englishman jumped out of his seat, not even stopping to think that if Moss, out in front, should break down he might become World Champion. It was a gesture of real nobility.

Fangio was overwhelmed. 'My anxiety and misery gave way to joy, so much so that I threw my arms around Collins and kissed him on the cheek and got into his car.'

Giambertone remembered that 'Fangio's eyes shone with emotion when he took off again.' He inherited the third place Collins had been in, Moss half a lap in front of Musso. Fangio launched himself into what Giambertone describes as a 'passionate, crazy pursuit'.

On lap 46 out on the back of the circuit Moss began to slow so much that Musso caught and overtook him. 'I was running out of fuel,' Moss says. 'Suddenly the Maserati faltered and died beneath me on the banked section. It happened on the back straight. No fuel! I spotted Luigi Piotti, an Italian Maserati privateer, coming up and I waved and gestured frantically for him to come up behind and push me to the pits. Somehow he understood. I suppose I would have been doing around 120mph and he did it gently, he didn't bang against me, he came up at 121mph. Our speed dropped to about 100mph with him pushing – that may seem a lot but really it's not so dramatic if you're a racing driver and naturally accustomed to much greater speeds. Piotti kept pushing me along the back straight until we reached the curve and about half-way round that he pulled away. He'd given me enough momentum to free-wheel to the pits.'

Moss took five gallons of fuel on board, sufficient to cover the last five laps, but the gap between himself and Fangio was now ten seconds. Moss came out of the pits very, very quickly.

Clearly Musso would win the race, itself a controversial thing. He had no remote interest in the championship with only four points from the first race, Argentina. He had disregarded Fangio's advice about how the race should be run. He had disregarded the signals telling him to give his car to Fangio. On lap 47 Moss came through followed by Fangio. Where was Musso? His steering arm broken, his front wheel badly buckled, he drifted slowly towards the pits.

And still Fangio forced the pace. The Maserati pit became a tightened place because the mechanics could see that Moss's tyres were badly worn and might give way at any moment. They adopted the attitude of prayer. And still Fangio forced the pace.

Moss responded by setting a new lap record, 2m 45.5s, an average speed of 135.4mph (217.9kmh) and that pushed Fangio back a little but on the last lap Moss had to slow. His tyres were virtually bald. He crossed the line 5.7 seconds ahead of Fangio who was sure:

Those guys [Castellotti, Musso] lost the race, and you could almost say they made me lose as well. I was all for winning it without fuss. Moss finished the race with a damaged engine, because some part of it failed on the Saturday and had to be repaired and he wouldn't have reached the pits when he ran out of fuel if Piotti hadn't given him a push – Piotti, a Maserati customer who later lent me his sports car to race in Portugal, where I won. But, you know, if I'd taken the Italian Grand Prix it would have been undeserved. Moss had run a very shrewd race, both fast and well thought out. He was the very best kind of driver.

Moss remembered that 'after the race the officials came to me and said I was disqualified because I'd been given a push. "But," I said, "Piotti is my team-mate, he is entitled to give me a push." Strictly speaking Piotti wasn't my team-mate, he was a privateer although we were both in Maseratis. The officials said, "Oh, well, OK."'

This is how, as long as records are kept, Stirling Moss will be the victor of the Italian Grand Prix, 2 September 1956 and on that same day Juan Manuel Fangio four times World Champion.

He hadn't finished.

1957

REQUIEM FOR A RINGMASTER

German Grand Prix, Nürburgring

The small Fairchild Argus plane came carefully into Cologne Airport. The pilot got out and wondered if there was another airport nearer to where he wanted to go. The Allied presence in West Germany was strong then and a Royal Air Force officer said yes. A telephone call was made. The French evidently controlled it but there were no problems.

The plane took off again, gained height and flowed over the woodlands and rolling hills of the Eifel region, landed at a tiny grassy strip about twenty miles from the Nürburgring. Mike Hawthorn, who owned and flew the plane, was given the signal to land:

> But the moment I taxied in I was surrounded by German airmen. It seemed the French had moved out and handed over to the new German air force and the German officers told me I must leave immediately and return to Cologne. I protested and was hauled before the commanding officer. I could not understand why I was being told to leave when I had been given permission to land by telephone but the telephone had apparently been answered by some luckless fitter who had no right to give permission.

It was the last thing Hawthorn needed. He'd joined Ferrari and all season had been urging and pressing to try and catch Fangio, now with Maserati. Nobody could catch Fangio: he won Argentina, Monaco and France before engine problems stopped him at the British Grand Prix. Contrast that with Hawthorn: the clutch went in Argentina, he crashed at Monaco, was fourth in France, third in the British.

Fangio could win his fifth championship at the Ring with two rounds to spare. This was heavy enough for Hawthorn to bear, Hawthorn who was still arguing with the Germans. There were many sides to him, not all rose-hued but he had a boyish English Public School sort of charm.

OK, they said, leave it here until Monday morning, the morning after the race. An officer gave him a lift to the track and Hawthorn secured a couple of guest tickets, one for the officer, one for the commander. Tactically, it was a shrewd move.

Others had their problems as qualifying began. Moss, who'd departed Maserati for Vanwall and won the British Grand Prix, found his car needed 'drastic work' on it. The car bucked all over the place. On the second day the sheer 'hammering' which the Ring dispensed so liberally caused small body cracks and broken engine mountings.

The Ferraris looked good after experimenting with variations on rear spring rates and axle ratios. Collins, partnering Hawthorn, found a fast combination through the endless corners, Hawthorn a fast combination on the straights and the Ferraris wouldn't need to stop for tyres or fuel during the 22 laps. Someone computed the advantage of that at a full minute.

Late on the Friday in the first session Fangio did 9m 25.6s destroying the lap record he set the year before at 9m 41.6s. Hawthorn couldn't get near it on the Saturday and neither could Collins.

Collins	Behra	Hawthorn	Fangio
Ferrari	Maserati	Ferrari	Maserati
9m 34.7s	9m 30.5s	9m 28.4s	9m 25.6s

A breeze that Sunday afternoon made the row of flags on their tall poles flutter like gentle hands. There was the usual bustle on and around the grid, Fangio drinking deeply from a bottle of mineral water, Moss nearby looking so young and fresh and polite. Easily, easily Fangio slipped into the cockpit, hands holding the steering-wheel to steady himself as he did. His goggles were up across the front of his heavy, solid helmet. He looked as he always looked, serene. A huge crowd waited.

In the pits, Maserati took a decision that Fangio would start on softer, faster tyres, the fuel tanks half full to make the sleek car significantly lighter and quicker. Fangio would stop around half distance for more fuel but by then he ought to have built up enough lead not to worry about the Ferraris, and if he was going that fast early on he might well have blown up the Ferraris if they tried to stay with him. A provocative notion and a powerful one.

At 1.15 p.m. the starter positioned himself in front of the grid and raised the flag, held it aloft so that all 24 drivers could clearly see it, backed quickly away to the rim of the circuit and let it fall. At the instant of release Fangio and Hawthorn pulled away faster than Behra and Collins while down the grid a couple of mechanics scampered clear of the rush and melted into the line of people standing in front of the pits.

Hawthorn surged and led by the Sudkehre, Collins tucked behind, Fangio third and running wider before he turned in to the corner. That was the order as they completed lap 1. Hawthorn had covered it from a standing start in 9m 42.5s. Thus, the pace of progress. Fangio had set 9m 41.6s the year before during the race.

This was going to be fast.

Fangio allowed the Farraris to go in front of him. 'I was surprised at the way they kept passing each other and not working as a team. Instead of thinking about how to get out in front together they were playing around for the lead. I kept behind for the first two laps and that allowed me to study their styles of racing.'

On lap 2 Hawthorn did 9m 37.9s, a new race record. It lasted a few moments. Fangio covered his second lap in 9m 34.6s and at the Sudkehre drew alongside Collins, moved through. Collins clung but couldn't counter-attack and down the long sweep into Adenau forest Fangio went past Hawthorn, dragging Collins with him into second place.

'On the third lap I took advantage of the fact that they had stopped dicing with each other and challenged and overtook both.'

On that third lap Fangio did 9m 33.4s and as he crossed the line to complete it had drawn five seconds from the Ferraris. He knew he needed much, much more than that. Fangio attacked the Ring.

Lap 5   9m 33.0s
Lap 6   9m 32.5s
Lap 8   9m 30.8s
Lap 10 9m 29.5s

The lead had become 31 seconds on lap 12 when he brought the Maserati into the pits. A mechanic in white overalls waved an arm to slow him, show him where to position it. Even before he was stationary another mechanic scurried forward with the jack.

I stopped the car and got out. While I was having a drink the team were putting me in the picture about the state of the race. My mechanics were working away but they weren't doing a good job. I don't know whether they were nervous or what.

They scrabbled here and there, they weren't co-ordinated, it wasn't smooth. By now Hawthorn was in front again. He'd remember:

I was leading Collins by a few yards, and as we rushed from the narrow road on to the vast plateau of concrete between grandstand and pits we could see the crowd standing, waving and cheering, which meant just one thing. Fangio must have stopped. But was he just ahead or had he broken down and we passed him somewhere? He was at this moment in the pit but at 140mph we could not spot his car, which must have been surrounded by mechanics, officials and photographers. We only knew we must motor as fast as possible until our pit could give us the position next time round.

As the two Ferraris moved into the Sudkehre, Fangio stood impassive and helpless. He heard the Ferraris pass close together. The seconds ticked – and ticked. No one knows how long that Maserati was stationary: 53.5 seconds, 52.0, 54.0, 56.0. Fangio estimated he had lost all he had gained and 48 seconds.

Giambertone leaned towards him and said, 'Listen ... can you take it a bit easy for two laps and not go flat out until Guerino Bertocchi [the team manager] gives you a go-ahead signal?' Giambertone:

The old racing fox Juan caught on and was about to smile. I tightened my grip on his arm and whispered 'don't smile. Look serious. Shake your head. You're being watched. . .' Fangio played his part marvellously and behind his goggles his eyes sparkled with joy.

The Ferrari pit was nearby, knowing eyes monitoring every nuance. Fangio clambered into the car and before he could slide down on to the seat two mechanics were shoving it as hard as they could. Fangio settled and moved back out on to The Ring. The Ferraris were that 48 seconds up the road and suddenly Collins covered lap 13 in 9m 28.9s. New record!

'Fangio's driving made it all too evident that his Maserati was not right,' Giambertone says. He had to bed the tyres in anyway, his tank load heavy. That stretched the Ferraris' lead to 51 seconds. The immense crowd sensed Fangio was in trouble. Even one of the mechanics in the pit, who didn't know that Fangio was setting a trap, danced with frustration and began shouting curses in Italian. Giambertone:

I must admit I was trembling inside. What if the tactics I had suggested proved too risky? If Fangio lost because of my advice I could never have forgiven myself. Tavoni, one of Enzo Ferrari's best men, was in charge of their team. How could I hope that he would snap at the bait?

Tavoni did. They hoisted a signal to Collins and Hawthorn:
STEADY. EVEN PACE, FANGIO LOSING TIME.

On lap 14 the lead was 48.5 seconds. As Fangio passed the pits Bertocchi made a slight gesture towards him and Fangio nodded, all enacted with such subtlety that nobody in the Ferrari pit realized. The hounds had been let loose. On lap 15 he took a full 7 seconds from the Ferraris, on lap 16 the gap had been sliced to 32 seconds. Hawthorn repassed Collins but the Ferrari personnel were now dancing up and down themselves urging the two Englishmen on.

Fangio would write:

I knew the Nürburgring very well. It's one of those tracks where you lose touch with things. You think you're going fast and you're not going fast at all. I began to use higher gears for some of the faster curves – if you went in at the right angle you came out with the engine revving at a faster rate on the straight. It wasn't very comfortable feeling the lack of grip as the car went round but I began to take nearly all the bends in a higher gear than I would normally have used. That's how I was driving when I came to the dip below the Bridge [at Adenau] where I had passed Froilan in 1954 in order to gain the lead on the first lap.

This time I didn't lift my foot off the accelerator. Normally we took that curve in fifth, trying to skim rather than jump, so as not to jolt the car and allow a margin of error when it landed. This time I took it without slacking at all, with my foot down. I tried to stick well to the inside above the dip, where the car 'took off', and I touched the ground again on the opposite side of the track, uncomfortably close to the wire fence. There were no guard rails in those days. In my mirror I saw the cloud of dust I'd raised at the edge of the track. I'd done it right. It was a risk worth taking. The curve linked two straight stretches and I had treated it as if it were just one straight. I knew I'd made up some seconds there.

Hawthorn took the bait, too. He wondered if Fangio had lost a gear or was his engine failing?

Whatever it was, victory seemed to be ours and as we roared along the straight I motioned to Peter to come alongside and pointed behind us with thumb down to indicate that Fangio seemed to be in trouble. He nodded, put his thumb up, then pointed to me with one finger and back to himself, with two. He wanted me to win and was prepared to come second, which I thought was a very sporting gesture and would save us racing against each other and perhaps breaking up both cars. Next lap Fangio pulled back a little time but at that rate he obviously could not catch us. Then as we came past the pits at the end of the next lap we had the fright of our lives. Fangio had cut our lead by 12 seconds in one lap.

That had been lap 14. The hunter drove faster and faster.

On lap 17 he did 9m 28.5s. New record! The lead was down to 25.5 seconds. Jack Brabham, whose Cooper-Climax had broken down, watched entranced from the pits. 'Fangio threw that Maserati round the Nürburgring like no-one I've seen before or since.'

On lap 18 he did 9m 25.3s. New record! He had become the first man to average 90mph (145kmh) on the circuit so many feared and he'd cut the gap to 20 seconds. The Ferrari pit was 'frantic', the crowd howling and cheering every time they glimpsed the Maserati. The cheering echoed from hill to hill and through the trees like a tribal chant.

On lap 19 a Ferrari mechanic held out a board with the single word FLAT on it: abandon everything for total speed. That lap 19, just as Hawthorn and Collins moved through the Sudkehre, Fangio crossed the line in 9m 23.4s. New record! He'd sliced the gap to 13.5. The crowd howled again when they heard that tumbling from the loudspeakers, the announcer 'shaking with excitement'. The Maserati pit signalled to Fangio that a Ferrari lay not far in front of him.

The crowd settled uneasily to their long wait listening to the wail of engines. Fangio saw 'a red blur disappearing round a bend among the trees and I said to myself, "I'll certainly catch that Ferrari." He assumed with the pit message still so fresh in his mind this must be Collins, Hawthorn far in front and out of reach.

I had no idea that Hawthorn was only a few metres in front of the one I had seen. On the descent to Adenau I saw two red cars, one behind the other. I knew I was going to catch them.

The crowd heard the wail beginning to come back from far, far out there, heard the wail rising along the immense straight from Schwalbenschwanz, the right-left-left-right which fed the straight, heard it rising and rising as the three cars moved towards the pits and the grandstand. When they saw the cars clearly there was Hawthorn, there was Collins perhaps three cars' length behind him, there was Fangio a mere 100 yards behind Collins. Stopwatches flicked. Fangio had butchered the gap to 3.0 seconds. Fangio: 'By the time we passed the pits I was tailing them.'

The announcer bayed over the loudspeakers. 'Achtung, achtung. New record for Fangio, new record for Fangio. Nine minutes 17.4 seconds!' The voice was lost as the crowd rose and howled again, flung a mass of hats in the air. It was probably the greatest lap ever driven.

Two laps left and as they headed towards the Sudkehre Fangio gained, gained, gained, almost up with Collins. Coming out of the Sudkehre Fangio thrust the Maserati alongside Collins, edged ahead – and Collins retook him.

Fangio: 'I had pressed the Maserati a bit too hard and it was too far over coming out of the curve. Collins gained some yards on me and he overtook me again and placed himself strategically for the next curve.' Fangio clung and at the Nordkehre, a bowl of a hard left-left-left just behind the pits, Fangio went through, two wheels on the grass and showering Collins with stones from the rim of the track. One of them shattered Collins' goggles. Hawthorn:

As Peter drifted in, Fangio pulled on to the outside of the bend and went past. It was an old trick from the school of long-distance inter-city racing in which Fangio served a hard apprenticeship in South America. Down the hill he went still clipping the grass all the way and Peter tried vainly to hold him.

Fangio: 'And there was Hawthorn's Ferrari directly in front of me going down into a right-hand bend.' This was not the moment. Fangio drew up to the Ferrari, primed himself and the two cars wheeled and turned, wheeled and turned through corner after corner. They had echoing names, Hatzenbach, Hocheichen, Quiddelbacher-Hohe, Flugplatz, Schwedenkreuz.

Hawthorn: 'It was now a fight between Fangio and me again and I was driving right on the limit as we rushed through the endless tree-lined curves to the Hocheichen and on to the Quiddelbacher-Hohe...'

Fangio calculated how many passing places remained this second last lap.

A short straight ended in a 90 degree turn to the left, followed by an equally sharp turn to the right. On the straight stretch Hawthorn pulled to the right to get his angle.

I saw my chance and cut in on his inside. Hawthorn must have seen a blur to his left because he suddenly pulled over as if startled.

The place was called Aremberg.

Hawthorn: 'Just as I was going in to the slow left-hander Fangio pulled the same trick, cut sharply inside me and forced me on to the grass and almost into the ditch.' As Fangio accelerated away he 'looked round almost apologetically'. Hawthorn thought: 'Right, now it's my turn to have a go at you.' As Hawthorn gathered himself for that a Maserati loomed ahead, but not that of Fangio; no, this one was blue and white and being driven by an American, Masten Gregory, a lap behind. Fangio nipped by but Hawthorn lost precious instants before he could.

There was a commentary point at Breidscheid three miles on from Aremberg and from there the news came back, from there that the voice on the loudspeakers bayed *Fangio leads, Fangio leads.*

Hawthorn: 'I gained on him again on the uphill sections but on the long straight back to the pits the Maserati was pulling away from me.'

Fangio: 'I made a point of getting away from him before we reached the straight because there he might have been able to take advantage of my slipstream and pass me.'

Tumult as they crossed the line to begin the last lap. Fangio had already squeezed enough to be clear of Hawthorn. 'As we started the last lap Fangio had the vital yards in hand which prevented me from getting to grips on the corners.' That last lap Hawthorn hammered, gaining a bit here, losing a bit there on the giant carousel but it was too late. Fangio made no mistake and won it by 3.6 seconds.

That was when the crowd saw it, there beneath the heavy crash helmet of the man in the Maserati: the smile on the face of the master.

The crowd carried him on their shoulders here, there and everywhere.

Fangio: When I managed to get to the podium Hawthorn and Collins were ecstatic as if they had been the winners. They never stopped congratulating me and shaking me by the hand even though my car had thrown up a stone and broken one of the lenses of Peter's goggles.

Hawthorn: Fangio told me afterwards that he was absolutely determined to win that race so as to make certain of the World Championship for the fifth time and on that fantastic 91.8mph lap which put him right on our tails he did things which were risky even for the greatest driver in the world.

Fangio (confiding to Hawthorn): 'I don't ever want to drive like that again.' Many years later Fangio said:

The Nürburgring was always my favourite track from the first day I drove on it in an Alfetta in 1951. I fell totally in love with it and I believe that on that day in 1957 I finally managed to master it. It was as if I had screwed all the secrets out of it and got to know it once and for all. I was trying out new things during those last laps of the race, pushing myself further at many blind spots where I had never before had the courage to go to the limit. I was never a daredevil, never a spectacular driver. I would go just so fast and no faster. I never tried to shoot far ahead or tried to be stylish for its own sake.

Quite simply I had always been a man with faith in my own abilities and in the machines that were prepared for me to drive. Until that race I had demanded nothing more of myself or the cars. But that day I made such demands on myself that I couldn't sleep for two days afterwards. I was in such a state that whenever I shut my eyes it was as if I were in the race again, making those leaps in the dark on those curves where I had never before had the courage to push things so far. For two days I felt delayed-action apprehension at what I had done, a feeling that had never come over me after any other race, a feeling that still returns to me this day when I think about that time.

1958

THE SHEIKH OF FARNHAM

Moroccan Grand Prix, Casablanca

Mike Hawthorn did wear a bow-tie during races and that suggested a style, a flamboyance. Once on his slowing down lap at the British Grand Prix he accepted a pint of beer offered by a marshal. Moss says 'just his presence did a lot for motor racing, I think, his being such a character. I liked him although we weren't close friends. You know, I've never been really close with another driver.'

A Londoner, Graham Hill, drove to Monte Carlo to make his debut in a Lotus. He'd remember driving down with his wife Bette 'on our old Austin A35' and doing the journey in thirteen hours from Calais 'which I thought was a pretty good time for such a small car.' The race was the first of a sombre season. Hill went seventy laps before a mechanical problem halted him.

However flamboyant Hawthorn appeared, he was worried and had been for long, nagging weeks. Tragedy stalked the season. His Ferrari team-mate Musso had been killed at Rheims in the French Grand Prix, the car snapping out of control in a corner and somersaulting. An America, Phil Hill, made his debut in a Maserati and finished seventh. He'd been at Le Mans during the crash of '55, now Musso had died and three years later Hill would know more tragedy.

Collins, team-mate and close friend of Hawthorn, was killed at the Nürburgring.

With nine rounds gone only Morocco remained and only Moss could beat Hawthorn to the championship, Moss in his very British Vanwall, but Moss had to win and get fastest lap and Hawthorn finish lower than second. Hawthorn was 29 and had decided to retire after the race.

The race before, Monza, had been five weeks ago. It gave Hawthorn time to reflect, although so many well-wishers coming up day after day asking their eternal, questions it preyed on him. The weeks gave Hawthorn time to reflect on a career and a life. He'd started in 1952 with Cooper, gone to Ferrari then Vanwall, Maserati, BRM and back to Ferrari. Amazingly in all that time he had won but three races, the last of them Rheims when Musso was killed.

As Morocco neared, smaller, more human anxieties began to prey on him. There'd been a race there the year before and Hawthorn still remembered the 'cramped and uncomfortable' flight on Air France 'with no food on board but cheese sandwiches'. This time Tony Vandervell, the moving force behind Vanwall, chartered a plane from Heathrow and offered Hawthorn a seat. The plane set course for the perfect place for a showdown – Casablanca.

The drivers gathered on the Thursday. Graham Hill remembered:

We stayed in a very smart hotel which had self-opening doors. I had never encountered such doors before and I was frightfully impressed that they should fly open when you stood on the mat in front of them.

That evening at dinner Hawthorn was shown the entry list by the Ferrari team manager.

The sight of it really upset me. I had been given number 2. No doubt it was partly due to nerves, but as Peter and Luigi had both been killed with the number 2 on the car I asked to have it altered.

The team manager soothed Hawthorn by saying he could have number 6 which had been allocated to another Ferrari driver, Olivier Gendebien, and the organizers would allocate Gendebien a different number altogether. Gendebien retorted that he wasn't superstitious and would take the 2. Phil Hill drove the third Ferrari and he'd stay with his number, 4.

After dinner, we must conjecture, drivers went out in search of diversions. Certainly Graham Hill discovered that 'in those parts they were able to provide some entertainments which one doesn't see elsewhere'.

The first session for the grid was on the Friday. The circuit lay on the Atlantic coast, a street circuit of 4.7 miles (7.6km) largely flanked by straw bales. From the start drivers went round a right-hand corner taking them inland and uphill to another right-hander on to the back straight, taken at high speed. That fed them to a 'vicious' – Hawthorn's word – right-hander, fast and potentially awkward towards the end of the race when the setting sun would be full in the drivers' eyes. A fast left and right-hander brought the drivers to the straight which ran parallel with the seashore.

Hawthorn arrived at the Ferrari pits and saw instantly Phil Hill's car had number 4 on it but Gendebien's still number 6. Hawthorn's own car had a cover over it. 'Oh hell,' he thought, 'number 2 is on it and I just daren't look.' He had to be soothed again: his Ferrari had had no number yet.

The first session was exploratory. Behra set fastest time in his BRM, 2m 25.2s.

Hawthorn remembered:

The sun was very tricky as also was the sea mist which would suddenly envelop the circuit. It didn't make the circuit dangerous but it was a little diffcult to see at times and the salt tended to stick to my visor. To counteract the glare of the sun we had the Perspex air-intake covers painted a matt black and also the top of the cockpit inside the wrap-round windscreen. I had a dark visor made to fight the glare and it worked very well.

Quite naturally the drivers went quicker on the Saturday, giving a front row of

Lewis-Evans	Moss	Hawthorn
Vanwall	Vanwall	Ferrari
2m 23.7s	2m 23.2s	2m 23.1s

That evening Hawthorn went to a party held by the British Ambassador and was in bed shortly after 11.30. He felt a curious sense of release from the tension – he'd even been worried about catching a cold, felt stomach pains and thought it was appendicitis.

Hawthorn heard the echoing of fog horns as ships slipped along the coast. He went into a deep sleep. Forgotten, even, was a wonderfully bizarre memory of that very afternoon's session for the grid. Gendebien's wife found a chameleon – a live one – and her husband carried it in the cockpit while he did 2m 24.3s. She offered it to Hawthorn for luck. 'It was an odd little creature and had a pair of beady eyes which could look in different directions at once.' Hawthorn declined. A bow-tie was one matter, livestock quite another.

When he woke he gazed out over the sea. It was a cloudy day and that delighted him because the Moroccan sun could burn a Briton – but, this 19 October 1958, the clouds began to clear...

Before the race the King of Morocco swept up in a motorcade flanked by bodyguards on motor bikes, was introduced to the drivers and made his stately way to the royal box in the grandstand. Bands played. The sun shone, hotter and hotter by the moment. Ferrari had number 6 on Hawthorn's car.

Moss, second in the championship in 1955 and 1956 and 1957, could virtually disregard tactics: win with fastest lap and hope either Stuart Lewis-Evans, a 28-year-old Briton in his second season, or Brooks in the other Vanwalls would come second forcing Hawthorn to third. Moss wrote:

> I must admit, it was a nerve-racking five weeks before the Morocco trip and I must confess the tension really got to me. I coveted that championship. After Fangio's retirement I felt I was his natural heir. Only his presence had kept it from me the previous three seasons. Does that sound like arrogance? I don't believe it was – I was still a young man, a very competitive young man, and it was a natural, almost instinctive attitude which developed in my mind. Mike sat his Ferrari on pole position after my engine blew in practice.

The starters didn't get the drivers into their cars until 15 minutes late and one of the Coopers wouldn't fire up. The starter used his flag to indicate the car should be pushed away but the other 24 drivers assumed the gesture meant go, and went, leaving the starter to run for his life. He made it.

'I made the best start,' Moss says, 'with Stuart in my wheel-tracks and Phil Hill leading Mike, driving very hard, wheel to wheel with me past the pits.' Moss took the first corner first, Hill directly behind him and already attacking. Hawthorn wasn't particularly worried that Lewis-Evans and the Swiss Jo Bonnier (BRM) were in front, never mind Moss and Phil Hill. Fifty-three laps to cover, 250.8 miles (403.6km) to cover. That would take more than two hours in this broiling sun.

Hawthorn moved up to third and delighted in watching Phil Hill maintain his assault on Moss, Hill coaxing the Ferrari alongside, Moss responding.

'I had a big battle from the start,' Hill says.

They crossed the line to begin lap 3 and travelled fast towards the right-hander at the end of the straight. Hill's drum brakes weren't as good as the discs on the Vanwall and, 'I brake-tested him,' Moss says, 'leaving my braking point very late just to emphasise my discs' advantage.' Hill plunged on down the escape road, turned and returned. Hawthorn was second, Bonnier third.

Hill hustled and on lap 5 re-passed Bonnier, a lap later was behind Hawthorn who immediately waved him through to 'have another go at Moss'. If Hill passed Moss and stayed there Hawthorn became champion. If Hill didn't he would be ordered to slow and allow Hawthorn into second place.

There was a problem. The deeply perceptive Brooks was at 26 already thinking of his career beyond motor racing and using the journey time between Grand Prix races to study for it – but in a car he was as dedicated as any and he harried Bonnier for fourth place. On lap 12 he went by and set off after Hawthorn.

The whole balance of the race began to shift. Moss pulled cleanly away from Hill, extending the gap lap by lap. 'We had finally dragged ourselves free of the rest but there was no way I could stay with Moss with the brakes we had.' Hill says. If Brooks – coming, coming, coming – overtook Hawthorn it made Moss champion. Brooks caught Hawthorn and harried him, Hawthorn holding on.

'I found I had the speed on the straights but out of the corners the Vanwall was quicker. If I passed him all he had to do was to get into my slipstream along the straights and then he would nip past me out of the corners.' That was Hawthorn thinking aloud, projecting what would happen if Brooks did get past. The balance shifted again. On lap 18 Moss moved to overtake a Maserati, lapping it for the second time, and they collided. The nose of the Vanwall buckled but Moss kept control and kept on. The air intake was damaged although not enough to affect the water temperature...

A lap later Brooks did pass Hawthorn. 'At one point Tony got a lead of about three seconds but I got it back and as we swapped places every now and then I noticed there was a little stream of smoke from the engine compartment by the exhausts, and occasionally Tony would have to wipe his windshield and his goggles. Well he's not going to last very long, I thought, nothing to worry about there.'

On lap 21 Moss pressed the Vanwall round in 2m 22.5s, an average speed of 119.5mph (192.4kmh): the one crucial point for fastest lap.

What Hawthorn saw on Brooks' Vanwall was a mirage which might have come straight from the desert, the little stream of smoke no more than quantities of oil gathering in the exhaust pipe and burning off. Hawthorn had to re-pass Brooks and stay there. They duelled, passed and re-passed but on lap 30, Brooks panting hard just behind, the Vanwall dropped a valve. The piston burst through the side of the car and with oil flooding on to the rear wheel Brooks slid, held it, came to rest at the side of the track. Gendebien, sixth, ran on to the oil and slid, too. A lapped Cooper-Climax went into Gendebien's Ferrari, ramming it off the circuit. It hit a rock, slicing the whole of the back away just behind the driver's seat. Gendebien suffered only bruising.

Moss held a lead of 30 seconds over Hill, and Hill held a substantial lead over Hawthorn. 'At a certain point I was given the order by the team to slow down and drop back and let Hawthorn through, which I did. I was a new boy, I wanted to stay on the team, I had to do what they told me and anyway I got along very well with Hawthorn.' On lap 40 Hawthorn accepted the second place but a problem remained: Bonnier in the BRM circling hungrily in fourth.

Hawthorn knew he had the protective shield of Hill between himself and Bonnier and he – Hawthorn – could use more of the Ferrari's power if he needed it. Hawthorn had been conserving the car and it was running faultlessly.

Maybe, some wondered, Lewis-Evans might find some speed, mount a late run, shift the balance again but on lap 42 the engine blew, the Vanwall went off into sand and was engulfed by fire. Lewis-Evans, badly burnt, struggled out but was so concussed that he sprinted away from the fire marshals. Hawthorn saw a 'huge column of black smoke' and when he reached the corner leading to the sea 'there was oil on the road and a car burning fiercely on the inside of the circuit. I could just see part of the bonnet hanging from the car with Vanwall written on it. I could see no number on the car'.

As Hawthorn moved past the pits his own board gave him a time gap and he knew then it must be Lewis-Evans. If Moss had been on fire the board would be announcing to Hawthorn that he led. Hill followed Hawthorn obediently home, Moss already over the line more than half a lap ahead. Moss won by 1m 24.7s. Immediately Hawthorn punched the air and regretted that somehow he hadn't savoured his last moments in a racing car more fully. He remembered exactly when he thought that: a hundred yards from the Ferrari pit, his lap of honour all but completed.

The Ferrari manager said 'next year we will do it again.' Hawthorn replied 'I won't be racing. I'm going to retire.'

On the podium Moss, magnanimous as ever, smiled and said 'you did it, you old so-and-so.'

Much, much later Moss would say:

I made fastest lap, I won the race by more than a minute but Mike was champion because Phil Hill, his team-mate, lying second, dropped back to third. One might say that it was Phil who beat me not Mike but I've never felt a trace of bitterness against Phil for it – if he hadn't done it he'd have been fired off the Ferrari team five seconds after he stepped out of the motor car. Ideally, of course, every driver would try his best all the time but that's not the way things are done. Some people like to say that motor racing is the cleanest game in the world, the cleanest sport. The older I get, the more

I distrust absolutes like that, but it is a clean sport and to me it's a saintly sport compared to any other ... Mike deserved it. My congratulations were genuine but I could not hide my deep depression because of poor Stuart's crash as well as my own disappointment. But within days the knot in my stomach relaxed and I realized it didn't matter. . . not that much. I became far more philosophical and, perhaps, more mature.

The aftermath of the race itself was as the season had been. Hawthorn returned to his hotel, shaved, accepted the trophy – 'a cup mounted on four little racing cars' – but his thoughts were on Lewis-Evans. He had to be persuaded to go to a little nightclub for a drink or two.

Some postscripts.

The next day they flew home. The plane Moss was on had to make an emergency landing at Paris, two engines gone. Lewis-Evans was on Hawthorn's plane, 'conscious and very cheerful despite his pain'. They strapped him across three seats and a nurse sat in attendance. Five days later he was dead. Four months later Hawthorn was dead, too. His Jaguar careered across the central reservation of a by-pass in southern England and struck a tree.

Far into the future, Moss 'was saying to a friend that I didn't know, really, when the championship had lost meaning for me. Katie, the friend's wife, was with us and she said, "I know when it was, it was in 1958." I thought about that for a long time and I realized she was right. I tried for it just as hard in 1959, 1960, 1961, but that was when the meaning went out of it for me. 1958.'

The last postscript? That, too, involved words, words which tumble gently in the background of life. A nightclub, a pianist, a beautiful lady and a hustling chancer in a creased suit.

It's still the same old story,
A fight for love and glory,
A case of do or die.
The fundamental things apply
As time goes by.

You know the film where it all happened. Casablanca.

1959

BRABHAM, FOOTSOLDIER

United States Grand Prix, Sebring

Jack Brabham had never driven on the other side of the Atlantic. When the offer came for a race at Nassau's Speed Week it made a lot of sense. He'd have a chance to relax in delightful surroundings and be handily placed for the United States Grand Prix at Sebring, Florida, a few days later.

Brabham shipped a Cooper over, raced and trying to get into the lead a stone was thrown up

smashing my goggles. The glass was safety reinforced but apparently these were an old pair. I whipped the goggles down and tried to drive with one eye, the other stinging. It was full of glass. A doctor rushed me to hospital where they extracted as much as they could but a specialist told me I had been very lucky. A piece of the glass had pierced my eye about an eighth of an inch off the pupil. I was worried for the championship.

Brabham, a taciturn Aussie with sharp edges as well as smooth in a racing car, did relax after that. He had to. The doctors were still not satisfied all the glass had been removed because the eye was so bloodshot they couldn't see into it properly. When he boarded a plane for the short hop to Miami on the Tuesday he was still worried. He had several reasons.

Sebring, originally scheduled to open the season in March, was the first United States Grand Prix to count for the World Championship. Some teams weren't ready that early so it was put back to 12 December. As late as November rumours suggested it wouldn't take place and, even if it did, Ferrari wouldn't go but the championship remained open.

Sebring became the last race of the season and the decider.

The best five finishes out of nine counted and Brabham (Cooper-Climax) already had five. From his total of 31 he faced dropping the four points he'd just won at Monza. Brooks (Ferrari) had 23 but from only three finishes. Moss (Cooper-Climax) had 25 but from five. He faced dropping only a single point. All this allowed permutations but Moss needed victory and fastest lap and Brabham not finish second. It was a replay of Casablanca.

Brabham spent the Tuesday night in Miami. On the Wednesday he headed up Federal Route 98 into deepest Florida, a journey of 200 miles. He didn't arrive until midnight. The next day he passed a medical and drove out to have a look at Sebring. The circuit was truly curious: about a third of its 5.1 miles (8.3km) ran round aircraft hangars while the remainder wandered across flat and featureless country. It was dull for both spectators and drivers and had the appearance of being set up for a driving test in a rally. There were rubber pylons to mark the edges of some parts of the circuit while the inside of some turns was marked by half-buried tyres, which were not easy to sight.

Sebring was flat, uneven and in the middle of nowhere.

When Moss arrived he found that his team had indulged in a little psychology. They'd stuck a vivid action photograph of Brabham taking a corner fast on Moss's rear-view mirror...

Autosport reported that not long after qualifying began the lap record 'went completely. Moss's existing time of 3m 20s in the DBR1 Aston Martin (93.6mph) was beaten by no fewer than thirteen drivers. Spectators gasped when Moss returned three minutes dead, a speed of 104 miles an hour. He made racing look ridiculously easy.'

Brabham had gearbox problems and indulged in some 'market gardening', running wide over the half-buried tyres and denting the side of the car. During the second qualifying session he decided to swap cars with his team-mate Bruce McLaren, a young New Zealander:

If we hadn't I would probably have put my car away and not practised any more in it. When we swapped, Bruce decided to do a couple of laps to see if he wanted to make any adjustments. He had only done half a lap when the crown wheel and pinion broke. Had I used that car I wouldn't have completed a lap in the race.

I took Bruce's car around for a few laps and found it would not handle well at all. When we checked up that night we discovered the chassis was twisted. This car was the one Masten Gregory had used in Lisbon [for the Portuguese Grand Prix] and during the race he hit a kerb with the result that the frame was now three-quarters of an inch out. We did our best to straighten it but it was an almost impossible task. I fiddled with the suspension and re-set it to suit the twisted frame. Then the brakes started to shudder. Having got the brakes working reasonably well we then dismantled the gearbox and discovered the mainshaft was cracked. Luckily we had a spare gearbox.

The work went on until one in the morning of the race.

Brabham began to concentrate on the tactic of getting fastest lap, something he judged 'the all-important factor'. Originally he'd planned to ask Gregory to sacrifice his own chances by going out and setting such a pace that neither Moss nor Brooks could risk blowing their engines trying to beat it. That would have kept the fastest lap point away from them, but Gregory had been injured before the Italian Grand Prix and wasn't driving at Sebring. Brabham would have to do it himself.

Nineteen cars lined up on the grid, Moss pole, Brabham next to him. With the minutes ticking to the start the world went mad. Schell (Cooper-Climax) had done 3 minutes 5.2 seconds in qualifying, a major surprise and one which the timekeepers couldn't believe. They said he'd done 3m 11.2s, which placed him on the fourth row. Schell was very angry indeed, berated the timekeepers and announced his intention of placing the Cooper on the front row alongside Brabham – forcing Brooks back to the second row.

The timekeepers argued, Schell argued and they eventually agreed he could have the front row. Beside the pits, the Sebring girls' band and some majorettes were lining up to give the crowd the showbusiness they like so much but the Ferrari officials, hearing that Brooks had been relegated to the second row, brushed through the girls and a fierce argument developed, people pushing and gesticulating. *Autosport* reported:

It looked exactly like a free-fight in a Glasgow dockside pub – only noisier. Then the majorettes started up the band and the girls stamped their shapely legs. As if by magic the jostling and shoving ceased. Both Moss and Brabham were trying unsuccessfully to keep their faces straight.

The Italians retreated. Schell took his place on the front row, Brooks on the second.

From the flag Brabham grasped the lead and held it for a hundred yards then:

Moss raced past me like a rocket. This suited me fine. There was no sense in chasing Moss in the early stages when we had full tanks because this is the easiest time to break a car. When I saw Moss go past me I almost relaxed completely. The way he went off down the road I could not believe his car would go far.

Moss of course was searching for that fastest lap. Further back a German, Wolfgang 'Taffy' von Trips (Ferrari Dino) and Brooks misjudged a corner, both went off and collided. Brooks had difficulty restarting his engine and limped to the pits to have his wheels checked. He rejoined fifteenth.

Moss led Brabham by a couple of seconds completing lap 1. Forty-one remained. Moss continued to pull away and after four laps the lead had become eight seconds, crossing the line to start lap 6 it had become 9.8 but all at once:

The gearbox went. There were many post-mortems and someone suggested 'both Moss and Phil Hill (Ferrari) rather punished their transmissions with sprint starts'. In my own view this had nothing to do with it. I like to be out in front because if you can get there and lose the field you are in a good position. After doing a lap of 3 minutes dead in practice, my lap times of 3m 5s showed that I was not hurrying all that much. I had fuel in reserve and I was prepared to drive the race of my life to win the championship.

That championship was now decided. As Brabham passed his pit they held up a sign MOSS OUT. He suspected it already. On that sixth lap as he rounded a corner called Webster Turn about half-way round the circuit – it was like a kink in a straight – he'd seen Moss off the circuit. Brabham assumed he had spun. On lap 7 Brabham carefully looked again to be sure Moss had not rejoined. The car was still there.

Brooks rejoined and created a powerful thrust out of the debris of his race. He had nothing to lose. After eight laps he was 81.5 seconds behind Brabham, after 11 laps he started cutting deeper at a second a lap. Brabham sensed that Brooks 'could still upset me'. Brooks couldn't sustain the thrust. He was gaining places – fifth now – but not gaining enough time.

'Five or six laps before the end,' Brabham says, 'I increased speed and Bruce McLaren stayed with me. The car was running perfectly and I could not see anything to rob me of the championship. My idea in letting Bruce slipstream me was that if anything did go wrong with my car he could take the lead and beat Tony to the line – Tony had to beat me and get fastest lap.' Trintignant (Cooper-Climax) set that on lap 39 and his time, 3m 5s, would take some beating.

Von Trips' Ferrari still ran as they moved towards the last lap but the engine 'more or less exploded' and the German pushed it to the line, oil dripping. He waited for Brabham to finish and would push the Ferrari over the line to be classified, albeit a lap behind.

As Brabham passed his pit to begin the last lap he nodded solemnly. It meant all was well. Then...

'I was about a mile from the finishing line when the car started to run on two cylinders. I was shocked. I just couldn't believe it.' The order: Brabham, McLaren, Trintignant storming round – Moss stood on the rim of the track urging him on with dramatic gestures – Brooks.

'I automatically put the gear lever into neutral as the engine went dead. I was out of fuel. We were cornering at the time at about 70 miles an hour. I coasted on down until we reached the second last corner'- a loop-corner which fed out directly on to the finishing straight. 'Bruce came alongside me, almost stopping. My reactions were quick and to the point. With much arm-waving and shouting I told Bruce to get going. Bruce was horrified. He couldn't work out what was wrong and had ideas of stopping to help me. Luckily he got the message and pressed on. Trintignant went past me at about the same time as I coasted along getting slower and slower. Eventually about 500 yards from the flag the car came to a standstill. Why must home straights always be uphill? I took off my helmet and goggles, got out and started to push.'

McLaren won, Trintignant a fraction under one second behind him and now there was consternation all along the pit lane. Where was Brabham? There, down there in the distance, a strong man in his blue overalls, pushing.

'I remember seeing Tony come past me then I just put my eyes to the road and kept on pushing. It was hot. They tell me the crowd went wild. Motor cycle cops tried to keep the crowds back ... it must have been the first time the new World Champion was escorted to the line by a motor cycle escort.'

Slowly, slowly under the pedestrian bridge he came and the man with the chequered flag waved it to encourage him but the line lay another hundred yards away. The pits were full of people and they moved in a current towards the man in blue who still pushed slowly, slowly, his body hunched over the flank of the car. The bustle in the pit lane became applause as Brabham pressed the car over the line and fell to the ground.

'Frankly I don't remember a thing except flopping down beside the car and reviving myself with a bottle of Coca-Cola. I lay there for a few minutes while people pumped my hand until eventually they helped me into an official's caravan. I flopped out for a quarter of an hour or so to get my breath back. Then suddenly it dawned on me. I'd won, I'd won the World Championship!'

Brooks was third, Brabham himself fourth, 4m 57.3s behind McLaren. That was how long he had had to push the car.

Relaxing in the bath at his hotel Brabham wondered quite how he'd run out of fuel and McLaren hadn't. More puzzling, McLaren had had four gallons left at the end. True, McLaren had been slipstreaming Brabham across large tracts of the race and that naturally saved fuel, but Brabham estimated the saving at two gallons. Then he remembered that just after the start the engine briefly ran on only three cylinders:

It must have lost a lot of fuel out of the overflow and the breather tube had been spilling the fuel down past the carburettor, making it run rich. Once the fuel had gone down a bit it started to run properly.

Never mind. Jack Brabham had become the only man to reach the World Championship on foot.

1960

IN THE TRAMLINES

Portuguese Grand Prix, Oporto

The defence began badly. A gearbox problem thwarted Brabham in Argentina and Monaco became a freak Grand Prix. It was wet, he spun into a barrier on the way up to Ste Devote and retired but more and more cars retired, too, and at one point only four were running. He decided to have another go. It didn't matter how many laps he'd lost because points were there for the taking but his Cooper-Climax needed a push start and he was immediately disqualified.

A genuinely great motorbike rider, John Surtees, made his debut at Monaco, 'quite an experience because I had only taken part in the occasional bike race on proper street circuits,' which meant he'd 'never encountered anything like the challenge' of Monaco. The transmission failed after eighteen laps.

After Monaco Brabham bestrode the mid-season winning Holland, Belgium, France and Britain.

A farmer from the Borders made his debut in the Dutch race. Jim Clark drove a Lotus, as he always would and 'took it very easy' in his first race with such a car. After a 'tremendous battle' with Graham Hill the gearbox failed. A new generation was at hand: Surtees, Hill, Clark.

After Britain three rounds remained. Brabham had 32 points, his nearest rival McLaren (also Cooper-Climax) 27, but only a driver's six best finishes counted and McLaren had already scored in five, Brabham in only four. Brabham was going to be hard to beat.

Two flights had been arranged from Gatwick to take the Formula 1 fraternity to what should have been a delightful place, Oporto, sun-kissed and famed for the port wine the British adored so much. Clark, still feeling his way into Grand Prix racing, travelled on one. He would write:

These trips to the races with all the drivers, mechanics and pit crews were really good fun. On this occasion, for instance, every passenger was given a little construction kit of a boat to make up on the flight. The man who made the best model got half a bottle of Scotch.

Brabham had his own plane, a Cessna, and flew that down himself taking wife Betty with him.

'Team Lotus,' Clark wrote, 'stayed at the Hotel Imperio in Oporto and someone hired a BMW 600 for us to travel about in. We drove out to have a look at the circuit because it was a fairly new one. A crowd of men with assorted bits of metal were trying to build a footbridge over it. It had fallen down the previous day. A young American millionaire had let Colin Chapman [creator of Lotus, of course] use his massive Fiat transporter. This was a real plush affair and Jim Endruweit, our chief mechanic, was so pleased with it that he elected to drive most of the way from England and let the other mechanics loll about on the two bunks or on the reclining passenger's seat.'

Oporto's 4.6 miles (7.4km) truly was a street circuit, paved with cobblestones and tramlines set into them. Fifty-five laps represented a long way to bounce – 256 miles (412km).

There was Moss in a Lotus-Climax, recovered after a crash at Spa when a wheel came off and the car cartwheeled into a horrifying crash. There was Surtees opening up another career in a Lotus, Graham Hill who'd left Lotus for BRM after two barren years, Innes Ireland, strong-willed Scotsman, in a Lotus, Brooks in a Cooper-Climax, Phil Hill and von Trips in Ferraris.

Qualifying began on the Friday at six in the evening because it was cooler then.

Oporto offered only bales of hay placed at intervals to keep the cars away from stone walls. Henry Taylor, a Briton in a Cooper-Climax, crashed in the left-hand corner leading to the long Avenida da Boavista straight and was taken to hospital with a cut shoulder, cracked ribs and damaged fingers. Moss was second quickest behind an American, Dan Gurney (BRM), covering the circuit in 2m 28.32s, an average speed of over 111mph (179kmh). Moss had had brake problems but you'd scarcely have known that. Brabham was fourth.

On the Saturday Surtees provided 'a sensation' and took pole with 2m 25.56s while Moss drifted back to fourth a place behind Brabham (2m 26.05s). Clark meanwhile had a moment.

On my second lap I tried a tight line on one corner when I was going too fast. I braked hard and skidded, missing a lamppost by inches but hitting a kerb which bounced me to the other side of the road and through the straw bales. The front end of the car was wrecked.

Chapman was determined not to sacrifice the starting money so he and Endruweit set out to build a 'starting money special' with the prime job of being capable of at least taking part in the race. They sent the other mechanics off to bed to get some sleep while they descended on a local Portuguese garage man who cleared his workshop for action. The man looked at the mess of the car and shook his head leaving these mad Englishmen to get on with it.

It was about 10pm and at midnight he came back to see what was happening and found the car almost stripped of everything. By 2am with the twisted chassis laid bare before them Chapman and Endruweit started to improvise as only they can. They straightened out the steering rack then they attacked the chassis with an oxyacetylene torch and hacksaws. They took two tubular jacks and chopped them up into frame tubes for the chassis. With yards of wire and much welding they put the front end together again and straightened out the remaining tubes, with masking tape they patched up the glass fibre nose cowl and at 6am they staggered off to get some sleep. I was really surprised when I got up in the morning to find I had a car to drive.

Innes Ireland was surprised to find the Irish flag flying above his car. The organizers hadn't realized he was Scottish and assumed, being called Ireland, that was where he came from. Meanwhile the workmen still worked on the footbridge and the organizers decided on the only possible decision: the bridge would be closed.

The two minute board produced a moment of rich comedy. Phil Hill naturally assumed that two minutes meant two minutes and ran full tilt from the pits to get into his Ferrari where he sat for twenty minutes waiting. As *Autosport* said, 'after a cavalcade of motor scooters had paraded, followed by officials with a police escort on motor cycles with shrieking sirens, it looked as if a race might start any hour.'

Graham Hill on the second row was determined not to be left. He began to edge forward before the flag fell and the others set off, too. Their estimated speed when the flag did fall: 30 miles an hour.

Brabham took the lead, Surtees and Gurney directly behind. That was done at the left-hander before the long straight. Brabham went wide and cut in front of Gurney but at the end of the straight, towards the left-hander, Gurney nipped in front and Moss nipped in front of Surtees; and they began the second lap.

That first lap, geographically, resembled no other in the long and improbable history of the World Championship.

'After the straight and the left-hander,' Brabham says, 'you go uphill and along the tramlines, then you have to turn left' – it was a 90° hairpin – 'but the tramlines go straight on. I came up and moved inside to overtake but I got myself into the tramlines going straight on like a tram and it was obvious I wouldn't be able to stop.' He thought *I'll have to stay in the tramlines all the way to the depot, wherever that is*. He stayed within them long enough to slow and extricate the Cooper, turn it round and head back towards the circuit, eighth, Moss up to second.

Gurney, Moss and Surtees regularly hammered the lap record, Phil Hill was catching them, Graham Hill was catching him. At the end of the fifth lap Surtees moved past Moss whose engine had developed a misfire. 'I hung on,' Moss would say, 'and Surtees closed up on Gurney who hit some oil letting us both through. Now Surtees led and I was back in second place.' Oil blew from Gurney's BRM engine on to the back wheels and on lap 11 he spun.

In the background Brabham was coming in a long charge, now fourth. Clark nursed the improvized Lotus expecting it to break at any moment and food poisoning gave him a 'terrible ache' in the stomach.

Moss attacked Surtees and cut the gap to a second but they couldn't pull away from Phil Hill, whose Ferrari engine was making a lovely noise. Moss took a lunge at Surtees, failed and came in for new plugs to cure the misfire. The time lost put him back to sixth.

Brabham attacked Hill hard, caught Hill and got through. Hill grasped second place back. On lap 29 Hill missed a gear – the clutch was damaged – and thundered into the kerbing, scattering the straw bales.

Surtees led by 20 seconds, Surtees so combative by nature. What Brabham didn't know was that petrol seeped from Surtees' fuel tank and fell on to Surtees' canvas driving shoes, burning. Moss overtook Surtees to unlap himself and Surtees took him back. Phil Hill reached the pits minus clutch. He would cover one more lap slowly and park the car just short of the finishing line, wait until the leaders had finished and limp across himself because if less than six cars were running he'd get points. The officials didn't like the idea, a fierce argument developed, the officials started to push the car away and then Hill was ordered back into the race. He couldn't make the engine fire.

The dripping petrol reached the soles of Surtees' shoes but he had stretched his lead to 28 seconds and Brabham couldn't catch that. On lap 37 as Surtees was negotiating a left-hand corner his foot, smeared with petrol, slipped on the pedal. He hit a high kerb hard and the impact burst the radiator. Suddenly, all Brabham had to do was finish. He led McLaren by 45 seconds, Clark nicely in third.

Brabham's engine was 'running pretty hot' but he made it 57.97 seconds in front of McLaren. John Cooper, who made Cooper cars, did a back somersault in celebration and landed on his feet.

A postscript.

Autosport: 'Brabham was taken round the circuit in a splendid white Rolls-Royce and then hurried to a local tram depot where Dunlop had arranged a TV interview.' He might have got there earlier if he'd stayed in the tramlines.

1961

PHIL HILL'S PHILOSOPHY

Italian Grand Prix, Monza

'It does not bother me one iota, not at all, never has in fact. The only thing that bothered me was when people were so busy analysing how I should feel. They got more muddled up than I did.' Many years later, Phil Hill remained ambivalent about the Monza race which gave so much and took away so much, but he had it in its context. He was, truth to tell, fatalistic about it and wondered how else you could possibly be.

This soft-spoken, erudite, charming man from Santa Monica, California – who died in 2008 – started his working life as a mechanic, raced an MG and progressed via Le Mans to driving a Ferrari in 1958. All his races from then until 1961 were with Ferrari, except the US at Riverside in 1960 where he drove a Cooper 'because Ferrari did not come. Enzo would go if someone was paying the bill...'

Hill had an ambivalent relationship with The Great Man, Enzo Ferrari, or as he put it, 'I never had a particularly pleasant relationship. He was so busy being the boss all the time and of course there may have been something about my personality and character that he did not warm to. I don't know whether there was or not. So – I never really had a good relationship. I don't think all that many people did have. I can't think of all that many people who did get along well with him.

'I know he liked Dan Gurney because Gurney always would have a big grin which put people off their guard, so to speak, and I didn't do that when things were going wrong, but really I don't know why we didn't get along well. It never got to shouting and arguments. I remember once I complained, in fact I think it was that week at Monza. I complained about the windshield on my car and Enzo made some crack that maybe I should get my foot down or something like that and I snapped back at him.

'With the elevated track, the banking which was flat out all the way round, it didn't take a genius to plank his foot down and hold it there. If your car is a second or a second-and-a-half slower than somebody else's going round there it's pretty obvious something's got to be wrong with the car.'

The Ferrari was the car to have in 1961 and after Moss (Lotus-Climax) won the first race, Monaco, von Trips took Holland from Hill, Hill took Belgium from von Trips and though Hill had a crash in France and von Trips' engine let go, von Trips won the British from Hill. That was the matrix of the season. By Monza and with only Watkins Glen to come, von Trips had 33 points, Hill 29. The five best finishes counted and Hill had those, the lowest a third place. Von Trips had those, the lowest a fourth.

'I got along fine with von Trips. He was happy-go-lucky, I didn't find him sort of serious enough. Maybe he was but not in my way of being serious. It wasn't that he hadn't come from Germany to do well, either, perhaps it was just a matter of degree although I did feel he was a little bit too light-hearted about everything. We were different, you know, people are different and very often you can't analyse the aspects of character which make one person completely a kindred spirit and another not. I never had much empathy for drivers who didn't have a key interest in the mechanical side of it and von Trips didn't have that. He knew what spark plugs were and that was about the end of it.'

I must, I feel, soften this impression of Phil Hill because the printed word faithfully recording a man's words cannot capture the timbre of his voice, the sound of the sentiments being expressed and thus how they are being expressed. That is important. Hill, long matured in the ways of the world, was recapturing something honestly and without a trace of rancour. He was not criticizing von Trips and barely criticizing The Great Man himself, just telling it the way it was. That is the key to the first paragraph of this chapter. You must not, please, read more into it than that. Or less.

Hill knew Monza. 'It was a bit the same as it is today, a very, very intense attitude on the part of the darned military there, well probably much more so than now. You know the feeling when you get off the plane at Malpensa Airport in Milan? That hard feeling, a lot of people in uniform. Out at the track they wouldn't take any guff off of anybody, which was unusual to the racing people whether it be mechanics, Enzo Ferrari himself or team managers or drivers or what. They were in the habit of being cow-towed to and the military wouldn't do that. There was always an incident with a journalist or someone getting kicked around by the military. Ferrari withdrew his whole team one year, I forget whether it was a team manager who'd been pushed around or what, but it was weird that sort of behaviour – although he put the team back in again.'

Even for Ferrari, even for the drivers, those God-heads instantly recognized and feted throughout Italy with mystical reverence, Monza was a place of no favours and no compromises. The military's conduct, which seems so mysterious and inexplicable, was based on military pragmatism. The unruly, empassioned crowd might become a Roman mob at any moment as the current of passion plucked them this way or that.

'I had great confidence in my car because I had a good idea what had been wrong with it and that was that we had probably broken some valve springs, a problem we had had throughout the year. We made some changes to the car the final week before coming up for the race and mine was the only one which didn't have a fresh engine in it. We increased the ride height and got rid of some of the negative camber in the back on the first day because the Dunlop people told us we had to – because of the temperatures on the inside edges of the tyres and in doing so we gained some revs.

'I felt that that had happened to my car with the work that we had done mid-week in testing, I'd got up into the break-the-valve-spring revs, and my whole first day of practice was a cock up because I drove off from the pits that first time and went from first to second and shifted over into the next track [gate in the gearbox, as they say] and went back to first again. It took me half an hour to convince the people that they had screwed up with the darned gating in the rod going back to the gearbox. So that was the end of my first day's practice, wasted. It wasn't until I didn't get the fresh engine that I made a fuss. I rarely ever behaved like that but this time it was so obvious that something was wrong with my car. I always did well at Monza.'

It had been unseasonally wet, von Trips snatching a dry moment to do 2m 46.8s. Saturday dawned sunny.

Autosport reported:

This year drivers were required to lap within 15 per cent of the best time, which worked out at a 25 seconds margin. The organizers also charged a 5,000 lire fee for observing conductors [drivers] who had not previously raced on the banked track. In the United Kingdom one had never heard of making invited pilots [drivers] part with folding money for the privilege of dicing.

Ferrari made sure of an all-red front row with von Trips returning 2m 46.3s and the incredible Ricardo Rodriguez [a Mexican in a Ferrari] being only one tenth of a second slower. Richie Ginther [an American, also Ferrari] had a best time of 2m 46.8s, Hill's 2m 47.2s and Giancarlo Baghetti [Italian, Ferrari] 2m 49s. The Italian nearly came unstuck in a big way on the South Bend of the banking, his Ferrari diving down from the top and all but spinning round. The surface on the banked sections was dreadfully rough and cars were seen to be leaping and bounding with dampers working overtime.

Phil Hill was seen to be slow and he was not a slow driver. 'I'd held the lap record there a number of times and suddenly to be on the second row – we kept the score, we broke our lap into two pieces, once around the banking and once around the track and they went together for our total time. I was slow around the banking and I made some of it up on the road part. So I got a new engine. I was out there early in the morning to help get it sorted out and make sure the throttle mechanism was working correctly and everything, I needed to be sure my car was going to be good and I felt just fine for the race. They told me they had found some broken valve springs, which again made me feel just fine for making all the fuss.'

As we have seen, Peter Collins had been killed in a Ferrari at the

Nürburgring in 1958 and Enzo Ferrari, who didn't go to the races, 'said he was going to be there but he didn't. He told Louise Collins he had returned to Modena for one reason or another. When I had a kidney cholic they both came to visit me, Ferrari and Louise Collins, and he said he was going to break tradition, Louise was going to sit beside him during the race and of course it never happened.'

Rodriguez crawled forward before the start, braked and 'waited' for Hill. They set off together, Rodriguez nipped ahead, Hill took him. The grid was so immense – 32 cars – that the last row of the grid crossed the line thirteen seconds after. Coming off the banking to complete the lap, Hill led Ginther, Rodriguez, Clark, Brabham (Cooper-Climax) and von Trips. Towards the end of the second lap *Autosport* reported:

Von Trips roared past Brabham and Clark but going into the Parabolica he seemed to lose control and collided with Clark's Lotus. The Ferrari overturned and reared up against a wire fence where many spectators were gathered. Von Trips was flung out, being instantaneously killed, but before the wrecked car finished up back on the track it had created terrible havoc amongst the crowd. Clark's Lotus also overturned but the Scotsman escaped injury. For some time there was confusion, with officials attempting to remove the crashed Ferrari and attend to the dead and dying.

The image was terrifying, the Ferrari riding up a bank which acted as a launch pad, rotating three times in the air, returning airborne towards the track, making another rotation and thrashing itself against the surface of the track.

Did von Trips lose control? Clark would write:

I remember nothing about the race after von Trips and I touched wheels. After pulling his car off the track and seeing his body I just felt sick through and through. I cannot describe the feelings I had. One minute I was racing and enjoying it, and the next I was walking away from a ghastly mess. I didn't want to see a racing car again...

Brabham judged the accident

*just one of those unfortunate things that can happen at any time at all
on a slipstreaming circuit. I don't think either Jimmy or Taffy were
carving each other up, as was suggested at the time. I'm not even sure
that theirs were the only two cars involved – it could have been a third
one, which touched one of the other two and caused the Lotus to veer
enough to touch the Ferrari. At that speed, early in the race on a
slipstreaming circuit, this kind of thing is a constant possibility. Jimmy
was always a driver you could really drive hard against and be quite
confident that he wasn't going to do something stupid.*

What is known is that fourteen spectators were killed.

Phil Hill, moving into lap 2 and well ahead of the crash, saw
nothing of all this. When he reached the Parabolica he did see the
Ferrari but didn't know which one it was, and he saw the Lotus. 'I
made it a point to pay no attention. Any racing driver wants to get
on, wants to pay attention to the things he is supposed to be paying
attention to. Nothing was blocking the road. Passing the pits that lap
– or it might have been the next lap – I watched the order boards.
Von Trips was missing so I knew it was him.' Hill did not, of course,
have any conception of the extent of the accident.

They slipstreamed, Brabham clinging to the Ferraris of Hill, Ginther
and Rodriguez. Ginther moved into the lead on lap 7, was third as
they came round to start lap 8: that slipstreaming. Brabham's engine
overheated on lap 9 and the race became a Ferrari procession.
Baghetti moved up to join the bunch. Ginther regained the lead and
held it for three laps but the Ferraris were so tight together it had no
particular significance.

Suddenly Rodriguez and Baghetti were in the pits together,
Rodriguez with oil all over the windscreen, Baghetti's engine gone.
Mechanics attacked the cars but could do nothing. Both retired. That
was lap 13.

Autosport reported that 'Ferrari were extremely worried and signals
were continually displayed to the two Americans. Consequently the lap
speeds dropped slightly and both Moss (Lotus-Climax) and Gurney

(Porsche) began to creep closer. The pair were having a monumental dice, passing and repassing all around the circuit.'

Some time after lap 20 Ginther began to fall away from Hill. His Ferrari's engine had lost its crisp note and on lap 24 he pitted, smoke belching from the engine. Hill was alone, nursing the quiet satisfaction 'of final vindication about the fuss I'd made because mine was the only Ferrari to finish, all the rest of them dropped out'. He won with perfect ease, 31.2 seconds in front of Gurney and gave an expansive wave of his right arm from the cockpit as he crossed the line while a tubby official flailed the chequered flag.

The Italian police were actively seeking Clark. According to Brabham 'the police moved in and wanted to arrest somebody, in this case Jimmy. He was forced to hide in his hotel and was later rushed on to a commercial flight before things could get difficult.' Another version suggests that Clark was flown quickly away in Chapman's Piper Comanche.

Hill meanwhile 'drove up to my pit. The mob was further up by the gate where they always congregated and where the finishers were supposed to go. I looked up at Carlo Chiti, the chief engineer, and though he was not a demonstrative man at all Chiti didn't seem quite as joyous as I'd expected. I said, "How is Trips?" He sort of paused and there was a certain look on his face and he told me, "go on up there in the car to the finish area, they want you to be up there" but I knew it was bad. I went through the motions of what I was supposed to be doing, I didn't have a great grin and I didn't laugh and all that stuff because I felt it was inappropriate or unsafe to dare to. I wasn't absolutely positive about what had happened to von Trips but I had a damn good idea. I knew nothing about spectators being involved. I found that out when the ceremony was over and I was able to talk to people.

'The accident took a chunk away from what should have been a sublime moment. I wasn't able to enjoy it in the same sort of way you'd have wanted. I had a feeling the world would recover but I felt a prisoner of the propriety of the whole thing.' In other words, what should a man feel, how should he conduct himself?

Question: how do you feel about it now, in 1992 [when the

interview for this book was done]? 'Oh gosh, I don't know, I don't
have any particular feelings. You know, in the end if you win you win.
All the rest of it sort of goes away. Don't ask me why that is, but
people don't like to dwell on the mortal aspects of things. I've seen
lots of people who I felt behaved inappropriately under nasty
situations and I didn't want to do that. It's amazing how indiscreet
people can be as far as laughing and carrying on within minutes of a
situation, forgetting how terrible the situation is.'

Phil Hill had been at Le Mans in 1955. He never did forget.

1962
GRAHAM HILL AND THE PENNIES

South African Grand Prix, East London

At an Easter meeting at Goodwood, a track in the south of England, the Lotus of Stirling Moss crashed very suddenly and very heavily. The cause is totally unknown and Moss can't help. He has no memory of it, only of his journey to the track that morning and regaining consciousness a month later in hospital. An era closed the moment the Lotus left the track on 23 April, stabbed itself into an earthen bank and broke itself to pieces. Moss recovered but his Grand Prix career was over. All else aside that altered the character of the season.

It was a long season embracing nine rounds from Zandvoort, Holland in mid-May to South Africa on 29 December. Approaching South Africa Jim Clark still had a chance of becoming champion although many felt he wasn't ready yet. He accepted this judgement. He'd taken his Lotus to three wins, Belgium, Britain and the USA at Watkins Glen.

Graham Hill, the man who finished 9.2 seconds behind Clark at The Glen was also British but of a very different temperament. Awkward, sometimes headstrong, he lacked Clark's grace in a car but compensated by fierce determination. He'd been driving since 1958 but curiously his first win was Zandvoort, mid-May. He was into his stride after that taking Germany and Italy, too.

The mathematics: five best finishes to count and Hill punished for consistency. He and Clark had three wins but Hill two second places, a fourth and a sixth, Clark only a fourth place. Clark, however, had to win South Africa. If Hill came second behind him, and had to discard that sixth place, both would have 39 but Clark the championship on the most wins tie-break, 4-3. It was an uneasy Christmas.

A wind swept in off the Indian Ocean to the track set among

hillocks in East London and this wind seemed to carry rumours within it. BRM had, one rumour said, built an extremely light new car for Hill. It could be decisive. Chapman heard, of course. Chapman always read the wind and spent a great deal of money making sure that Clark's Lotus 25 was lighter, too.

Chapman went to scrutineering to see exactly how light the BRM was and when he read what the weighbridge said – only 2.27kg less than normal – he was very angry. He'd fallen for the rumours. They'd said it would be 22kg lighter...

Hill wrote:

The winds on the first day of practice were terrific. The circuit is right on the edge of the Indian Ocean and the winds were seriously affecting the cars on some of the faster corners, making them especially twitchy to go through. There were two fast ones just past the pits and the track itself was very exposed. In a big cross-wind these two corners were very tricky – the car might be moving sideways two or three feet and when you're working to within two or three feet of the edge of the track you just haven't got that sort of room. The wind also affected our gear ratios. It was all very confusing.

The circuit measured 2.4 miles (3.9km), the race 82 laps (199.9 miles/321.7km).

Clark was glad to be in South Africa.

The two weeks before the race were terrible because people kept coming up to me and asking if I was worried about it and if I thought I could win.

Clark, by nature modest, found that uncomfortable. Public attention always seemed to sit uneasily with him.

Hill fretted:

The first day's practice was on Boxing Day, traditionally a time for hangovers. The way practice went it looked very much as if Jimmy was going to win and we were just not going to be able to do anything about it. You can always tell by practice what sort of chance you have. You must be within 0.1 or 0.2 of a second. In fact I was something like 0.7 slower. I could see it was going to be very difficult for me to hold on to him at all.

Although Clark and Lotus 'changed a number of things to get the car running and handling properly', he was not devastatingly faster than Hill when qualifying ended: faster, yes – Clark 1 minute 29.3 seconds to take pole, Hill 1 minute 29.6 to take his place alongside Clark on the front row of the grid.

On 29 December *Autosport* reported:

The little seaside town had filled to capacity and it was absolutely impossible to find any accommodation anywhere. South African Airways were putting on special flights from Johannesburg to cope with visitors and over 150 Pressmen had arrived to cover the race. The Hill-Clark rivalry was the sole topic of conversation, but a bearded Stirling Moss refused to commit himself to a forecast.

As a crowd of 90,000 gathered an excited American television commentator rushed up to Hill and asked, 'Well, Graham, what is it that bothers you on a day like this?' Hill: 'It's people like you coming up and asking me questions like that...'

Before the start the drivers were taken round in procession in the backs of little sports cars so that the crowd could see them. Hill would write:

The crowd are terribly enthusiastic. They climbed over the barriers and came to pat us on the back and shake us by the hand. Eventually we were driving through an avenue of people. On the far side of the track there was one particular section which was wired off for coloured people. They saw all the white people patting us on the back so they thought they'd do the same. In the end we were cowering in the backs of the cars under a rain of blows from very enthusiastic Africans. I got pretty badly bruised and there was no way of telling them to stop.

At the flag Ireland (Lotus-Climax) got away first from the second row but maddeningly couldn't engage gear properly. Hill had a moment of wheelspin when he put the power down and that gave Clark – who made what Hill described as a 'fabulous start' – he lead. They were already under the Dunlop Bridge on the start-finish straight, Clark to the right, Hill to the left and fractionally behind him, Ireland behind Hill. By the first corner, Potters Pass Curve, Clark was clearly and cleanly ahead. Hill got in 'just behind Jimmy but I was not able to challenge him although I was driving as hard as I could.' They flowed into the start-finish straight to complete lap one, Clark a second in front.

Lap 2: 2.5 seconds
Lap 3: 4.0 seconds
Lap 4: 5.0 seconds

'Jim Clark was certainly determined to leave everyone else behind,' *Autosport* reported, 'All round the circuit the crowds were breathless with excitement and spellbound by the skill of the world's top road-racing man.'

By lap 8 Clark had lapped a couple of cars and was pulling clear of Hill at a consistent, remorseless rate. By lap 11 he'd stretched the gap to 11.0 seconds. Clark settled, let Hill press on as hard as he could and yet, and yet, however hard Hill pushed Clark held the gap at 11 or 12 seconds. Always it seemed he manipulated a car with an economy of movement, always he had more speed if he needed it. Nobody knew how much, perhaps – because he was so intuitive – not even he, but it was there, an ever-present reserve and resource.

They circled like that for seven more laps, eight laps, nine laps. Hill, true to his character, remained fierce. Consistently he took the same line through all the corners. At quarter distance Clark was moving through back-markers and the gap had gone out to around 13 seconds. The times on that lap: Clark 1 minute 33, Hill 1 minute 34 – and that was the second Clark drew from his reserve when he needed it. On lap 25 he'd drawn it out to 18 seconds and lapped Carel de Beaufort, whose Porsche weaved about, for the third time.

Clark moved within a groove, the engine sounded 'glorious' and without question his car was the fastest in the race. Hill was isolated in second place, impotent. On lap 36 Clark moved past Ireland to leave just five cars on the same lap and his lead stretched to 24 seconds. Clark would write:

Steadily I had been drawing ahead until at half-distance I had a lead of about 27 seconds over Graham. It must have been a very dull race to watch.

Crouched on a low wall and wearing a flat white cap Chapman held a stopwatch in a gloved hand and gazed in an agony of suspense for Clark to keep coming round. Chapman's wife Hazel stood behind the wall, her face serene. Chapman and Lotus had been in Formula 1 for five years. They had yet to win the World Championship.

On lap 50 the gap stretched to 30 seconds.

The BRM pit became tense. As they gazed they sensed that Clark was not exploring the limits of the Lotus, he was simply maintaining a very fast and consistent pace. What hope had Hill? Clark was most unlikely to make a driver error.

On lap 59 Clark glanced in his wing-mirror and noticed 'a puff of blue smoke'. He remained very calm. 'I checked and sure enough there was smoke coming from the exhaust pipes. I didn't really know what to do but I pressed on for another couple of laps.'

Autosport reported:

With the dramatic suddenness which makes motor racing the most unpredictable of all sports the whole picture changed. A wisp of smoke appeared at the tail-end of the Lotus and rapidly increased in density until the car was virtually laying a smoke-screen. Oil started to be spattered over his rear tyres. Gamely he kept going as everyone in the Lotus pit anxiously awaited him.

'Then it looked too bad and I didn't want to wreck the engine so I dashed into the pits,' Clark wrote.

Still smoke was being pushed out from the back of the Lotus as Clark eased it along the pit lane. The mechanics ran into position.

They ripped the engine cover off and dug into it trying to find out what was wrong. There was nothing visible at all and the smoke was coming from oil burning on the exhaust pipes. But where was it coming from? As we looked Graham Hill swept past into the lead and I knew it was all over.

Hill wrote:

It was not until I saw Jimmy stop at the pits for two consecutive laps that I realized I was going to win the race. In fact I didn't even have to win it – with Jimmy out it didn't matter whether I finished or not. The pressure was right off and I was able to cruise home. It was very lucky for me that Jimmy broke down.

Three postscripts.

A few minutes after the race finished torrential rain fell. What effect would that have had if it had fallen half an hour earlier?

As Hill did his lap of honour the crowd came on to the track and, all unknowing, Hill ran over the leg of a small boy and broke it. 'This upset me of course and I corresponded with him for some time after the accident.'

The oil leak on Clark's car had been caused when a small bolt in the distributor shaft housing worked loose and fell out because it hadn't been provided with a lock washer. The championship had gone for the want of something costing a few pence.

1963

CLARK, IN HIS SORROW

Italian Grand Prix, Monza

The horror of von Trips and Clark colliding was a two-year-old memory now. In 1962 the police posed no problem although an official enquiry proceeded in the background. Clark had no fear of returning.

He had much else on his mind after a season of great superiority. Graham Hill (BRM) won Monaco, he took Belgium, Holland, France and Britain, was second behind Surtees (Ferrari) at the Nürburgring. Now his first World Championship lay within his grasp although Clark would write:

> It is terribly easy to get depressed when you are driving a car. Even one meeting can put you off. Before the crucial race at Monza in 1963 I was very depressed. I was truly beginning to doubt my own ability and I remember thinking: Hell, what happens if I can't get this car to go any faster? I had the quickest Climax-engined car but it was half a second slower than Hill's BRM and about two seconds slower than Surtees' Ferrari, and normally I had been as quick as them. This fighting with yourself leads to most drivers having a basic insecurity about the cars being prepared for them. That is one reason why you see drivers fussing around with their cars.

Before Monza there had been a non-championship race at Enna. Clark didn't go but his team-mate at Lotus, Trevor Taylor, did and returned with the information that Surtees' Ferrari was much faster. Three rounds remained after Monza but if Surtees and Hill were decisively faster, where would that leave an even more depressed Clark? 'Things,' he would remember, didn't look at all good.'

Nor did they look good at Monza. The organizers decided to use the full banking-cum-road circuit again. Bob Anderson, a Briton, crashed his Lola and car after car returned to the pits with suspensions hammered by the uneven concrete. A deputation of drivers and teams pressed the organizers to use the road course only and, even before this, the Commission Provinciale di Vigilanza, responsible for safety, told the organizers that spectators were not sufficiently protected if a car went over the banking.

The first session for the grid was thus halted half way through and the times declared void. The second session would be on the road circuit and extended to a full three hours.

It rained hard overnight leaving damp patches under the trees where the sun couldn't get at them. In these conditions Surtees lapped in the astonishing time of 1m 37.3s, averaging more than 132mph (212kmh), Hill 1m 38.5s. Clark's worst fears were coming true. His 1m 39.0s put him on the second row.

The fact that I was so much slower than Surtees really sapped my confidence and I felt so bad that before the race started I had fitted a new engine, gearbox, gear ratios and changed the tyre sizes. This meant that I started the race not fully knowing what the car would be like when it arrived at the first corner.

The teeming thousands came, more than for a decade, drawn instinctively by the magical element of Surtees in the Ferrari on pole. The thousands created their own tension. Clark tried to ignore that, concentrated on forgetting his troubles and doing the race. 'I had to keep up with Surtees and Hill at all costs.'

When the flag fell Hill surged away in front of Surtees but as both drivers reached for second gear Clark – aimed squarely between them – was already ahead. Cheeky, as someone with a nice sense of understatement noted.

At the Curva Grande Surtees went by. Surtees, Clark and Hill struggled and jostled at the Lesmo Curve, Hill burst through in a violent surge which carried him past Clark then Surtees. That was the order as they crossed the line to complete lap 1. On the next lap all three broke the lap record held by Phil Hill. On lap 4 Surtees made his power-play and took the lead. Clark used Surtees' slipstream and it sucked him past Hill.

'I hung on grimly, determined not to let Surtees get away. At Monza slipstreaming is almost second-nature for everyone. In my case slipstreaming Surtees down the straight gave me an extra 500 rpm.'

Surtees towed Clark, Hill towed Gurney (Brabham), Ginther (BRM) towed Lorenzo Bandini (Ferrari). This created a weaving and darting match, each driver behind trying to use the tow to gather speed, flick out and get in front.

At ten laps Surtees led Clark, Hill and Gurney but on lap 17 Clark noticed an 'ominous' puff of smoke coming from Surtees' exhaust pipes. 'A few yards further on and there it was again so it was no surprise to me when he dived into the pits.' The engine of the Ferrari had blown and Surtees did not re-emerge but it left Clark with a problem: no tow. He made a judgement that it wasn't worth 'stretching' the car to try and maintain the lead because sooner or later Hill and Gurney would overtake him. This was so inevitable – Hill decisively quicker in qualifying and Gurney only a fraction slower – that Clark felt he could have profitably used the time to nip into the pits for a cup of tea.

Gurney broke the lap record and when he overtook Clark on lap 23 did it with such devastating speed that Clark was almost taken by surprise. A lap later Hill overtook them both, Clark third. Another classical Monza match unfolded, Gurney retaking the lead, Hill retaking it, lap after lap. Clark watched and waited. At moments under the tremendous suction of the slipstreaming he'd take the lead himself knowing that he wouldn't be there long.

On lap 49 Hill's clutch began to slip and he angled the BRM into the pits taking his championship hopes with him. The race was between Gurney and Clark but the championship was surely Clark's.

We came up behind Innes Ireland (BRM) and his car was much quicker than ours down the straights but we had him on the corners. I tried on one bend to get past on the inside but Innes blocked me, then I tried again and the same thing happened. The next time I thought I would play it craftily so I waited until Gurney had come up close behind me and I made a pass at Innes. But I eased off slightly and let Gurney go through. Innes thought that the car coming inside him was me and he moved over again but he found out it was Dan and no-one did that sort of thing to Dan. In the ensuing battle of wits Dan eased Innes out and while he was doing that I passed both of them...

Jim Clark was truly a very great driver. He and Gurney lapped the entire field, Clark held the lead for long periods and on lap 63 Gurney slowed, his fuel pump failed. This left Clark isolated and with a cushion of a whole lap. Across the final stages Ginther tried to unlap himself and Clark permitted this.

When Clark crossed the line he'd won by 1m 35s from Ginther. The Lotus pit presented a sight Clark could barely believe, all manner of people crowding into it and Chapman, clutching the silver trophy, fighting his way through to reach Clark. He clambered on to the Lotus and they did a lap of honour, stopping to pick up Mike Spence, also in a Lotus, who'd broken down.

By now the spectators packed the track – they'd run on after Clark crossed the line but other cars were still racing – and, the lap of honour completed, they mobbed Clark. The crowd in the Lotus pit had grown so overwhelming that Clark escaped to the sanctuary of the Dunlop enclosure. While he stood there 'someone came up and informed me that the Italian police wanted to see me immediately in the race organizers' office.'

Clark went there, the chanting of the crowd still loud in his ears, and was requested to sign a document written in Italian. He could not read it. They explained that this document was an undertaking he would appear before the local magistrate the following morning to answer questions about the accident with von Trips. 'I naturally refused to sign a document I could not understand and I asked for it to be translated. This, I was informed, was not possible.'

Clark had already made arrangements to fly back the following morning with Brabham. He had given the police a signed statement in 1961 and co-operated in a three-hour interrogation in 1962. What new information, he reasoned, could he now be expected to remember a full two years after the accident? He negotiated a compromise. He could depart Italy provided he left the name of an Italian lawyer to act for him.

'Coming as it did on what should have been a night of triumphant celebration the affair depressed me so much that all I wanted to do was get out of Italy and I didn't care if I never returned to the place. Consequently it was a very subdued victory party, enlivened only by a bun fight in the hotel between the Lotus and Cooper teams. This then was the rather miserable end to what should have been the most memorable day of my life.'

1964

SURTEES, TWO PLUS FOUR

Mexican Grand Prix, Mexico City

He'd put the car on the ninth row of the grid. Of the 19 drivers who would set off in the Mexican Grand Prix that hot and humid afternoon he'd been second slowest during qualifying. He'd already won races on a Honda. On a Honda, not in a Honda.   To drive a car, he would say, 'I had to learn a completely different set of techniques, a different approach, with vastly varying mechanical hazards to master. I was almost dizzy trying to unravel the mysteries.'

The words are those of Mike Hailwood and they capture exactly the chasm between riding a bike fast and driving a car fast, or rather the width of the chasm. Only with that perspective can you appreciate what the strong, self-assured Englishman up at the other end of the grid was achieving.

This October afternoon John Surtees could look back on World 500 cc Championships in 1956, 1958, 1959 and 1960 just as Hailwood could look back on championships in 1962, 1963 and this year of 1964. Riding an MV Agusta, Hailwood had won seven of the nine rounds, the last at Monza only the month before, but no man had ever done the big double by adding the Formula 1 car championship. Nor could Hailwood now. A whole season of trying to unravel the mysteries in his Lotus-BRM had brought but a single point.

An angular Austrian, Jochen Rindt, had made his debut in the Austrian Grand Prix driving a Brabham. Of this, Heinz Prüller wrote in his biography Jochen Rindt:

Photographers were at the airport – Rindt and Clark, then Rindt with Hill – but Jochen was determined to avoid being obtrusive; he didn't yet feel like master in his own home, but more like a guest in his own country.

At the drivers' briefing, held in English, Rindt didn't understand one of the points made but another driver turned and said 'don't worry, just follow us.' In the race the steering failed.

Surtees went to Mexico with 34 points in his Ferrari. Graham Hill (BRM) had 39, Clark (Lotus-Climax) 30 but the permutations were more subtle. This was the last of the 10 Grands Prix of the season and you could only count six finishes. Hill had already used those up and would have to drop the three points he'd got from Holland. Surtees had five finishes, Clark four. Whatever they got would count fully. The permutations after that went on and on and would constantly alter during the race itself.

Because of its altitude – more than 7,000 ft (3,534m) – Mexico presented an awkward examination of an engine. Hill explained:

There just isn't the air about to get sucked into the engine. Roughly you end up with the engine 25 per cent down on power, about 100 horsepower. This affects every car the same way, or is supposed to, but we normally find that the multi-cylinder cars – the 12-cylinders, for instance – are slightly better off than the 8-cylinder cars. They have four more pots to suck the air in at every stroke so it looked as if the V12 Ferrari was going to have a slight advantage.

Surtees had been using a V8 all season and continued with it here but the other Ferrari driver, Bandini, had the new V12 and out-qualified Surtees, 1m 58.60s against 1m 58.70s.

'We'd had discussions about it,' Surtees says, 'and I quite wanted to use the V12 but there had been problems with reliability and fuel consumption and although the latter should not have been a factor in Mexico it might have been. What decided it was that at the time Ferrari were in discussions with Fiat [who eventually bought Ferrari] and there were possibilities of putting the V8 into a road production car so the team decided to use Bandini in the V12 as a hare.

'In Mexico you had to be careful about how you lived. You watched what you ate and drank – you didn't touch the water – and that was one of my concerns. The other was technical, the altitude.'

On the hot and humid afternoon of 25 October the 19 drivers faced 65 laps of 3.1 miles (4.9km).

Autosport reported:

The cars were wheeled out on to the dummy grid just after 1.30 pm and then the drivers were summoned over to await the arrival of Mexico's President, A Lopez Mateos. The drivers seemed unusually disciplined as they lined up to shake hands with the President. At 2.15 thousands of coloured balloons were released and a private plane amused the crowd by carving through them and sending many bits of deflated rubber hurtling to the ground. The warm-up lap provided its own drama – a dog was loose on the circuit and Mike Spence managed to spin his Lotus.

The front of the grid, pole on the right:

Gurney (Brabham-Climax)   Clark (Lotus-Climax)
Surtees (Ferrari)   Bandini (Ferrari)
Hill (BRM)   Spence (Lotus-Climax)

Hill would remember

Just as I pulled my goggles down before the start, the elastic gave way and my goggles fell over my face so there I was sitting on the start line for the final round of the World Championship, in which I had to finish third or higher to win irrespective of what anyone else did, with my goggles on my lap and no means of getting them to stay on. I began fiddling with the elastic but as I had my gloves on it was a bit difficult to work the tiny adjustment catch. While I was doing all this the starter dropped the flag. I lost four places...

Surtees, too, was engulfed. The 'reliable' V8 had a misfire and the Ferrari crept forward, almost stalled, crept again before it did fire. Clark, calm and consummate, knew what he had to do: win the race. He took the lead and kept it on lap 1 as the cars rounded the banked circuit which Hill described as 'terribly tight and twisty with lots of funny little bends in the middle'. Crossing the line to complete the lap Clark had already opened a two-second lead over Gurney, Hill tenth, Surtees thirteenth. The first six: Clark, Gurney, Bandini, Spence, Bonnier, Brabham.

'My strategy was two-fold,' Surtees says. 'I would let the race develop, wait and see what happened but at the same time keep in reserve a barnstorming run at it if I needed that. Mexico was not the place where you wanted to do any barnstorming unless you really had to. I kept in my mind that when the Ferrari ran warm it lost performance. It didn't like the heat.'

The misfire cleared and he, like Hill, began to move through the field. On the second lap he overtook Phil Hill (Cooper-Climax), the Swiss Jo Siffert (Brabham-BRM) and Ginther (BRM). On lap five Graham Hill took Bonnier (Brabham-Climax) but became embroiled in a struggle with Spence and Brabham. Clark led the race by 5 seconds from Gurney, Surtees eighth. On lap 9 Hill made his decisive move, taking Spence, and that was fourth. Only Clark, Gurney and Bandini lay ahead – specifically Bandini. The moment Hill took him, third place was all he needed for the championship. He did that on lap 11 although immediately Bandini came back at him. Surtees was much further away and locked in a struggle with Spence and Brabham. Surtees needed six laps to get past them.

By lap 21 Clark led Gurney by seven seconds running smoothly, well within himself. Gurney was twelve seconds ahead of Hill, now third, and Bandini. That didn't matter. 'I was leading the championship and if I stayed in third place that was enough to ensure I won it.' Surtees, fifth, was four seconds behind Bandini who, feeling all the advantage of the V12, launched a heavy attack on Hill who described some of what Bandini did as 'wild attempts', particularly at the hairpin.

On one lap he dived straight in underneath me and I had to move out to give him room. It was a bit of a desperate effort and as I was coming out of the hairpin his front wheel hit my back wheel and spun me round into the guard rail.

Hill had been so angered by Bandini's attack that, mere moments before, he'd shaken his fist at him.

The crash was on lap 30.

'There is no question that Bandini did anything deliberate,' Surtees says. 'People simply don't in open-wheeled racing cars. If you do you risk flipping, you risk anything. I sensed that Graham didn't like Bandini so close to him, sitting there on his tail with me behind Bandini, and he started to make mistakes. The hairpin was banked and if you took the inside line – which Hill did – you could find yourself thrown up to the top of the banking. Hill got the hairpin all wrong.'

Surtees went through while Hill and Bandini recovered. Hill got the BRM going again but 'it sounded most peculiar'. He'd rammed the guard rail hard backwards virtually closing the exhaust pipes. The engine could barely produce power and Hill chugged round to the pits where jack handles were rammed in to break off the 'crumpled' ends of the exhaust pipes. His championship was gone unless Clark and Surtees didn't finish. Hill came back out and drove in hope.

Bandini made a full recovery and within three laps of the crash overtook Surtees. That meant that if Clark kept on and won – and Surtees stayed fourth – Clark had the championship. What would Bandini do? He was an Italian in a Ferrari...

Surtees had been competing on bikes since 1952, in cars since 1960 and he understood all the mechanisms of self-control. 'I was getting full information from the pit signals, of course, and I knew that Colin Chapman was a man whose cars were in advance of the others but the reliability of the Lotus was not, let us say, brilliant; and Bandini must soon have fuel problems. Normally you didn't in Mexico but the V12 driven at full steam surely would have.'

Surtees watched and waited.

Graham Hill had been into the pits a second time – the throttle spring came off, a late symptom of the crash on lap 30 – but he was still moving.

Clark drove majestically, his lead over Gurney out to twenty seconds. He couldn't concern himself with what Surtees was doing so far behind because he couldn't affect that. All he could do was win the race. With ten to go he noticed oil on a corner. Surtees noticed it too and thought, 'well, something is happening to somebody.' The next lap Clark altered his line to avoid the oil and on the lap after that noticed more oil but on exactly the new line he had been taking. There could be only one explanation: oil from his own car.

Two laps remained. The order: Clark, Gurney, Bandini, Surtees. A lap later Clark's oil pipe broke completely, the Lotus crippled. Chapman and the mechanics stood poised in the pits waiting to acclaim him because, if Clark could keep on, Surtees had to be second – and that meant overtaking Gurney as well as Bandini. Clark did keep on, treating the Lotus so gently but unable to make it go other than slowly. Gurney went by, then Bandini, then Surtees, who felt 'sure Hill was getting pit signals that Surtees was only third.'

Hill did think he'd become champion again. 'The four points for third will leave Surtees short of one point to beat me ... he had to get into second place and the six points to beat me.'

Bandini now held the championship in his hands. Surtees thought clinically 'Bandini has never beaten me yet in a race.' Gurney was over a minute in the lead and out of the equation. He would win the race. The equation came back to Bandini and Surtees. As they crossed the line to complete lap 64 all the Ferrari mechanics were on the side of the track gesturing for Bandini to slow and let Surtees through. Bandini obeyed. Or did he? Surtees does not accept that Bandini slowed. It is as if even all this time later he does not accept he might have needed the indignity of help. 'I believe,' he says, 'that Bandini had simply shot his bolt.'

Surtees began the last lap and out at the back of the circuit saw Clark's Lotus halted. A few moments later Spence came upon it and thought briefly of moving in behind and nosing it all the way back to the pits. He decided against because it would have been futile.

The crowd angled their heads towards the semi-circular corner feeding the cars out into the pit lane straight and the finishing line. Gurney came round and won. Long seconds passed. Would it be Bandini? Would it be Surtees? Then the crowd saw the snout of a car with a big number seven. Somewhere out there amid the tight twists and funny little bends Bandini slowed – or shot his bolt – and Surtees moved into second place.

Graham Hill came in eleventh and couldn't know Surtees had

overtaken Bandini. When Hill 'arrived back at the pits after the slowing-down lap I looked at all the faces to see whether or not I was champion.' That's when he knew.

In the evening Surtees had a quiet dinner in Mexico City with his father-in-law and a girl from a television company who had been making a documentary about him and the race. 'In qualifying, I'd burnt my foot and there were no medical people around. This girl had gone off and found her own cold cream and I'd used that, smearing it on my sock to keep my foot cool until the cream was all used up.'

The way it was.

1965

SPEEDMASTER

German Grand Prix, Nürburgring

It Happens. You take the best driver in the world, the best car, you take a new 32-valve engine pouring out a lot of power and every race is there for the winning, every lap there for the taking. You can of course simply scan the statistics, shrug and pass on. The statistics alone are monumental and suggest a domination so complete that the interest in the season was only how it was exercised – how, so to say, the mechanisms of mastery played themselves out. Of course it wasn't quite like that. It never is.

On 1 January Clark driving, as ever, a Lotus powered by Coventry-Climax won the South Africa Grand Prix from Surtees (still at Ferrari) by 29 seconds: a lot. Coventry-Climax had produced the 32 valves for their V8 engine, giving an estimated 215bhp at 10,500 revs although with that came the perennial problem of reliability. In its early days the engine tended to blow up.

A Scot, Jackie Stewart, made his debut in a BRM and finished sixth but two laps down. He and Clark were kindred souls and would become close.

The calendar was curious, the second race five months further on – Monte Carlo, 30 May – but Clark and Lotus didn't go there. The Monaco Grand Prix was run on a Sunday, the Indianapolis 500 on the Monday. Clark and Chapman had almost won Indy twice before and they intended to win it this time. Chapman, by nature a showman, burned to do it.

A New Zealander, Denny Hulme, made his debut in a Brabham and finished eighth, eight laps behind Graham Hill, who made his traditional and imperious progress round the Principality – he and Monte Carlo might have been created for each other.

Clark prepared himself for the Brickyard. Next day the Indy 500 tumbled into his lap.

Mario Andretti, an Italian-American who finished third, chatted with him and asked if he'd have a word in Chapman's ear 'about keeping me in mind for a ride sometime. Jimmy reported back to me that Colin had said he would. I was delighted but I didn't really believe it.'

Whatever Clark came to feel about Indianapolis, he hated Spa and said it frightened him. You have some understanding of Clark when you reflect that he could distance himself from such feelings and win the Belgian Grand Prix three years in a row. Returning from Indianapolis he added a fourth. It was a wet race which made Spa a nightmarish ordeal and extremely dangerous. Only one other driver finished on the same lap, Stewart.

Clark won the French Grand Prix from Stewart by 26.3 seconds, won the British – although the engine developed a misfire when he was half a lap ahead of Hill – won Holland by eight seconds from Stewart. The Nürburgring was next.

Speed drew them in their thousands. All through the Saturday night and Sunday morning they came, column after column stretching back towards the distant autobahn; came down the wooded roads from Belgium and Luxembourg and France. They parked their cars and in the darkness moved cautiously towards their chosen place to watch. The campers were already here in their tents. The mid-morning estimate was 300,000 inside the Nürburgring.

Clark sat on pole, and this is what the engine was giving: the year before, Surtees had pole with 8m 38.4s. Clark had now covered The Ring in 8m 22.7s. The days of Fangio and 9m 25.6s seemed much further away than 1957.

Even missing Monaco, Clark had rendered the rule about counting your six best finishes from the 10 rounds meaningless. He'd won all five he competed in, set fastest lap in four of the five, missing the fifth only because of the misfire at Silverstone. He had led every lap of every race except Holland where amazingly he'd taken five laps to catch and overtake Ginther (Honda) and Hill. Clark had 45 points, Hill 26 but from his full quota of finishes,

Stewart 25 but also from his full quota. Surtees had 17, nobody else near double figures.

Stewart faced The Ring for only the second time and in the Friday morning session, with damp patches under the trees, did 8m 30.6s, an eye-blink under 100mph (160km/h). No man had ever gone round at that. Clark meanwhile fiddled with the suspension of the Lotus because it was 'bottoming'. Three other drivers got under Surtees' lap record of 1964, Surtees himself, Hill and Gurney (Brabham-Climax). Clark was saving himself for the afternoon. He plundered The Ring: 8m 22.7s – through the 100mph barrier (101.53/163.36kmh).

Parts of the track had been resurfaced, which smoothed it and made it a little faster. On that same Friday afternoon, Hill, Surtees and Gurney all went through the 100mph barrier, too. Saturday was wet.

Speed. On the Sunday that was what the 300,000 really waited for. The first nine drivers on the Grand Prix had brushed Surtees' 1964 time aside. The crowd was so immense that, as *Autosport* noted:

One tried in vain to get lunch in the poorly organized Christopherus restaurant in the Sport hotel, much to the fury of Dunlop's Ralph Home who was entertaining a party of guests. By now the favourite vantage points were packed and the public address announcers were busy giving information.

The start was clean, the four cars on the front row moving away in unison although by the Sudkehre Clark led by a few yards from Stewart, then Hill, Gurney and Surtees. Hill edged past Stewart – Surtees already in trouble, fumbling to find gears. The Ferrari faithful made their throaty noises of despair, compounded when the public address announced that Surtees had stopped at the Karussel, were mollified when it announced he was moving again, although very slowly, towards the distant pits.

Clark pulled away giving no impression of urgency, Clark pulled away at every point on the circuit. He came out of the Nordkehre on to the pit straight and stoked the Coventry-Climax up, up, up towards 160mph (257kmh). The crowd rose in unison because they had to see this. Clark went across the line three seconds in front of Hill.

He'd done 8m 36.1s. He'd destroyed Surtees' record set on lap 11 of the 1964 race. Clark had done it from a standing start. On lap 2, while Surtees sat captive in the pits, Clark became the first man to lap The Ring at 100mph in a race, 8m 27.7s. He led Hill by 7.2 seconds after lap 3. The mechanics drained fuel from Surtees' tank to make the car lighter and he emerged to attack the record Clark now held. The Italians roared. They knew, surely, what was afoot.

Hill was combative, too, and by lap 4 had cut Clark's lead to 6.2 seconds while Surtees was on the move. The Ferrari's 12 cylinders 'snarled'.

8m 26.1s.

Clark pulled away from Hill and on lap 10 gave Surtees his reply. He scattered every statistic. It was of such magnitude that the journalists there babbled 'fantastic', 'scorching', 'unbelievable'.

8m 24.1s.

Clark lowered his pace and had a pleasant Sunday afternoon run over the remaining five laps, beating Hill by 15.9 seconds. He averaged 99.7mph (160.5kmh) and this was more than Surtees' 1964 fastest lap. Clark won his second World Championship in the most comprehensive way.

Some postscripts.

Lotus had quite a party that night, one of those times when Clark relaxed and shed his inhibitions about being a public persona. The party was held in the Christopherus restaurant and Lotus got served, all right.

After the race – perhaps at this party, perhaps not – Clark confessed that during the first lap the Lotus hit a bump, was pitched full into the air and he'd had a flash reading of 11,600 from the rev counter. That should have blown the engine apart.

Three rounds remained and this is what happened:

Monza, 12 September. Clark out, fuel pump.

Watkins Glen, 3 October. Clark out, engine.

Mexico City, 24 October. Clark out, engine.

Always win the championship the earliest you can.

I wonder where Mario Andretti was that autumn. Winning domestic races in the United States, no doubt, and wondering if Colin Chapman ever would call. No, he wouldn't. Would he?

1966
MIRACLE IN THE PARK

Italian Grand Prix, Monza

The sky was leaden, always ominous at Spa because it invariably means rain. On the first lap of the Belgian Grand Prix the drivers found themselves breasting the brow of a hill when a cloud burst. Bonnier spun off and came to rest hanging over the wall of a farm. Rindt did a sequence of spins before somehow gathering up the car safely. A few moments after that Bob Bondurant found himself upside down in a ditch. Stewart hit a post sideways breaching the petrol tank. Graham Hill ran back and found Stewart trapped unconscious. The ambulance taking him to hospital lost its way...

Stewart, driving a BRM, was 26, only in his second season of Grand Prix racing. He decided that he would begin a campaign to make racing safer. It drew much abuse on him but the days when drivers might find themselves suspended on farm walls were numbered. It would take time, of course, a long time.

Stewart had won the first race, Monaco, Spa was the second but after it Brabham seized the season, winning France, Britain, Holland and the Nürburgring, whose days were numbered, too.

Brabham was forty.

After the Dutch Grand Prix I decided to have a bit of a go at the Press for labelling me the old man of motor racing. They were giving me a hard time. My wife Betty went off shopping and bought me a false beard and I got hold of a jack handle. Just prior to the start of the race I went out to the car with the beard, leaning heavily on the jack handle. I just had to win after that.

Brabham was driving superbly.
There were two rounds after Monza, the USA at Watkins Glen and

the Mexican at Mexico City, and with only a driver's five best results counting from the nine rounds Brabham had constructed a very strong position. He had 39 points, Surtees and Rindt 15, Stewart – who missed France because he was still recovering from Spa – 14.

Surtees had departed Ferrari after an explosion over pairings at the Le Mans 24-hour race and Cooper-Maserati. Ferrari replaced him with a young Englishman, Mike Parkes, who finished second on his debut in the French Grand Prix. Ferrari also had the experienced Bandini but 1966 was not his season. He had only 12 points.

The team's number three driver was also Italian and he had had an extremely undistinguished career thus far, all with Ferrari. In 1963 he drove only in the Dutch Grand Prix and finished sixth but two laps behind the leaders; in 1964 drove only once, at Monza, and starting from the seventh row finished ninth but a lap behind the leaders. He did not race in 1965, was now drafted in for the Nürburgring and, such was the power of the Ferrari, qualified fourth quickest. In the race the electrics went. Ludovico Scarfiotti was already thirty-three.

At Monza, the crowd would treasure the Ferraris of course but they'd probably spend the 68 laps watching the fast men: Surtees with his Maserati who would want, given his character, to win here more than any place on earth to show Enzo Ferrari, Brabham, Clark having an awful season with Lotus but capable of winning anywhere, Rindt of sublime speed, Stewart visibly close to becoming a great driver.

Monza was clearly going to be a hell of a race.

Parkes had pole, Scarfiotti startling all Italy by qualifying second quickest. They formed the front row with Clark (it was three abreast), Bandini next to Surtees on the second, Brabham next to Ginther (Honda) on the third.

At the flag Clark had both hands out of the cockpit gesturing, seemed to have stalled, hadn't, set off in pursuit. By then Scarfiotti held the lead, Parkes behind, Bandini coming strong behind him. Ferrari, Ferrari, Ferrari. Scarfiotti would be brushed aside by the fast men and almost immediately was. On that first lap Bandini overtook Parkes for the lead, Surtees harrying. They crossed the line Bandini,

Parkes, Surtees, Ginther, Brabham, rugged New Zealander Denny Hulme, Scarfiotti, Rindt, Stewart.

At the end of lap 2 Bandini was in the pits with a broken fuel pipe. He'd come back out as a duty but clearly not to figure in the race. At lap 2:

Parkes, Surtees, Brabham, Hulme, Scarfiotti, Ginther, Rindt.

They were in a traditional Monza bunch slipstreaming furiously. Surtees overtook Parkes and Brabham overtook Parkes. The Old Man knew all about pacing himself and overtook Surtees, who didn't like that and kept the Cooper-Maserati right up Brabham's exhaust pipe. Parkes and Hulme were travelling wheel-to-wheel. Parkes re-took Surtees.

By lap 5 Brabham led Parkes by 0.6 of a second, Parkes 0.2 in front of Surtees who was 0.3 in front of Hulme in a Brabham-Repco who was 0.1 in front of Ginther. Stewart's petrol tank split and he retired.

The Old Man began to pull away driving, as someone noted, just like a World Champion. His hands were powerful, his mechanical knowledge profound, his experience of racing rich, he knew all about Monza but.. . as he crossed the line to complete lap 7 smoke was being plucked from the engine. A lap later he was in the pits with an oil leak which couldn't be repaired. He had essentially won the championship with that mighty run in mid-season and what did Monza matter now? Monza mattered a lot if Surtees won it...

He might. The leaders were still locked into the tight bunch and then the miracle happened. Scarfiotti suddenly burst all the way through into the lead hauling Parkes with him. Ginther burst through into second place from a long way back, urging power and more power from the meaty Honda V12 engine. Ginther was poised to overtake when inside the Curva Grande a tyre threw a tread and the Honda snapped completely out of control, bashing and beating itself until it was wrecked.   At lap 15:

Scarfiotti, Ginther, Parkes, Surtees, Rindt, Hulme.

By lap 20 that had become Scarfiotti, Surtees, Hulme, Parkes, Rindt. Twelve laps later Surtees was gone from the race – fuel leak – and the championship decided.

Who in the crowd noticed that? Scarfiotti was still leading and on lap 49 set fastest lap while behind him Parkes and Hulme struggled over second place. Clark had been into the pits for repairs and now although many laps down flew past Scarfiotti before dropping out for good on lap 59 when the gearbox failed.

Scarfiotti ran to the end and Parkes held Hulme.

Who can tell the future? Ludovico Scarfiotti would only drive six more races and finish no higher than fourth. He had less than two years to live.

Mike Parkes drove only two more Grands Prix races, both for Ferrari in 1967. He gained a single point from them. He was killed in a road crash in 1978.

A full decade after Parkes died I was sitting in the back of a motor home at Spa chatting to Jackie Stewart. Qualifying was going on for the Belgian Grand Prix. The circuit was unrecognisable from the one where Stewart lay trapped soaked in petrol and at any moment the whole car might have been consumed by fire.

Stewart's son Paul was taking up motor sport much to the consternation of mum Helen. She'd accepted that her son would race although she hoped and believed she'd left all those sort of anxieties behind years before when Jackie retired. Stewart himself had ambivalent feelings. He knew he couldn't stop Paul doing what he wants to do because a man is always going to do that. Towards the end of the interview Stewart suddenly paused, reflected. 'Perhaps my legacy to my son is that I helped make motor racing safer for him and his generation.'

In time Paul Stewart would tackle Formula 3 where amongst others he'd find himself racing against a chap by the name of Brabham – David, son of Jack.

Who can tell what the future brings?

1967

HULME IN THE BULLRING

Mexican Grand Prix, Mexico City

'I didn't like the press putting their noses into my office on race day and my office was my car. If someone came up and thrust a microphone at me I'd crunch it. If someone thrust a camera at me they'd end up with the maker's name imprinted on their forehead where I'd rammed it back at them.' To Hulme, motor racing was pleasure and business, and that was never more true than at Mexico City on 22 October 1967.

It had been a season of themes, distinct and yet inevitably interweaving. Hulme was in his third year with the team which bore the name of Brabham. The cars had Repco engines and were clear favourites. As if to announce that, Hulme set fastest lap in South Africa although he and Jack Brabham were hampered by mechanical problems. Hulme won Monaco, by a lap.

They came to Zandvoort, 4 June and the story of Grands Prix was to be fundamentally altered amid the dunes of the pleasant seaside resort. The Lotus team had been waiting to take delivery of a new engine. Ford, in active association with a duet called Keith Duckworth and Mike Costin, had created an engine for a whole era: the Cosworth.

In the hands of Clark it won at Zandvoort beating Jack Brabham by 23.6 seconds and Hulme by 25.7. In the 2h 14m 45.1s Clark took to win the race the era began but the engine lacked reliability. Clark either won the races or didn't finish. That was one of the themes, the Brabhams strong as their drivers.

Hulme pressed solidly forward racking up points: Gurney won Belgium, Brabham won France, Clark won Britain, Hulme won Germany, Brabham won Canada. Two rounds remained, the United States at Watkins Glen and Mexico.

That night in the hotel near the Glen a council of war was held. Colin Chapman attended, Walter Hayes the senior Ford executive who had instigated the Cosworth programme attended, the two Lotus drivers, Clark and Graham Hill attended. Hill would write:

Although this was an English Ford enterprise, and nothing whatsoever to do with American Ford, Walter was particularly anxious that we should do well in the United States Grand Prix and therefore he didn't want the two of us scrapping together. We agreed that the fairest thing to do was toss a coin to decide who should cross the line first if the two of us ended up dicing in front of the field. The one who lost would have the privilege, assuming we were both in front, of winning the Mexican Grand Prix. I won the toss.

The Cosworth had shown itself eminently capable of projecting Clark and Hill far beyond the reach of the others. The council of war represented what might well happen. At The Glen, Clark took the lead but obeying the toss of the coin allowed Hill to go by. Hill's Lotus developed clutch problems and Chapman signalled for them to forget the agreement. Clark won, Hill second, Hulme third but a lap down, Brabham fifth but four laps down.

The scoring system in Formula 1 had been completely altered, eleven rounds and the season in two parts. A driver could count his five best finishes out of the six rounds up to and including the British at Silverstone, his four best out of the five after that. Approaching Mexico, Hulme had 47 points and could keep whatever he got there. Brabham might have to drop the two points from the Glen and that gave him a working total of 40. Brabham had to win and hope that Hulme finished no higher than fifth.

There was another theme, this one unstated. 'I'd been driving for Bruce McLaren in Can-Am on alternate weekends to the Grands Prix races.' Hulme said. McLaren also had his own Formula 1 team. 'I hadn't made a decision about what I was going to do the following season but I was leaning towards joining Bruce, who was promising Cosworth engines which seemed good.'

Jack Brabham and Denny Hulme had done a lot of racing together.

There was perhaps a natural affinity between them because Australia and New Zealand are neighbours.

'It was pretty common knowledge that I was interested in joining Bruce. I remember the atmosphere in the Brabham team was tense. I don't think I even had breakfast or dinner with Jack during the Mexican meeting.'

Brabham would remember that 'Denny had not agreed to drive for us again the following year. We asked him half a dozen times during the autumn and the answer we got was that he hadn't decided yet and we were in no position to screw his arm over it.' In Mexico Brabham faced another problem. He had to beat Clark and Hill and the Cosworth engines or the championship was gone.

Hulme stayed in one of those imposing hotels on one of those imposing city centre streets. He was, however, shocked by the poverty just a few paces away.

Clark set the pace early in qualifying, moving down into the 1m 50s with Jack Brabham a second slower. Both were well inside the record set by Ginther in the Honda during the race the year before, 1m 53.7s. After an hour the annual dog stories started, Spence (BRM) reported that two were 'rushing round on the other side of the circuit' and as he spoke another trotted on to the track by the pits. Jean-Pierre Beltoise flung his Matra on to the grass to miss it.

The Friday session finished Clark 1m 48.97s, Hulme 1m 49.79s, Hill 1m 50.63s, Brabham 1m 50.90s. Saturday was hot, Clark set 1m 48.62s and nobody else could reach under 1m 50s for a long time. The teams waited until late afternoon when the cooler weather came. As *Motor Sport* reported, Surtees, meanwhile, was

> *trying very hard. His engine was on all 12 cylinders down the straight but the pick-up from the corners was still suspect and was losing him at least a second a lap. Brabham and Hulme both did a few laps but nothing serious until the last hour.*

In the last hour they reached under 1m 50s but Clark went quicker still, 1m 47.5s despite a faltering engine pick-up as he emerged from the hairpin. If that cured itself Clark's next lap ought to be the pinnacle but as he passed Hulme near the pits he lifted off so that Hulme couldn't get a tow...

That lap might have been a 1m 46s.

Chris Amon, a New Zealander in a Ferrari was flying, Gurney (Eagle-Weslake) was flying and that put Jack alongside Hulme on the third row of the grid. Hulme knew what he had to do. 'I wasn't exactly going to drive a percentage race in the accepted term,' he says. 'My plan was simple. I would stay as close to Jack as I could and hope my car made it to the end.'

That Sunday morning Hulme drove himself to the track in a courtesy car provided by Renault. Each driver had one with his name emblazoned on the side. At the circuit there was nothing much to discuss between himself and Jack, and anyway Jack had other matters to weigh. *Motor Sport* said:

Race day was clear and had all the symptoms of developing into a very hot day, which in fact it did. This added to the last minute frenzy to cut more louvres and extractors in bodywork and enlarge radiator openings [the altitude]. Jack Brabham went one stage further and two hours before the start his mechanics were shaping a new water pipe which they fitted along the outside of the cockpit.

Three saloon car races laid oil on the surface of the track, and oil already lay on the surface of the track anyway. *Autocar* reported:

It is two o'clock on a Sunday afternoon. A mid-engined pick-up truck has just finished doing wheel-stands (wheelies) and the public address system is churning out the theme music from the film Grand Prix. Small groups of drivers are talking casually in the shade of the pits and officials in sombreros are hustling the mechanics to bring their cars out.

 In a few minutes it will be time for the Mexican Grand Prix. A colourful crowd is ranged all round the circuit, kept out of harm's way by an army of brown-shirted soldiers – every one of them carrying a loaded rifle. There are spectators in every tree and on every hoarding, and hundreds on top of the swings and roundabouts which are a feature of the Sports Park through which the circuit runs.

These swings and roundabouts and see-saws stood in a special area for children, arranged on a massive scale. The crowd was estimated at 125,000. The cars covered the parade lap and drew up on to the grid. The starter did not raise the flag. Without any warning he waved it in front of his knees. This took Clark and several others completely by surprise. Clark almost stalled. Hill would write:

There was a bit of confusion at the start. Gurney hit Jimmy up the backside when he didn't get away and Jimmy's exhaust pipe went into Dan's radiator so that put Dan out of the race straight away.

Hill moved off fast, Amon behind, Clark chasing Amon. Gurney limped away last with water gushing from the radiator. The immediate order: Hill, Amon, Clark, Brabham, Moises Solana (a Mexican in a Lotus), McLaren, Surtees, Hulme. On the second lap Clark took Amon and closed up on Hill while further back Surtees and Hulme moved past McLaren. On the third lap Clark took Hill but at the very instant of doing that his clutch went. For the remainder of the race he would average more than 100mph without it.

Gurney trundled round gushing water.

Clark pulled away from Hill and on lap 5 Surtees and Hulme closed on Solana. Hulme couldn't afford to let Jack Brabbam get too far away but equally he didn't want to risk blowing the engine or straining any part of the car trying to catch him. Hulme was sixth but he needed fifth. On lap 6 he got it, moving past Surtees, but Surtees stayed with him. Both were some fifteen seconds behind Clark. Hulme advanced on Solana quietly, holding the balance between racing and conserving, tracked him, pressured him but Solana – who only ever drove a couple of Grands Prix a year – resisted, driving competently. On lap 12 Hulme cautiously slipped by, six seconds behind Brabham. Next lap Solana dropped out when, according to *Motor Sport*:

The pin which connects the lower link of the suspension to the left front upright broke on braking for a left-hand corner and, in turning, the

whole thing broke the top of the upright. Fortunately in a left-hand bend
all the weight was on the right-hand wheels so he was able to stop on the
grass without doing any further damage, nor scooping up those spectators
sitting in front of the safety banks.

By lap 20 Clark led Amon by 21.5 seconds, Hill out of it altogether
(dead engine), Brabham 29.5 seconds behind Clark, Hulme 43.5
seconds behind Clark, and what might be of much more significance
Surtees only 7.5 seconds behind Hulme. The Honda delivered power,
Surtees could use it and Hulme had to consider that.

Brabham wondered about the Lotuses. Two had failed. Could Clark
go the distance? That wouldn't alter the geography of the race:
Brabham would still have to get past Amon. On lap 30 Clark led
Amon by a full minute and Amon led Brabham by twelve seconds,
Hulme travelling prudently in fourth. Thirty-five laps remained and
the leaders strung out, nobody advancing, nobody retreating.

The race was ebbing away to nothing.

On lap 52 and perhaps to amuse himself Clark set the fastest time
of the race, 1m 48.1s. On lap 62 he lapped Hulme, which didn't
disturb Hulme at all. The next lap Amon's Ferrari choked at the
hairpin over on the far side of the track. Hulme flowed past where
Amon stood. 'I'd been chasing Jack all the way and now all I could
do was hope that nothing went wrong with the car.'

Clark won the race. Brabham crossed the line 1m 25.5s later,
Hulme crossed the line but still that lap behind. *Autocar* caught the
mood beautifully:

Jim Clark is surrounded by photographers and receives his trophy from a
local beauty queen but Hulme wanders off along the back of the pits and
seems totally unconcerned about his World Championship. The crowd
begins to drift away and the drivers pile into their borrowed Renaults and
head for the prize-giving, somewhat daunted by the fact that it is being
held in a bull ring and they have been told they will have to fight for
their prizes.

However the bulls turn out to be very small and with a bit of
persuasion most of the drivers go into the ring. The danger of it all is

shown by a local photographer, who stands in the middle of the ring and shoos the bulls away with a wave of his hand. Clark insists on wearing his crash hat but Graham Hill and Jo Bonnier wear more traditional headgear and a good time is had by all – even the bulls. Guy Ligier, riding a donkey, puts up a good performance as a picador and Lotus mechanic Alan McCall becomes the star of the evening by riding a bull.

'They gave me a proper matador's cape,' Hulme would say many years later. 'I wasn't frightened, oh no. They weren't really bulls, they were calves. It was quite an evening.' He'd remember something else. Guess what the Mexicans paid prize money in? Gold bullion.

Every World Champion had been worth his weight in gold and these days that statement may be literally true.

1968

THE HALL OF MIRRORS

Mexican Grand Prix, Mexico City

That Monday Graham Hill 'flogged' round Rome in a Formula 2 race. It was largely meaningless but Lotus had obligations and were honouring them. The background was much more important.

French company Matra entered Formula 1 in 1966, competed in three races in 1967 and now supplied Ken Tyrrell's team with cars. Tyrrell, an affable Englishman, had a rare talent for running a racing car team.

Tyrrell fully understood what Clark and Hill had done with the Cosworth engine in 1967 and had got them himself. After a difficult start Stewart, who'd joined from BRM, slipped into his stride and mounted a sustained campaign towards the championship. Hulme did join McLaren and he had the Cosworth. Hill, of course, was already in his second Cosworth season but carried a burden from April when Clark was killed in a Formula 2 race at Hockenhcim.

Now, in the autumn, Stewart won the United States Grand Prix at Watkins Glen while Mario Andretti, who'd asked Clark at the 1965 Indy 500 to have a word with Chapman, made his debut in a Lotus. The clutch failed.

Only Mexico remained and a driver's ten best finishes (out of twelve) counted. For once nobody would have to drop anything, not Hill on 39, not Stewart on 36, not Hulme on 33. Mexico was a three-way stretch, but Mexico was days away and Hill flogged round Rome enjoying himself on the way to finishing seventh.

Matra side-stepped Rome and spread the word to Hill it was because 'they weren't offered enough start money'. Hill thought no more about it until after the race. He heard whispers. Matra were already in Mexico, Stewart doing extensive and secret tyre testing.

After Hockenheim Hill worked to rebuild Lotus's faith in themselves. He was old for that, 39, but in another sense the maturity helped. He was not at all pleased when, nearing the climax to this effort, he heard of this tyre testing. He need not have reacted: it never happened.

Stewart said he and Hill shared the same sense of humour although publicly they adopted 'postures to emphasize our rivalry'. Stewart knew how important this race was for Matra and Dunlop – they were returning after they'd missed most of the 1967 season and had lost Le Mans to Ford and Firestone. Dunlop flew £4,000 worth of tyres to Mexico for the testing but the authorities at the circuit changed their minds and said no.

Hill wrote:

The Olympic Games in Mexico were all over and the athletes had gone home a couple of weeks before so we missed all that. The Mexican Grand Prix was going to be the needle-match in the championship. Denny Hulme had won in Canada and at Monza, so he was a contender. I had the best start with 39 points but if Stewart won the race he would win the championship. Even if I came second to him he would still get it because although our scores would have been 45 he'd have won more races than I. It really boiled down to this: I had to go out and beat both of them by winning the race myself. We turned up on the Thursday to get in some unofficial practice but there was nothing doing as the officials couldn't seal off the circuit, which is in a park.

Changes had been made since the year before. The sawn-off tyres which marked the corners were now low kerbing, a wire-mesh fence charted the hairpin instead of a guard rail, other fences had been put up here and there but not sufficient to stop the dogs. The memory of just missing one still haunts Stewart and so does another memory, of people crossing the track.

Stewart could cope. He'd been teaching himself self-control and noted what a difference that made in his performance during the races. At the flag he'd move cleanly off 'without emotional interference.' He'd found a complete aspect of himself: if he could control his mental processes he could go out and do fast times immediately. He constructed a mental build-up towards this starting the day before. The build-up actively involved staying away from noise, from parties, not permitting himself to become optimistic.

As a consequence, on the eve of the race he was not at all pleased to discover he'd been committed to chatting to a group of French journalists and told Ken Tyrrell in no uncertain terms as they drove back to their hotel. Stewart would remember the mood on that journey, Tyrrell full of confidence, himself pessimistic and the difference in their moods 'irritated' him.

Hill wrote:

Mexico is very high up and so we had all our usual problems over the fuel mixture and loss of power. The course is twisty, for which you need power. We were about 25 per cent down on power and this affects your handling. And our wings were only of real use when you were trying to transmit full power to the road. Lotus had three cars. One was for Jackie Oliver and I was to take my pick of the other two. Whichever I didn't choose would be driven by Moises Solana. We had one car without wings just to see what effect they had and also to baffle the opposition – 'now why are Lotus running without wings? Perhaps we ought to try'. The idea was to baffle them a bit without baffling ourselves.

It was understood that Solana wouldn't get a car until after I made my decision, which would be towards the end of practice. He was always in the background hoping to hop into a car. The Press were of course pretty pro-Mexican and when it was seen that Solana wasn't going to get in a car while I was driving it they began to get a bit nasty. Colin Chapman's face was getting a bit grim and so Jackie Oliver volunteered to share his car with Solana, who actually went very well. I settled for the car with the wings and we got down to making it work.

On the Friday, Siffert in a Lotus run by privateer Rob Walker was quickest, then Hill, Stewart and Surtees. Hulme, tenth, had clutch problems. Hill ventured on to the circuit and found the wing didn't work because the pressure was in the wrong place. The wing had to be re-made:

Beautifully constructed, real aircraft stuff. When we tried it the next day it was better but it still went flat when the wind pressure built up. We were using bungee rubber cord to hold it down and we went on adding to the thickness until we got it right. At last we got it strong enough.

There was an odd moment each time I pushed the pedal – it would need a strong shove and then the wing would flip through dead centre and the pedal would go soft as the wing went flat. If I took my foot off it would go back to the down-load position – which is very important. The brakes are set up to work with the wing pressing on the back wheels and if it isn't the braking ratio between front and rear is thrown out, your back wheels lock up and your car goes all over the road – very nasty.

Hill struck a kerb towards the end of the Saturday practice which meant changing the wheel.

That second day Siffert stayed quickest from Amon (Ferrari), Hulme, Stewart and Hill. Stewart had his own troubles when a driveshaft shattered, hitting the roll-bar which hit a wheel at some 160 miles an hour. Stewart wrestled the car to a standstill.

Race day was sunny. Spectators climbed trees overlooking the circuit and clung there or wedged themselves between branches. On the grassy banks they sat in shirt sleeves. Some of these banks directly bordered the track and the people there were totally unprotected. Some were behind wire mesh fences.

On the warm-up lap Hill realized the wheel which had been replaced was out of balance. As he brought the Lotus into the pits he was being filmed and when he subsequently watched it he could see his mouth opening and closing but no word audible until he said 'out of balance'. He concluded that the words he'd used immediately before had had to be censored.

They rolled gently forward from the dummy grid and the starter lowered the flag instantly. Hill, matured in the ways of it, had his eyes locked on to the starter, almost not allowing himself to blink.

Hill made a 'fabulous start with Surtees' Honda coming up beside me like a rocket – the Honda has a fantastic amount of power'. Siffert botched his start from pole, not using enough revs. Hill pounced on that and went by, bringing Surtees with him. Surtees, accelerating through the Honda's power 'steamed' (Hill's word) into the first corner too fast. Hill followed him, overtook him coming out of the second corner and did not see him again. As they crossed the line to complete the first of 65 laps Hill led from Surtees and Stewart, then Amon and Hulme. Stewart took Surtees on the second lap and tracked Hill.

On the third lap Hill thought the championship had been taken from him. As he entered the straight he stabbed the pedal to flatten the wing and felt the pedal go light. He thought *we're in trouble*. He reached out and seized his wing mirror – habitually he had these mounted loosely – and twisted it so he could see the wing. He saw the 'old bungee rubber band waving in the breeze'. He twisted the other wing mirror, adjusted it so he could see the other strut of the wing knowing that if the rubber there had gone too the car would be undriveable. Without the bands to haul the wing to its maximum download setting the Lotus oversteered 'like a pig'.

Hill watched and now saw that, although the remaining rubber band wouldn't give him the maximum download for braking at the far end of the start-finish straight, the instant he lifted from the brake pedal and the speed dropped the wing moved into position by itself. 'It was all a bit hairy under braking but it held.'

During qualifying Hill had made a careful study of the new kerbs. They were only a couple of inches high and not particularly effective but you could take short-cuts across them. Others would be doing that and so would he. He'd driven the first lap the 'proper' way but now he saw 'everyone carving straight across all the corners. When Jackie started attacking I thought blow this.' The danger was that the kerbs might damage the transmission. Each time Hill flowed over one he changed gear to take the load off the transmission.

Stewart, nestled behind Hill, sensed an 'epic race' unfolding between them. Hulme had overtaken Amon on lap two to hold fourth but a distance back from the epic.

On lap 5 Stewart passed Hill who clung for four laps but lacked outright speed. Hill wondered if that was the problem with the wing and then he 'started to be a little unkind' to Stewart. 'I would pull out to make a pass and then go back and pull out the other way. I could see him looking in his mirror and thinking where is Hill now? You can press on someone this way and it worked. He made a bit of a mistake and ran on to the dirt.'

Hulme went out of the race and the championship on lap 10 when a damper broke as he came onto the straight. By now Siffert had recovered and was moving on the leaders. Stewart, struggling to stay with Hill seemed to have decided, as one reporter noted, 'on a war of nerves'. That was an illusion. Stewart's car developed a loss of power when he had it flat out and this worsened to the point where the engine 'cut out' when he rounded the corners. He kept on, of course, but prudently. On lap 17 Siffert caught him, outbraked him at the hairpin and took second place.

Hill made a tactical decision. He too wanted to handle his car prudently and, glancing in his mirror again, saw that Siffert was only what he estimated to be four or five seconds behind. Why not let Siffert take the lead? Hill could then control Stewart – and Stewart had to pass him.

Hill reduced his pace and on lap 22 Siffert outbraked him at the hairpin. Stewart moved up as best be could and tried to cling but Siffert towed Hill:

We both began to draw away from Jackie. It was lovely and Jackie was getting smaller and smaller in my mirror. And then Siffert packed up – his throttle linkage came adrift. That's nice, I thought, here we are back to square one, all my plans ruined. Then I really had to pile the pressure on. I put in a few fast laps but it takes a bit of doing when you can perhaps only make a fifth of a second each lap. And then all of a sudden Jackie disappeared. I was pulling out three seconds a lap so obviously he was in trouble.

He was. The power ebbed from the Matra and towards the end Stewart lost perhaps six, perhaps seven seconds in the space of a single lap.

Hill cruised it. Towards the end he eased off so much that a couple of drivers unlapped themselves – then Hill noticed something alarming. The crowd, some using hacksaws, were pouring through the wire mesh fencing and standing on the edge of the track. The organizers had not dared to use armed troops because, during the Olympics, students had demonstrated, the army fired on them and at least 267 people were killed. The organizers of the Mexican Grand Prix had decided to avoid any risk of provocation – and repetition – by having only unarmed police.

Hill wrote:

I had already lapped Pedro Rodriguez (BRM) and Oliver, who were battling for third place and they were gradually catching me. Oliver was of course my team-mate so I thought I would hold position to the last lap and then, if Oliver was in front of Rodriguez, I would cross the line ahead of him; but if he was not I would allow both cars to pass me before the finish line and that would give Oliver one more lap to catch Rodriguez before their race finished. So I watched and I saw Rodriguez slip past Oliver. Well, I thought, I'd better let them both past to give Oliver that other lap to try and catch him.

Rodriguez (older brother of Ricardo) was Mexican, he was fired up and so was the crowd still gathering on the edge of the track. As Hill went into the hairpin half way round the last lap – he glimpsed Rodriguez arriving with his tyres smoking. Rodriguez had made his approach very, very fast, braked hard and was heading straight for Hill.

'I did a big swerve and he just missed me, leaving me scrabbling round the outside of the corner. I had been robbed of the championship on that very corner four years before – someone had knocked me around, bending my exhaust pipes so I had had to make a pit stop. And now the same thing had very nearly happened again.'

Hill cantered home 1m 19.32s ahead of McLaren, Oliver third, Rodriguez fourth, Stewart seventh and a lap behind. Chapman rushed on to the track to salute Hill and his wife Hazel burst into tears. When Hill emerged from the car he was tightly hemmed by people. They gave him the laurel to drape round his neck and as he stood he raised the bottle of champagne he held in his left hand, drank briefly. Chapman applauded and looked round as if he had suddenly become a cheerleader and was telling all the others to applaud, too. Hill reached out his right hand and touched Chapman lightly on the shoulder, a gesture of warmth and thanks and comradeship. Chapman took this hand and held it in both of his, shaking it so firmly that his whole body rocked to and fro in time to the motion.

After Clark, life had meaning again.

Two postscripts.

Hill's wife Bette was not present at Mexico City 'because it was too expensive to go to all the races. You had to pay your own fare. I did get to most of the European ones and I'd been to America and South Africa but, you see, drivers weren't paid what they are now. I suppose in another way it was a good thing I wasn't in Mexico because with all the tension if something goes wrong you'll be the first to be balled out.

'I had a system for finding out how Graham had done in the races. I'd telephone Reuters [the international Press agency in Fleet Street] and ask for the motoring desk. They got reports cabled from their people at the race. Reuters were very nice about it and very helpful. If they didn't have the result they'd tell me when to telephone back.'

That's how, late on the evening of 3 November 1968, she discovered that her husband had become World Champion for the second time.

Stewart reflected that a tiny fault had halted his Matra. Gauze came loose and infiltrated a pipe leading to a petrol pump so that it caused a blockage on the corners, then infiltrated further. In retrospect he wouldn't be too sorry. He knew he wasn't ready yet as a man.

1969

STEWART AND THE HARE

Italian Grand Prix, Monza

O nce upon a time Stewart, making a speech in London long after his career ended – it was 1991 – said 'I reasoned that as a driver I was being paid for my skill, I wasn't being paid to risk my life.'

He had just received the Labatt's Safety Award for his contribution to trying to keep all Grand Prix drivers alive, which began at Spa in 1966. It hardly matters that the award was made in 1991. In some ways it's actually more appropriate. Formula 1 has never been safer. I wonder if, as he stood there, his thoughts strayed not just to Spa but to Monza three years later. Of the first six in the Italian Grand Prix, 7 September 1969 four subsequently died in crashes.

That season Stewart's great talents reached maturity. Tyrrell still had Matra, and Cosworth, allowing Stewart to paralyse the first half of the season. He won South Africa and Spain, took pole and set fastest lap at Monaco before the driveshaft broke, won Holland and France and Britain. It gave the points table a stunned look: Stewart 45, McLaren 17, Hill 16, Siffert and Jacky Ickx, a neat and thrusting Belgian in a Brabham, 13. Stewart had defeated the fail-safe designed to keep a season alive – you could only count your nine best finishes from the 11 races. He was poised to complete the season with immensely more points than any man had ever scored before. Potentially he could total 90 and count 81.

And the season faltered...

At the Nürburgring he had gearbox troubles and although he finished second he was almost a minute behind Ickx. The sheer impetus of Stewart might be drifting away. Nor had he yet won the championship, of course, and that can prey on the driver.

The Italian Grand Prix at Monza was five long weeks after The Ring.

To have peace of mind Stewart booked himself and his family into a very elegant – no, opulent – hotel on Lake Como for the duration of the Grand Prix meeting. The staff took some of the pressure off by making a fuss of his two young sons, Paul and Mark, as Italians do. Como, one of those towns fading into its own ornate splendour, offered many advantages. It was near enough to Monza to be a pleasant drive, far enough away to be removed from the Formula 1 incubator.

The pit lane was quiet as the drivers watched the moments tick away towards the end of the final qualifying session. Each was waiting for the weather to cool. Stewart wandered over to Rindt (Lotus) and said, 'I see you're using the rear wing again but you weren't yesterday.'

Rindt smiled and pretended to be surprised.

'I saw you, I saw it all,' Stewart said.

During the first session Rindt tried without the wing and discovered he could pull an extra 300 revs down the straight. Immediately he slotted his Lotus into the pits and had the wing put on so the other drivers wouldn't realize; but Stewart had seen and realized. This might well be important. If Stewart didn't take the championship here he faced the long and uncertain trek to North America: Mosport, Watkins Glen, Mexico City.

Stewart spent qualifying searching for the correct gear ratios because he knew how evenly matched so many drivers were. This amazing man projected his thinking all the way to the last three corners of the race and the ratio which would bring a decisive advantage from there to the finishing line. He was thinking across the whole 68 laps, playing pictures in his mind of the inevitable slipstreaming. If he could escape from the bunch at the Curva del Serraglio, get further away on the flowing left-hand Curva del Vialone, get to the Parabolica he'd be difficult if not impossible to catch.

All this might have been thrown by a typical Monza incident. Stewart arrived at the paddock entrance wearing his overalls and holding his drivers' badge. Officials scanned it and decided it did not entitle him to entry. A crowd gathered and their temperature rose at this piece of lunacy. They demanded that Stewart be allowed in and eventually he was.

Rindt and Hulme (McLaren) occupied the front row, Stewart alongside a Briton, Piers Courage, in a Brabham Ford on the second, while Ickx – who had had desperate mechanical troubles – was at the very back, row eight. Stewart was not unduly concerned about his position with all the slipstreaming to come.

Cars took up wrong places on the grid and Rindt and Hulme lurked instead of coming full up to the starting line. The official with the flag panicked and waved it without warning. Rindt was fast away, Hulme was not – the McLaren hesitated in second gear – and Stewart thought he might just have brushed against it as he went past. He tucked himself in behind Rindt and after the Lesmo curves overtook him, holding that lead into the second lap.

Then ... there was a bizarre incident which, Stewart has said, graphically shows the 'slow motion camera' effect a driver can have if he's taught himself how to do it. Stewart saw a 'tiny movement' far in the distance – a hare. Startled, it flitted towards the cars bearing down on it, flitted into Stewart's path: no chance to evade it with other cars around. He'd remember a front wheel striking the hare and instantly thought *has a bone sliced into the tyre? Are the hare's teeth being ground into the tyre?* He kept an eye on the wheel, glanced regularly in his mirror at the back wheel, too, monitoring their shapes, deliberately heightened his senses to every movement the car made.

The slipstreaming was so extreme that Rindt estimated you could get a tow from a car 250 yards in front. Eight drivers – Stewart, Rindt, Hulme, Beltoise (Matra), Hill, Courage, McLaren and Siffert – formed the bunch: Stewart might lead over the line, Rindt would re-take it before the first corner, Stewart would follow all the way to the Parabolica when he'd take Rindt and lead over the line; as they reached the first corner again Rindt would re-take him...

Stewart and Rindt knew each other as men and drivers, knew the price of folly at Monza. Simultaneously Stewart made the Italian Grand Prix a laboratory. He gauged which of the cars was faster, watched with infinite care where it was faster, conducted experiments.

He needed to find out that, come the last lap, if he reached the Parabolica in the lead and left it in the lead, none of the others could reach the line before him. The crucial gear: second, sharp enough to give him complete freedom of movement within the Parabolica, high enough to take him out of it with the right number of revs to flick to third to flick to fourth for the final rush.

On lap 18 Courage made his move and took the lead although Stewart took it back from him. The bunch was still eight-strong on lap 20 but Hulme drifted away when his brakes began to fail. Rindt led on laps 25, 26 and 27, Stewart third behind Courage, Stewart retook the lead on lap 28. Moves, moves, moves. Hill, travelling strongly, was up to fourth and by lap 36 third. It meant Stewart had two Lotuses behind him.

Stewart's tactic was to take the bunch through the Parabolica slowly to maximize the second gear advantage, get away from the bunch fast. He wondered about Hill in the bunch and what he'd do. Occasionally he'd let Hill lead so he could monitor how Hill's car performed. Would Hill help team-mate Rindt or would Rindt help him? Rindt had only three points from a frustrating season, Hill 19 including a win at Monaco. The question was answered almost as it was posed. With five laps left, in Hill's own words, 'I was in second place and a half shaft broke.'

On lap 66 – two to go – the bunch had become four, Stewart, Rindt, Beltoise, McLaren and that held as they began the last lap. Rindt pulled out and took the lead but he had no idea this was the last lap. He didn't see the signal the Lotus team held over the pit lane wall and he didn't see the official leader board either. Rindt led through the Lesmo Curves and the four cars flowed down the straight to Vialone before the Parabolica.

As they came out of Vialone, Stewart pitched the Matra to the left and drew alongside Rindt. Exactly as he made his move Beltoise moved too, snaking out, letting his Matra be sucked by Stewart's slipstream. Perhaps 200 yards from the entry to the Parabolica Stewart was still on the left but cleanly ahead of Rindt. Beltoise had a brief look outside Stewart and flicked to the inside into a gap – barely wide enough but Beltoise went into it anyway and for a millisecond was moving across the front of Rindt. Beltoise drew level with Stewart and Beltoise had the racing line. Stewart braked early, not weighing Beltoise in the equation. Suddenly there he was.

The Parabolica: Beltoise the inside, Stewart level, Rindt directly behind, his Lotus bucking and twitching under braking. Stewart made an immediate alteration to his line and that put him on to the gravel near the edge of the track. Stewart thought: *Rindt's going to get through*. They turned into the Parabolica, Beltoise mid-track, Stewart at his elbow but having to go the long way round the outside, Rindt poised, McLaren a car's length behind Rindt.

Half-way round, Beltoise's impetus took him wide and a window opened. Stewart held his car in mid-track and that opened another window outside him for Rindt – but Rindt's rear wheels slithered and the window closed. Beltoise's power came full on and he led as the quartet came from the Parabolica but he was still far over to the outside. Stewart's power came full on, too. Rindt put the Lotus deep into Stewart's slipstream.

They raced towards the winning line: Beltoise on the left, Stewart leading but Rindt moving out of his slipstream and already up to his rear wheels. As they crossed the line Rindt was almost level.

Stewart beat Rindt by 0.08 of a second, Beltoise by 0.17 and McLaren by 0.19.

The crowd rushed the track, Stewart retreated to drink champagne but, curiously, he didn't feel like World Champion. That came the next day at the hotel when he asked a porter to book him a flight. The porter called the airline and requested a ticket for Mr. Jackie Stewart, Champion of the World.

I hadn't intended to end two chapters of this book, 1966 and this one, with Stewart and safety. It just happened. and now we must face 1970. We must do it with care and a proper regard for many sensibilities, not least because Jackie Stewart asked that it be phrased like that. I hope within my abilities it is.

1970
RINDT, IN MEMORIAM

United States Grand Prix, Watkins Glen

Somewhere out there amidst the corners with such strange names – Loop Chute, Big Bend, Hard Right – the neat Belgian felt something wrong with his Ferrari. On lap 56 of the United States Grand Prix at Watkins Glen, he was in second place and, if he won, could take the championship at the final race in Mexico.

'It was a fuel leak,' Ickx says. 'What I felt was a sense of release. I was saying to myself: *you're not going to win this race any more, you're not going to be champion.* If I had won that it would have given me no satisfaction, no satisfaction at all.'

A month before, Ickx attended a sponsor's party in the parkland of Monza after first qualifying, Rindt among the guests. Ickx remembers the party as 'an attractive occasion. Jochen was very funny, also very wise.' Ickx liked Rindt, 'although no, I don't really think I was a friend because in an individual sport like this you don't really have friends among the drivers'.

Rindt, in his second season with Lotus, had reason to be happy. He was leading the championship with 45 points, Ickx only 23. All Rindt had to do was win the Italian Grand Prix to become the first Austrian World Champion.

His Lotus 72 carried a rear wing although Rindt didn't use it in the Friday session. Team manager Peter Warr says:

My own opinion is that Jochen felt he just had to win that race and had built himself up mentally in order to do so. On the Friday he had been very quick although it had taken about six laps to warm up the tyres. It was obvious he was becoming bolder and bolder and intended to give the opposition no chance at all. He just wanted to destroy them. We all had dinner together and Jochen was telling everybody about his plans for using his name to build up a sports clothing company, and that he was going to make a fantastic success of it. Then the car became the subject of conversation and he would keep coming back to the fact that he wanted to race it without the wing, as he had tried in the afternoon.

The other Lotus driver, John Miles, ran the wing and said:

Just before the practice session was due to end I found myself with Jochen who by this time – and probably at Colin Chapman's instigation – was running without wings. For the first time in my life I had actually been able to keep with Jochen although his car looked quite a handful.

I came in a few minutes before the end of practice and Colin came over, I think to look at my times. Although generally about half a second slower than Jochen's, our comparative times were somewhat closer than they usually were after that amount of practice. Colin then said: 'You've got it wrong with that wing. You've got to take the wings off your car.' 'I don't really want to, the car already feels a little spooky.' However, at his insistence I took off the wings and drove only a lap and a half or so before practice ended, and it wasn't a flying lap. I had never driven such an awful race car in my life. It was very, very unstable with what felt like a huge amount of lift at the back.

Miles spoke to Chapman who repeated that the only way he was going to be quick was if he took the wings off. Miles replied, 'I don't want to because this is the first time in my life that I was really frightened in a racing car.'

That Saturday Rindt had his wings off for second qualifying. The air ducts leading to the front brakes were covered, but Rindt didn't like that and Chapman agreed to have them uncovered. The Lotus was fitted with different gearing which, says Warr, gave 'a top speed of 205 miles an hour – 15 miles an hour more than anyone had used before'. The weather was superb and some 50,000 were there to see if Ickx or the Swiss Clay Regazzoni in the other Ferrari could get pole.

Rindt had a brief conversation with a mechanic. 'Well, you've got your title now,' the mechanic said.

'You know, you can never quite be sure of that.'

A few moments later he said in English, 'I must go.' He stepped into the Lotus, left foot first, the way he always did. He covered four laps, building the pace from 1m 40.7s through 1m 27.5s and 1m 27.2s to 1m 26.7s. On the fifth lap he moved past the orange McLaren of Hulme on the exit to the Curve di Lesmo and Hulme followed. They travelled together towards the Parabolica. On the approach to the Parabolica Hulme noticed the Lotus 'weaved slightly' as Rindt braked down from perhaps 190mph (306kmh).

Chapman, sitting on a blue metal chair in the pits and wearing a light pullover, couldn't see that. The pits weren't positioned so he could. He had sunglasses on and waited, pencil in one hand, stopwatch in the other and a time sheet across his lap for Rindt to come round. Nina, Jochen's wife, sat nearby.

The Lotus snapped out of control, swerved and rammed the Armco. Warr:

The barrier was lifted out of the ground by the left front wheel, which then went underneath it. The right wheel, which also passed beneath the armco, then caught the next supporting post – one carrying a public address loudspeaker and therefore somewhat stronger and heavier than the others. As a result, this tore the front bulkhead off the car together with the suspension and the steering.

The savaged remnants were spinning on to the sand on the far side of the Parabolica. A marshal, standing in the sand, ran. A wheel was flung off towards Hulme. The sand settled very quickly. What remained of the car was a ragged piece of metal. Four marshals ran towards it, another ran on to the track flailing a flag to warn approaching cars.

Hulme had been travelling behind but was already round the Parabolica and had no way of knowing the full extent of what happened. He took the McLaren straight to the Lotus pit, reported the accident and added he believed Rindt was all right. Bernie Ecciestone, a close friend of Rindt, was in the pit and started running towards the Parabolica. When he reached it Rindt had been taken

ABOVE: *Giuseppe Farina has just won the very first race in the new Formula 1 Championship, the British Grand Prix, in 1950. With three victories from the six races that season he gained 30 points to Juan Manuel Fangio's 27 and became the first World Champion.*

BELOW: *Reigning champion Alberto Ascari masters Silverstone in 1953.*

LEFT: *The gentlemen of Monza, 1956. Juan Manuel Fangio leads from Stirling Moss (36) and Peter Collins (26) – who will give his car to Fangio to win his fourth crown.*

MIDDLE LEFT: *The serenity of the master as he tames the Nürburgring, August 1957. Juan Manuel Fangio takes the Maserati to one of the greatest victories.*

BOTTOM LEFT: *The aftermath at the Nürburgring. Peter Collins (left) and Mike Hawthorn seem as happy as Fangio.*

TOP RIGHT: *The sweet taste of success, and Jack Brabham would enjoy it three times.*

MIDDLE RIGHT: *Phil Hill, the first American champion, saw everything clearly.*

RIGHT: *Phil Hill, alone at Monza. Only later would he learn about the death of his team-mate Wolfgang von Trips in a racing accident that also claimed the lives of 14 spectators.*

ABOVE: *Graham Hill at East London, South Africa, 1962, winning.*

LEFT: *Graham Hill, stiff upper lip.*

BELOW: *Jim Clark wins his first championship, at Monza in 1963, and gives Lotus boss Colin Chapman a lift.*

RIGHT: *Chapman speaks, Clark listens. This is 1965, on the way to Clark's second title.*

RIGHT: *Big John Surtees, master of two worlds.*

BELOW: *Denny Hulme in his pomp in 1967. This is the Nürburgring, which he won.*

ABOVE: *Jochen Rindt and his most famous victory, Monaco, 1970. He would become the only posthumous World Champion – in a season marred by the deaths of Piers Courage and Bruce McLaren, Rindt was killed in practice for the Italian Grand Prix.*

BELOW: *A beautiful study of Jackie Stewart in the wet in Canada, 1971, his second championship year.*

ABOVE: *Stewart interviews Emerson Fittipaldi at Watkins Glen in 1974 after the Brazilian's second championship. Two years earlier he had been crowned the youngest ever champion, aged just 25.*

BELOW: *The calm before the storm at Fuji, 1976. From left, James Hunt, Niki Lauda, Ronnie Peterson and Jean-Pierre Jarier.*

TOP: *Mario Andretti wins the Dutch Grand Prix in 1978, setting up the championship and returning Lotus to glory. Peterson is on his right, Chapman his left.*

ABOVE: *Jody Scheckter leads Ferrari team-mate Gilles Villeneuve in the crucial Italian Grand Prix, 1979.*

LEFT: *Scheckter, contemplating the championship?*

from the car. Three men, trotting, were bearing him on a makeshift stretcher, a white sheet draped over him. They took him to an ambulance. Ecclestone stooped and picked Rindt's helmet and a shoe from the sand of the run-off area.

Stewart was in the Tyrrell pit waiting to go out again. He'd already done a fast lap and mechanics were making small adjustments. Ken Tyrrell came over and said he thought Rindt had had 'a shunt'. Stewart went immediately to Peter Gethin, Hulme's team-mate, who had just come past the accident. 'The car is all over the place,' Gethin said, 'but it's on its feet. The cockpit looks pretty right and there's no sign of Jochen.' Stewart and Gethin both made an assumption: Rindt had walked away from it.

Chapman wanted Miles to drive round to see what had happened. The marshals at the end of the pit lane wouldn't let him out. Stewart remonstrated with them, explained why Miles wanted to go. They said no. They must have known by now.

Stewart went to the control tower only a few yards away. Closed-circuit television cameras covered the whole of the track. The track manager wouldn't look Stewart in the eye. Stewart explained that he needed to know because he had to go to Nina. The manager said he believed Rindt was OK but had been taken to the track's hospital. Stewart moved back towards the pits, asked Nina to remain where she was and ran towards the hospital. An ambulance stood outside, sirens shrieking, lights flashing. Stewart elbowed through a group of photographers and saw a second ambulance, its doors partially open. He saw a stretcher and men working, saw Rindt's left foot, saw the condition it was in – bad – and concluded that if the men working inside were ignoring that something more serious must be happening.

He returned to Nina and together they went to the hospital but were stopped at the gate. They were told they must not go in, everything was being done. Then Nina saw a priest entering the ambulance. The priest emerged, draped an arm round Nina's shoulder and said, 'courage, Mrs. Rindt.'

Chapman arrived and Ecclestone told him that Rindt was dead. 'Oh God, not another one,' Chapman said.

Stewart needed solitude. In the pit area he struggled to keep control of himself. Ken Tyrrell came over and said there were fifteen minutes of the session left. Stewart was in the act of buckling his helmet when he broke down, wept in a corner, did get into the car, wept again. He could taste the salt of his own tears. Out there he became a racing driver again. He spent a few laps examining the Parabolica, searching for clues then drove the fastest lap he had ever done at Monza.

Emerson Fittipaldi was a young man and in the third Lotus. Initially the confusion had been so great that Warr had told him that Rindt had had an accident and would need his car.

After I knew, it was the hardest day in motor racing I had in my life. I went straight to the hospital but when I arrived I heard the news and I just went straight home. There is nothing you can do. You feel so bad you don't want to meet anybody, you don't want to talk to anybody.

Nobody will ever know why Rindt began to weave and hit the Armco. Warr:

My own feeling is that, considering the no-downforce configuration, he started to go quickly much too soon. I believe that he was caught out because the tyres had not warmed up and the aerodynamic and brake balance was miles out due to having no rear wing. Also the Monza circuit then consisted almost entirely of right-hand corners, so the left-hand tyres would be the first to warm up. I think that the first time he hit the brakes really hard the car became totally out of balance.

The Lotuses were withdrawn and the transporter left almost immediately. Ickx dropped out of the race on lap 26, clutch, but could still become champion if he won Canada, Watkins Glen and Mexico.

Fittipaldi waited to see what Lotus were going to do. He was told the team wouldn't compete in Canada but might go to The Glen.

It was not sure. Colin had talked of retiring from motor racing altogether. But I waited. Then two weeks before the United States Grand Prix they called me and told me to go to Snetterton [a local track] to test the car and said we would be going to the States. The Press kept asking me a lot of questions and I was not happy. I was under a lot of pressure. This was only my fourth Formula 1 race.

Lotus missed Canada and Ickx won it. 'It was not a difficult situation,' Ickx insists these many years later, 'because I thought Jochen deserved the championship and I had no wish to win it in circumstances like that. It never hurt me in the sense of doing what I was doing, driving on. Of course I did my best...'

Rindt would get the title on merit.

Fittipaldi remembers that the surface of the Watkins Glen track was 'dirty. It had been raining heavily on the Saturday evening and people who were camping there were walking all over the track in dirty boots on Sunday morning. There was mud everywhere on the track. They let us have three or four warming up laps and I could scarcely believe that this was America, so modern and so rich.'

Before the race Chapman said, 'Emerson, whatever you do, you must finish in front of the Ferraris because of the championship'. Fittipaldi 'told him I would do what I could.'

Stewart intended to do what he could to beat Ickx and make the title safe for Rindt. He led and on lap 16 Ickx moved up into second place. That lasted until lap 56 and the problem with the Ferrari. Repairs took three minutes and cost ten places. Ickx emerged and paid Jochen Rindt one final compliment: he charged. Stewart dropped out on lap 83 – out of 108 – and with twenty laps to go Fittipaldi was into second place behind Rodriguez (BRM) and Rodriguez pitted, a fuel problem. Fittipaldi led, Ickx still charging. Fittipaldi:

I didn't know, but Colin had made a mistake on the lap chart. He thought Ickx was on the same lap as me and was catching me. I was trying hard at the end of the race to keep Ickx behind me but he was catching me, driving very hard – he did the quickest lap of the race.

At last I came into the pit straight and down towards the finish line, and I saw Colin jumping in the air and throwing his hat. When I finished the race I saw everybody was – not crying, but with drops on the

eyes, you know. It had made sure Jochen was World Champion. From all
that disaster at Monza had come something good.

In mid-October 1970 Nina wrote to Ickx. 'First of all I want to congratulate you on your win in Canada. To be honest I was a little worried that you might win Watkins Glen and Mexico City as well, which would have meant Jochen had lost the championship. I am very happy Jochen managed it after all. It was his only burning wish.'

Ickx reflected on all this many years later and contented himself with three words. 'Jochen deserved it.'

1971

STEWART WALKS IT

Austrian Grand Prix, Österreichring

'TO WIN THE World Championship never becomes easier, it always becomes more difficult because of the professionalism which has come in to the sport. This was particularly so in 1971. We had the year of the young lions. A lot of young drivers came along who were incredibly good, incredibly good.' Stewart had trendy long hair then and seemed a creature of the 1960s, those years when we thought all the barriers came down and the world belonged to youth.

Inwardly he was what he had always been, crisp and concise, perceptive to a remarkable degree and disciplined: the opposite of a hippy.

Young lions sharpening their claws? There were some of those, the Swede Ronnie Peterson driving a March and in only his second season, the Austrian Niki Lauda; Gethin (McLaren) who, like Peterson, was in his second season. Frenchman François Cevert who partnered Stewart at Tyrrell was in his third. Andretti (Ferrari) had yet to drive a full season.

Over them and everybody else Stewart exercised almost complete mastery, rarely lowering his guard. Andretti took South Africa, Stewart second but then the little Scot won Spain, Monaco, was eleventh in the wet at Zandvoort (his Goodyear tyres didn't like the conditions), won France, Britain and the Nürburgring.

Four rounds remained but Stewart already had 51 points, Ickx only 19, Peterson only 17. Nobody else could catch him. For Ickx to win the championship he needed a second place and three firsts, for Peterson to win he needed four wins – and in both cases Stewart gaining no points at all.

There was a strange feeling of inevitability hanging in the hills and woodland which surrounded the Österreichring.

'When I start a race I'd best describe it as like being a rubber ball,

I'm mentally deflating that ball to the point where I personally am in control of it without any difficulty at all. Finally when I get into a racing car the rubber ball has totally deflated and it's just a heap of rubber in the bottom of the cockpit.'

Lauda, a well-bred Viennese, made his debut in a March but would retire after twenty laps with a handling problem.

Conditions proved ideal for the first day of qualifying – there would be three days, giving nine hours altogether – because although the plateau surrounding the circuit held dampened, cooled air after earlier rain the temperature suited the engines perfectly.

Rindt set the lap record the year before at 1m 39.2s but to general amazement Stewart moved swiftly into the 1m 39s then the 1m 38s. *Motor Sport* judged this 'almost too much for the opposition'.

Fittipaldi made a shrewd move towards the end of the session tucking in behind Stewart and getting himself towed into fourth quickest. Interestingly Stewart's time, 1m 37.6s, was as fast as he would go in the three days. It put him on the front row. On the Saturday Stewart complained that the gearbox wasn't functioning properly, it was taken apart and inspected and that gave him only a brief thrust at the very end of qualifying. He couldn't overhaul the 1m 37.4s by Siffert (BRM) for pole. Of more significance were the plights of Ickx and Peterson. Their cars were just off the pace, Ickx on the third row, Peterson on the sixth.

Austria was at its best on Sunday, 15 August 1971, sunny, clean as an essentially rural country should be. The circuit was a delight, too. The rolling, undulating hills fashioned it into an amphitheatre populated by 130,000 spectators. Siffert got away quicker, Stewart's Tyrrell dragging itself over towards the centre of the track under acceleration, its left rear wheel laying a dark swathe of rubber behind it. Going up the hill from the startline Regazzoni (Ferrari) went to the inside, Stewart clinging to Siffert who had now assumed the centre of the track. Cevert tracked Stewart.

Siffert breasted the hill and led into the first corner, Stewart behind, and they moved out into the loops of the Österreichring for the first of 54 laps. Round the fast right-hander to the start-finish line Siffert held the lead, then Stewart, Regazzoni and Cevert. Poor Ronnie Peterson was far back, his car understeering badly and on the fifth lap everyone heard the rough gurgle of trouble from Ickx's Ferrari engine.

Siffert moved away from Stewart and as *Motor Sport* said:

Stewart was in slight trouble with his car understeering too much because he was using narrower Goodyear tyres on the front wheels than he normally does and the decision to experiment was a wrong one.

Stewart, unable to close the gap to Siffert, eased off and Cevert went past on lap 23. By now Ickx ran eleventh and Peterson slogged on but nowhere near the points. On lap 32 Ickx's engine let go altogether.

Stewart was champion – and gone himself in a rotating cloud of dust, the left rear wheel off, the short stub axle broken. Stewart walked back to the pits as Peterson struggled by, ninth, walked to the championship.

Siffert, an extremely popular man, won the race although for the last three laps he had a puncture and by the last lap the car was almost beyond his control in the slower, sharper corners. Fittipaldi crossed the line 4.1 seconds later.

The crowd mobbed Siffert as if they wanted to be part of this, the second win of his career. It would be his last.

Peterson, for all that he hadn't won the championship, became a celebrity in Sweden and so much was being written about him – by no means all of it accurate, and with a heavy concentration on his wealth – that he decided to call a Press Conference. During it he explained how the money came, didn't divulge how much (nothing changes) and added, 'Now I hope all this has been sorted out once and for all, but I don't want any nosing about to find out how much I earn.' Peterson would spend another seven years in Grand Prix racing, would know pole positions and front rows and ten wins but never the championship; and sad it is to contemplate him now.

Stewart had his second championship. Even then, placing him in a broader context was difficult because he had made himself arguably the first technocratic driver. Flamboyance, risk, daring cavaliers: that was the public perception of the champions. They weren't all like that, of course, but Stewart represented a fundamental change. He didn't even look like that – and never mind the long, trendy hair.

1972

FITTIPALDI'S LOVE STORY FILM

Italian Grand Prix, Monza

The rugged man with the hewn face moved across the paddock to the medical centre wearing a white, tight-fitting shirt open at the neck, sunglasses and a broad, toothy smile. He wore a brown leather belt with an ornate buckle and blue jeans. He paused, signed an autograph mechanically and moved into the medical centre to complete the preliminaries for the Italian Grand Prix.

Fittipaldi was 25 and those who thought he carried the Brazilian ease about him were mistaken whenever he got on to a race track. When he took the United States Grand Prix at The Glen to give Rindt the championship he'd been the third youngest race winner of all time.

A strong year, 1972, Stewart in the Tyrrell, Hulme in the McLaren, Ickx in the Ferrari but Fittipaldi proved quick as well as consistent – second in South Africa, victory in Spain, third at Monaco, victory in Belgium, second in France, victory in Britain and Austria. As he strode across the paddock that September morning he'd pushed himself to the verge of becoming the youngest champion. He needed only three more points.

Two rounds remained after the Italian Grand Prix but he sensed that somehow Monza might be 'crucial'. If he didn't do it here what awaited him in Canada and at Watkins Glen?

The lady on the reception at the Hotel de Ville in Monza said 'oh, Signor Fittipaldi, it seems there has been an accident to your transporter.' Checking in, he was tired. There'd been so much traffic that the drive from his home in Switzerland took four hours. He'd arrived deliberately early – the Tuesday – because he felt a need to stop doing business and start concentrating on the race. Standing there at the reception the worrying began. His race car was of course in that transporter. Peter Warr had already left for the scene and nobody could tell Fittipaldi anything.

He went to dinner with some Italian friends where he met two other drivers, Henri Pescarolo and Carlos Pace, and Frank Williams, then a man struggling to keep his small team in existence. The dinner was fine but inevitably Fittipaldi's thoughts kept straying to the transporter. When he returned to the hotel he found Warr there 'very upset and very nervous'. Warr told him the transporter's right front tyre punctured on the Turin-Milan autostrada, the transporter hit the guard rail and almost overturned, the driver was hurt and one of the mechanics, thrown through the windscreen, was in hospital. The racing cars and spare parts had been flung all over the place. Two more mechanics had arrived and were spending the night guarding everything.

Fittipaldi had a friend at an Italian company called Novamotor and at 1.0 in the morning telephoned to see if he could organise another transporter to bring the pieces. Half an hour later Fittipaldi's phone rang. A Novamotor transporter would be at the accident at eight in the morning.

He drove there and 'it was a really terrible sight. My racing car was damaged. It was a shame to look at it.'

Legal proceedings continued after Rindt's death two years before and Chapman suspected that the Italians might confiscate his cars. Lotus had debated whether to go to Monza at all but were given assurances by the organizers. Lotus could afford to ignore Monza and still win the championship but not if the cars were impounded and, as it might be, held indefinitely. Chapman decided to send the spare car in a separate transporter and keep it over the French border at Chamonix. If the police impounded the race cars he'd still have that. Now Chapman's hand had been forced. He needed the spare and urgently.

Someone had to take a driver up to this reserve transporter and Fittipaldi volunteered. Then he set off for Turin and the annual prizegiving for the best Constructor and best Chief Mechanic, both won by Lotus. With the team spread all over northern Italy and the French Alps, Fittipaldi accepted the prizes on their behalf.

The team 'gave up trying to salvage the race cars and concentrated on the spare because in a crash like that you don't know exactly what is broken. The monocoque might be bent, the chassis cracked – anything,' he'd say. They had the spare ready for the Thursday afternoon.

Under the weight of drivers' complaints that all Monza offered was the slipstreaming the organizers had built two chicanes. The Thursday session allowed time for the drivers to learn them. Fittipaldi would write:

I drove round for a few laps and then Ickx passed me and I got a tow from him. I could see the right braking points by this time and I got a comparison between my car and the Ferrari. I did 1m 27.3s and we were very pleased because the car wasn't even set up properly. It was oversteering very badly coming out of the chicanes and the braking wasn't very good, though I didn't know why. At first the car weaved about a lot so we put more braking on the front but then the front started locking and I had to try and find a balance.

This preoccupied Fittipaldi for both grid sessions, holding him to sixth fastest. Race day morning was wet. After the untimed session he sat by the motorhome looking at the weather. The rain stopped and probably wouldn't come back. He felt 'completely relaxed'. He wasn't going to win the race in the spare car so why not relax? This cosy line of reasoning was disturbed by Chapman, who pointed out that every time Lotus won a World Championship they did it by winning the decisive race. Fittipaldi said he'd naturally do his best but this time it wouldn't be easy. Chapman strode urgently off towards the pits.

Ten minutes later and 35 minutes before the start of the race Chapman returned. 'Look, don't get too excited,' he said, 'but we have a bit of a problem with your car. There is a fuel leak in the cockpit from the main tank.'

The mechanics were already pumping out the fuel so that a new tank could be installed but Fittipaldi knew that that normally took two hours. He was out of the race. He announced that he would watch it from the grandstand. In the pits Warr used reams of absorbent blue paper to mop the petrol while a mechanic struggled underneath the car. Chapman sat with Fittipaldi in the motorhome keeping him calm and only ventured to the pit once. He was shooed away. Fittipaldi cleaned his visor, just in case. He heard the cars going out to come round to their places on the grid, where they'd stay until they were signalled on to their warm-up lap perhaps a quarter of an hour from now. With ten minutes left, Lotus told Fittipaldi his car was ready. Fittipaldi understood the importance of a good start because the chicanes had made Monza into an orthodox race. At the 6-second signal, he held the revs at 9,500. Stewart, on the second row, felt the transmission go and cruised limply forward, out of it.

Ickx took the lead followed by Regazzoni in another Ferrari, then Fittipaldi, nursing the Lotus because he had softer compound tyres than the Ferraris and didn't want to overheat them. He drove 'very gently, very smoothly'. Ickx pulled away, going so hard that once or twice he locked the brakes and had the Ferrari sideways. Regazzoni reeled Ickx in at half a second a lap.

Fittipaldi began to put pressure on Regazzoni just as Regazzoni was putting pressure on Ickx. On lap 14 Ickx made a small mistake at the Parabolica, slid on to the dirt and Regazzoni nipped through. Ickx recovered fast enough to be second, Fittipaldi behind him. Fittipaldi was mildly surprised at how easily he caught Ickx, but getting past... not easy. Fittipaldi fretted that Regazzoni was easing away and on lap 17:

We came to the second chicane and there was a yellow flag being shown, I put my arm up to show that I was slowing down more than normal and Ickx did the same. I think Regazzoni, who was leading by six or seven seconds, went too quickly into the chicane under those conditions – because if there is a yellow flag you never know what might be round the corner and the approach to that chicane is absolutely blind. When I was in the chicane I saw the Ferrari going out of it, spinning over the kerbstone on the outside of the track.

It had begun when Pace's March spun in the chicane. Pace was trying to re-join with the help of the marshals, hence the yellow flag.

Three cars had already threaded their way past him but Regazzoni arrived fast. He hit the front wheel of the March with his rear wheel and it was torn off. The Ferrari rotated into the barrier and burst into flames. Regazzoni sprang out.

As Fittipaldi went by he saw the flames and glanced back fearing a firestorm because the Ferrari's fuel tanks still had a lot of petrol in them. He didn't see Pace and he didn't learn until after the race that Regazzoni had hit him.

Ickx led Fittipaldi by 1.5 seconds. At half distance after a long struggle to lap Surtees (Surtees-Ford) Fittipaldi launched his assault. In himself Fittipaldi had no particularly strong feelings either way: second place was good enough for the championship. Somewhere around lap 35 and with twenty remaining a feeling started to grow: he could win the race. He watched to see where Ickx might be vulnerable and where he would be strong. He focused that down to two places, outbraking him into the first chicane or coming out of the second chicane faster. Three times Fittipaldi tried and each time Ickx kept his nerve. Fittipaldi knew the assaults heated his tyres far too much so he'd back off after each, let the tyres cool.

With eleven laps left he tried to out-brake Ickx at the first chicane, didn't, tried to power through at Lesmo, didn't, and hounded him all the way to the Parabolica when 'suddenly Ickx lifted his left arm to show me he was slowing down. There was something wrong with his car. That was very good of him to raise his arm because he knew I was close behind. So I found myself in the lead.'

The Ferrari's engine was dead, an electrical short circuit.

Immediately Fittipaldi transferred his thinking. What if I haven't enough fuel? There had been the drama of the spillage as the countdown to the race went on and Fittipaldi must assume the leak had been cured but he slackened his pace. He knew that Mike Hailwood (Surtees-Ford) was catching him although he still had a substantial lead.

The last lap was the longest lap of all.

He reached the Parabolica and suddenly accelerated so that even if the tank ran completely dry he could freewheel to the line. Hailwood would still be too far away.

Fittipaldi's Cosworth engine kept on pumping power. Chapman vaulted the low pit lane guard rail winding his right arm round three times as if he was winding himself up for a lift-off. Then, arm erect, he flung his famous black hat into the air and flung his arms around Warr.

As Fittipaldi emerged from the cockpit Chapman stood at one side of the Lotus, Warr at the other, the crowd jostling tightly around them. On the podium, a garland of flowers round his neck and the chunky silver trophy in his hand, Fittipaldi smiled a great deal but he still looked calm.

I didn't see my mother and father until I reached the motorhome. There was champagne, which I don't like, but I drank a very little bit to please everyone because they were all congratulating me and my mother was really crying, she was so happy. I was happy. Everybody was happy. It was like a love story film.

1973

EXITS AND ENTRANCES

Italian Grand Prix, Monza

'I'm very nervous.' Stewart, wearing shorts and a running vest, grinned as he said that. Around him other drivers, mechanics and team managers milled. They too wore shorts and running vests. They were at Monza.

Sunlight fell across this strange group creating mosaics of shadow. It was -inevitably, perhaps – Frank Williams who organised them, pointed out the starting line, directed them to it, told them to form up two men to a team for a four kilometre fun run. In the background James Hunt, a tall, stooping Englishman, limbered up by high-kicks of his long, lean legs and took the lead with a loping stride. He'd made his debut at Monaco in a March but didn't finish, an engine problem. Williams overtook him and, accelerating, won. Stewart caught the informality perfectly, reached the line doing an impression of the Highland Fling. He was sixth.

It was also typical of the man to be in this race, held after the final grid session for the Italian Grand Prix, at all. He had a headache from a cholera immunization injection and he had influenza. That gave him pains across his chest.

All was not well with his Tyrrell, either. It had been inexplicably slow in qualifying and he would start from the third row of the grid behind two very fast men, Peterson and Fittipaldi in John Player Special Lotuses.

Two rounds remained after Monza, Canada and the United States. In the mathematics of it Stewart, Fittipaldi, and Cevert, Stewart's team-mate, could still take the championship, but Stewart only needed fourth provided Fittipaldi didn't win. Fittipaldi had made a very strong start to the season before Stewart dominated the central part of it.

Something else favoured Stewart. Fittipaldi and Peterson were locked into an extremely uneasy relationship. Warr said:

Emerson had already been World Champion in 1972 and was now assuming the attitude consistent with that high office. He was no longer the 'tiger' he had been when he first joined the team. Ronnie, on the other hand, was every man's dream of a racer. He just breathed, walked and talked motor racing the whole time. He was a marvellous guy to work with, the only difficulty being that he was so good he was able to 'drive around' any problems which arose with the car.

We very quickly ran into a problem of a different sort when everywhere we went Ronnie demonstrated that he was basically quicker than Emerson. In some places he was staggeringly quicker, and I felt sure that without a shadow of a doubt Ronnie would have won the World Championship but for gearbox trouble at both Barcelona and Zandvoort.

All this would have a direct impact on the Italian Grand Prix and Fittipaldi going for the championship with his 42 points. What would happen if Peterson out-drove him again? Team orders? Would there be any? Warr says:

What people didn't understand is that a deal was struck in Brazil at the beginning of the season where it was agreed that Emerson would have the Brazilian race while Ronnie would take the Swedish. And Emerson did win the Brazil whereas Ronnie lost out in Sweden when he had a puncture on the last lap. When we came to the half-way point in the season the situation had got so bad that in practice sessions Ronnie's car would be set up one way and Emerson's another. Then, with only about five minutes left, Ronnie would be totally confused and so we would have to adjust the settings of his car to those of Emerson's. Things would then become very tense because not only would Ronnie be quicker but he was doing it by pinching Emerson's settings as well.

What actually happened was that it had been agreed that if Emerson had any chance of taking the World Championship Ronnie was to be prepared to give up the lead. But all this came to an end in the Austrian Grand Prix [the race before Monza] where Ronnie was giving the race to

Emerson in order to help him win the championship and Emerson dropped out due to a broken fuel pipe so that Peterson won the race after all. At that point Ronnie still had a chance of winning the championship, albeit a remote one...

In the Sunday morning untimed session Stewart's Ford engine dropped a valve, the first engine failure Tyrrell had had the whole season. There was just time to change it. While the mechanics worked, Stewart's influenza seemed to worsen, making whatever he said into a throaty croak.

Towards 3.30 in the afternoon thinning cloud shielded the sky. At the start they used the long straight, bypassing the chicane – they would use that from the second lap on – and the chicane had traffic cones placed carefully around it to direct the cars away. As they passed these cones Peterson led, Fittipaldi behind, then Hulme (McLaren), then Stewart who had edged past Peter Revson (also McLaren).

That was how it was on lap 1 ... and 2, 3, 4, 5, 6. Revson stayed as near to Stewart as he could. Stewart's car wasn't handling properly and he drifted back from Hulme towards Revson. The Tyrrell looked almost vague in the corners. They crossed the line to complete lap 7 and, going towards the chicane, Revson went through on the outside.

Stewart took the Tyrrell slowly around the 3.5 miles (5.6km) to the pits. Whenever he glanced in his mirror he could see the left rear tyre slowly deflating. A nail had sliced into it and, as he stopped, mechanics rushed to that wheel, stooped, probed. 'The tyre hadn't gone down with a bang, it was a slow puncture. I really felt it at the Lesmo Curve. What happens is that the back end gets loose, the car gets loose and there is nothing you can do about it. Everybody was doing the best they could but they couldn't get the nut off.' As Stewart sat, car after car went by – the German Rolf Stommelen in a Brabham, the Argentinian Carlos Reutemann in another Brabham, Ickx (Ferrari), Hailwood (Surtees), Beltoise (BRM), Lauda (BRM)...

To remove the nut and replace the wheel took more than sixty seconds, and Stewart rejoined twentieth. How far behind the leaders he was had become so academic that nobody seems to have bothered to check the gap. As he crossed the line to complete lap 9, and with 46 left, only a couple of backmarkers lay behind him.

'What you do is try to be as smooth and gentle with the car as you can to make it go quickly,' Stewart says, 'but I knew of course that Monza was a difficult circuit to make up time because it is not a difficult circuit to drive.' Monza was a straightforward speed bowl and in theory those nineteen cars in front could run as consistently fast as he could.

Hulme crashed at the chicane and limped towards the pits, Stewart swiftly overtook David Purley (March) so that on lap 10 he was eighteenth. The pit stops began and on lap 12 Stewart took Gijs van Lennep (Williams) to be fifteenth.

'I hadn't thought of giving up,' Stewart says. 'You can never do that. If you give up once you will always give up. I was driving as hard as I could and I sensed much faster than the front runners. In fact I knew I was because I was breaking the record almost every lap – but what I didn't know was how fast the opposition was going.'

On lap 17, Pace (Surtees) had a puncture, Regazzoni pitted for tyres and that was thirteenth. 'I was getting pit signals, of course, but I still wasn't thinking in terms of clawing all that distance back and the team weren't either. I was getting signals from Ken Tyrrell and on the board it said I was minus 50 seconds from the car in front. I assumed they were doing that to keep me going because maybe they thought I might lose interest. I started to get minus 30 on Graham Hill (Shadow), then it would come down and down until I could see him, then I knew I was in twelfth position.'

That was lap 18.

On lap 19, Lauda pitted and that was eleventh. On lap 20, he moved past Jackie Oliver (Shadow) and that was tenth. On lap 21, he moved past Georges Follmer (Shadow) and that was ninth – but the pit signals told him he was a long way behind Beltoise (BRM). On lap 25 Beltoise pitted and that was eighth – but the pit signals told him he was a long way behind Ickx and at current speed would need seven laps to catch him.

Ickx had his own problems, the water temperature rising because a piece of tyre from Pace's puncture damaged the radiator. They crossed the line to complete lap 36 and at the chicane Stewart went effortlessly past. That was seventh. He tracked Hailwood (Surtees) for four laps and Hailwood had problems. He'd bent a wheel at the chicane and on lap 37 Stewart took him. That was sixth.

Now Reutemann in a Brabham. He needed five laps to catch and take him. That was fifth. He needed seven laps to catch Cevert, his team-mate, and when Cevert clearly saw him he waved him through. That was fourth.

Warr in the Lotus pit moved urgently across to where Chapman stood.

The main problem was that if we had given the race to Emerson [running second behind Peterson] he would also have to be allowed to win in both Canada and at Watkins Glen. This would have meant he would have been 'given' a total of five races during the season. Despite what people said at the time, I briefed Colin on the up-to-date points position now Stewart had fought his way up to fourth. We then realized that the championship would be Stewart's unless Emerson won the race and the remaining two. Colin quite rightly felt that the chances of Emerson winning all three, particularly in view of Ronnie having to agree, it was pretty obvious we would not be winning the championship.

Stewart began to catch Revson in third place and on lap 51 broke the record again, 1m 35.3s. Across three laps Stewart closed to the point where Revson could distantly glimpse him. One lap remained.

Ken Tyrrell, headphones to his ears, arms folded in front of him, stood impassive.

Coming to the Parabolica for the last time Peterson still led. What would he do? Fittipaldi was behind him, poised. Half a minute behind and out of their sight Stewart had drawn up to within five seconds of Revson. Peterson came towards the line, giving Fittipaldi nothing. Peterson saw Chapman fling his cap into the air and thought that was the line and he'd won. Wrong. He lifted his foot from the accelerator and it brought Fittipaldi virtually up to him. Peterson had enough impetus to cross the real line 0.8 of a second before Fittipaldi did.

Stewart, fourth, had the championship.

Fittipaldi, deeply enraged, decided immediately to leave Lotus.

Stewart reflects that 'technically that was the best race I ever did. To me it was as satisfying as winning any race. I'd thought we'd actually had a chance of winning before the puncture and I'd have gone for the big win. As it was I was concentrating hard to make the car perform well. What did I do afterwards? I went back to the hotel where I was staying, changed, I drove to Milan, had dinner with a whole bunch of Elf people and I drove back to the hotel. I was exhausted then.'

In Canada he was fifth but deep into the second session for the grid at Watkins Glen Cevert's Tyrrell broke out of control and struck a guard rail at enormous speed. Cevert was killed.

A week later Jackie Stewart announced his retirement.

1974

FROM THE EMBERS

United States Grand Prix, Watkins Glen

A pall of black, acrid smoke drifted across the circuit. Nobody paid much attention. It was only a Greyhound bus which had been overturned and set on fire. Watkins Glen attracted weirdos and hippies in large numbers as well as the dedicated Formula 1 followers. The weirdos staged car burning ceremonies to pass the time in an area called The Bog.

The season had been hard-fought, swaying this way and that, and after fourteen rounds the balance was perfect.

Fittipaldi did leave Lotus (for McLaren) but 'it was hard for me to do that, very hard inside. I started with Lotus, always I drive with Lotus'. He had 52 points, Regazzoni (Ferrari) 52, an eager young South African, Jody Scheckter (Tyrrell) 45. All could win the championship in this last race.

The Greyhound bus now reduced to a charred carcass had brought a noisy and passionate group of Brazilians from New York to watch Fittipaldi, who, as the drivers gathered at The Glen was a bit nervy, didn't much want to talk. He could contemplate a good year studded by wins in Brazil and Belgium and Canada, second places in Britain and Italy and four other finishes in the points but they didn't mean much now.

Regazzoni was lucky to be alive after a fiery crash in South Africa the year before, Hailwood hauling him out. In 1974, McLaren ran cars for Fittipaldi, Hulme and Hailwood. At the Nürburgring, Hailwood's car battered the Armco and he was lucky to be alive, too. He would not race a car again. Regazzoni won that German Grand Prix and could contemplate a solid season with four second places and six other finishes in the points but like Fittipaldi he was a bit nervy, didn't want to talk much.

Scheckter was eleven years younger than Regazzoni and four years younger than Fittipaldi. He'd driven one race for McLaren in 1972, five for them in 1973 and joined Tyrrell. He'd remember:

When I took that decision, a lot of people felt I was making life unnecessarily hard for myself by following after Jackie Stewart and exposing myself to the natural comparison that would be made between us. On the other hand there were people who felt I was in need of a good tight rein in Formula 1 and that Ken Tyrrell was just the man to control it. I suppose both views had some merit. In fact I think Ken Tyrrell and I both had doubts about the wisdom of our decision to join forces in the early months of the year.

Scheckter gained no points from the opening three rounds but by mid-season was a front runner, winning in Sweden and Britain. That was good to contemplate but approaching Canada, 'the worst part was the waiting. I stopped playing tennis and took ridiculous precautions when I walked upstairs or around the house. I was ready to shoot myself if I threw the title away because of the strained ankle or a broken bone.

'Then during the Canadian race, at about half-distance, I began to get bad vibrations through the brake pedal. Normally I would have stopped to investigate but the brakes were holding up and Clay was still chasing points in fourth place. I was third. At one of the faster bends the brake drive straps on one of the front wheels let go and spun me into the guardrail. End of story.'

Scheckter was a bit nervy, didn't want to talk much.

For me the arithmetic was now quite simple. To beat Emerson and Clay I had to win the race and hope that neither of them finished in the first five. Any other result would hand the title to one of them. The odds were very long.

The first qualifying session provoked astonishment. Mario Andretti in a Parnelli car was quickest, to his unconcealed delight, then Reutemann (Brabham), Pace (Brabham), Lauda (Ferrari), Scheckter, the Ulsterman John Watson (Brabham), Regazzoni, Fittipaldi. Scheckter had felt something 'funny – maybe the clutch' on his race car and switched to the spare.

Regazzoni had already been pre-testing here just after Canada, put a wheel off and crashed heavily. He suffered a bruised leg but the Ferrari was also very badly bruised. 'Regazzoni came back on foot and his car came back on a lorry, its engine having blown a big hole out of itself on the top side,' *Autosport* said. Ferrari flew a spare chassis from Italy for the Grand Prix.

Fittipaldi moved quietly in the background, pleased with his car.

Two qualifying sessions on the Saturday, Scheckter on the pace but 'I was getting too many confusing messages from the car. I couldn't even tell the designers what it was doing.'

Meanwhile Teddy Mayer, a small, neat man running McLaren, made sure the car-to-pit radio he'd brought from domestic American racing worked. He wanted to be able to talk to Fittipaldi. Mayer anticipated a tactical race...

At the end of Saturday the whole thing seemed wide open. The Brabhams were flying and Hunt in a Hesketh – the car financed, built and raced by an English nobleman, Lord Hesketh – flew, too. Reutemann took pole with Hunt alongside; Andretti and Pace; Lauda and Scheckter; Watson and Fittipaldi; Regazzoni and a Frenchman Jean-Pierre Jarier (Shadow).

Still Fittipaldi and Regazzoni and Scheckter said little while some of the crowd amused themselves by pouring petrol on a section of road over by The Bog and lighting it so that those on motor bikes could do wheelies through the flames.

When the twenty-seven starters formed into the grid Andretti was missing, his engine misfiring. As he came round he peeled into the pits where the mechanics diagnosed an ignition fault. This was Upstate New York, Andretti was American, the Parnelli team was American and who was going to start the United States Grand Prix without them? The grid sat there while the mechanics cured Andretti's car and it did a lap in lonely isolation.

The drivers faced fifty-nine laps of the 3.3 mile (5.4km) circuit, a total of 199.1 miles (320.4km).

A clean start, Reutemann and Hunt together, but Reutemann holding a clear advantage. Pole position was on the right of the track and the first corner a right. All Reutemann had to do was stay abreast of Hunt and hold his line. He did.

Far behind Andretti's car hadn't started at all. *Autosport* reported:

Hunched there totally helplessly, Andretti lived through the experience of cars flashing by on either side in a cloud of grit. Mechanics swarmed upon the Parnelli and pushed it away to one side and attacked it.

Hunt pressed Reutemann hard all the way round that first lap and at the end of it they were clear of the rest: Pace, Lauda, Scheckter, Fittipaldi, Regazzoni – a truly desperate situation for Scheckter, who had to win but equally desperate for Regazzoni because the Ferrari's nose was wallowing. It had a defective damper.

Reutemann moved away from Hunt, Pace on his own in third but for twenty-three maddening laps Lauda rode shotgun in front of Scheckter, holding him there, pressing him back, holding him there. Lauda's Ferrari was no match for Reutemann or Hunt or Pace, but he could help team-mate Regazzoni. Each time Lauda looked back he could see Scheckter, then a group but no Regazzoni. He slipped to ninth, his championship over. The Ferrari pit hung out a pit board telling Lauda to forget about holding the others up so Lauda pulled out 2.5 seconds on Scheckter, who now found Fittipaldi directly behind him. If Fittipaldi tracked Scheckter to the end he was champion.

Scheckter went flat out, the only option left after a whole season of proving himself, of earning Ken Tyrrell's respect, of fashioning himself into a contender. 'I was driving too hard,' he would say, 'I think Emerson must have been flat out as well even though he had those people behind him. There were some bends where my car was faster than his, much faster, and I would pull out a ridiculous margin, about a second, but in other bends he'd pull it back again so we stayed even.'

Three times Fittipaldi challenged Scheckter at the end of the straight. Scheckter fought him off. 'I wasn't flat out,' Fittipaldi would insist, although he added with a mischievous twinkle, 'but pretty close to flat out.'

Hulme had long gone from the race, the engine blown. He changed and walked over to a helicopter. Someone asked him what had happened but, he said, 'you're talking to an ex-racing driver.' This was the last of his 112 races and he flew away, his eight victories and the 1967 championship only memories.

Regazzoni kept the Ferrari moving although he pitted three times and with fifteen laps to go Scheckter was out.

I hadn't been able to get higher than fourth place anyway because the race belonged to the super-quick Brabhams of Reutemann and Pace. Clay was plagued by handling problems and lost several laps. Then I had a fuel line break. The odds against me winning the championship lengthened to infinity at that moment...

Fittipaldi reduced his revs to under 10,000 and cruised it, a safe fourth behind Reutemann, Pace and Hunt.

A postscript.

During the race Fittipaldi had a picture of his daughter in the breast pocket of his overalls for luck. Afterwards Fittipaldi's wife Maria-Helena brandished it and gushed, 'Emerson carried her with him today.' Sometimes lucky mascots don't bring luck.

Sometimes they do.

1975

LAUDA'S CHANGE OF LIFE

Italian Grand Prix, Monza

At first there were just dark clouds. It had been raining and the damp, dewy odour of that lingered in the air. It was not raining now. At 10 o'clock twenty-six cars went out for the warm-up session before the Italian Grand Prix. Niki Lauda knew that if he finished no higher than sixth his life would be changed forever.

Lauda was in his fifth season of Formula 1, his second with Ferrari. Everybody knew that Ferrari had not had a World Champion since Surtees eleven years before, the last time they took the Constructors' title, too.

For 1975 Lauda had what he described as the 'magnificent 321T, a gem of a car'. He was mature enough to exploit it, although Fittipaldi (McLaren) made a strong start winning the first race, Argentina, and coming second in Brazil two weeks later.

An Australian, Alan Jones, made his debut in the Spanish Grand Prix in a Hesketh and he'd remember 'some drivers came up and said hello and made me feel welcome; others walked right past me as if I weren't there.' He'd remember how the ones who 'snubbed me' would be 'going out of their way to be nice' – but years later, when he started winning.

Lauda gripped the mid-season. He won Monaco, Belgium, Sweden, was second in Holland, won France and by Monza only Reutemann (Brabham) could catch him but it wasn't quite that simple. The Canadian Grand Prix, due after Monza, had been cancelled because of financial problems so that only Watkins Glen remained. If Reutemann won Monza and The Glen and Lauda got no point in either, Reutemann was champion by half a point – the Austrian Grand Prix immediately before Monza had been stopped in a deluge,

177

Lauda running sixth. Half points were awarded. That gave Lauda a total of 51.5. Theoretically Reutemann could finish with 52.

And now on the Sunday morning at Monza, with all the fervour of Italy bearing down on Lauda and Ferrari, another deluge tipped its load from the skies. A few minutes after the warm-up session began the track was so flooded that even wet-weather tyres offered no grip.

Many years later Lauda, sitting becalmed in his office at his own airline on the fringes of Vienna Airport, would describe the mechanisms of winning a championship. You ignore nationalism, emotion, flights of fancy, you isolate all your thinking to the art of the possible. Flags and anthems, he would say, mean nothing. You win the championship with your throttle and your head.

During first qualifying he'd taken provisional pole from team-mate Regazzoni with 1m 32.8s, Reutemann third (1m 33.9s). Early in the second session Lauda rapped out 1m 32.2s – *Autosport* described it as 'almost stunning' and returned to the pits to watch. Nobody was going to beat it. Regazzoni dipped to 1m 32.7s but Reutemann, determined to fight until the end, overdid it at the Parabolica, spun off into the sand-trap and that put him on the fourth row.

Scheckter, in his second season with Tyrrell, was emerging as a potential champion although obviously it wouldn't be this year. He'd put himself on the second row and represented a problem for Reutemann. Hunt was emerging as a potential champion amidst the romance of Hesketh and his team. Hunt lined up alongside Reutemann, another problem.

Peterson struggled with the 'old' Lotus 72 and had wanted to leave early in 1975 but Chapman kept him to a contract. Peterson's faith in Chapman 'disappeared' and he needed the new car, the 77. He'd been promised it for Monza but it wasn't ready. He could place the 72 no higher than the sixth row.

And it rained in the Sunday morning warm-up. The paddock lay under water, people wading through it crouched beneath umbrellas. A vast puddle formed at the apex of the Parabolica and cars moved far off the racing line to miss it, another formed at the second chicane, another in the dip under the old banking. The first chicane was, as *Autosport* reported *terribly greasy and slippery, but most discomforting of all was the way water was gathering in a sheet along the straight in front of the pits.*

'You can't see it at all,' one driver explained, 'but the car hits it and goes crazy.' But everyone in the pits could see it. Cars were appearing out of the Parabolica in a ball of spray and simply cruising at part-throttle along the straight, twitching and fish-tailing wickedly at speeds that could not have been as high as 70mph (113kmh). Hans Stuck (March) came in with the metal nose spoiler half ripped off. That had happened as the nose dipped into a puddle of water. Tom Pryce (Shadow) and a couple of other drivers came in to say that in the puddle at the second chicane the nose wings were completely submerged. Jim Crawford (Lotus) came in to add force to their tale by saying that his chisel nose had gone under the surface and a 'wave of solid green water' had shot up the nosepiece and flooded his helmet...

Around midday the rain stopped and the clouds began to lift. By three o'clock, 30 minutes before the start, the sky offered a patchwork of blue and dark, the sun glinting through the windows of the blue. Lauda and Fittipaldi toured the circuit in a sports car inspecting the conditions and pronounced it fit. The race started a few minutes late with the grid forming up far over to the left of the wide starting area to bypass the first chicane and the possibility of a mêlée there.

Regazzoni led from Lauda, the German Jochen Mass (McLaren) third. Mass nipped by Lauda who responded and retook him but behind there were already casualties. Vittorio Brambilla (March) and Bob Evans (BRM) pulled off on to the grass with mechanical problems, while someone hit Crawford.

At the front Scheckter followed Lauda past Mass and that was the order as they crossed the line to complete lap 1. The chicane beckoned. Regazzoni passed safely through and so did Lauda but Scheckter overdid it, his Tyrrell gave 'a burst of white tyre smoke and a vicious weave' and plunged on down the escape road.

What followed was wild. Mass bounced his way through over the kerbing with such force that he risked breaking the suspension. Reutemann rode the kerbing so hard that he subsequently admitted he'd been 'several feet in the air'. Fittipaldi and Hunt did thread through but someone hit Peterson up the back and Tony Brise (Hill) spun and spread his car sideways across the mouth of the chicane. The rest of the pack, seeing this, poured on to the escape road to where Scheckter was positioned. Scheckter later told a reporter he'd been 'sitting there in the escape road patiently like a good boy waiting permission to rejoin the race' but 'when he looked up and saw a wide frontal assault on the escape road he thought he'd be safer taking his chances on the track and got himself out of there fast.'

A very narrow opening in the Armco allowed him back onto the track but Pryce had the same idea. Only room for one. A marshal stood near its entrance and directed them while another fled. Scheckter and Pryce went through nose-to-tail missing both.

The lap chart exploded.

Lap 1: Regazzoni, Lauda, Scheckter, Mass, Reutemann, Fittipaldi, Peterson, Hunt, Brise, Frenchman Patrick Depailler (Tyrrell).

Lap 2: Regazzoni, Lauda, Reutemann, Fittipaldi, Hunt, Depailler, Pace, Frenchman Jacques Laffite (Williams), Pryce, Stuck.

Regazzoni and Lauda had avoided the chaos and completed lap 2 six seconds in front of Reutemann. The Ferraris circulated alone, the gap to Reutemann was 7.5 seconds next time around and he saw in his mirrors the disquieting arrival of Fittipaldi, then Hunt.

Scheckter meanwhile got the second chicane wrong. 'The car just jumped away from me, they will do that sometimes.' He brought the Tyrrell into the pits where they diagnosed a bent steering arm and fixed it by someone using their boot to straighten it. That was lap 5, Regazzoni and Lauda more than ten seconds in front of Reutemann, whose brakes lacked consistency.

Fittipaldi went by on lap 14 and set off after the Ferraris.

Regazzoni ticked off the laps and Lauda followed him, showing no interest in trying to overtake. No reason to do that. Ignore nationality and emotion, don't risk the championship by trying to win the race. That would be an emotional decision and a wrong one. Forget the flags and the cheering.

Lauda had been maintaining a precise gap to Regazzoni but slowly drifted back from him. A rear damper had failed and the Ferrari oversteered. Lauda drifted so far back he was mid-way between Regazzoni and Fittipaldi; and Fittipaldi was coming very hard.

Autosport reported:

Fittipaldi. How that man was driving. The big red bait in sight ahead. Emerson was doing everything his muscular body could do to haul in the slight usurper of the title. He was driving the McLaren hard enough to lose control of it but when he lost it he caught it again incredibly quickly. When the car weaved and waggled in the braking areas it weaved and waggled so quickly that it seemed to vibrate. He was not, really, making any impression on the race leader – that gap stayed steady at around 10 seconds – but he certainly was catching Lauda in second place and with 15 laps to go he was in his slipstream. With 10 laps to go he was nose to tail. With six laps to go Fittipaldi whipped over to the left as they braked for the first chicane. As Fittipaldi drew level the two men seemed to look over their cockpit sides at each other – were their faces spread in broad grins? – and Niki gave in.

Regazzoni won, Fittipaldi 16.6 seconds away, Lauda 23.2 seconds away. Niki Lauda showed his extreme pleasure as he sprayed the crowd with champagne, the way winners do. At Monza on the evening of 7 September 1975, Andreas Nikolaus Lauda was just another champion on the ever-lengthening list.

Immortality would have to wait, but not for long.

1976

HUNT RIDES THE STORM

Japanese Grand Prix, Mount Fuji

Mist hung like a shroud over Mount Fuji. It seemed to be uncoiling, drifting down to the ribbon of track where workmen tried to brush grey lakes of water off the surface. For long moments these brushes could be seen scraping at the water and flinging it away like spray. Then the mist swallowed the workmen.

On the first floor of the control tower drivers argued. 'We were,' John Watson says, 'like a group of lemmings. We could see that the main straight was flooded the worst but we all knew that racing drivers are racing drivers and ultimately that's what most of them will do whatever the conditions.'

Most felt that to run the Japanese Grand Prix in this represented an act of madness. Rain had fallen during the night, rain had fallen in the early morning making the untimed session a slipping, slithering, frightening thing. Now, moving towards 1.30 when the race was due to begin, the arguing went on. The drivers wanted to be told something, anything. More rain mingled with the mist. Who dared risk 73 laps of a 2.7 mile (4.3km) circuit, who dared imagine they'd be able to cover nearly 198 miles (318km)? 'In the wet,' Watson says, 'with no visibility you only want someone in the bunch to lose control and you might have a massacre.'

Lauda pondered it gently, too. He could retain the championship here but in the morning session:

Even at 20mph (32kmh) the car had simply been flushed away at the corners because the tyres could not cop. with that volume of water.

Of the twenty-five drivers only Brambilla (March) and Reggazoni

(Ferrari) said they would go on to the grid. That feeling broadened and others – Peterson (March), Stuck (March), Pryce (Shadow) – were prepared to race, too. While this was happening a tall, well-spoken Englishman said to Lauda, 'I think it should be postponed to another day but if the race does start I will be in it.' James Hunt was saying something very important because whilst Lauda had three more points – 68 against 65 – the championship lay between them and only them, Lauda still with Ferrari, Hunt now with McLaren partnering Mass.

Fuji was drawn in another dimension: a widespread disbelief that Lauda was actually alive never mind driving his Ferrari. The German Grand Prix at the Nürburgring two months before had been 'one of those iffy races where it was raining at the start a little bit,' Guy Edwards says. Edwards had qualified a Hesketh on the last row of the grid. 'The Nürburgring is long and you can't see what is round the first corner or two. Everyone with the exception of Mass started on wet weather tyres. He must have had the balls of an elephant. It was quite clear after the first lap that it wasn't raining all the way round. The front runners decided to stop and change to dry tyres because by then Jochen had a huge lead. I went past the pits to start the second lap thinking that maybe I'd come in next lap or whatever. As I was going past the pits Lauda came out on his dries.

'He was behind me for a while, he overtook me and started to pull away—he was in a Ferrari, I was in a Hesketh. Then it got very damp again, very twitchy. He was having trouble with the car sliding all over the place and because I was still on wets I was catching him up. There is a part of the Nürburgring where you go down, down to Adenauer Bridge. I was 50 yds behind him. You accelerate up the long climb to Karussel and there's a slight left-hand kink which is normally no problem flat. Lauda turned in and I was right behind him.

'All of a sudden his car went shooting off to the right totally out of control. The car switched ends and went left. It went through the catch fences like a knife through butter, hit a rock and earth bank and just sort of exploded straight away, exploded in fire. Then it came hurtling back towards me. I thought *Oh God, it's going to hit me*. I was doing maybe 150mph. I aimed left, I was off the track, I just clipped the Ferrari. I was trying to sort out my problems and avoid the barriers. Immediately behind me were Brett Lunger (Surtees) and Harold Ertl my team-mate. Lunger could not avoid the Ferrari which by then was in the middle of the track. Bang. Ertl also I think hit it. He certainly had an accident. It took me between 200 and 300yds to stop and I ran back.

'Lunger was out of his car. There were a couple of marshals and they were in ordinary jackets but they had small hand-held extinguishers. Ertl got one of them and by that time Merzario (Williams) had stopped. It was a big fire. What Ertl managed to do was direct the extinguisher into the cockpit for about six to ten seconds. That was enough to dampen the fire down so we could see Lauda. We dashed in, Merzario, Lunger and myself, we were all heaving and pulling. I thought *we can only stay here another couple of seconds because it's so hot I can't tolerate it*. A petrol fire turns your guts to water because at any instant the whole thing can go up and we'd have gone with it in a very, very unpleasant way.

'Lauda came out like a cork out of a bottle and we all rolled on to the road in a heap. By then the fire was really going again because the extinguisher had run out. We supported Lauda and hauled him away from the fire, which was out of control. Lauda was sort of walking, he was very incoherent but we did get him away.

'Then I saw a great big river of fire and it was coming towards one of the tanks which had broken away. The tank was still full of 20 gallons of fuel. The river was coming from the wreckage of the car licking along the road towards the tank. I left Lauda to the others and ran to the tank and physically pulled it clear.'

Lauda survived, recovered, was driving again by Monza.

As the rain fell at Fuji and the drivers argued in the control tower Hunt had to think of winning, nothing else. James Simon Wallis Hunt was 29 and to many outsiders the essential example of an Englishman, educated at an expensive boarding school, married to a stunning blonde. He appeared to embody two of the traits which the English believe set them apart: inspired amateurism and a devil-may-care approach. Privately Hunt was the obverse of all this. He worried enough to make himself physically sick before races and drove a car pragmatically.

Still the rain fell, still the workmen struggled with the water. The crowd, listening to the drumbeat of the rain on their umbrellas, waited like the drivers for something to happen.

Lauda would write:

In normal circumstances, the last two or three races in a season are madness even for a strong and healthy driver. In my case the physical and mental trauma of the Nürburgring was an added burden, not to mention the pressure piled on by Hunt.

Watson noticed how tired Lauda seemed, how the new eyelids didn't seem to blink properly, how desperately irritating that must have been – like driving a car without windscreen wipers or even worse, because it hurt. Lauda understood the demands a wet race would extract from him and concluded: 'I have no such reserves. I am finished. The rain has totally destroyed me.'

An official opened the door in the control tower and announced the rain had ceased, the workmen had cleared the worst of the water and the race would start at three o'clock. Any delays beyond that would run the race into nightfall.

Watson felt a sense of relief and thought he saw the same reflected in the other drivers. 'I wasn't happy at the prospect of racing but once we knew we were going to the professional attitude took over and we put all other thoughts out of our minds.'

As Brambilla led them from the control tower towards the pits Lauda didn't feel like that. He made a straightforward decision. He'd take part in the race so Ferrari could collect their start money and then he'd drop out.

The drivers waited on the grid almost ten minutes and set off on the warm-up lap. Tyres sliced through standing water. They re-formed.

Hunt (McLaren)	Andretti (Lotus)
Watson (Penske)	Lauda (Ferrari)
Pace (Brabham)	Scheckter (Tyrrell)

Brambilla (March)   Regazzoni (Ferrari)

Hasemi (Kojima)   Peterson (March)

In the grandstand spectators were holding up so many umbrellas they made a complete roof-top of them.

At go Hunt's McLaren wobbled fractionally as the power came on. He angled it towards the middle of the track, Watson moving in behind him, Lauda third. In less than two seconds the twenty five cars churned a vast, rolling ball of spray. Hunt moved into the right-hand corner at the end of the pit lane straight and through it, moved into the right-hander immediately after that. Watson – attacking because racing drivers race – slithered wide, came back, followed. Hunt accelerated towards the loop at the back of the track, the whole car twitching. 'I got a terrific start and I was doing about 140mph when the skirts of the car hit the water and I thought the bottom was going to fall out of it.'

Coming back on to the straight to complete lap 1 Lauda felt the Ferrari aquaplaning and whatever doubts he might have had about his decision were confirmed now. The whole thing was absolutely unbearable, sitting there panic-stricken, seeing nothing, just hunched down in the cockpit waiting for somebody to run into you. There are more important things in life than the World Championship.

At this moment fourth place would make Hunt champion. Watson still attacked him. 'James was on the dry line, I tried to go outside him, I flicked the edge of a puddle and spun.'

Lauda halted the Ferrari in the pits after three laps. Mechanics in yellow waterproof jackets, glistening from the rain, dipped their heads over the cockpit directly into his, that scalded face lurking behind the helmet. Lauda was gesturing, small gestures and suddenly all the heads were gone, the mechanics wandering away. Lauda's hands felt for the catch on the safety-belt and unbuckled it. He prised himself out and as he walked away someone put a comforting arm round his shoulders but Niki Lauda needed no comfort from any other man. He would live with his decision.

The rest was formality. Hunt really need only finish fourth now to have the championship and on lap 10 he held a nine-second lead over Andretti. He dropped his pace and when Brambilla passed

Andretti and attacked he, like Watson, spun. Not that it mattered. Hunt could have afforded, this lap 20, to allow Brambilla through and stroke the McLaren for the remainder of the race but the umbrellas were coming down, the rain was easing, the mist was crawling back up Mount Fuji.

Every car wore wet tyres. As the surface of the track dried, friction heated them and would eventually destroy them. Some drivers already weaved as they went, searching for water on the track. Andretti, slipping back through the field, watched bemused because Hunt didn't seem to be trying to do that. Hunt stayed strictly on the racing line, by definition the driest route. Not that it mattered. At half-distance he still led comfortably, Mass second and as Hunt's team-mate a shield from any attackers. It was all anti-climax, all a procession.

And still the track dried...

On lap 36 Mass found himself on a wet patch as he was coming towards the straight and the car floated away from him into a guard rail. Depailler in the Tyrrell was second now, Pryce third. Not that that mattered, either, not with Hunt so far away – except Depailler was coming hard and Pryce was coming hard. Across the middle of the race Pryce advanced and on lap 40 stole past Depailler but his engine seized seven laps later.

Autosport reported:

The track was now dry enough for the rain tyres to become seriously overstressed. In fact all the wet air was gone, the clouds had blown away from the circuit, some blue sky had appeared overhead and the lowering evening sun had begun to glow warmly over the scene. Incredibly Mount Fuji began to loom through the clouds, showing hints of snow-covered slopes. Cars began to sparkle. The still-wet tyre treads began to glisten. They were shredding and chunking, too. Instead of the treads cutting through the water to get at the road, the road was biting into the rubber. The soft rain compounds were wearing away at a frightening rate.

With twenty laps to go Hunt sensed the front left tyre beginning to wear. 'I didn't know what the hell to do.' The inevitable logic was a pit stop but that would cost him a lot of places and probably the championship. Depailler closed and Andretti was on his way back up.

Each time Hunt passed the pits he looked for a signal to bring him in and didn't see one. Worse, he felt the left rear tyre deflating. That fractionally lowered the chassis which ground against the bumps of the circuit churning cascades of sparks in its wake.

Mayer, running McLaren, 'figured James should know best how long he could run on that tyre. We weren't about to over-rule his own opinion and signal him in for a change. He was waiting for us to tell him when to come in but of course because we were further away from the car we couldn't judge how bad his tyres were so we were more or less telling him to decide. It was down to him.'

Hunt would write:

I was waving at the pits, begging them to call me in. No signals came and then it got so dark I wouldn't have been able to see them.

The weather was turning again. Hunt slowed and slowed, Depailler plunged past on lap 62 and Andretti followed. Hunt lived on the knife-edge – third place, Regazzoni behind him. On lap 64 Depailler was a long way up the road when his left rear deflated and as he limped awkwardly towards the pits, Andretti took the lead, Hunt back in second place. Still he waited for the signal.

On lap 68, as he prodded the McLaren round towards the pit lane straight, the front left gave way completely and started to break up, the tread shredding from it with every revolution the wheel made ... but he was near the pits, approaching them. If it had happened just past the mouth of the pit lane he'd have had to do a complete lap, the 2.7 miles (4.3km) to reach the pits. The tyre wouldn't have survived.

He slipped along the pit lane and stopped. Fevered hands struggled to thrust the jack in but the chassis was too low. 'One of our guys, a guy named Howard Moore, did a super job,' Mayer said. 'We couldn't get the jack under the wishbone. Howard didn't muck about, he lifted the car with his bare hands and we did a good tyre change in the circumstances.'

In the spray on the other side of the pit lane wall – the track wasn't that dry – Regazzoni passed. The seconds melted, fifteen, sixteen, seventeen. Jones in a Surtees passed. Twenty, twenty-one, twenty-two. Depailler, charging after his pit stop four laps before, passed.

Twenty-five, twenty -six, twenty-seven. At last the McLaren moved along the pit lane towards the track spewing spray of its own. Hunt had no conception of where he was in the race but he felt certain the championship had gone. Only five laps remained.

As he completed lap 69 he glimpsed a signal through the murk telling him he was sixth. 'It was a little bit difficult to catch up our lap chart,' Mayer says with superb understatement. In fact Hunt was fifth but even if McLaren had known and he'd known, fifth was useless. This is what they didn't know: Andretti, then Regazzoni a lap behind followed by Jones, Depailler, Hunt, Gunnar Nilsson (Lotus).

James Hunt was an angry man. He had sweated the championship out and been denied through what he believed was no fault of his own. He surrendered to the anger and the anger drove the car. With three laps left he caught Regazzoni and Jones, both trying to conserve their tyres.

'All I could do,' Hunt would say, 'was drive as fast as it was possible to drive and pass any car that I saw.'

On the short, sharp hill behind the pits – a right, a descent, a left – Hunt pitched the McLaren outside Jones, kept it on that line to go outside Regazzoni and was through. He had no idea what that meant because he didn't know where they had been never mind where he was. Jones and Regazzoni were just cars.

With two laps to go pit signals all along the wall reflected the mounting chaos. Hardly any team had any idea what it all meant. 'We didn't have computers or anything like that and the position was changing all the time,' Mayer said, 'but before the end we had sorted out his position from memory.'

Hunt gained on Depailler and Depailler closed on Andretti in the lead, but the anger was undiluted. On the final lap Hunt went savagely after Depailler but never did catch him. They rushed at the line, Andretti with Depailler right behind him and Hunt twenty, thirty yards behind Depailler.

Hunt came down the pit lane and now the spray from his tyres was eddying in gentle little waves. His foot stabbed the accelerator and the engine howled a last time. That was a gesture to vent his anger. He braked in front of an arc of mechanics, snapped the seat belts open and rose, roaring abuse at Mayer.

'I couldn't hear the words because of his helmet,' Mayer said. 'James had quite a temper and he was hot. He was yelling and screaming. I realized he thought he'd blown it from the expression on his face. We were telling him it had all come right but he couldn't hear because of the helmet. Then he dragged it off and paused for breath and I just said "You've won it ... you were third ... you've done it."' Mayer held up three fingers splayed rigid, thrust them towards Hunt. Mechanics grasped him and pitched him into the air. Other people made wild whooping noises. Hunt landed from the mechanics' throw and he didn't believe it. He lurched into a clearing among all those people, rasping 'give me a drink, give me a drink, give me a drink' and then 'did we really win?'

He calmed himself, thrust a hand through that shaggy hair to smooth it and still he didn't believe it. 'I want proof,' he said. 'I want to see it in writing.' He would remember this moment vividly.

I was absolutely determined not to think that I was World Champion and then get disappointed because there were 300 good reasons why something should have gone wrong. It was only really when I checked the lap charts and when the organizers said I was third – and there were no protests in the wind – that I allowed myself to start believing it. I still didn't feel that good when they put me up in third place on the rostrum because I wasn't sure if I was going to be dragged off it. The championship win came to me slowly.

Lauda still wonders about keeping on because a safe and prudent fifth place would have been enough to rewrite history but on the evening of 24 October 1976 he reached Tokyo airport and rang Enzo Ferrari before boarding the plane home. Lauda would recall that Ferrari was 'less than dignified. Officially he supported me and accepted my decision but the conversation was non-commital, heartless. He never seemed to wonder how I was.'

Everybody knew how Hunt was and the chapter heading in his book on the championship tells you everything. It is called The World's Most Famous Hangover.

1977

THE COMPUTER, RIGHT?

United States Grand Prix, Watkins Glen

'Two years ago Niki Lauda went all out for a win in America because, he said, he wanted to end a triumphant season in triumphant style. He did just that. But the Lauda of today is a different man. He has always been a thinking racing driver but now there is an almost alarming degree of calculation in everything he does on the track. There is no evidence of passion in his driving but instead a relentless, cold determination which, day in day out, adds up to more.'

This was how *Autosport* saw the man deep into the autumn.

Lauda himself expanded on the theme and at the same time explained himself. 'I am a human being like you are, there's no problem there. I don't think I'm a computer. The only difference is when I go to the race meeting I am there to race, I am not there for fun, for jokes, for enjoying myself. I go to Argentina or Brazil or wherever not to play tennis and to go swimming but to race. That means from the first moment I arrive there I think about my race car, I think about the race and when I go away I think about the next race.'

You need take only the most casual glance at the statistics of 1977 to imagine you know what happened. Lauda, in his fourth year with Ferrari, led the first half of the season with 33 points from Scheckter (Wolf) 32, and Andretti (Lotus), also 32. In the next five races, while Scheckter and Andretti faltered, Lauda won twice and was second three times. He came to the third last race – the United States East at Watkins Glen – needing a single point.

In one sense your casual glance told you the truth, in another the truth was extremely different. A bitter year, 1977, Lauda versus Enzo

Ferrari himself. This began with that telephone call from the lounge of Tokyo airport in late October 1976, Lauda anticipating some understanding from Ferrari. Instead Enzo Ferrari judged Lauda has lost the stomach for it and once Lauda was back played an interesting game. He said Lauda could become team manager. At that moment Lauda did become a computer, clicking out the reason. Ferrari wanted to make sure he couldn't drive for anybody else. Lauda left Ferrari's office, went to his car and got out the contract he had signed for 1977, returned, demanded whether it should be torn up.

Once that's done, Lauda said, *I'll be free to drive for McLaren* – Lauda plucked the name out of the air. Lauda was sent from the office while Ferrari and his advisers raked the matter over. Lauda returned. He could stay as a driver but number two to Reutemann. Lauda knew that was nonsense: numbers are meaningless, status is decided on the track.

His first task was to establish his superiority over Reutemann, which he began to do after the third race. Now Lauda faced the rest of the season battling against Scheckter, Andretti and Hunt. Lauda would not forget what he considered Ferrari's 'breach of trust' and he knew that Ferrari could be vindictive. For entirely personal reasons Ferrari might decide that Lauda should not win the championship. That could have been arranged with a word in the right place.

By the Dutch Grand Prix at Zandvoort, Lauda had signed for Brabham. Five rounds remained, Ferrari were anxious to re-sign him for 1978 and he had to fend them off with 'one lame excuse after another'.

He won Zandvoort, was second at Monza and came to The Glen needing only that single point, but the word was out by Zandvoort because on the day after the race Ferrari asked a young Canadian, Gilles Villeneuve, to fly from Quebec to Modena for a chat.

While Lauda calculated the championship the drivers' market was thrown into turmoil. Ferrari hadn't signed Villeneuve and after Monza invited Andretti for a chat but he stayed with Lotus because his heart was there. Lotus meanwhile might find themselves swapping one Swede for another, Nilsson for Peterson. Andretti didn't want Peterson – two stars in one team was too much, he decided – and made what were described as 'great efforts' to persuade Nilsson to stay. But no, Nilsson wanted to go. Peterson had a possible chance of joining Ferrari but Reutemann said no to that.

Four days after Monza, Andretti turned down Ferrari officially and Villeneuve's phone rang again but only for another chat. Alan Jones, working his way into Formula 1, eyed the Ferrari himself and one of those days left the Modena office with what he thought was a contract.

Thus the background to Watkins Glen and Lauda had to face the most basic question: what would Enzo do now?

Watkins Glen was wet although the rain didn't fall until immediately after the first session on the Friday. By then Hunt had provisional pole, Lauda only seventh. On the Saturday the rain fell hard and long and Lauda managed only a few laps before the engine let go. He needed a tow to the pits.

Scheckter would start the race from the row behind him. 'It's something we have not come across before,' Wolf team manager Warr, who had left Lotus, said. 'Jody says the car is well balanced, braking well and the speed trap times are no better and no worse than anybody else's, yet he is a second and a half off the pace. The only thing we can put it down to is a small engine problem that's losing us a bit of time all round the circuit. He used the spare car in the untimed session and was quickest in that.'

When final qualifying had drowned a hushed whisper grew in intensity. Will it be like Fuji? What would the implications of that be? Might Lauda do a few token laps then withdraw again?

Such questions were themselves drowned. On the Saturday night, the eve of the race, Ferrari fired Lauda's mechanic because he intended to follow Lauda to Brabham. This enraged Lauda. The timing represented a vindictive act but after a row Lauda controlled himself again: disregard emotion and nationality, drive with your throttle and your head.

That Saturday afternoon during final qualifying Lauda had described the conditions as undrivable. He had to control his memories of Fuji, too.

On the Sunday the sky darkened, the surrounds of the track still sodden from the day before, the car parks a muddy morass. Cars sank as they came in and a tractor was needed to haul them.

The morning warm-up stayed dry but drizzle fell after it, just enough to be tantalizing. Every time the clouds opened the drizzle stopped and the track began to dry; then it came back. A wet race? Dry? Wet weather settings? Dry? Most teams settled for an uneasy compromise.

Stuck (Brabham) sat alongside Hunt on the front row, he liked the rain and immediately took the lead through the banked Turn One, through the chicane and out along the straight, Hunt hounding him, then Andretti and Reutemann. Peterson, next, went into a vast slide just in front of Lauda but corrected it, held his Tyrrell steady. If he hadn't, if he'd struck Lauda...

Stuck led a Grand Prix for the first time and had the posture of a man who intended to stay there. He of course had a clear road and, as someone noted, 'he powered the Brabham through the puddles like a rally driver on ice.' Hunt eased back to a 'safe distance where I could see what was happening before it happened'.

Lap 1: Stuck, Hunt, Andretti, Reutemann, Peterson, Lauda, Scheckter coming with a rush. On the second lap he took Lauda and the next lap Jones took Lauda, too. That was eighth.

Peterson constantly struggled to control his Tyrrell and needed a lot of the track to do it. Jones, tracking him, ducked and darted but found no way through. Jones launched another attempt but, he said, Scheckter 'had already put me on the grass twice trying to get by and in the end I tried so hard I lost it myself. The catch fencing stopped me well and the car was not too bad, although when the marshals left it sticking out almost on the edge of the track I didn't think it was going to stay that way for long.'

Lap 4, Lauda seventh.

Lauda's Ferrari suddenly snapped sideways in front of Brambilla (Surtees) who lifted off to miss him and spun himself. If...

On lap 6, Lauda took Peterson and that was sixth: the point he needed. The order: Stuck, Hunt, Andretti, Scheckter, Reutemann, Lauda. They ran like that through to lap 11 when Lauda took Reutemann. They'd had a brief battle and Reutemann spun. That was fifth and he'd reached it comfortably because Reutemann spun well clear of him. Scheckter lay ahead but Lauda didn't need to worry about that. All Lauda had to do was finish.

Stuck's clutch had gone on lap 3 and now deep into the perils of Turn 1 the Brabham jumped out of gear and Stuck left the track, Lauda fourth.

Soon enough a dry line formed and teams were holding out pit boards to tell their drivers to cool tyres – like Fuji. Lauda was eminently intelligent enough to drive to the end keeping good and clear of all obstacles. He was still fourth when the flag fell and had 72 points. No man had scored more.

'When I'd got the three points I felt how hard the pressure had been being short of one point. Even when you take the point you feel how much pressure comes off you. The 1975 championship was difficult but thinking back the championship of 1977 – the year I had, all the things I went through – was a hundred times more difficult.' Lauda was happy that his departure from Ferrari represented a 'slap in the face' for Enzo, who responded with some abuse of his own.

Lauda did not feel inclined to tolerate any of this one moment longer and said he didn't feel well enough to drive in the last two races.

One of those days Lauda flew himself down to the nearest airport to Modena and entered Enzo Ferrari's office a last time. *That's it*, Lauda said, *finished, nothing more to say*. He returned to his aeroplane and sat in it for a long, long time waiting for permission to take off. Other planes were, he wasn't. He radioed the control tower. Silence. He radioed again. A voice crackled, 'you leave Ferrari, you stay there. No permission.'

The computer clicked. 'But,' Lauda said, 'I'm going to Brabham and they have your Italian Alfa Romeo engines.' Silence, then 'OK, you can go.'

He went.

1978

ANDRETTI, IN HIS SORROW

Italian Grand Prix, Monza

They'd hardly spoken that weekend, itself a curious thing. As we've seen, Andretti hadn't wanted Peterson to join Lotus for 1978 because he thought that somehow such a pairing wouldn't work out. Instead they became friends to the point where Peterson publicly wished all human beings were as straight as Andretti.

Between them they dominated the season from Reutemann (Ferrari), Lauda (Brabham) and Depailler (Tyrrell). During this, however, there were two significant debuts – Keke Rosberg in South Africa driving a Theodore (clutch, engine and fuel leak problems), and Nelson Piquet in Germany driving an Ensign (engine problems). These debuts were as anonymous as debuts generally are.

By Monza, the third last race, only Andretti or Peterson could win the championship.

Normally they'd chat, exchange information, level with each other. This time they didn't. Andretti would write 'it was not that there was anything wrong between us, just that he was a little uptight about his position and I was the same about mine.' Andretti led by twelve points. 'Exactly what was happening there between us I don't know. It was nothing bad, just something of the moment.'

Andretti would never forget that.

All across the weekend of the Italian Grand Prix there were omens. Two qualifying sessions on the Friday: in the morning Peterson was second quickest behind Andretti but an engine blew in a big way towards the end forcing him to use the spare car, the Lotus 78 from the year before, during the afternoon. He could urge it no higher than thirteenth.

In the untimed session on the Saturday the Lotus 79 had a new engine but the brakes weren't right, the clutch wasn't right and Peterson said 'there was a lizard in the car. I tried to catch it and put it out of the car but it kept getting away from me. After practice it was still there.'

The car wasn't ready until ten minutes of final qualifying remained. Peterson set off down the pit lane in a furious rush to make up lost time but he couldn't. Andretti had pole, Peterson only on the third row. Andretti told Nigel Roebuck of *Autosport*, 'no, no problems, not yet, anyway. You know the race is incidental in this god-damned place. The race I can handle, no sweat, but getting my family and friends in here. . . Jesus Christ. I go to Forest Hills for the tennis and Jimmy Connors snaps his fingers and there's a box for me. Here I can't get my own family in.'

On the morning of 10 September, the sun up hot and getting hotter, Andretti made stately progress to the track – someone had lent him a Rolls-Royce Corniche – from the superb hotel he was staying in at Lake Como. At the track Peterson stayed in the shade. Most of the others did, too.

A few moments after the morning warm-up session began Peterson, who had assured those around him that surely nothing further would happen now, walked back with his helmet in his hand. The brakes failed at the second chicane and he'd ploughed straight on tearing his way through so many layers of catch-fencing he had no idea how many (it was four) before he hit a tree. The Lotus 79, badly damaged, could not race.

Peterson bruised both legs and sought the privacy of the Lotus motor home to examine the extent of that. Frederick Af Petersens, a Swedish journalist, wandered off to have a look at the car and Peterson joined him after some fifteen minutes. They remained in silence for a long time and then Peterson said 'someone made a mistake with the brakes. There was a split pin missing but don't tell anybody.'

He'd race the Lotus 78 and got in to make sure he was happy with the pedal positions. A new engine had been fitted here, too, and Peterson said in a brisk way that he wasn't unhappy: the 78 could probably deal with everything except Andretti in the 79, and if Peterson finished second the championship remained in play.

They set off on the parade lap and Andretti, sharing the front row with Villeneuve, came to rest then inadvertently crawled fractionally forward, braked, came to rest again. The light flicked to green. The rear of the grid were still nosing towards their places on the grid. They were moving...

Villeneuve dipped the accelerator hard. Peterson made a poor start – hesitant, someone called it – and the pack swallowed him, a big pack because those from the rear had already joined those who had been stationary.

No man truly knows the exact and definitive sequence of events which followed.

The track, so broad at the start-finish line, narrowed towards the first chicane. Villeneuve, Andretti and Lauda were already safely ahead of the pack. Somewhere in the pack Riccardo Patrese (Arrows) and Hunt seemed to have been in collision. Hunt's McLaren was then in collision with Peterson who spun into the guard rail. Peterson was struck by Brambilla (Surtees). A terrible sheet of flame seared into the air and another seven cars crashed. The flame was so strong that it singed the face of Regazzoni whose Shadow had tyre marks criss-crossed over its back.

Peterson's ravaged Lotus burned in the middle of the track.

Brambilla sat unconscious in the Surtees.

Hunt and Regazzoni ran to Peterson and Hunt dipped into the flames to try and haul him out. Depailler kicked wildly at the steering wheel of the Lotus to make more room. A fire marshal sprayed the car, more fire marshals arrived. Hunt and Regazzoni did get Peterson out and laid him on the surface of the track.

Red flags were being waved at the start-finish line to stop Villeneuve, Andretti and Lauda, Villeneuve had an arm out of the cockpit to warn those behind and the crowd cheered him – a Ferrari in the lead. Villeneuve and Andretti motored quietly up to the scene and Andretti got out, stood hands on hips surveying it. A battleground of tyre marks spread all around him.

Nigel Roebuck wrote this:

One by one the drivers began to walk back to the pits. To a man they looked grave and angry. In the opposite direction marched a collection of

soldiers, rifles in hand. Just what you need after a major racing accident,
boy soldiers with guns and a sense of importance. Peter Briggs, of Team
Surtees, set off to the scene of the accident to find out about his driver's
condition and was rewarded with a truncheon blow to the side of the
neck. There were plenty of people down at the scene of the devastation.
What there was not was medical help, a fact Clay Regazzoni lost no time
in communicating in words of one syllable. The Swiss was beside himself
with rage and justifiably so.

Freddie Petersens noted that when Hunt reached the pits he could
do no more than shake his head and when with almost unbelievable
lack of sensitivity a policeman asked him for his autograph Hunt
brushed him away.

The ambulance arrived eighteen minutes after the crash. Peterson
and Brambilla had been lying on the road for those eighteen minutes.
Both were flown to hospital in Milan and while the wreckage was
being cleared away the public address system announced that
Peterson had broken his legs.

Towards five o'clock nineteen cars set off on the second parade lap.
During the course of it Scheckter's Wolf lost steering in the second
chicane and he severely damaged a guard rail. An official was
dispatched to examine the guardrail and when he returned the
drivers gathered round him. Five drivers – Andretti, Lauda and Hunt
among them – boarded a Fiat estate car and toured round to inspect
the damage for themselves. They said, repair it or no race. Lauda was
evidently poised to leave the circuit altogether.

The race, cut to forty laps, started shortly after six o'clock.
Villeneuve jumped it and Andretti thought better be on my way, too.
'The guys behind me had seen him go and I figured they'd be over
the top of me if I didn't.' Both were penalized a minute although, as
Andretti pointed out, every time he glanced at the big official
scoreboard it didn't show anything like that.

On the thirty-fifth lap Andretti literally slid down his seat to reach
his brake pedal fully – it had gone deep – and rammed the Lotus past
Villeneuve who gave him enough room. The kid's thinking, Andretti
thought. The race finished like that although the penalty meant

Andretti was classified sixth. It gave victory to Lauda who, completely uninterested, asked his Brabham team-mate Watson to collect the trophy for him and headed for his helicopter.

What mattered was that Ronnie Peterson had no worse than the broken legs and might well drive again, however long that would take.

Freddie Petersens journeyed to the hospital hoping that he might even be able to speak to him that night. The condition of the hospital shocked Petersens – dirt, cigarette ends – and photographers hovered. Petersens spoke quietly to a doctor and didn't enjoy what the doctor told him.

One of Peterson's old mechanics, Ake Strandberg, became so concerned he phoned Chapman during the night but Chapman said all was well, Ronnie was in good hands.

Petersens returned to the hospital the following morning and they told him that during the operation on Peterson's legs bone marrow had entered the blood stream, he was in a coma and all hope had gone. Fittipaldi rang Andretti to say there was a 'problem' and Andretti headed for the hospital. He met Petersens there. Petersens told him that Ronnie had just died, and there were so many journalists and photographers he shouldn't even get out of his car. Andretti was looking straight ahead, full past Petersens. He drove some way down the road and stopped. The journalists and photographers pursued him and he would remember saying only 'unhappily, motor racing is also this.'

1979
SCHECKTER AND THE ARITHMETIC

Italian Grand Prix, Monza

The helicopter lifted from the lawn of a magnificent chateau on the outskirts of Milan and moved high across the web of factories, roads and workers' apartment blocks. Soon enough it began its descent over the parkland of Monza and the columns of foot soldiers bearing their flags and banners as they tramped towards the circuit. They were the Ferrari faithful. Jody Scheckter wasn't necessarily the kind of human being to inspire passion in them but he didn't have to be. In Italy the car did it.

He'd joined from the Wolf team at the end of 1978 and was 29. He'd surveyed 1979 and settled upon a simple philosophy. You must, he told himself, be consistent. A driver could count only eight finishes and with a refinement: four from the first seven races, four from the last eight. Scheckter fully appreciated that a tremendous run in one segment could be negated by a poor run in the other, which is exactly what had happened to Jones in the Williams. He managed only third place at Long Beach to reach the mid-point – it fell after Monaco in May – with a mere four points. In the second segment he was fourth in France and back-to-back won Germany, Austria and Holland. That already filled his quota. As Scheckter's helicopter landed he knew that Jones could not win the championship.

Courtesy of the 'cut', Scheckter faced dropping only the fifth place he'd got at Silverstone. Two men could overhaul him, Laffite at Ligier and more pertinently Villeneuve at Ferrari – Villeneuve who did inspire his own faithful. Scheckter had 44 points counting, Laffite 36, Villeneuve 32.

On that helicopter journey Scheckter reflected. 'We'd been testing and as normal Gilles was trying to do the fastest lap all the time, he was always trying qualifying tyres. I was working on different configurations with the chassis because that was obviously very important for the Italian Grand Prix. We'd done a lot of the testing at Monza itself, which Ferrari normally do anyway, but we'd done extra. We experimented on the undercarriage, which gave us more revs, we experimented with some different braking systems which were an advantage compared to what we had been running before.'

Villeneuve was a pure racer. You gave him a car, he drove it as fast as it could be made to go and what happened after that was all part of the great adventure.

Scheckter calculated.

'What I wanted to do was win the championship and so my object in all of the setting up of the car was making sure that I finished in the highest possible position in the race. It seems like the obvious thing to do but, well, Gilles had concentrated on setting fastest laps. All the Press were saying during the build up: Gilles fastest lap! Gilles lap record! But, you know, you've got to ignore all that, you've got to say to yourself *I'm working towards a goal to make sure the car is in the best possible shape for the race*. At that stage of his life Gilles didn't really care about the championship. It depends what's important to you.'

There remained, of course, Laffite, in his sixth season of Grand Prix racing. He'd started the season by rapping out wins in the first two races, Argentina and Brazil, faded but was now rolling again, third in Germany and Austria and Holland. Whatever he got at Monza he'd keep.

Scheckter had other matters on his mind as the helicopter touched down and the faithful wanted a glimpse of him. 'Am I a calm sort of man? No, I don't think so, and that year was different from all the other years because during those other years the tension would drop off and come up again. Across 1979 it seemed to stay at a high all the time, even between races. It was tough, that, but I think it got to me in a positive way. I concentrated more, I tried harder but that takes a lot out of you. I judge that the tougher you make it on yourself in the short term the better you do' – but Monza was round thirteen and the ninth month of the season, the long term.

During qualifying Scheckter did lap after lap using the car as a laboratory, checking, adjusting, fine-tuning. 'I qualified quite well. The guys I thought would be the problems were the Renaults (Rene Arnoux and Jean-Pierre Jabouille). They were going very fast. Laffite could be another problem and don't forget Gilles could have won the championship. I was faster than him in qualifying by quite a margin (1m 34.8s against 1m 34.9s) and that was not normal. Gilles was usually very, very fast in practice. So I was in good shape from that point of view.'

You might think 34.8 against 34.9 isn't much across the 3.6 miles (5.7km) of Monza, but over Villeneuve it certainly was.

The Renaults filled the front row, Scheckter and Jones the second, Villeneuve and Regazzoni (Williams) the third, Laffite and Piquet (Brabham), in his second season, on the fourth.

The sun was out, shades were being held over the cockpits to shield the drivers from it. The noisy crowd perched and clung on homemade grandstands but the calculator kept that from himself. 'Frankly it didn't strike me as any different because I was looking at it this way: a race is a race, but I was worrying do I have the right setting? I put all of my nervous energy into trying to make sure that I had the car set up properly. I always felt more relaxed once I had made the last decision on what setting to use, what tyres to use and everything else. Then I could relax until the race because all I had to do was race. That's the way I regulated my tension.'

Arnoux was so impatient that while he waited for the green his Renault crept. At the green, both Renaults set off down the centre of the track, Scheckter hugging the barrier on the left. He took them both. Jones had a problem with his battery and moved slowly, Villeneuve took Jabouille.

That was the order as they rounded the Parabolica and moved towards the start-finish line to complete the first lap, but Arnoux, young and aggressive, caught Scheckter, nibbled at him. As they moved towards the chicane he ducked left and went through. Laffite passed Jabouille and settled into fourth behind Villeneuve.

Arnoux had turbo-power and turbo-power adored Monza's bends, sweeps and fast corners. Scheckter could do nothing against it.

Laffite attacked Villeneuve, darting one way, darting the other along the start-finish straight. Laffite had to win. With only four of the 50 laps gone this was a clinging race, Scheckter trying to stay with Arnoux, Villeneuve with Scheckter, Laffite with Villeneuve. 'It was really very easy to lead,' Arnoux would say. 'I had never led a Grand Prix before but there was no pressure on me. I was sure I had the quickest car.'

On lap 13 Arnoux's engine stuttered into a misfire and at Lesmo he pulled to the side of the track, waved the three cars behind him through. That drew a roar from 100,000 throats – Ferraris first and second – but Laffite clung and Scheckter tracked Laffite's progress behind Villeneuve in his mirrors. Scheckter couldn't know that Laffite's rear brakes were overheating and that he'd adjusted the brake-balance bar to transfer as much of the load as he could to the front of the car. Regazzoni, somewhere back there, was coming. He'd be another shape in Scheckter's mirrors at some moment.

On lap 30 Laffite fell slowly back towards Regazzoni and by lap 41 Regazzoni was on him, next lap past. 'It was very hard for many laps,' Laffite would say. 'I had put on more front brake and the pedal went further and further down. Then I came to a corner, changed down, the clutch was jammed by the brake-balance cable and stayed there.' The rev counter flicked to 12,000 and oil bubbled from the exhaust.

'Once Arnoux had gone,' Scheckter says, 'immediately I was watching Laffite. I was pushing very hard and as soon as Laffite went backwards from me I slowed up, brought my revs down, I started changing gear slowly, I wasn't using the kerbs. That's when Gilles just stayed on my tail...'

So we have it, and it is a very delicate thing: out there amid the roaring and cheering and waving of flags Scheckter had Villeneuve filling his mirrors.

'Gilles and I had a very honest, straightforward relationship. As difficult as it was, it was open to the extent that we would tell each other if we found improvements. This was very painful to do but better than fighting amongst ourselves. It was typically Villeneuve to be honest but I like to think I was honest, too. We both had to be honest the whole year. You lie to somebody and that's that, you break the trust once and it's all over right through to the end. The difficulty comes when you've just found something on a car and you have to say to your team-mate, "hey, look at this" but if you don't you know he won't and so on and so on and so on.'

It was their first season together.

The Ferraris circled Monza, the roaring swelled lap by lap but Regazzoni sustained his charge. Scheckter held to his tactic, kept 'off the pace, I don't know how far off the pace but all I wanted was to get the car to the finish'. What would Villeneuve do? How strong was the honesty and trust now, how strong or brittle? Scheckter could wind the pace up but Villeneuve could, too. Villeneuve followed. Regazzoni cut one-second-a-lap chunks. On lap 46 he blasted the track record with 1m 35.6s, enormously quicker than the fastest in the race so far, Jones 1m 36.2s, itself a record. How long would Villeneuve follow with all this going on behind him? Might not the threat of Regazzoni's charge release him from all moral obligations? He would, after all, be making the race safe for Ferrari by winning it himself.

'There were always team orders,' Scheckter says. 'The person in front stayed in front unless the other person was going to lose a position because of that. I'd tried to get them changed but Ferrari wouldn't. If Arnoux was leading the race and I was holding Villeneuve up he could pass me or I had to let him through. If Arnoux dropped out and it was just Gilles and I, whichever of us was leading stayed ahead – after all we both had a chance of the championship so that was fair to both of us. At Monza my tactic had been to get in front so that if the position arose where I was in the lead and Gilles behind me it would stay that way. I didn't want to race the whole race if it was just Gilles and me, and I knew I could trust him to whatever extent I needed to trust him.'

Villeneuve lurked perhaps three cars' lengths behind but consistently there. Regazzoni responded to more and more urgent signals from the Williams' pit who saw victory themselves. On lap 48 he'd cut the gap to a fraction over two seconds but Scheckter continued to calculate. 'Regazzoni was not an issue because I had chosen to drive off the pace.'

Regazzoni burned to win. He'd been fired by Ferrari three years before and bitterness lingered. Enzo Ferrari, he would remember, 'was not correct with me, he didn't speak clean'.

Regazzoni was low on fuel and all at once the engine sounded rough, cut out, fired again. He'd lost power and lost time. He could afford neither.

'The only time I pushed the car after Laffite broke down was on the second last lap. I wanted to make sure that even if Gilles wanted to pass me he couldn't. I waited, pushed as hard as I could to make sure I didn't have to trust Gilles on the final lap. I couldn't leave it to anybody else, I had to do it. Even if he'd wanted to pass I made sure he couldn't.'

A man within sight of the championship thinks like this. Jody Scheckter deliberately removed the burden of trust from Villeneuve.

Scheckter crossed the line and 'I felt the year's pressure fall from my shoulders. It hadn't been like a race's pressure, it was a year's pressure. It was tremendous pressure. There'd been such a big build-up to the race and afterwards you never really shout and scream, it takes time to sink in.'

Mass hysteria was played out below the podium the way it always is when Ferrari win. The police used their batons and for a moment it might have turned ugly. One young member of the faithful had blood running down his face but that didn't stop him standing cheering with the rest.

'Marco Piccinini, the team manager, came to me and one of his regular jokes was that they'd disqualified the car because the wing was too high. He said it again now. The cars had gone into the paddock and were being checked, all of this pressure which had been draining from me shot straight back up and then he said "I'm only joking." I gave him a mouthful for that. I don't mind a joke but the tension was too much, the moment too painful for that. It's like saying "your wife's died" or "your child's died" and two minutes later saying you're only joking. Is that a joke?'

That evening the helicopter rose from Monza's parkland and angled itself back towards the web of factories and roads and workers' apartment blocks. The static panorama had not altered. On the return journey Scheckter had a great deal to reflect on but all different now.

Later that evening he went 'to dinner with the mechanics at a restaurant outside Milan. Obviously Ferrari doesn't go to bad restaurants – that's one of the pleasures of working with them – but this was a wonderful restaurant. I felt I needed to go. We had a couple of little speeches and I made one of them. I thanked everybody because the car hadn't broken down once and I appreciated that.'

He still does.

1980

JONES ON THE NOD

Canadian Grand Prix, Montreal

The struggle lasted more than a decade and a journalist acquaintance of mine used to wield a poignant anecdote to prove what a struggle it had been. 'It's damned hard to believe,' he'd say, 'that we gave Frank lifts in our hire car because he couldn't afford one of his own.'

Frank Williams came to motor racing entirely by chance. One school holiday he went to a race to have a look and, curious, leant over a car watching a mechanic work. 'The mechanic handed me a screwdriver so I could help him and I had begun in the business.' The consuming passion of his professional life was born. Whatever it entailed, and that would be virtually the complete register of human experience, the passion was never diluted; rarely questioned.

In time Williams ran his own team. It's a familiar theme, the passion, the ambition but no money. When the Post Office cut off the factory telephone – unpaid bills – they used a public telephone box. Williams hung on.

The team reached Formula 1 in 1973 and for years ran an anonymous assortment of forgotten drivers. Williams corrected this with the stroke of a pen. He persuaded Saudia, the Saudi Arabian airline, to sponsor them and the struggle was over. The first win came at Silverstone in 1979, Regazzoni beating Arnoux (in the Renault turbo). That same year Regazzoni's team-mate Jones won four rounds after Silverstone to give him third place in the championship.

For 1980, Williams would say 'we knew that many other manufacturers would have worked no less hard than we, and I personally was far from being sure that the superiority we had shown at the end of the 1979 season would still be ours. And I was right.'

The season had a broad spread of variables: Jones won Argentina where a Frenchman, Alain Prost, made his debut in a McLaren and finished sixth. He'd remember the asphalt starting to melt in the heat. 'I vividly recall a painful scene during the pre-race briefing. Fangio – the great Juan Manuel Fangio, for me a living legend – suggested, although perhaps not in so many words, that we make a special effort to keep our speed down in the early laps. Keep our speeds down?' Fangio had to say this, Prost concluded, because as an Argentine he was 'acutely embarassed' by the circuit but had to be diplomatic.

Arnoux won Brazil and South Africa, Piquet (Brabham) won Long Beach, Didier Pironi (Ligier) won Belgium, Reutemann won Monaco, Jones won France and Britain. Laffite won Germany, Jabouille won Austria where an Englishman, Nigel Mansell, made his debut in a Lotus and suffered agony when he had to sit in some spilt fuel as the race began.

Piquet won Holland and Italy. That left Canada and Watkins Glen.

As they boarded their aeroplanes to Montreal, Piquet had 54 points, Jones 53, Reutemann 37. The scoring system changed again: ten best finishes counting out of the fourteen rounds, five from each half of the season. Jones would write:

I went to Montreal in a marvellous and serene mood, absolutely full of confidence. The only thing in my favour, apart from the conviction that the championship belonged to me, was that with points being awarded on the basis of the best results in the two separate halves of the season for Piquet to win the title he had to win at Montreal and I had to finish out of the first three. If he won at Montreal and I still placed high enough then a good result at Watkins Glen would still see me home.

The Williams and Brabham teams arrived with four cars each, an unusual number, almost like bringing your own reinforcements. With its seventeen corners Montreal might be merciless on brakes. 'It will certainly be our biggest worry for the race, even though the ambient temperature here is not as hot as it was at Imola earlier in the month for the Italian Grand Prix,' Brabham's designer Gordon Murray said before the first qualifying session. Wind dragged rain across the circuit, ruffling the waters of the lake behind the pits into patterns of waves.

The morning untimed session set the tone for the whole weekend, the rain so hard that standing water lay all over the track and most of the drivers huddled in the wooden cabins which served as pits. Eventually Villeneuve flung his Ferrari at the circuit in what one observer judged 'suicide speeds'. Others slipped and slithered. Jones snapped sideways near the pits but caught it; at the tight hairpin before the pits Piquet got his braking wrong and punted Jabouille.

For the first twenty minutes in the afternoon the wind dried the surface, but Arnoux spun off and the session was halted to recover the Renault. That helped Jones who had stopped out on the circuit, no fuel. 'I was on a quick lap and I tried to stretch it to one more lap,' he said. Almost immediately the rain began again, ending the session.

The quick lap gave Jones provisional pole from Reutemann, Piquet sixth. 'I hope it stays dry tomorrow morning and rains again in the afternoon,' Jones said mischievously.

Tomorrow was cold but dry. Suddenly Piquet, whose Brabham had a longer wheelbase and revised weight distribution, went really fast. The handling was superb, Piquet braked later into the corners, used more power in and out of them. He did 1m 29.9s running on full tanks, and settled to a tremendous rhythm: seven laps under 1m 28s. Piquet had found an extra second and a half which prompted Jones to become cryptic not mischievous. 'That surprised everybody, to put it mildly.' He battled and at one stage was only sixth. Towards the end he attacked and you could see he was on the limit.

Piquet	1m 27.3s
Jones	1m 28.1s

That was the front row. 'I was held up on my best lap, maybe a couple of tenths, but there was no way I was going to get near Piquet's time,' Jones said. 'The race' – seventy laps of 2.7 miles (4.4km) – 'is going to be a case of survival.'

The green light seemed to take a long time coming on. When it did, Pironi from the second row powered down the inside, Piquet in the centre of the track, Jones abreast but on the outside. Piquet pulled across in front of Pironi, Jones still abreast. They rounded the right-hander, Jones now in the lead. Because of that he didn't see Piquet. Bits of cars were flying everywhere. *Autosport* reported:

> *Jones bounced back into the middle of the track, while the impact spun the wheel out of Piquet's grip, gave his elbow a nasty bang on the side of the monocoque and sent him spinning down the road. Piquet turned at right-angles and rammed the Armco head on. Keke Rosberg braked hard in his Fittipaldi and 'I don't know what happened. I was heading for the wall.' Derek Daly (Tyrrell) was braking hard. 'I looked up and saw Andretti upside down over my head and then I hit Jarier's back. There were cars going everywhere.'*

'We screamed down to the first corner and I got the jump on him,' Jones said. 'We touched and he went into the fence and damaged his car severely.'

'It was very sad for me,' Piquet said, 'because Alan pushed me into the wall and I had to change to the spare car.' Jones emerged with no more than damage to one of his car's skirts.

The debris took a full hour to clear. On the grid waiting for the restart Williams repaired Jones' skirt. At the re-start Pironi edged forward under the red light but didn't get away as fast as Jones, who'd taken great care to position the Williams precisely on the twin strips of rubber he'd laid at the first start. That gave him adhesion. They crossed the line after lap 1, Jones, Pironi, Piquet. Jones saw Piquet do 'exactly the same thing to Pironi but Pironi had the common sense to back off.' Piquet moved past Jones along the straight.

If Jones and Frank Williams hoped that the spare Brabham might be slower they were wrong. For the next twelve laps Piquet moved away from Jones at a second a lap. Pironi had been locked into a fierce argument with Bruno Giacomelli (Alfa Romeo), neither conceding anything. The argument was settled when they moved into a right-hander together and both went straight on. Pironi found himself on the grassy run-off area and resumed, but Giacomelli's side skirts were broken. This gave Jones a comfortable cushion over Pironi.

On lap 20 Piquet already threaded through the backmarkers cruising the race. Jones couldn't narrow the gap. People in the pits instinctively calculated what that result – win for Piquet, Jones second – would mean for Watkins Glen the following weekend. Then on lap 23 Piquet slowed. 'The engine blew. One minute it was perfect, the next it went bang.' Piquet walked back to watch knowing that if Jones won the race he won the championship but if he was second they'd have to go to The Glen.

Brabham now applied psychology to Pironi. Brabham didn't care that Pironi drove a Ligier, Brabham didn't care what Pironi was driving. They did care that Pironi could catch Jones. They hung dollar signs over the pit wall to him and the Ligier began to close the gap. Just then the announcement came through that Pironi had been penalized a minute for jumping the start.

Williams signalled that to Jones but, 'I didn't slow down at all until they gave it to me for the third time and I saw Frank nodding his head at me over the barrier.' Jones had already suffered: at the Spanish Grand Prix he fell victim to the warfare between FISA, the sport's governing body, and FOCA, the Constructors' Association, Jones won, the race was declared void and no points awarded.

On the afternoon of 28 September 1980 Jones was not about to take the risk of throwing the championship away on the strength of pit signals but he regarded the nod as conclusive. Jones knew Williams the man.

He slowed to protect the car.

Still Pironi came and on lap 44 Jones allowed him by. It was a nice calculation and a careful one but it carried an inherent risk. He had to hold Pironi's lead to less than sixty seconds or Pironi would have recovered the time he'd lost with the penalty. Pironi tried to do it. On lap 62 he beat the lap record with 1m 28.7s. Jones tracked him.

Pironi finished in 1h 46m 4.6s but that became 47m 4.6s with the penalty, Jones 1h 46m 45.5s and the championship. The Williams team had taken the Constructors' title at Imola two weeks earlier. Frank Williams had won his struggle.

Someone ventured to Jones that this had been a flawed finale because Piquet's engine blew and Pironi got the penalty. Jones said: 'The championship? You take it any way it comes.'

1981

PIQUET'S PAIN IN THE NECK

United States Grand Prix, Las Vegas

The three-way split exercised those who enjoy figures because you could play the permutations this way and that after a tug-'o'-war season. Piquet started strongly – he won Argentina and Imola – Reutemann (Williams) peppering in points and Laffite (Ligier) making a late rush by taking Austria and Canada. A carpark at Las Vegas beckoned for the fifteenth and final round, the United States Grand Prix, with Reutemann on 49, Piquet 48, Laffite 43. The permutations are more easily digestible in table form:

	1st	2nd	3rd	4th	5th	6th
Reutemann	58	55	53	52	51	50
Piquet	57	54	52	51	50	49
Laffite	52	49	47	46	45	44

The three-way split could become a three-way tie with, successively, the most wins in the season deciding it. That favoured Piquet. If Laffite won and they all finished on 52 Laffite would get it because he'd have the same number of wins as Piquet but more second places. If Piquet didn't score, and Reutemann and Laffite finished on 49, Laffite got it. He and Reutemann would have the same number of wins, the same number of second places but Laffite more thirds.

And what was a Grand Prix showdown of such intriguing and varied promise doing in a place like Las Vegas, anyway? Jones, poised to retire after the race, took one look and said it was 'like a goat-track dragged down from the mountain and flattened out.' Its outline may have struck Jones like that but in outline it resembled the vertebrae of some dinosaur, anti-clockwise, essentially 2.2 miles (3.6km) of corners and loops.

Part of it was in the carpark outside Caesars Palace Hotel. That didn't present a problem because the track was wider than people had anticipated. What did present a problem was that the anti-clockwise corners placed an enormous strain on Formula 1 necks which had spent most of their lives taking the G-loading the other way. And 75 laps if the weather was very hot...?

Reutemann felt that strain early and was already under strain. During the Brazilian Grand Prix, the second of the season, he and Jones were one-two and a clause in their Williams contracts stipulated that if they led with no more than seven seconds between them Jones would be allowed to win. The team hung out a pit board sign reminding Reutemann of that but he ignored it. Jones said: 'Now I know the situation I shall treat him just like any other driver, too, and bang wheels to go past him instead of sitting back praying he's a gentleman.'

At Las Vegas, Laffite went about his business quietly and with good humour, as he habitually did, although that changed by the end of qualifying. He had understeer, briefly flirted with his team-mate Patrick Tambay's car, and qualified twelfth.

Piquet seemed at an obvious disadvantage because while all Formula 1 drivers are by definition strong men, strength is relative. Piquet was almost slender. Worse, during the untimed Friday session – the race on the Saturday – he had an accident with Reutemann who, flying along, punted Piquet's rear and was airborne, spinning but not striking any of the special interlocking concrete blocks which marked the boundary of the track.

Piquet suffered severely from the neck strain and spent a lot of time with a masseur who, anxious to soothe, applied his art with such zeal that he bruised Piquet's neck. The team built him a special head-support.

Reutemann took pole, Jones alongside. What would happen at Turn 1? Piquet might be able to watch from the safe distance of the second row he shared with Villeneuve but Laffite, so far back, would see nothing of it.

Late on the eve of the race Reutemann wandered into the pits to see if all was well. The mechanics were working on the car. The accident with Piquet had damaged the brakes, they'd been replaced and, his engineer said, Reutemann would have to spend a large tract of the morning warm-up session bedding the new brakes in. From Reutemann's viewpoint this represented a necessary but punishing loss of time.

Before the race Reutemann said only 'I will be driving 100 per cent to win and so will Alan. I don't want to make predictions because I think this race will be one of chance, just like spinning the roulette wheel.'

Villeneuve crawled before the green but Jones made a tremendous start, Reutemann a bad one, Piquet a bad one and by Turn 1 Jones led from Villeneuve, then Prost (Renault), Giacomelli, Reutemann, Watson, Laffite and Piquet.

By the end of the second lap the race had a beautiful poise: Jones clear of Villeneuve who was holding up a bunch, Laffite swarming Reutemann and Piquet swarming Laffite. Prost took Villeneuve on lap 3 and set off after Jones, Laffite took Reutemann. A lap later Laffite took Watson. At lap 5:

Jones, Prost, Villeneuve, Giacomelli, Laffite, Watson, Reutemann, Piquet.

Behind Reutemann, Piquet ducked and dived searching for a way through. At this stage Laffite was most unlikely to win the race but if he finished second that opened everything up, and anyway Piquet had to finish in front of Reutemann. Piquet laid pressure on Reutemann and took him on lap 17, a mystery born within the moment. Whatever was Reutemann doing? He'd say fourth gear kept coming out as the Williams rode the bumps on the surface of the track but all witnesses are agreed that Reutemann's performance became inexplicably ordinary. At lap 17:

Jones, Prost, Villeneuve, Giacomelli, Laffite, Watson, Piquet, Reutemann.

A lap later the Reutemann mystery compounded itself when Andretti (Alfa Romeo) got by, too, took Watson and went after Piquet. Villeneuve's Ferrari caught fire (although he'd been disqualified anyway for the crawling). At lap 23:

Jones, Prost, Laffite, Giacomelli, Andretti, Piquet, Watson, Reutemann.

If it finished like that, Piquet and Reutemann would have 49 points, Laffite 47. Four laps later Giacomelli spun – 'the tyres were picking up a lot of rubber and the handling was very bad' – hoisting Reutemann to seventh and two laps later Watson pitted for tyres:

Jones, Prost, Laffite, Andretti, Piquet, Reutemann.

On lap 32 Prost pitted for tyres and Andretti was gone with rear suspension failure.

Jones, Laffite, Piquet, Mansell, Reutemann, Prost.

What did that mean? Piquet 52, Reutemann 51, Laffite 49 but it wouldn't finish like that and everyone in the high, temporary, and very expensive grandstand seats sensed it. The showdown in the carpark wasn't that sort of race. Nobody knew how much was being extracted from Piquet's body and neck. He began to fight the car.

Prost, luxuriating in fresh tyres, rode through every calculation. He picked off Reutemann and Mansell in successive laps, tracked Piquet across another eleven and, in a sweep of a gesture, took Piquet and Laffite. At lap 46:

Jones, Prost, Laffite, Piquet, Mansell, Giacomelli, Reutemann.

By now Piquet had seen the pit board telling him thirty laps remained and he asked himself *how can I keep going that long?*

At least Giacomelli, recovering from his spin, had pushed Reutemann out of the points. Piquet could not know what was happening to Laffite who slowed and slowed with a tyre problem. 'I was waiting for a board to say come in and they were waiting for me to come in,' Laffite said. Piquet went past and Laffite did pit. He emerged eighth.

Piquet need only run to the end, but to the end of eternity. Giacomelli took him but that didn't matter with Laffite eighth. Then Watson re-took Reutemann.

A pit board told Piquet twenty laps remained. At one point he was physically sick in his helmet, the product of fatigue and heat and dehydration and pain.

With seven laps left Laffite made a gesture of no surrender and took Reutemann:

Jones, Prost, Giacomelli, Mansell, Piquet, Watson, Laffite, Reutemann.

By now Piquet was floating in to total exhaustion and floating out of it. The calculations and permutations ceased to exist. He drove the Brabham by instinct. And then ... the whole rear of the car started to vibrate. *It's over*, Piquet thought, *it's all been useless, all of it* – but the instinct held him, corner merged with corner, he was down the mini-straight, corner merged with corner, he was down the mini-straight, corner merged with ... is that a chequered flag?

Jones crossed the line twenty seconds in front of Prost, Giacomelli slightly over four hundredths of a second away, Mansell at 47.4 seconds, Piquet at 1m 16.4s, Laffite at 1m 18.1s. Reutemann was eighth.

Piquet was virtually unconscious in the cockpit when the car came to rest. He had to be lifted from it and was unable to go to the rostrum for fifteen minutes. Even a man as strong as John Watson had been claimed by the exhaustion, Laffite summoning whatever he had left to take Watson's sixth place on the very last corner. Laffite had lost but he hadn't surrendered.

When Piquet did reach the rostrum he was close to tears. The exhaustion had given him the same feeling as delayed shock. He'd suddenly realized what he'd done.

Some postscripts.

Las Vegas had been 17 October and Piquet called himself World Champion 'until the last day of December. Then it was another year, another championship. What would I have wanted to call myself the champion after the last day of December for?' Some would say to make a lot of money, some would say to glory in it, some would say to take personal satisfaction from it until the precise moment it was taken from you. Piquet cared about the championship in a quite different way. He saw it for what it was and nothing else.

After the race Reutemann said to Jones 'let's bury the hatchet,' and Jones replied 'yes, in your back, Carlos.' Some people thought that was a funny old quip. Some didn't.

Many people misunderstood Reutemann, stuck one of those handy-sized labels on him: moody. He was sensitive. It didn't prevent the labellers judging he'd been in the wrong mood at Las Vegas. Privately he told friends he'd been slogging his guts out in a car which was barely driveable. The aftermath cut so deep that for years he felt it hung heavy over his whole life. In December 1991 he was elected the political governor of a whole region of Argentina with a $2.8 billion budget, control of the police force and responsibility for 2.5 million people. When he got it he confided to one of those friends that he felt 'released at last' from the carpark.

1982

ROSBERG RIDES THE BIG WHEEL

United States Grand Prix, Las Vegas

John Watson was sitting becalmed in the Marlboro McLaren motor home. All around dozens of Italians swarmed past the guards and the Alsatian dogs into the paddock, and now they gabbled and gesticulated and looked for any souvenirs they could lay hands on. It was the evening of 12 September. As Watson sat, his eyes seemed far away, almost dreamily so. Perhaps they saw the carpark at Caesars Palace where he would go in two weeks. 'It's a long shot,' he said in his gentle, lilting Ulster accent. He didn't say much else. No need.

The whole season had been shocking, etched into sadness, completely unpredictable. Prost (Renault turbo) won South Africa and Brazil, Lauda (McLaren) won Long Beach, Pironi (Ferrari turbo) won Imola but a lot of teams boycotted that because of the FISA-FOCA struggle; at Imola, Pironi broke Ferrari's team orders and lured Villeneuve into a trap. When the Renaults blew up Villeneuve led, Pironi second. Pironi overtook him. They exchanged the lead and Villeneuve thought Pironi was indulging in this so they'd put on a show for the crowd because not much else remained to watch. Of only 14 cars which started the race five were still running. Crucially too late did Villeneuve realize Pironi intended to take the race for himself and did. In the remaining two weeks of Villeneuve's life he exchanged no further word with Pironi.

Watson (McLaren) won at Zolder. Villeneuve was killed in qualifying. Patrese (Brabham) won a bewildering Monaco – cars to the left of him, cars to the right of him dropping out on a chaotic last lap – Watson won Detroit, Piquet (Brabham) won Montreal. Pironi won Holland, Lauda won Brands Hatch, Arnoux (Renault turbo) won France, but that was the race where he ignored team orders and wouldn't wait for Prost, convulsing Renault and France. Tambay (Ferrari turbo) won Germany, but that was the weekend when Pironi almost died after crashing in an untimed session.

The next race was Austria.

Keke Rosberg, in his first year with Williams, remembers the background to the racing. 'It was the last time you went to a Grand Prix and didn't have a clue who was going to win. The turbos were already there and they were going to beat you in qualifying but in the races you could compensate. Williams had a fantastic chassis, the factory was very, very good. Williams had a strong team. Neal Oatley and Frank Dernie were brilliant young engineers, Patrick Head was brilliant, too, Frank was at the height of his life.'

Already, eight different drivers had won, Rosberg not among them. His season had been solid, not more, and normally that would preclude thoughts of the championship but 1982 was in no sense normal. Nobody could put together enough wins to break clear. Nobody had won more than two.

Up and down and round the sweep of the Österreichring's undulating hills a magnificent race unfolded between Rosberg and Elio de Angelis (Lotus). As they reached the final corner, a ferociously fast and long-looping right, de Angelis led. 'I still to this day think I wasn't brave enough in that last corner,' Rosberg says. 'I should have won the race. I question myself: Did I go to the wrong side? Should I have gone to the outside? If I'd gone to the outside would we both have ended in the armco? Anyway it was a great climax...'

De Angelis reached the line 0.05 seconds ahead.

Rosberg had yet to win a race at all after four years of trying and forty-nine races for five teams. 'In a way I didn't really mind what happened in Austria because I knew that the win was going to come. We were so close to it, second all the time and on the other hand my best friend – Elio – won his first.' Rosberg's win was not long in coming: the Swiss at Dijon, the next race. Rosberg had 42 points, Watson 30.

At Monza, Rosberg says, 'I knew I would be struggling. The opposition in terms of the championship was Wattie [Watson], but Prost – 31 points – was still very much in the hunt. Monza is never easy. The fanatical crowd makes it a very intense place. The circuit is very fast, the weather is hot and there always seems to be that little extra bit of pressure – and anyway there was a lot of pressure on me because I could have clinched the championship in the race.' He anticipated Monza would favour the turbos and Prost had one, he hadn't and neither did Watson.

Rosberg ran seventh in a 'tactical' race for any points he might inherit if someone broke down. On lap 25 he heard a bang as he moved along the start-finish straight and he thought, naturally enough, he had a puncture. Wrong. 'The bang I heard was a rear wing which came off. If you lose a rear wing on a normal flat-bottomed car it swaps ends.' This time it didn't. The pit stop to replace it took two minutes and Rosberg came out fifteenth, Prost third, Watson fifth. Prost changed his tyres and promptly spun out of the championship. It automatically moved Watson to fourth, where he stayed. Rosberg came eighth. 'The race,' he concluded, 'produced nothing but disappointment for me but at least the title was now between two men. There was still hope.'

Rosberg had 42 points, Watson 33.

'There shouldn't have been a showdown at Las Vegas,' Watson says. 'There were a number of drivers who could have won the championship. The two McLaren drivers [himself and Lauda] were obvious candidates for that, and so were the two Ferrari drivers, and Keke of course. I had a very good season up to the Dutch Grand Prix then I went all the way to the Italian Grand Prix at Monza and, for a number of different reasons, I failed to score points. After Monza I had a mathematical chance at Las Vegas but that was based not just on what I did but on what Keke did, too. If we'd finished with equal points I would have taken the title on more race victories. I faced this: you go and do the best you can because there were factors – namely what Rosberg did – over which I had no control and that made it a lottery. If I'd scored points between Zandvoort and Monza that would have altered the percentages.'

Rosberg said that 'if only it hadn t been for that wing I suppose I would have been fifth and that would have been that. Still Prost could have won and that would have meant he and I went to Vegas only two points apart so I guess you could say that of all the bad things which could have happened at Monza it was the best of the bad things which did happen.'

There might still not be a showdown at Las Vegas. Rosberg had finished second in the Brazilian Grand Prix in March but his Williams was disqualified for a weight infringement. The team protested but the FIA Court of Appeal rejected it. The team took it to a civil court in Paris. They were due to hear the case on the Monday before Vegas. If Williams won, Rosberg had the championship.

On this Monday the FIA Court of Appeal were due to hear an appeal by McLaren. Lauda finished third in Zolder but was disqualified for a weight infringement. If McLaren won and Lauda got his four points he'd have 34. If Williams didn't win their case Lauda came back into it.

A ruling in both was postponed...

Immediately after Monza, Rosberg made a decision. He'd spend five days in the seclusion of his home and then go to California to rest and recover his 'mental equilibrium'. California was a good place for that, sun, good food, complete anonymity.

I had to do a job at Vegas and I wanted to be calm and relaxed, so I went to California early, did some flying, just to keep myself free from tension.

Rosberg checked into his hotel at Vegas at the last possible moment. The first qualifying session was so hot that he could 'barely breathe' in the cockpit. He estimated the temperature in there at 130 degrees. He was fifth and Watson only tenth although that might mean little. Watson's special qualities were pacing himself from the upper mid-field of the grid, overtaking with greatest precision and winning from there. The heat meant the same as in 1981. Who could physically tolerate the 75 laps? Some drivers spoke of a communal tactical race with everyone taking it easy until an undefined moment towards the end. How did Rosberg intend to drive it? 'Balls out – from the start. All these guys say they're going to go easy in the first half. You wait until that light flashes green then watch them. No way are people going to coast along. I don't believe it.'

Rosberg faced the American press who scattered 'idiotic' questions all over him, mainly wanting to know if he was driven only by money, although that was a reasonable line of inquiry at Las Vegas. The questions irritated. Almost without his sensing it the pressure mounted.

In second qualifying he fell back to sixth, Watson rose to ninth. It was the sort of position where Watson might be comfortable and Rosberg knew that. Rosberg knew equally that he could disregard every move Watson made provided he – Rosberg – came fifth, taking him beyond anything Lauda could total, courts or no courts. Rosberg fell to thinking what might go wrong with the car and somehow couldn't stop thinking about that.

McLaren had to make a delicate decision. 'On the Sunday morning Ron Dennis spoke to Niki and explained the facts of life to him, or as Ron was keen to say Niki had to bite the bullet,' Watson says. 'Niki was asked – or he was told – to co-operate in the team winning the championship. It wasn't just a question of me, it was a question of the team. For Niki it was a difficult bullet to bite and understandably so because he, too, felt he had a mathematical chance. To give that up and support his team-mate was, I think, a new experience for him. In the end he accepted the situation but it was difficult, a man of his stature – and in a race anything can happen.'

The grid:

Prost (Renault)	Arnoux (Renault)
Michele Alboreto (Tyrrell)	Eddie Cheever (Ligier)
Patrese (Brabham)	Rosberg (Williams)
Andretti (Ferrari)	Tambay (Ferrari)
Watson (McLaren)	Derek Warwick (Toleman)
Laffite (Ligier)	Piquet (Brabham)
Lauda (McLaren)	

An overcast Sunday, the morning punctuated by fitful stabs of rain but enough to make everyone wonder what a downpour might do in a carpark with Formula 1 cars going round it. Just then the sun came out.

In the untimed session, Prost went quickest and Watson second quickest, the difference between them one hundredth of a second. That turned the pressure up another notch. What had canny old Wattie been up to? Playing a waiting game?

At the green light the Renaults went clear but behind them Alboreto, an Italian, and Cheever, an American living in Italy, touched at Turn 1, bending Cheever's wheel. Order at lap 1:

Prost, Arnoux, Alboreto, Patrese, Cheever, Andretti, Rosberg, Piquet, Warwick, Daly, Watson, Laffite, Andrea de Cesaris, Lauda.

'Inevitably,' Watson says, 'Niki wasn't called up to assist me. You know, as happens in these situations when the green light goes, the best laid plans are only that: plans. I did my normal thing, coming through the field.'

He didn't do that immediately because on lap 2 Laffite overtook him. Arnoux swapped places with Prost. Alboreto tracked them, thinking 'I know I can stay with them but there is no point in going harder just for the sake of it. Tyre wear might be a problem towards the end.'

It settled. At lap 14:

Arnoux, Prost, Alboreto, Patrese, Cheever, Andretti, Rosberg, Watson.

Across four laps Watson had been gaining on Rosberg and was with him. On lap 15 Watson flew by. 'I couldn't keep up with John when he passed me,' Rosberg said. 'I knew there was no way I could stay with him and it was quite clear to me at that stage that he could win the race. If he did that my points position became critical. Now I really needed points and for the first time I concentrated my attention on the championship rather than the race.'

When Watson flew by he put Rosberg back into eighth and far from the points. Watson set off with the maturity of a man covering familiar territory. He'd always gone well in the constriction of street circuits. Now he went quicker and quicker.

Lap	Time	Position
16	1m 22.8s	Sixth, taking Andretti.
17	1m 24.0s	Fifth, taking Cheever.
18	1m 21.1s	Fourth, Patrese out, engine.
19	1m 21.2s	Fourth.

20	1m 21.3s	Third, Arnoux out, engine.
21	1m 21.7s	Third.
22	1m 22.2s	Third.
23	1m 21.1s	Third.
24	1m 20.8s	Third

'Everything seemed to fall into place. I tell you, the car was just fantastic. I could drive it anywhere on the track...'

In the background Rosberg moved. On lap 18 Patrese's exit lifted him to seventh, on lap 20 Arnoux's exit lifted him to sixth. He tracked Andretti and battled with him. That lasted six laps before Andretti's suspension broke on lap 27 – Rosberg fifth, shifting all the pressure on to Watson who nibbled towards Alboreto in second place. 'I faced this: you go and do the best you can,' Watson says.

Rosberg: 'Fifth place was all I needed...'

Although Alboreto was thirteen seconds behind Prost, Watson was fifteen seconds behind him. Around this stage, 'I was getting very bad tyre vibration,' Watson says. 'The fronts were picking up rubber from the surface of the track and going out of balance. I think they also may have turned on the rim a little. When a car is like that there's not much you can do because suddenly you can't lean on it like you could before. Actually it was so bad under braking that I had trouble focusing.'

Prost, too, picked up rubber. 'Under braking I felt as though I would be shaken out of the cockpit.' Alboreto went into the lead on lap 56. If Watson could get to Alboreto he would at least win and if Rosberg had a problem...

'I'd come through but then really progress stopped,' Watson says. 'I just couldn't make any more inroads into Alboreto. He had grip above and beyond the call of duty.'

Rosberg felt that perhaps he might have looked 'cool but those last twenty laps seemed awfully long. I took it easy because by then whatever Wattie did didn't matter. It didn't matter if I was fourth or third or second. I knew I was fifth and I knew where everybody else was so I sat in fifth, hoping, praying that nothing would break on the car. It's hard to keep your concentration. Sometimes, you know, when you're just cruising you lose concentration.'

The chequered flag:

Alboreto	1h 41m 56.8s.
Watson	1h 42m 24.1s.
Cheever	1h 42m 53.3s.
Prost	1h 43m 05.5s.
Rosberg	1h 43m 08.2s.

Rosberg had been very safe indeed and was now given a kiss by Diana Ross, no less.

That night was quite extraordinary because it was Mansour Ojjeh's thirtieth birthday [he was the major Williams sponsor apart from Saudia]. So there was a big celebration in San Francisco and TAG were paying. It was really fun on the plane there from Vegas. Derek Daly was on it, Elio was on it, it was my Formula 2 generation there. We had one section of the plane and we went crazy. When we landed at San Francisco we were on a downer. We were tired, the season was over, the race seemed far away. We went to the hotel, checked in, waited for the limos and before we got to the party it was history, finished.

This did not prevent Keke Rosberg enjoying himself. The party was in a pub where amidst the hamburgers and beer he was given a cake with a 'great shark's fin' protruding. Finn, fin, get it?

Watson couldn't avoid his downer. 'I was tired, physically and mentally. I'd been so tantalizingly close to the championship, closer than I'd ever been.' Or ever would be again.

I posed a question of my own to Rosberg years later and in quieter times. Many drivers have said that because the pressure of expectation is so great they are unsure when they actually realized they'd made it and some needed until the following morning to absorb it. When was the moment for you? 'It hit me when I crossed the line. The morning after? Hit me the morning after? No. I was busy then, starting work, starting capitalizing on it.'

1983

OUT ON THE VELDT

South African Grand Prix, Kyalami

Logically it ought to have been something else, a consummation, a celebration, a vindication, a perfect last act to the play which had been running for six years. Logically it ought to have been everything but what it really became.

From 1977 Renault spent a staggering and undisclosed sum of money to win the World Championship with, for preference, a Frenchman driving the car which did it. To have a Frenchman was not de rigeur as one of their senior management, Jean Sage, insists. Renault's Grand Prix team were free to hire from any country where Renault had a market but the inclination was always, and naturally, to lean towards someone holding a passport with the words République Française on the cover.

In 1977 it was Jabouille, in 1979 Arnoux joined him, in 1981 Jabouille left to join Ligier and Prost partnered Arnoux. Arnoux departed for Ferrari at the end of 1982. Renault broke the mould and hired Cheever. This did not dilute their primary purpose, Prost to take the championship, Cheever to support him.

Renault introduced turbo engines to Formula 1 (to some initial derision) and could already claim to be major innovators. They lacked, however, their World Champion. Prost came closest, fourth in 1982. Prost had been a rare talent for years – since the day he began, in fact – and by now was an experienced Grand Prix driver journeying towards greatness. He approached 1983 with a prime chance.

Renault might also be a burden: not the car, not its engine which delivered so much power so consistently but the situation teeming with chauvinism. France expected and demanded that Prost win it. His contract enshrined his status, number one driver, a position he hadn't held before.

To fulfil the expectations of a team is essentially an enclosed matter, almost an in-house matter, you and them. To fulfil the expectations of 54 million people who may know nothing about the difficulties you face but have a great suspicion that Renault, as a nationalised company, are spending their money – that's several dimensions and beyond motor racing.

Immediate problems loomed. Brabham's BMW turbo engine would be measured directly against Renault's and the Brabham would be driven by Piquet who knew all about winning a championship.

Prost won France, Belgium, Great Britain and Austria; Piquet won Brazil, was second in France, Monaco and Britain. The Ferrari drivers were in there, too, Arnoux and Tambay. After the Dutch Grand Prix, which Arnoux won from Tambay, the points tightened to Prost 51, Arnoux 43, Piquet and Tambay 37. Prost sensed the burden becoming heavier for Renault and subsequently wrote about in-fighting and senior management taking decisions which ought to have been left to the race team. Prost complained that Renault were capitalizing on him, making too many press relations demands on him. Sage vehemently disputes it but that's only partially relevant. Prost thought it.

Three rounds remained, the next Monza. It was the last place Prost wanted to go. The Ferrari faithful didn't (of course) like him, didn't like Renault and saw both as a direct threat to their men Arnoux and Tambay.

There in the paddock you could see it, the face of a haunted man. During testing some days earlier the faithful had thrown straw on to the track to try and make him slide off, had even thrown stones at the car. In the race the electrics went on lap 26. Piquet won at a canter, Arnoux second, Tambay fourth and that tightened it even more, Prost 51, Arnoux up to 49, Piquet up to 46, Tambay up to 40.

In the more genteel surrounds of Brands Hatch – the European Grand Prix – Prost finished second but to Piquet. Arnoux, ninth, still retained some sort of remote chance but Tambay had an accident and spun off taking his chances with him.

Prost 57, Piquet 55, Arnoux 49, Tambay 40.

Prost has said publicly that he was fatalistic before the South

African Grand Prix at Kyalami on 15 October. Pitching his hopes too high would have been a 'futile exercise in self-deception'. He escaped the burden by spending time on – amazingly – Piquet's boat, which Piquet habitually moored off Monte Carlo.

Prost had been telling Renault for weeks that Brabham and their BMW turbo were making dramatic progress and he wasn't at all sure Renault fully appreciated that. He wondered about the legality of the fuel Brabham were using. Contemplating all this depressed him.

The connection between Kyalami and East London, where Graham Hill had won the only other decider in South Africa in 1962, was only geographical. They were more than 500 miles apart and East London hadn't been used since 1965. Kyalami, custom-built in the bleached veldt between Johannesburg and Pretoria at an altitude of 5,000 ft (152 m), held its first grand prix in 1967. It became tradition that the race was run at the beginning of the season and 1983 was the first time it hadn't been.

At Kyalami on the Wednesday Prost sat surrounded by Renault people locked into what was obviously deep conversation. He seemed vulnerable, looked haunted. Only the day before he'd tried to relax by playing golf but so many journalists and camera crews tracked him that he'd abandoned it. Now he sat and as I approached Sage moved quickly over to intercept. 'Please don't go near him. He bites people at the moment.' Prost gazed through glazed eyes and murmured, 'I'm OK.' Pause. 'I'm confident.' He looked anything but that. 'I think we are quicker than they are on the twisty sections.' End of interview.

A couple of miles down the road at the Kyalami Ranch Hotel pretty girls frolicked round the swimming pool and a handful of drivers sunned themselves in deck chairs. Where was Piquet? 'Up there,' someone said, jerking a thumb towards the second floor of the hotel, 'in his bedroom asleep.'

Tambay was quickest in the first qualifying session from Piquet, Prost and Arnoux and thereby hangs a tale. On his second run Arnoux's Ferrari stopped out on the circuit – electrics – and he had to persuade the marshals to push it to a safer place. As they did that they pushed it over his right foot. I happened to be taking a short cut through the Ferrari pit some minutes later and there in the half-shadow Arnoux sat with his foot in a bucket of cold water, already beginning to swell. He glanced up when I asked how he was and fired an expletive. End of interview. I didn't know they'd pushed the damned car over him.

The grid wasn't what we'd anticipated when the second session ended: Tambay and Piquet, Patrese and Arnoux, Prost and Rosberg (in the Williams but for the first time with a Honda turbo).

'I'm happy enough,' Piquet said. 'For sure Tambay is very strong here but if it is very hot for the race I think Michelin will be in better shape than Goodyear.' (Piquet on Michelins, Tambay on Goodyears; although Prost on Michelins, too.)

'You know, if you look at our season you can see that usually we have been qualifying fourth or sixth, something like that, where last year we were usually first or second,' Prost said. 'In the races, though, we have been more competitive and much more reliable than last year. The balance and handling are perfect.' He added that he liked the circuit, always had. This was as up-beat as he could get.

Saturday, 15 October. Piquet put a large sticker on Prost's car: Nelson Piquet Fan Club. Prost peeled it away and stuck it on to the front of his overalls. He smiled.

In the morning warm-up Lauda (McLaren) went quickest, then Patrese (partnering Piquet at Brabham), Piquet, Prost. What might that mean? Prost must win to be sure, Piquet must win to be sure and for both men the equation was the same. Whichever won, it didn't matter what the other did.

Piquet had had a small problem with the brakes on the race car, flirted with the spare, rejected that option. The Brabham mechanics, someone observed, had time for a 'leisurely lunch'. Not so at Renault. Officials, worried about how narrow the pit lane was, suddenly decided to remove everyone except those they deemed essential – and one to be removed was François Guiter of Elf, a major Renault backer. Ugly scenes, strong words within the Renault pit; and that wasn't the atmosphere you wanted.

At the green Piquet and Patrese burst past Tambay and reached Crowthorne Corner at the end of the long, long straight in that order. A pattern was being established and it held as they crossed the line:

Piquet, Patrese, Tambay, de Cesaris, Prost.

Piquet was almost two seconds up on his team-mate, a deeply astonishing statistic. Piquet and Brabham were working to a plan: run the first part of the 77 laps on half tanks. That saved an enormous amount of weight and enabled the Brabham to build a lead large enough for Piquet to pit for more fuel and still emerge with the lead. 'We had decided that I would really go for it in the beginning,' Piquet said. Tambay dropped back to fifth. Meanwhile...

	Piquet	Prost
Lap 2	1m 11.4s	1m 12.7s
Lap 3	1m 11.3s	1m 11.8s
Lap 4	1m 10.5s	1m 11.5s
Lap 5	1m 10.1s	1m 11.3s
Lap 6	1m 09.9s	1m 11.2s

Prost didn't get past de Cesaris until lap 8 and on that lap Arnoux eased his Ferrari into the pits, engine blown. Only two left now, Piquet and Prost. Once Prost did pass de Cesaris he found the gap to Patrese at fully four seconds, Piquet a continent further away and in the background to all this came Lauda, crisp, utterly precise – at the tricky left behind the paddock they would rattle the kerb as they flung their cars on to it, he took the McLaren to within an inch each time but never on. Lauda wasn't hustling, just travelling very quickly and in very great control. On lap 17 he overtook Prost, shed him and began to catch Patrese at a second a lap. It was a psychological and physical blow for Prost. He simply couldn't make the Renault go faster.

Piquet was covering the 2.5 miles (4.1km) in drum beat 1m 10s lap after lap, and at no stage could Prost get near. His fastest lap (on 9) had been 1m 11.1s.

On lap 28 Piquet came in, the tyres were changed – Piquet selected the hardest compound for his opening gambit – and the fuel put in. Piquet was stationary for 11.8 seconds, enough to get him back out still holding a four second lead over Patrese who now had Lauda attacking him hard.

As Piquet completed his first lap after the stop the team signalled that he still led. Piquet disbelieved it. The stop must have cost him places, he thought, and accelerated. His next lap was 1m 11.2s, clearly quicker than Patrese, Lauda and Prost were travelling. If Lauda won and Piquet was second and Prost was third, he and Prost would have 61 points. It would go to the most wins tie-break. Who had that? A hell of a time to be trying to remember.

Prost lived through 'absolute torture' – his phrase – and at the end of the lap 35 heard a sound which could not be mistaken, a 'snort-cum splutter.' The turbo had gone. Prost brought the Renault to the pits and instinctively the mechanics started to change the wheels. Prost unbuckled his seat belts and levered himself from the car and then watched, because Piquet might break down.

Brabham signalled to him that Prost had gone and Piquet slackened the pace. With Piquet's kind permission Patrese moved through into the lead. 'I eased off for sure and I think maybe I eased off a little bit too much' Piquet said. 'Eventually I let Niki through because I knew I could afford to finish fourth if necessary. Then de Cesaris caught me and I began to worry about how far Derek Warwick (Toleman) was behind him but the pits gave me the gap and I knew I was safe. I was not concerned about winning the race. The only thing in my mind was the championship.'

Lauda broke down on lap 72, which automatically made Piquet third and impregnable.

The Renault aftermath was a bitter one. Some French journalists wounded Prost by suggesting he'd chucked it when he realized he couldn't win. Prost did not forget some of the words written.

Within a very short time after the South African Grand Prix. Renault informed Prost that his services were no longer required.

These postscripts.

Kyalami was only the second win of Patrese's career and he had already driven ninety-eight Grands Prix races. He was very, very happy occupying centre stage on the podium, all grinning and champagne-spraying. He would not take centre stage again for seven years and a further hundred Grands Prix.

De Cesaris drove until 1994 and never finished second again.

The final postscript is a hard one. France did get their World Champion and he'd win it four times but all with British teams.

1984

The Living Legend

Portuguese Grand Prix, Estoril

'The hotel stinks. The rooms are terrible. Prost moves out after the first day but I can't be bothered.' Niki Lauda was in a stretched mood, detuning himself towards relaxation but simultaneously trying to keep his motivation sharp and fresh. He understood how you did it, none better. The throttle and the head, remember?

Estoril ought to have been a haven, strategically placed far enough from Lisbon to be tranquil, near enough to the seaside resort of Cascais to soothe although it was a drive from the circuit through the barren hillocks and narrow lanes to the coast and who was going to waste energy on that? Lauda wasn't. No, better to stay at the hotel at the Autodromo do Estoril and find the balance.

Just this once it might be elusive. In the eyes of other people Lauda was no ordinary human being after the fire at the Nürburgring in 1976. You only had to mention his name and everybody knew who you were talking about. The showdown to any championship is intrinsically gripping enough to seize the most casual sportswatcher but the legend reached far beyond that. Lauda was front page news as well as back page news.

After 15 rounds he had 66 points, Prost now partnering him at McLaren – 62.5. Between them they'd won every race except four. Prost's unusual total came from the Monaco Grand Prix which was stopped in a thunderstorm after 31 laps, only half points awarded. He led that race at that moment. If he'd had the full nine the season would have altered, especially here at Estoril. He'd need only finish anywhere in front of Lauda. As it was, all Lauda needed was to finish anywhere in front of him or, if Prost won, finish second. This had to be drawn against the unknown: no Grand Prix had been run at the Autodromo do Estoril before.

For Lauda qualifying became a 'nightmare'.

On the Thursday session to get to know the track Prost liked it, albeit with reservations. He went quickest and said, 'I think it's going to be a tiring track because it's bumpy and also seems slippery but overall it's not bad at all. At first I was worried about the lack of grip – I thought it was a problem with my car – but I was quickest so it must be the same for everyone.' Lauda was fourth.

On the Friday hard rain swamped the carparks and left two parts of the track too dangerous for use, truncating the untimed session. It dried enough to allow some sort of first qualifying and Prost went quickest again, de Angelis (Lotus) a whisker behind, Lauda a whisker behind that. On the Saturday Prost got down to the serious business of putting the McLaren on pole. Piquet (still Brabham) took it but Prost alongside on the front row. 'I am happy with that,' Prost said. 'My main worry was that Niki would be right behind me. All I can do here is attack, attack from the start. I must assume he will finish and finish in the points.'

Lauda was eleventh, the sixth row of the grid.

He felt he was watching himself in a 'second-rate movie' while the team struggled to correct 'incredibly stupid defects'. He lost his mental balance, began to make mistakes and at the end lost his final run on qualifying tyres because of an electrical problem. *The situation is so bad*, he concluded, *there is simply no point in worrying about it*. That Saturday night his 'guru' Willy Dungl cooked him a special meal and Lauda slept the sleep of a babe. He woke and reflected that every other driver will be prey to nerves so why should he? He moved methodically down his checklist, isolating his priorities – self-control, concentration, avoiding any more mistakes, not thinking about the championship.

At the circuit he glanced at Prost and sensed Prost hadn't slept properly. 'He keeps biting his nails; he is pale and haggard.' Lauda moved through his checklist again.

The nightmare went on that race morning. Lauda set fastest time (from Prost) in the warm-up but his engine suffered a water leak and he decided to have it changed. The replacement was the engine he'd used to win the French Grand Prix at Dijon. While this was being done he tried to compose himself again – not easy because the paddock at Estoril was a tight maze of narrow corridors threaded between the motor homes. An excited cohort of reporters and radio men and TV men and photographers stalked him, lurked for a glimpse, a word. The world wanted to know.

A current stirred in the paddock soft as a whisper. Lauda needed second place and would have to do a great deal of overtaking to get it. The configuration of the circuit argued that only one place was safe and convenient to do the overtaking, the long start-finish straight. The rest was all wheel-and-turn, wheel-and-turn, through the rises and dips out the back, follow-my-leader unless you were prepared to take big risks. The current became a question. Who dares baulk the Living Legend, who dares take history away from him by getting in the way?

Hundreds of millions would be watching on television and they'd see the minor players spoiling the whole thing. That was no comfort to any of those minor players, either, because if they weren't at the Autodromo do Estoril to race what were they doing there? Different drivers found different answers. A young Brazilian in only his first season, Ayrton Senna – he had made his debut in Brazil and almost won Monaco – said trenchantly that no, he wouldn't be getting his Toleman out of Lauda's way or anybody else's way. Others weren't so sure. Some would compromise, perhaps put on a bit of a show for the cameras before letting him go. Lauda anticipated it. Leaving Prost out of it – because he knew what Prost would do – he had no way of knowing which of the nine men ahead of him might love the exposure of going round lap after lap demonstrating how they were quicker.

Without warning a different whisper stirred. Marlene, Lauda's wife, arrived and word of it spread through the paddock like a very big current indeed. Marlene could never quite understand why grown men bothered with such a thing as motor racing, didn't ever come to races and here she was, her face bearing all the dignity of a Hapsburg princess as she moved serenely along the back of the pits with courtiers in attendance. She wasn't serene inside but she wasn't nervous enough to make Lauda nervous. The photographers engulfed her.

Still the clocks ticked away and now Lauda started to feel tense. He took his place on the grid, put his helmet on. 'Whether it is pure joy or an indescribable feeling of power I don't know but tears come into my eyes. I have never felt as strong as this in my whole life.'

Prost concentrated on the only possible objective: to win. He could do no more.

Mansell, on the third row, nursed disquieting knowledge. This was a circuit where you needed large brake pads but the team only had them for one car and gave them to de Angelis. Mansell would have to press on with the smaller ones although his mechanic transmitted the even more disquieting judgement that 'no way' would they last the 70 laps – the 189.2 miles (304.4km). Not that that mattered in the slightest except to Mansell himself and possibly Lauda when and if he caught Mansell.

To take second place Lauda had to pass the anglophile Swede Stefan Johansson (Toleman), Warwick (Renault), Alboreto (Ferrari), Tambay (Renault), Mansell, de Angelis, Rosberg (Williams), Senna and Piquet, theoretically in that order. He wouldn't push for a couple of laps, keep clear of trouble then size it up. The tension became a calm. He had re-found the balance.

At the green Prost beat Piquet away but Mansell and Rosberg beat him to the first corner, Rosberg leading. Out the back and near the end of the lap Piquet spun at a right-hander and when Lauda saw that he felt almost betrayed. Piquet, his friend, ought to have been winning the race – from Prost. At lap 1:

Rosberg, Mansell, Prost, Senna, Alboreto, de Angelis, Tambay, Warwick, Johansson, Cheever (Alfa Romeo), Lauda.

At the precise instant Lauda crossed the line he was 7.6 seconds behind Prost never mind that seven drivers were between them. The pit signal gave him his position although the surface was so bumpy he only saw the signal as a blur. Mentally he shrugged, his position not yet important.

Prost moved past Mansell on the second lap, Lauda moved past Cheever on the third. As Prost gathered speed so did Rosberg. They both did 1m 28s on that third lap, 1m 28s on the fourth, 1m 27s on the fifth. Lauda moved past Tambay: Renault were running an experimental electronic injection engine and it didn't give him enough power down the straight.

While Prost caught Rosberg but couldn't take him – once, twice, three times he flirted with that – Lauda faced another nightmare. Ahead Alboreto, de Angelis, Warwick and Johansson argued in a bunch, perilous to anyone searching for a path through.

On lap 9 Prost moved closer to Rosberg and towards the end of the straight moved by. The gap to Lauda had gone out to 15.0 seconds, Lauda still behind the bunch. He saw a blurr from the pits: PROST 1 – Prost leads. With a clear track Prost set out to build on the lead, a clock running in his mind. Each lap he increased it by a second over Rosberg and, of course, Lauda captive so far back.

Lauda followed Johansson and on lap 13 Warwick spun with a brake problem. That lifted Lauda to eighth and thinned the bunch but Lauda couldn't get past Johansson because the Toleman was faster down the straight. Lauda assumed Johansson was putting on a show for the cameras and frankly didn't blame him. Lauda remained captive on lap 18 and by then Prost had stretched the gap to 26.5 seconds. Johansson and Lauda moved past de Angelis, who'd selected tyres which were too hard.

For another nine laps, well towards half distance, Johansson held Lauda. Lauda sensed his engine wasn't giving him the power it should and disregarded caution, turned the turbo boost up. He couldn't sustain that for long because it drank fuel and he'd never see the end of the race. What he needed was a burst to get by. He hustled Johansson and Johansson, with this pressure mounting behind him, braked too late for a corner. As Lauda went by Johansson's wing clipped his left rear wheel. Next lap Alboreto spun. The core of the bunch had destroyed itself.

At lap 28, Lauda was fifth but the gap to Prost mounting, now 41.3 seconds. Lauda could no longer win. He concentrated on Rosberg and Senna between himself and the second place. For the next three laps he hauled Rosberg in and then took him. Increasing the pace he caught Senna in two laps and, on lap 33, went safely, wonderfully into – as he thought – the second place. From the blurr he saw his pit signal.

P3
LAUD

He hadn't known Mansell was up ahead, so far up ahead that at no stage had he seen him. Lauda was third and Mansell thirty nine seconds ahead. There were thirty-five laps left and Mansell pounded out steady 1m 25s. Lauda judged the thing was possible. He accelerated, taking the McLaren into the 1m 24s and kept it there. John Barnard, who'd designed the car, watched from the pit. He knew Lauda and how rational he was, how carefully he weighed each risk. This, Barnard concluded, is one of the few times Lauda has gone to his limit and maybe a bit beyond his limit.

Prost's eyes scanned his pit board nervously every lap.

And Lauda got stuck in traffic – what he has described as a really tough group – all about to be lapped but all, as Lauda suspects, putting on their show for the cameras. Only Gerhard Berger (ATS) moved aside. Lauda was losing time and getting angry, something extremely out of character in a car. From those 1:24s he went back to a 1m 25s, a 1m 26s. When he's shed the group the anger produced 1m 22.9s, the fastest lap of the race. A lap later he saw a Lotus come into focus – de Angelis, to be lapped, obviously. As the Lotus travelled through the right and lefts at the back of the circuit Lauda noticed a front wheel locking each time it braked. He caught it quickly and went by – Mansell whose mechanic had been right about the smaller brake pads. A lap later (53) Prost saw

P2
LAUD

It was a difficult moment in the life of Alain Prost. How could he sense that Lauda was now worried? Lauda reflected that he'd almost certainly used too much fuel dispatching Johansson. He reached for the boost knob and turned it down for the run home, slowing to 1m 27s and 1m 28s. Senna was travelling between two and three seconds a lap faster and no man on earth should have doubted what he would do if he got within reach of Lauda. With this pressure mounting Lauda very rationally set aside the calculations and increased his pace again by two seconds a lap: enough to hold Senna.

The rest became history, Lauda agonizing all the way round the final lap and only relaxing when he rounded the last corner with enough speed to freewheel it. He didn't have to. Piquet pulled alongside, seemed to be enquiring if Lauda had made it, Lauda signalled and Piquet punched the air.

The rest was a scrummage of historical proportions, the media of the world besieging him and from somewhere within the push-and-shove mélée he said 'this championship means more than the others. I liked my win in 1977 coming back after the accident but this was much harder. When you win the title against a man like Prost and the equipment is the same you can't relax for a single race. There has been pressure all the way.'

On the podium Lauda saw the state Prost was in and said that in 1985 Prost would be champion and he'd help him.

Two postcripts.

Later Lauda was given an explanation about the fuel crisis, for which I'm indebted to his own book To Hell and Back. His left turbocharger had somehow been damaged early in the race, which was why he'd been between 100 and 120 horsepower down chasing Johansson. The instrument panel showed only the optimum turbo performance – it did not differentiate between the two chargers, took its information from the one functioning normally. So it didn't know and Lauda didn't know. The moment he turned the boost up he restored the 'approximate values' of both chargers and wasn't using more fuel than he should. He'd been all right all the time.

The team held a big party that night and shortly after midnight Lauda went to bed 'pretty sober.'

Normally, you see, he was absolutely sober and none more so than in a racing car.

1985

PROST'S VOYAGE OF DISCOVERY

European Grand Prix, Brands Hatch

A different pit lane and designer John Barnard was watching the timing monitor with his customary care as the Belgian Grand Prix unfolded. Prost's McLaren hadn't been completely right and adjustments were still going on when it took its place in pole position. As Barnard watched, 'the car was actually going quite well. I got a feeling: hang on, this guy's cruising.' At that moment Barnard knew.

He'd produced what he'd describe as a conservative car, efficient and reliable. With it Prost won Brazil, Monaco, Britain, Austria and Italy and that was 65 points, his nearest rival Alboreto (Ferrari) with 53. Four rounds remained, the next at Spa.

Alboreto's clutch went on the third lap and Prost finished 55.1 seconds behind Senna and twenty-six behind Mansell. After five years in Formula 1 Mansell had not been as high as this before and was suddenly a front runner.

Almost diffidently Prost approached Barnard and said 'I'm sorry, it was quite possible to win but I wasn't going to take that risk. I wanted the points for the championship so I thought *it's safe to finish third and I'll do that.'* The weather had been wet-dry, itself a reason for caution.

Barnard appreciated how Prost thought. 'When you get to know racing drivers you know that when the helmet goes on and they form up on the grid, for so many of them there is nothing in their head but the first corner and how they're going to blast past someone and that's it. The good guys have a little room inside their heads which is still thinking about the whole race, about the championship. They're reading a season.'

Prost 69, Alboreto 53.

At the European Grand Prix at Brands Hatch, Prost needed only two more points than Alboreto, clearly a formality because, if he failed, South Africa and Australia remained. To Prost this was not a formality at all. No man knew the vagaries better than he – he'd lost to Piquet with a turbo failure, lost to Lauda by half a point only the year before when he'd scooped up seven wins, Lauda only five. What if Alboreto stormed Brands Hatch and Kyalami and Adelaide? Prost had enough experience of the 'agony' to know how self-doubt 'starts to grip you like a vice.'

He arrived at Brands having made a decision. 'Unless the weather is chaotic as it was in Belgium I will go for the win. I want to win the championship with style.'

Qualifying might – ought – to have been better than the third row. 'I can't understand it,' he said. 'I can't get near the time we did in testing a little earlier. There really is not much grip and it can't be the track because look how fast the others are going, and we've tried the same settings we used in the test, but I'm not going to get upset about it. At least I've got the car's set-up for the race right and I think that's what matters. I know the public would like the championship to go to the last race but I've been through all that. I want to settle it here.'

Alboreto was all over the place: the eighth row. This normally chirpy and cheerful chappie said 'the traction is terrible, just wheels spinning everywhere.' He worried about how reliable the Ferrari might be even when the wheels weren't spinning everywhere. He hadn't finished at Spa and here at Brands two engines blew, one on each day of qualifying.

The race sold out, which meant every seat was taken in the stands spreading round the vast curve from Clearways through the start-finish line to Paddock Hill Bend. They liked Prost but they'd love to witness a race win for Mansell.

Still the mind games played their delicate variations on Prost. The trivial amplifies towards the big and the big amplifies towards the monumental. A man's very perspective can be distorted. As the minutes ticked to the start he made a final decision. *I will race normally and see what happens.*

ABOVE: *Alan Jones on his way to winning the Canadian Grand Prix, 1980, his rival Nelson Piquet long gone with an engine problem.*

RIGHT: *Jones tells Stewart all about it.*

RIGHT: *Keke Rosberg rides the roulette wheel at Caesars Palace, 1982. John Watson (garlanded, behind) looks emptied.*

ABOVE: *At Kyalami, Nelson Piquet adds the 1983 championship to the crown he won in 1981. Riccardo Patrese is on his left and Andrea de Cesaris beyond.*

BELOW: *The Return of Superman. Niki Lauda at Estoril in 1984, where second place would be enough.*

ABOVE: *The ten-championship podium at Estoril. Lauda has his third crown while Alain Prost, who'd win four, and Ayrton Senna, three, share the moment.*

BELOW: *Prost wins his second title at a bizarre, almost unbelievable Australian Grand Prix, Adelaide, in 1986, after Nigel Mansell's tyre exploded.*

ABOVE: *I will make this my world. Senna, on his way to winning the 1988 Japanese Grand Prix.*

LEFT: *After he'd done it. Podium, Suzuka.*

BELOW: *Mansell's moment. Second place in Hungary, 1992, is enough to give him an overwhelming championship and vindicate his life.*

ABOVE: *Everything under control as Alain Prost takes his fourth championship in the Williams in 1993.*

RIGHT: *Georgie Hill says you're my World Champion, Damon – Japan, 1996.*

RIGHT: *Jacques Villeneuve, 1997, achieving what his father, Gilles, never could.*

LEFT: *Mika Häkkinen, smokin' at Suzuka as he wins the 1998 Japanese Grand Prix – and the big prize.*

MIDDLE LEFT: *A familiar gesture, Michael Schumacher, fist clenched in victory. This is France in 2002, his fifth championship.*

BOTTOM LEFT: *Schumacher's seventh and final title, Spa, August 2004 – Ross Brawn to his right, Jean Todt to his left.*

TOP RIGHT: *And they said he didn't smile much? He did.*

RIGHT: *Fernando Alonso and the intoxication of a second championship, Brazil, 2006.*

BELOW: *Triple champion gallery: Kimi Räikkönen (2007) taciturn, Alonso (2005, 2006) bubbling, Lewis Hamilton (2008) circumspect.*

ABOVE: *The crucial moment for Hamilton at Interlagos. Timo Glock (behind) has just made him champion without even knowing it.*

BELOW: *Hamilton's patriotism and his pride for all the world to see, Interlagos, 2008.*

Green.

Senna, pole, led the rush to Paddock Hill from Mansell but Rosberg couldn't get his Williams moving and Prost, laying power down, saw frozen before him the whole of Rosberg's rear. He churned the McLaren on to the grass to miss Rosberg and used opposite lock to bring it back. By then the backbone of the grid was going by and any one of them could have struck him.

Miss me, Prost thought instantaneously, miss me.

They did and he nestled into the pack, Senna already drumming his way up the incline out of Paddock towards the horseshoe of Druids, Rosberg now going with a terrible venom, reaching and overtaking Mansell before Druids. Mansell drifted wide and Piquet stole through in Rosberg's wake. Rosberg set off after Senna and at lap 1:

Senna, Rosberg, Piquet, Mansell, de Angelis, Marc Surer (Brabham), Warwick, Johansson, Alboreto, Philippe Streiff (Ligier), Laffite, Martin Brundle (Tyrrell), Thierry Boutsen (Arrows), Prost.

He felt very, very annoyed although it was directed at no one in particular. A disaster, he concluded. No tactics remained to him now. He'd simply drive. On the second lap he overtook Streiff and Boutsen, moved past Warwick's Renault which was developing a misfire.

Alboreto eighth, Prost eleventh.

A lap later Prost took Brundle to be tenth, Alboreto still eighth. The crowd noted all this as moves within the body of the race, something to monitor across the 72 laps which remained. The sharp end of the race was the front, Rosberg conducting a struggle of wills with Senna for the lead, Piquet holding off a very abrasive Mansell. On lap four Prost moved past Laffite (Ligier) – ninth, and better Alboreto falling towards him. Rosberg went beyond the limit to take Senna and spun on lap 7. Piquet was so close he couldn't avoid hitting Rosberg. Piquet retired and Rosberg made his way to the pits.

Alboreto sixth, Prost seventh.

Rosberg emerged with new tyres directly in front of Senna, who was coming round being tracked by Mansell. Rosberg decided that he'd see how Senna liked a little bit of blocking himself, which in any case helped Mansell, his team-mate. Rosberg hampered Senna, Mansell took the lead to a reverberating roar.

On lap 9 Prost took Alboreto to go into the points but now faced a trio locked in combat of their own, de Angelis (Lotus), Surer and Johansson (Ferrari). Prost sensed danger mixing it with them, particularly since the handling of the McLaren wasn't perfect. He glanced in his mirrors and saw an amazing sight: his friend Laffite's Ligier coming at him like a missile. Prost had to keep him at bay.

On lap 12 Alboreto pitted for new tyres and half-way round the next lap his turbo blew, fire under the car wreathing it in smoke. He toured back so anxious to get out of the car that he stood in it as he brought it down the pit lane: a surreal sight. The smoke was a shroud.

Prost only had to run to the end. He pitted for tyres mid-way through, the team put on the softest compound and that improved the handling immediately. He was eighth, seventh when Brundle retired on lap 40 with a water leak. Laffite pitted for tyres and that was sixth. No pressure now. Johansson went on lap 59 – alternator – and very prudently Prost took de Angelis to be fourth. Surer had run the mid-part of the race second to Mansell but vanished on lap 62 – turbo – Prost third but deep into traffic.

Autosport reported:

Prost had become embroiled in a battle between Streiff, Boutsen and Patrese (Alfa Romeo), none of whom was about to co-operate with him. For several laps Alain – his lap times suddenly four seconds slower – was trapped. In normal circumstances he would simply have cut through them but this was not one of those days. He had to finish.

Rosberg moved up in a long, sustained lunge and Prost did not oppose him. With Surer gone Rosberg pressed Prost back to fourth, just where he needed to be and just where he stayed. He completed the European Grand Prix 1m 6.1s behind the winner, Mansell. While Brands Hatch surrendered to Mansell, Prost scampered up to the podium because they'd made a special place for him there.

Later he'd say in his own quiet way that although France would be surrendering themselves he didn't have particularly strong 'nationalistic feelings' and was just as pleased to win it here in England where he liked the people and they liked him.

Brands Hatch would prove to be a voyage of discovery. Very English Mr. Mansell had discovered how to win races and Anglophile Monsieur Prost had discovered how to win championships. Neither would forget.

1986

NIGHTMARE ON THE HIGH STREET

Australian Grand Prix, Adelaide

The simplicity of it. All Nigel Mansell had to do was keep going round the agreeable contours of Adelaide making sure he didn't hit the walls. Adelaide wasn't like Detroit where the walls seemed to move over on you, it offered ample room. Of course you needed to concentrate but any experienced driver can do that.

Few seasons chart a man's rise quite so sharply as 1985 and 1986.

On 8 September 1985 Mansell did not finish the Italian Grand Prix at Monza. From the twelve rounds that far he had seven points, making him – and this is a nice piece of symmetry – twelfth in the table. Monza was the seventieth race of his career and he had never finished higher than third. From the seventy races he had only 45 points. To set this in its context, after Monza Prost already had 65 from that season alone, Alboreto 53.

Mansell altered his career at the next race, Spa, won Brands and Kyalami and projected that impetus full across into 1986. He won five races and was second twice. The line on the graph rose and rose. The man many had dismissed as a loser altered the professional perception of himself entirely but, looking at the championship, he faced a problem: Piquet with the same Honda power, and he was the Williams number 1.

Towards the end of the season Prost hoisted himself to within striking distance and Senna fell just short of being in contention. By then the matter of number 1 and number 2 at Williams had imploded when Mansell won the British at Brands Hatch from Piquet by 5.5 seconds in Piquet's spare car and Frank Williams refused to put a signal out to tell Mansell to give way.

A driver could count his eleven best finishes from the sixteen rounds. As Mansell kept going round Adelaide he'd already 72 points (70 counting), Prost 65 (64 counting) and Piquet 63. All Mansell needed was to keep going.

He'd gone to Adelaide early, Rosanne with him to share the 'psychological pressure'. He relaxed by playing golf with Greg Norman, a close friend. A couple of times Mansell out-drove him and that gave him enormous, undisguised pleasure.

Meanwhile Prost hovered between confidence and the certain knowledge that whatever happened it wouldn't be easy. He had to win the Australian Grand Prix and even then Mansell finish out of the points. Prost wasn't particularly worried about Piquet. If Mansell dropped out, he need only finish anywhere in front of Piquet; and Prost had an ally, Rosberg partnering him at McLaren and driving the last race of his career. Rosberg told Prost in his usual direct way *I will help you.*

Prost knew Rosberg as a man of his word. Privately Rosberg told himself (in the same direct way) that the consummation of his career would be to leave it in a magnanimous way. He thought *If I have to finish seventeenth to get Alain the championship I'll make damn sure I am seventeenth.*

Prost knew that Piquet did not warm to Mansell (I'm being very diplomatic) and Mansell did not warm to Piquet. Both the Williams drivers faced the 82 laps (192.4 m/309.7km) with no allies. Prost took some comfort from imagining what Mansell would be going through. He'd been there himself those three times before he finally won it. He would never find himself under that pressure again and nor, he knew, would Piquet. Prost subsequently wrote that people were 'amazed' at the confidence this gave him but that didn't disturb him. 'In many ways,' Prost said, 'this is the ideal race for me. I have to win. No need to plan, really. It's the same for Nelson but maybe it's not so straightforward for Nigel...'

Mansell said 'I've got to try and win. I want to win. There's no way I'm going to think in terms of trying to finish third or anything like that. It's too dangerous for one thing, because it means you're going to be running with other cars around you and maybe getting mixed up in someone else's shunt. No, I'm either going to win this thing properly or I'm not going to win it at all.'

Before every race that year Mobil, a Williams sponsor, put out a complete preview. For Adelaide the preview offered in the most public way Frank's thoughts. 'Nigel goes to Adelaide with a big chance of coming home the World Champion. Obviously it's his number one target and he knows he only has to finish in the top three to do so while Nelson and Prost can only take it away from him by winning. This year we know about Adelaide [1985 had been the first time].

'It is desperately hard on cars and last year the field was decimated by half-distance. However, Adelaide could be different this time, it's two weeks earlier and that is the rainy season in South Australia – there is the possibility of it being a wet race. I doubt that that will worry Nigel. This business of dropping points and only counting the best eleven scores was pushed through in the early days of turbochargers by the turbo teams because they didn't have much reliability. It's obviously unfair and confuses the public. Nelson's task is much more difficult but he still has a chance and the three-cornered fight is very good for Grand Prix racing. Another matter is still unresolved, whether we can beat McLaren for the all-time record Constructors' Championship points. We need nine points from our two drivers to overtake them. That, and Nigel winning the championship, a British driver in a British car, could add up to one of the greatest days in my life.'

Team orders? Precisely the opposite.

In Friday qualifying session Mansell was quickest from Prost and Piquet; on the Saturday Prost was introduced to Soichiro Honda who 'no doubt was intrigued to meet this little Frenchman who was making life difficult for his cars.' The Saturday finished Mansell, Piquet, Senna, then Prost who had concentrated on what his tyres were doing and how long they might last because it was an aspect 'you had to get scrupulously right'. This little comment seems so ordinary and obvious as to be completely unremarkable, particularly since he, Mansell and Piquet were all on Goodyears.

Barry Griffin of Goodyear charts the background. 'During a season it can happen that problems with tyres are masked by other events – drivers making stops for new ones in the races, for example, so you can't judge how much further the tyres would have gone. The race before Adelaide – Mexico – was won by Gerhard Berger (Benetton) on Pirellis and he ran the full distance on one set. We hadn't been able to do any testing there and our runners were in time and again. At Adelaide, Williams, McLaren and the other teams we were supplying approached us and said 'for God's sake, if Pirelli go non-stop here can we?" We said no way, our teams would definitely need to make a stop' – but Goodyear can only offer advice. You don't have to take it. Williams certainly would try and go the distance.

That Saturday night in his suite at the Adelaide Hilton, Prost played cards with friends and then went to bed. The fire alarms sounded and he, like every other guest, gathered in the lobby before the all-clear came.

Sunday morning was decorated by blue sky but with the race two hours away dark cloud began to move towards the circuit. A wet race would alter everything and a light shower did fall before the start.

Mansell sat in the cockpit sheltering under an umbrella.

Prost looked fresh even after broken sleep.

The shower stopped.

Mansell led the procession off on the warm-up lap by giving his Williams a bootful of acceleration for an instant or two, so fast that he burned off a skin of tyre and left it there, two equidistant marks directly in front of where he would start the race. He'd noticed some dust and the acceleration blew that away; and when he came back, when he repositioned the Williams for the start he'd have the adhesion of the rubber he'd laid. In the potential mental turmoil he was thinking like a champion.

At the green he took the lead and moved into the first corner, a left-hander, in front of Senna, Piquet and Rosberg. That left-hander flicked right and when they emerged the road straightened to a right-angled right-hander. Mansell positioned the Williams in the middle of the road, allowing Senna to take him on the inside, then Piquet, then Rosberg. Mansell held fourth staying out of trouble, letting things settle. Prost, directly behind, started to swarm and just at that moment Piquet overtook Senna for the lead. At lap 1:

Piquet, Senna, Rosberg, gap, Mansell, Prost.

On lap 2 Rosberg stole past Senna and attacked Piquet because

Piquet had to win to take it from Alain. It forced Piquet to go hard to hold him off. Before the race Williams had been concerned about their rate of consumption and now, on the fourth lap, that became a sub-plot.

On the straight Mansell overtook Senna, Prost fifth. At lap 5:

Piquet, Rosberg 0.9s behind, Mansell 9.7s, Senna 10.6s, Prost 11.2s, Berger 12.6s.

Now Prost swarmed all over Senna, Rosberg had pitched himself to within striking distance of Piquet and Mansell was safely into no man's land between the two groups. He could afford Piquet to win if he held third. At the beginning of lap 7 Rosberg took Piquet on the pit lane straight and, into the lap, Prost took Senna. Piquet had to get back at Rosberg and re-take him.

All this activity resolved itself into simple equations.

On lap 11, Prost took Mansell for third and Rosberg left Piquet in his wake. Prost was fast, would surely catch Piquet and take him. Rosberg would then help Prost by giving him the lead. Mansell, running fourth, would then have to take Piquet for third.

Prost began catching Piquet, calmly, precisely, skittering over a kerb here, flowing over a kerb there but always in control. He could see Piquet clearly when he reached a backmarker – Arnoux (Ligier), no friend of Prost. Arnoux moved over and, urgently, Prost cut the gap to Piquet to three seconds. At lap 20:

Rosberg, Piquet 14.21s behind, Prost 14.8s, Mansell 19.1s, Senna 37.7s, Johansson (Ferrari) 56.1s.

Prost couldn't find a way past Piquet, however, and each lap brought Mansell closer to the championship. As Piquet turned into the right-hander on the short section after the chicane he locked his brakes – wisps of smoke from the tyres betrayed that – and he spun, coming to rest facing the wrong way. Prost was through and even while Piquet rotated his car Mansell was through. Now Mansell could see Prost a hundred yards away, maybe more. Rosberg, clear of all this, ticked off the laps and wondering why he was retiring. The last race of his career was proving to be the easiest.

On lap 32 Prost had a puncture in his right front. It deflated on the long straight and gave him a 'small moment'. He knew that three laps previously he'd brushed against Berger at the hairpin while he lapped him. Perhaps that was the cause but on balance Prost judged it a 'normal puncture'. He limped towards the pits, each second a long and important one. He'd been going round in the 1m 22s: this lap lasted 1m 53.7.

Mansell was second.

In the pits Goodyear carefully examined Prost's tyres. The puncture did not seem significant – anything could have caused it – and they concluded that with the race already at third-distance the wear-rate wasn't enough to prevent Rosberg, Mansell and Piquet going the distance. Griffin remembers 'Frank Williams and Patrick Head saying "what are Prost's tyres like, what are Prost's tyres like?" Goodyear told them.

Prost remained stationary for 17.13 seconds, double the normal time because the McLaren was so low with the puncture that the mechanics had difficulty getting the jack under it. Prost returned to the race in fourth place but twenty seconds behind Mansell and Piquet, and nearly a minute behind Rosberg. At lap 35:

Rosberg, Mansell 25.2s behind, Piquet 32.4s, Prost 49.1s, Senna 1m 09.8s, Johansson at one lap.

Some short while later Mansell would have liked to come in for tyres but because Piquet didn't Williams decided he shouldn't either. Williams of course knew what Goodyear had said. On received advice alone it was the correct decision. Any pit stop is a risk, especially if you don't have to take it.

On lap 44 Piquet caught and took Mansell, a move Mansell did not resist because he had no reason to.

Prost tried to launch an attack despite mounting concern over his fuel. 'Even when I came in for tyres the gauge read minus five and in an ordinary race I would have backed off until it had come back on to the plus side again. Maybe I would have settled for a safe third place or something like that. But on a day like this there was no way I could back off. I thought if I don't win the race I don't win the championship. I kept pushing.'

On lap 49 Prost got himself down into the 1m 21s but Mansell and Piquet did, too, and each of them for the first time in the race.

Prost stayed in the 1m 21s and set fastest time on lap 54 with 1m 21.0s. Inside ten laps he had drawn up to Piquet and Mansell. They ran together.

Rosberg meanwhile was musing quite how he could give the race to Prost, assuming Prost got past both Williamses. Should he park his McLaren just short of the finishing line and wait for Prost? *No*, he thought, *you risk stalling the engine and what would that look like?* Rosberg decided that towards the end he would slow progressively and demonstratively so that Prost caught him whilst making sure everyone understood what Rosberg was doing.

Moving into laps 60 and 61, Rosberg's tactics seemed irrelevant because Mansell held third, making him World Champion – although Prost was there, directly behind. On lap 63 Rosberg heard a brrrr and thought the engine had let go. Twice he angled his head to his left wing-mirror looking for smoke. He pulled off at the side of the track – there was a small, wedge-shaped enclave in the concrete wall – got out, moved left round the car and peered underneath the left rear of it for any signs of the oil he'd anticipated from an engine blow. He didn't see any but thought no more about it.

'I was coming at Mansell with a vengeance,' Prost said. 'As I pulled level I saw Rosberg, who had been hidden by Mansell's car. Not Rosberg's car but Keke himself standing at the side of the circuit.' As Prost went past, Rosberg shrugged. Prost saw this shrug and assumed Keke was saying *sorry, I did the best I could to help*. Rosberg flipped a thumbs up towards Prost but Prost doesn't remember that. Very likely he was already gone. Two marshals beckoned Rosberg to come to safety and he walked briskly through an opening in the concrete wall. Lost in all this was the singular fact that Prost had taken Mansell.

Mansell, in third place again, saw Rosberg's McLaren parked but had no idea what had happened to it.

At precisely this instant Griffin was on the pit lane wall watching one of the small television monitors. He knew what had happened to Rosberg. He'd just seen it. The right rear tyre had shed its tread and flap-flap-flapped against the bodywork. That was the brrrr Rosberg heard. Griffin turned and set off but others at Goodyear had seen, too. Every Goodyear runner was potentially vulnerable.

Already someone from Goodyear headed towards the Williams pit to tell them bring Piquet and Mansell in. Mansell moved into lap 64.

Williams listened to Goodyear and said they'd bring both drivers in at the end of the lap. By now Mansell had reached the long straight, the Williams in sixth gear, the speed moving up towards 200mph (320km/h). He ducked out from behind a backmarker – Philippe Alliott (Ligier) – and was abreast of him. His left rear tyre exploded. A fountain of yellow, molten sparks were flung up as the wheel rim gouged the surface of the track. The whole wheel was being sucked from the car, this car which bucked from side to side in a frenzy.

In the control tower the race director, a 57-year-old American called Burdette (Berdie) Martin watched the bank of television screens horrified as Mansell fought the car and fought for his life. He had a phone directly in front of him and words were forming. He did not touch the phone but he was poised to. Still the Williams bucked and kicked, chased – Martin's word – to and fro as it came on at such terrible speed towards the sharp right-hander at the end of the straight.

Berdie Martin was a very experienced Race Director. He thought fast:

We've already discussed that corner, it's the narrowest part of the track and one of the most dangerous. If the Williams stops anywhere around it I'll pick up the phone and tell the official on the platform at the finish line to put a red flag out. He held his hand over the phone but still he did not touch it.

The Williams slowed, dancing now, weaving like a snake towards the right-hander, passing the point where Rosberg's McLaren lay parked, and still it had the speed to stab Mansell's head left-right, left-right. It slithered full across the mouth of the right-hander into the escape road. Mansell had hauled it there by strength, instinct and almost fantastic sensitivity. The Williams ebbed to a crawl and bumped gently against a wall far, far up the escape road. He was safe. The car was in a safe position.

Martin took his hand away from the phone. If Mansell had stopped twenty-five yards further back, near the apex of the corner 'I'd have red-flagged the race instantly, a red flag means every driver has to stop racing and because more than 80 per cent of the race had gone it couldn't be re-started.' Martin's mind was still moving fast. 'If I'd have red-flagged the race the positions were frozen at where the drivers were on the previous lap. My God, I'd have made Mansell World Champion...'

Mansell held his arms aloft from the cockpit, a motion of great despair.

Piquet was a couple of seconds ahead of Prost but the on-board radio crackled its fateful message. *Come in for new tyres immediately*. Prost gained on him and as Piquet peeled off towards the pits went through.

'Goodyear were right to say what they did on the information they had,' Piquet would say. 'I knew I was losing the championship but I didn't care. I was alive.' He was stationary for 8.3 seconds, emerged but completing lap 65 was 15.2 seconds behind. He had sixteen laps to get that back.

Rosberg was walking back towards the pits when a spectator said *shame the same thing happened to you and Mansell*. 'His engine blown, too?' Rosberg mused. *No, no*, the spectator said, *tyre blown just like you*. 'Tyre?!' Rosberg couldn't believe it. Purely by chance he hadn't examined the *right* rear of his car. He did remember he had seen no oil. If the engine wasn't blown it must still be running. He hadn't switched it off, no point assuming it was blown, and he hadn't been able to hear it running because passing cars drowned all that. If he'd known he'd have made the pits somehow. They were only just over half a mile away. Rosberg would have got back out there and quite possibly still been in the lead. Rosberg walked on, out of Grand Prix racing.

Prost assessed fuel as a 'critical factor' and because of the nature of the race had had no chance to husband any. As Piquet dipped towards the 1m 20s Prost matched him and on lap 69 did 1m 20.9s. Probably that decided it. The gap was out to eighteen seconds and increasing.

On the final lap Prost waited for the engine to cough and start to die. Piquet came at him and in a supreme effort set a new fastest lap destroying the track record. It was not enough. As Prost crossed the line Piquet was already round the corner at the end of the start-finish straight but 4.2 seconds away.

Prost stopped immediately, clambered out and clapped his hands to his helmet. He waved both arms back towards the team in the pits, took his right driving glove off and flung it on to the car as if he was saying well, what about that?

Mansell, long back in the pits, was so visibly distraught the posse of journalists – some of them his friends who had lived the years with him – followed a few paces behind, hesitating to go nearer and intrude into private grief. They did eventually, of course, but that's another story.

There is a postscript.

In December at the annual FISA prize-giving ceremony in Paris, Nigel Mansell happened to be sitting next to Berdie Martin and they chatted of this and that. At some point Martin explained how close he had been to the red-flag, how the order to hoist it was forming in his mouth. Mansell had had no knowledge of this, of course, but he suddenly saw the full consequences.

'Oh my God,' he said.

1987

THE RACE THAT NEVER WAS

Japanese Grand Prix, Suzuka

If Nigel Mansell chose to see his career as a sequence of ironies Suzuka would fit. Suzuka wasn't a race at all, Suzuka was about a broken handful of images two days before the Japanese Grand Prix.

This had been a Williams Honda season with Mansell and Piquet pitted against each other. That's a smooth and comfortable sentence to write. The partnership was anything but comfortable and that tone had been repeated in the build-up to the first race, Brazil, where an interview with Piquet appeared in Playboy magazine. In it he said some unflattering things about Mansell's family which enraged another driver so much he said 'tell Nigel I'll hold Piquet while he hits him.' Their co-existence sharpened because only Senna (Lotus Honda) and Prost (McLaren) were capable of mounting a sustained challenge. After Mexico, the third last race, Piquet had 73 points and Mansell 61. Senna (51) and Prost (46) were out of it. As they all flew home from the Autodromo Hermanos Rodriguez on the evening of 18 October, Piquet had made himself clear favourite. If he won at Suzuka he was champion. If he was second and Mansell didn't win he was champion. There were other permutations but only grouped around these.

This was the first Japanese Grand Prix for a decade and reflected that country's growing power in the sport. 'Suzuka is a complete unknown as far as a race is concerned. We have tested there but I think that what we learned will be almost obsolete because the track has been altered and it will be totally different with all the other teams present.' Mansell weighed his words carefully long before he boarded the plane for Japan. Naturally he'd tested there – Honda owned Suzuka – but a race meeting was something else.

Twice before, Japan had hosted a Grand Prix, 1976 – the Hunt year – and 1977, but both at Fuji and a complete generation ago. Of the twenty-seven drivers who gathered now only Patrese spanned the generations. Piquet said the track was 'very narrow, very bumpy and very quick'.

Mansell was very quick, too. On the Thursday during the introductory session nobody went faster, and on the Friday during the morning untimed session nobody went faster, either. Piquet had a stomach disorder which prevented him doing many laps on the Thursday, he'd barely slept that night and on the Friday seemed weary. 'I don't feel great,' he said, and didn't have to say much else. You only had to look at his face to know.

Five minutes into first qualifying Mansell did a prudent warm-up lap of 2m 9.0s then a hot 1m 43.0s, cooled the tyres, took it down to 1m 42.6s. Tactically this was perfect. Provisional pole would likely be in the 1m 42s although if it did dip into the 1m 41s only he and Piquet seemed capable of that. Piquet went out to see what was what (1m 59.9s) and judged his run exquisitely: 1m 41.4s.

Ann Bradshaw, a shrewd judge of any motor racing situation, handled publicity for Canon, a major Williams sponsor. 'I was standing next to Charles, a friend of Nigel's, and Piquet was in the garage. He'd just come back from the quickest lap. We'd seen the time flash up and Nigel had seen the time flash up and you knew: Nigel just walked away and got ready. I remember Charles saying to me, "he's going for it now." We felt he was going out to be a lot faster. It was the way he got in the car.'

Around twenty minutes of the session had gone and Mansell continued to behave with great tactical awareness. He monitored the track, gauging how much faster it was getting. Being new in a Grand Prix racing context, Suzuka hadn't acquired a film of rubber scrubbed off so many tyres as they went round and round, giving adhesion and speed.

The lap concluded, the conclusions drawn, Mansell accelerated. Moving quickly he reached towards the S-shaped section behind the paddock, a right, a swift little surge, a left.

On the pit lane wall Ann Bradshaw kept her eyes on the small monitor which gave laps' times. 'Piquet and a lot of the guys were in the pit itself. The TV was up on the wall and they were watching that.' Mansell rounded the right-hander using the kerb nicely, the impetus naturally carrying him across the track towards the kerb on the left. He ran marginally wide and passed on to the kerb a fraction deeper than usual, only a few inches but deeper. Dust lay there. Two soft, small wisps of it were churned, one from the front wheel, one from the rear.

The car has no adhesion.

Instantly Mansell thought *something is happening, I don't know why but something is happening*.

The car had already snapped sideways. He hit the brakes hard and the car slewed as it turned, the movement so savage it burnt black strips from the tyres full across the width of the circuit. Wisps of smoke were coming from the tyres now. The car corkscrewed completely but the impetus carried it on. The car screamed backwards on to a narrow grassy verge towards a seven-layer tyre wall. The car was still rotating when it struck the tyre wall sideways. Mansell estimated the impact at 140mph (225kmh).

The tyre wall burst as if a bomb had gone off within it. The tyres were flung in a violent cascade. The impact pitched the car into the air and it corkscrewed again. For a millisecond it dipped at a crazy angle and nearly flipped. It landed with immense force on the kerbing, bounced and the whole rear wing tore away, bounced again – not so high – but the impetus still strong enough to haul it back across the track.

No other car was coming.

The car rolled gently on across the track like a wounded animal and came to rest on its rim, Mansell's head cast full against the rear of the cockpit.

Bradshaw heard 'a gasp from the pit. Somebody said "Nigel's gone off." I went across and everybody was transfixed looking at the television screen. At that point they hadn't shown the replay. All I saw was Nigel in the car with his head back and looking in a lot of pain. Without the replay I didn't know how bad it was although he seemed to be in agony. Then they showed the replay. There was silence in the pit. Piquet went white, he drained. There have been all sorts of comments about what he said but I can tell you nobody said anything.

Everybody had gone very quiet. There was nothing anybody could say.

'The moment we got the replay we really got the impact of how much it must have jarred his back landing on the kerb, then we watched the scenes of them taking him out of the car. A lot of people walked away to try and find out how he was. You often see accidents and thankfully they look worse than they really are but with this one you had no way of knowing. Nigel might have had broken arms or legs, might just have had a bit of bruising. I don't think it had crossed Piquet's mind at that moment that he was World Champion.'

Other drivers passing the scene didn't realize the gravity. They were presented only with the aftermath. Certainly Derek Warwick (Arrows) didn't because 'if I had I'd have stopped to help immediately.'

Mansell's spine was seriously jarred, his right leg damaged. The rescue team needed five minutes to get him from the cockpit and by now, his crash helmet removed, his face portrayed a stunned semi-conscious look. He'd remember suffering the most excruciating pain he'd ever known. They stretchered him to the track's medical centre and by helicopter to hospital in the town of Nagoya.

Nelson Piquet was World Champion 1987. 'It didn't come across Piquet until appreciably later, an hour, an hour and a half after the accident when they took Nigel off to hospital,' Bradshaw says. 'By the end of the day it was obvious Nigel wasn't going to race again that weekend. We had a lot of pressure from journalists wanting to speak to Piquet, we were being hounded by people who wanted to know how Nigel was.

'I spoke to FISA and they said we could use the press room, which they don't normally do, on the Saturday. (Piquet qualified fifth and was not therefore obliged or entitled to attend the usual post qualifying Press Conference.) I organised to take Piquet up there. People said he should, people said he shouldn't, but I think it was best because it got everybody off his back and the team's back. We had a race to do. We were still pretty much in a state of shock because we were very worried about Nigel and all sorts of rumours were going round. Who can say what a back injury might mean long-term?

'From what I saw, Piquet handled himself very well in this situation. I felt he had let himself down in various things he had done over the year and I didn't think they were necessary. He and Nigel having that battle didn't do anybody any good. Nelson likes to rev people up but slagging off families, you can't get any lower than that.

'I suggested the Press Conference, he did it and I wasn't surprised. I knew he was capable of carrying off things like that. He went up and spoke to the journalists and he did say that this was not the way he wanted to win the championship. In no way did he gloat.

'I know that the press had built up the ill-feeling between them and I won't pretend they were the biggest of buddies – by the nature of what they do they are all loners – but Piquet reacted like he was thrilled to have won again but would have preferred to have done it on the track.'

Piquet said that 'when someone has worked all year to beat you and then you see them go up in the air and get hurt is not very pleasant. I've been very consistent and I've taken very few chances. I've finished the races and that's why I have won the championship.'

Piquet spent the evening of Friday 30 October 1987 at a sponsor's reception. His face portrayed solemnity. 'Celebrations? No, it wasn't that kind of deal,' Bradshaw says. 'Nobody felt like celebrating and anyway Piquet was leaving for Lotus so we wouldn't have the number 1 on the car next season. It would have been lovely but that was it, one of the status symbols was being taken away.'

Mansell spent the night in hospital. 'All I heard were screams. Someone in the ward died. At that point I didn't know if I had internal bleeding. When you are exposed to that kind of trauma your thoughts are vulnerable.'

He woke on the Saturday morning and seriously contemplated retiring. He was visited by Professor Sid Watkins, FISA's doctor, who diagnosed concussion, a crushed vertebra, a pounding of the spine. All Mansell wanted to do was go home. He rearranged his air ticket and, heavily sedated against the pain, slumbered most of the way back to the Isle of Man. He watched the race on television but felt oddly detached from any emotions about it.

The sequence of ironies in the career of Mansell continued even in his absence. Piquet ran third in the Japanese Grand Prix but the engine failed. He ran second in the Australian Grand Prix but had brake problems and didn't finish.

It left a question Mansell might always have had to ask himself. If...

1988

SENNA ON A ROLL

Japanese Grand Prix, Suzuka

A paragraph suffices to encompass a season. Prost won Brazil, Senna won Imola from Prost, Prost won Monaco after Senna had led, Prost won Mexico from Senna. And so on. Rarely in motor racing has a team put such a grip on a season as McLaren Honda. Only one race escaped them, Monza, where Prost had mechanical problems and Senna became involved in a crash with a backmarker when, of course, he was leading.

Coming to Suzuka, Prost had 84 counting points and Senna 79, but in such a season punishment for consistency – 11 best finishes counting of the sixteen rounds – couldn't be avoided and while Senna had 'only' 11, Prost found himself already beyond his quota: 12, the lowest second place. You don't need to perplex yourself with the permutations and neither did Senna. If Senna won Suzuka he'd vindicate his life and be champion wherever Prost finished.

Prost was regularly and habitually mobbed at the Suzuka Circuit Hotel whenever an autograph hunter or a photographer caught so much as a glimpse of his shaggy hair and oft-broken nose. He'd grown accustomed to that because for most of the decade he'd been a celebrity but this mobbing was hysterical. The world crowded Alain Prost and he could do nothing except keep perfect control of himself. He'd grown accustomed to that, too.

On the Friday, Prost 'slept for about an hour last night, no more than that. I should have taken a sleeping-pill, I suppose, but the later it got the more I was afraid to in case I was drowsy through the morning.'

Prost had Senna to cope with: they had almost crashed in Portugal when, down the start-finish straight, Senna moved over on him, a frightening moment which created a furore. Between Suzuka and the race after, Spain, Senna spoke publicly about this and Prost responded by calling him 'just a spoilt brat'. Their relationship was ceasing to exist.

Jet-lag and an upset stomach did not prevent Prost from being quickest in the morning untimed session, 1m 44.6s against Senna's 1m 44.8s. Prost said his chassis and engine were perfect.

In the afternoon it went wrong, paradoxically 'a combination of chassis and engine problems. I think the track changed from the morning but I am finding that the power is coming in very suddenly and then fading along the straights. I am sure it is something which can easily be cured and I expect to be faster tomorrow.' Prost was third fastest behind Senna and Berger (Ferrari).

Senna took provisional pole with his first run and became the only driver to dip into the 1m 42s. 'Unfortunately on my second I could not get a clear lap before the tyres were too far worn. It is best to wait until tomorrow when the track should have more grip to try to improve.'

The Saturday session was wet-dry, Prost repeatedly baulked by slower cars while Senna found a clear lap for 1m 41.8s. It seemed the decisive gesture. Prost made a last run at it but 'I missed a gear at the last corner and I have to say that it was my own fault. We also had a problem with the pop-off valve which gave me less boost than normal.'

Senna had his twelfth pole of the season.

Prost spent the Sunday morning warm-up checking everything on the car and reached into the 1m 47s in race trim – as did Senna – but Prost found the engine 'stuttering' lower in the rev range. The technicians and mechanics quickly rectified that. Prost felt confident.

Drizzle fell and though it looked permanent no time remained for anyone to change to wet weather tyres. By the parade lap the drizzle stopped. Very deliberately on that parade lap Senna and Prost set off at high speed to see how their cars behaved, approached racing speed until suddenly Senna slowed. No doubt he had seen enough.

At the green Senna felt the McLaren hiccup forward – a sort of stammer – and coasted gently. He flailed both arms to tell the onrush behind. 'Stalling,' he would say, 'was partly my fault and partly a very sharp clutch.' He could think only *It's all over, it's all over*. The start line sloped. The McLaren coasted, cars flicked left and right. When he felt the power he was fourteenth, Prost long gone.

As they crossed the line to complete the first lap Senna was up to eighth. 'I started to find my rhythm and I was going quicker and quicker.'

Lap 2	sixth
Lap 3	fifth
Lap 4	fourth

That was done by elbowing past Alboreto (Ferrari) in a move you might call muscular. It put Senna 12.9 seconds behind Prost but, his boost turned up out of necessity, he'd be using more fuel than he should.

Prost began to have difficulty with his gearbox. 'I was missing a gearshift maybe once every two or three laps.' Ivan Capelli (Leyton House March) took Berger and closed on Prost, Senna closed on Berger but at ten laps Prost held the gap to 11.6s. Capelli tracked Prost, caught him and Prost couldn't afford Capelli to overtake; he had to win.

By lap 14 the drizzle fell again from an ever-darkening sky, just enough to make the tyres glisten. Senna was the fastest man on earth in the wet. Capelli swarmed Prost, took a slingshot at him and actually led going over the line before Prost stoked the Honda engine and re-took him. By now Senna had passed Berger, cutting the gap to 6.11 seconds. Worse, Prost's gearbox denied him second and third gears. He had to alter his whole approach to corners.

On lap 20 Senna moved past Capelli, came up to Prost and tucked in behind him.

'In two laps I lost eight seconds to Ayrton because of the gearbox,' Prost would say.

Capelli's engine let go and he left the classic duel unhindered. Senna stood off for a lap and on the straight powered through clean. He pulled away.

It was all over.

The drizzle stopped and after thirty three laps Senna squeezed the gap out to 3.6 seconds. For long moments Senna became trapped behind Satoru Nakajima whose Lotus also had Honda power. Senna took a risk and ducked inside at the entry to the chicane. Prost drew up but faced the same problem and, when he'd dealt with Nakajima, Senna had re-established the gap. Spots of rain fell, not drizzle, rain.

As Senna passed the start-finish line his hand was out of the cockpit pointing to the sky, saying stop the race! Prost launched a final assault and cut into gap but the rain defeated him. The gap moved out to 6.6 seconds and, after forty-nine of the fifty one laps, 9.4 seconds.

Senna was entirely justified in demanding the race be stopped. The Japanese Grand Prix was officially a dry race and slick tyres offered the most minimal grip. It did run to the end, Senna nursing his McLaren home with exquisite care. As he crossed the line you could see his emotion, see his right fist out of the cockpit pumping the air in taut, powerful short-arm jabs. He was releasing the tension of a whole season, perhaps a whole life. He flipped his visor up and as he slowed his eyes seemed narrowed by crying.

On his way to the Press Conference he rounded a corner and found a certain Dennis Rushen, the Englishman who'd run him in Formula Ford 2000 six years before, standing there – this same Dennis Rushen who had taught Senna many naughty English words because they are the ones you may need to understand. One of them was very naughty indeed and they'd used it as an affectionate term of greeting.

'You're still an expletive,' Rushen said to Senna, a lovely echo of 1982 and other, more modest triumphs that had led all the way to here. Senna looked at Rushen and Rushen will never forget that Senna 'didn't know whether to laugh or cry'.

At the Press Conference Senna, looking suddenly wearied, said: 'It's over. It's been a long season for me and I think for Alain. Amazing fighting between us, a lot of pressure on both of us and, although we always try to minimize the pressure to make it less painful, it's impossible. It was very hard and I still cannot believe it's finished.'

Prost, sitting next to him, said, 'I am quite happy for Ayrton. I am not too disappointed by this championship but I am a little bit disappointed by the way the race went on. It was quite easy in the first part, I was controlling the race very well, no problem with the fuel, no problem with the car, then I had the problem with the gearbox. Also I lost too much time in traffic for two or three laps. Ayrton overtook me, I had three cars in front of me, I lost maybe four, five seconds a lap. I could catch Ayrton but with the gearbox problems sometimes I was catching him, sometimes I could lose one or two seconds in a lap. Then when the rain came at the end I gave up. That's it. Ayrton did a very good season.'

Towards sunset, Senna was being interviewed by a clutch of Brazilian journalists. As it happened the race was being replayed on a giant television screen. One of the journalists said that Senna had been so single-minded he'd sacrificed many friendships along his journey and would this now change?

Tears tumbled from his eyes.

Prost telephoned his wife Anne-Marie at home in Switzerland and she hoped he wasn't too sad. No, he said, but he was concerned that his son Nicholas might take it hard. Anne-Marie said Nicholas was asleep but she was already sorting out in her mind how she'd help him to cope with any taunts at school on the Monday.

On the Monday, Prost telephoned Nicholas and hoped the other kids at school hadn't given him too rough a time. No, Nicholas said, not too bad, anyway...

Worse was coming, much worse.

1989

CHICANERY

Japanese Grand Prix, Suzuka

Coming towards the corner called Tosa, Senna pulled out and overtook Prost. To every spectator, official, journalist and fellow driver at the Autodromo Dino e Enzo Ferrari, Imola on 23 April, this move seemed most ordinary – a racing move, the kind drivers habitually make at the beginning of a race. Prost did not resist.

Senna executed it safely enough, a great relief in an atmosphere necessarily charged with foreboding. The race had been stopped when Berger's Ferrari kept straight on at a corner called Tamburello, struck the barrier virtually head on and battered itself into pieces while fire consumed it. For long moments as Berger remained unconscious inside it, this was as shocking as the Nürburgring, 1976 and Lauda. Berger escaped with comparatively minor burns.

At Tosa Senna did his overtaking and they ran like that to the end, Senna winning it by 40.2 seconds. Prost did not attend the post-race Press Conference. He was, so the rumours said, a very angry man.

Only later did the background become the foreground. Prost and Senna had struck an accord based on the superiority of the McLaren Honda in 1988 which, you could reasonably assume, would endure in 1989. Why fight amongst ourselves at the start of the races, risk eliminating ourselves? The accord stipulated that whichever driver reached the first corner first took it, minimizing the risk. Prost reached towards Tosa and believed the accord guaranteed him the corner. Senna, moving more quickly, believed that they were not near enough to Tosa for the accord to come into effect.

A chill descended.

By Monza in September Prost had headed himself towards Ferrari for 1990 and was making plaintive noises about equal treatment.

By Suzuka in October Prost led the table with 81 points (76 counting) from Senna, 60, but Senna had only seven finishes in the points, Prost thirteen. With, again, eleven best finishes counting of the sixteen rounds, if neither finished the Japanese Grand Prix Prost became champion. Moreover Senna had to win Japan to keep it alive.

Publicly everyone said the right things after Senna took provisional pole on the Friday.

Osamu Goto, Honda's Project Leader: 'I am really surprised and impressed at Ayrton's time (1m 39.4s). I thought that might be possible on the second day but not on the first. We have tried both engine specifications today, but we have not yet made up our minds which to run in the race.'

Senna: 'I missed second gear coming out of the hairpin on my best lap. Without that problem I think I could have managed a 1m 39s dead. I also blistered my right front tyre mid-way round the lap and understeered over a kerb on the return leg of the track.'

Prost: 'The car was not at all bad on race tyres. For sure I can be much, much quicker on qualifiers. I had a slight oil leak on my spare and a fuel pick-up problem at the wrong moment on my race car.'

The background remained more complex with Senna enjoying a Specification 5 Honda engine while Prost was restricted to a Specification 4, but that doesn't explain why Prost hadn't run on qualifiers. The explanation? Evidently McLaren had made a small but genuine mistake and over-filled Prost's petrol tank, making the car crucially heavier. As Prost built the pace for a fast lap he sensed this, came in to have the excess fuel drained and ran out of time.

On the Saturday, Senna blitzed Suzuka, 1m 38.8s although, 'my fastest lap wasn't a smooth one. I fumbled a couple of gear changes but it was a great lap nonetheless. Since chassis settings are so important here I chose to use one set of C racing tyres and one set of E qualifiers which enabled me to continue working for the race during second qualifying. Tomorrow the priorities are a well-balanced car and a good start.'

Prost: 'My first run was spoiled by traffic. I got stuck behind a Brabham and just couldn't overtake. On my second set of qualifying tyres I was particularly anxious not to make a mistake because it was so important to qualify second. There was just no way I could beat Ayrton. My only tactic in the race will be to push as hard as possible.'

Prost also said that in the past he'd left the door open for Senna but he wouldn't be doing that this time.

On the grid did Prost crawl the start or was he anticipating the green? If he wasn't it was close. He pressed the power down and it flung him over to centre track so strongly that within fifty yards he led, Senna behind. Prost flicked the McLaren left to position it for Turn One, the right-hander, and took that clean. As the necklace of cars strung out Senna harried briefly but Prost drew away. At lap 1:

Prost	1m 49.3s
Senna	1m 50.7s

Prost increased the gap to 2.2 seconds on lap 2, 3.2 on lap 3 – before Senna tried to respond on lap 4 but

Prost	1m 46.6s
Senna	1m 46.7s

Prost increased the gap to 4.8 seconds and with the cars and drivers so beautifully matched this might be a race of fractions. On lap 11 Prost set fastest lap, 1m 45.7s, on lap 15 Senna responded, 1m 44.9s and by lap 17 Senna had cut the gap to 3.6 seconds. The McLarens were now essentially alone, Berger in the Ferrari 20.3 seconds off the pace.

Prost drove with extreme accuracy, creating each lap in the image of the lap before. For eight consecutive laps his time varied by no more than seven hundredths of a second, but now on lap 19 they were deep into the traffic. Prost lapped three of them comfortably enough, marooning Senna behind them.

When Senna had shed these backmarkers Prost had already reached more of them, Alex Caffi and de Cesaris in the BMS Dallaras. Prost moved past de Cesaris and turned into the pits for his tyre stop. Senna waited a couple of laps for his and the gap stood at 4.6 seconds.

Twenty-nine laps were left but Senna had to make his move, catch Prost and win. He increased his tempo, set a new fastest lap on lap 25 and now, as Prost moved into traffic again, was there, clearly visible. He'd cut the gap to under three seconds. He set a new fastest lap on lap 27 coming through the traffic with awesome certainty.

Another backmarker – Brundle (Brabham) – flogged along ahead of Prost, Senna closing. Prost went through, Senna looking down the inside at the hairpin then Brundle moving aside. The gap at lap 36 was 3.3 seconds. Next lap Senna brought fastest lap down again, the gap 2.9 seconds. Prost however felt 'very comfortable, in control of the race, very calm'.

Senna looked sharper in the corners, Prost quicker along the straights. You could see it at the hairpin, Senna coming almost fully up to Prost, see it as they moved from the hairpin, Prost re-establishing the gap. A gap flicked up – 0.4 of a second – and the thing had become physical. Another gap flicked up – 0.5 of a second – on lap 42, the cars stretching and closing, inhaling and exhaling.

Senna could stay with Prost but, lap melting into lap, had to overtake and only one place in all the 3.6 miles (5.8km) seemed a possibility, the chicane. If Senna could get his car inside and alongside before they reached it he might do it – but he'd have to be alongside. On lap 43 he had a look, had another on lap 44. Out at the back there was a flash reading of the gap, 0.643. At the hairpin Senna had cut even that but on the long sweepers Prost re-established it.

At the chicane Senna hauled himself very close. At the apex of the 90° right he was no more than the length of a car behind Prost but Prost prodded the power and moved comfortably away. Senna decided: this lap.

They rounded the unfolding left which pitched them at the chicane. Prost held mid-track, Senna inside him, so far inside him that he had his car over the white line of the pit lane entrance. He kept straight ahead and, as Prost turned into the chicane, the two cars hammered together and went up the escape road in front of them.

Prost flipped his seat belts, glanced across towards Senna, got out of the car and walked away. At that instant Senna waved both arms to the marshals who'd sprinted up. Push me, push me. Six marshals hauled at Prost's car. Prost, pulling his gloves off, wandered almost casually in front of it until he was in front of Senna's car, glanced across at it, turned to face it.

Three marshals were shoving Senna's car. His hands cut the air mimicking again push me, push me. Prost saw and stepped aside. Seven marshals gathered at the rear of Senna's car and did push him deep into the escape road. The engine coughed, the marshals scattered and Senna threaded down the escape road to rejoin the track.

Prost walked back, World Champion for the third time. As Senna pitted for a new nosecone Prost, on foot holding his helmet in one hand, glanced at him. Prost was curious about that: Senna keeping on, Senna who'd had a push which was illegal, Senna who'd missed the chicane which was illegal.

Senna did keep on to the end despite giving Alessandro Nannini (Benetton) a heavy and torrid moment at the mouth of the chicane, and was disqualified.

Prost said 'I was sure I was going to win or have an accident because I knew that he wanted to win absolutely. You know the problem with Ayrton is that he cannot accept not to win and he can't accept that someone might resist one of his overtaking moves. I have to be careful because my life is more important than the championship.'

Senna murmured about someone being at the chicane 'who shouldn't have been there'.

McLaren lodged an appeal arguing that Senna's car was being pushed from a dangerous place and there were precedents for missing chicanes. Theoretically that kept the championship in play until the final race, Adelaide. FISA meanwhile issued a statement. Part of it read: 'The events which have occurred in the last few months during several Grands Prix prove that even if A. Senna is a talented driver, he is also a driver who endangers the safety of other drivers.' They gave him a six-month suspended sentence and fined him $100,000.

Two postscripts.

FISA rejected McLaren's appeal.

Adelaide was a wash-out, Senna crashing on lap 13. It's not a lucky number.

1990

POLES APART

Japanese Grand Prix, Suzuka

Senna in his McLaren Honda had won six races, Prost in his Ferrari five, which brought them to Suzuka with the main pressure on Prost. If neither finished, Senna took the championship. To keep it alive until Adelaide, the next and final race, Prost had to score at least one more point than Senna.

They did not like each other. That happens and it's no big deal unless the dislike assumes a ferocity which might override reason. The aftermath of the crash at the chicane in 1989 lingered through 1990 until the post-race Press Conference at Monza when a journalist asked quite how long this was going to go on – Prost and Senna studiously ignoring each other. Suddenly they were shaking hands and Senna was saying 'we are both professionals and we are both doing the same job. Maybe we don't have a lot of other things in common but we share the same passion and that is very important for us.'

Peace.

It held to Suzuka.

On the first day of qualifying Senna could get no higher than third fastest. 'My car was OK but it bottomed out badly at one point just as I was changing from fourth to fifth and I got a little sideways because I was glancing at the rev counter at the time. I feel quite satisfied with my performance as a whole.' The order: Berger in the other McLaren, Prost, Senna.

On the second day and, with only moments of the session left, Prost waited and Senna waited. Senna's mind worked like this: 'I wanted to be out at the right time in terms of traffic and the other factor of course was Alain. I realized that the best situation was to be slightly ahead of him. When I was ready to go, waiting, I was playing with him. When I heard his engine fire up I switched mine on and went, to be ahead of him. It was just a psychological factor, nothing else.'

Senna	1m 36.9s
Prost	1m 37.2s

Publicly Senna said predictable words. 'The whole team really contributed to my performance, men and machine working extremely well, but the race is a long one and anything can happen. I'm sure it will be the most exciting race of the season. We and Ferrari are really close now. Despite the pressure I am under I feel really fit. Naturally I am thinking of the championship and this one would mean more to me than 1988.'

Privately what would subsequently prove to be a great, bitter and decisive drama was being enacted. Senna felt deeply unhappy that pole position was on the right. He judged the track had more grip on the left – occupied by Prost. Senna insisted that pole should confer the advantage it implied and wanted it moved. Evidently Jean-Marie Balestre, President of FISA, was among those who said no.

Subsequently – in fact, a year later – Senna would explain: 'Before we started qualifying, Gerhard and I went to the officials and asked them to change the pole position because it was in the wrong place. The officials said yes, no problem. I got pole and then what happened? Balestre gave an order that we don't change pole. We said that it had been agreed. They said no, we don't think so. This was really [expletive].

'I said to myself, "OK, you try to work cleanly and do the job properly and then you get [expletive] by stupid people. All right, if tomorrow Prost beats me off the line at the first corner I will go for it and he better not turn in because he is not going to make it."'

As the cars came round to form up on the grid, only Senna knew this. Meanwhile, Prost revealed to John Watson, now doing television commentary, that the Ferrari could take Turn 1 flat out in fifth gear. Watson sensed that Prost became completely concentrated on that:

Prost said that what Senna had done was 'disgusting. I am not prepared to fight against irresponsible people who are not afraid to die. In Islam for someone who is about to die death is a game. The problem today was we have seen Senna take all the risks to win the championship. I am not ready to play this game.'

'I was coming faster than him,' Senna said, 'because I had more acceleration. In the first corner when you are with cold tyres, low pressure, the car heavy, you normally brake earlier and if you try hard you can overtake. It's difficult, it's risky but in my position I had to that. I think he made a big mistake to close the door because he took a chance that went wrong. In his position it was the wrong tactic in the first corner, just ignoring that I was coming tight on the inside. If he hadn't shut the door nothing would have happened because we would have been through the corner. I cannot be responsible for his actions. He is always trying to destroy people. He tried to destroy me in the past on different occasions and he hasn't managed and he will not manage because I know who I am and where I want to go.'

The world of Formula 1 raked over the wreckage and conducted its own inquest. There were many, many points of view, some around the notion that the crash of 1990 was a direct result of the crash of 1989 at the chicane, others claiming that the modern car had become so strong and safe that a driver's first consideration was no longer preserving his life. Cynics added *funny, wasn't it, that taking Prost out gave Senna the championship. Suppose it had been the other way round…*

Ron Dennis was interviewed on British television and explained patiently that the door had been opened. A slo-mo replay captured that: the instant when Prost's Ferrari lurched and straightened a second time. If you freeze-frame it, you do have a door – not ajar and not closed, either. The opening existed for one frame, perhaps two, a desperately short space of time and distance.

Some murmured about ethics because this was, after all, a sporting contest. Wasn't it? The ground rules of Formula 1 said that an overtaking car had to be level with the car it was taking. At no stage, even frame-by-frame, had Senna been that.

Prost had done a most normal thing, made a better start, taken the

lead, helped himself as he was sure
to the racing line. A sense of profou
not taken the most direct route to it
remember – getting across fast to t
three choices:

> To run into the back
> To back off and foll
> To try and take him

Perhaps Watson holds the key.
getting to fifth gear and going thr
than anything Senna might do onc

Senna's anger remained undilu
don't care if I upset Balestre. I th
what we feel. That's how it shoul
rules which say you cannot speak
allowed to say someone made a m
We are racing professionals. There
image and we cannot say what w
get banned, you get penalties, yo
you lose your licence. Is that a f
thought and what took place after

'If you get [expletive] every si
your job cleanly and properly, by
advantage of it, what should you
you, yes, thank you"? No, you s
right. And I really felt I was figh
because I was [expletive] in the
I got pole. I tell you: if pole h
would have happened. I would
result of a bad decision. And we
the first corner accident. I did
my responsibility.'

The dec
improb

Senna t
feat never
knew a hu
the fuel, b
is extreme
Imola and
Prost in the

There h
Senna kn
behind hir
That's take
instant he
Williams is
lot of power
full use of

He'd bee
late season
at the Cana
sight of th
snapped in
running. H
because a v

In Belgi
Schumache
Prix commu

the Ferrari was quicker and if Prost reached Turn 1 in the lead and emerged from it in the lead he'd win. So: arrive there first, go flat in fifth, take the race.

It was a warm and sunny Sunday afternoon.

At the green, Senna and Prost moved instantaneously but both were dragged by their acceleration towards the centre of the track. They came closer and closer. Behind, the twin columns of cars dug smoke from their tyres. They were travelling fast, too, already. Senna held the McLaren pointed directly forward, Prost still coming across and fractionally ahead.

Prost felt for the racing line.

Senna angled the McLaren across to centre track then held it pointed directly forward again. They might have been 6 feet apart, Senna hugging the centre, Prost almost half a car's length ahead and still coming across, still feeling for the racing line.

Within an instant the Ferrari's mounting acceleration pressed it clearly ahead of Senna: the length of the whole car. As Prost came across, Senna moved in behind him but not fully behind him. The precise positioning: Senna holding the McLaren to the right of the Ferrari's rear, poised to fling it inside the Ferrari and grasp the racing line for himself. And still Prost came across. Prost reached centre track, the Ferrari aimed into the mouth of Turn 1. Senna did fling the McLaren out from behind and to the inside.

Prost could have blocked if he'd kept coming across but he lurched a fraction to the outside and that created a gap on that inside. Senna went for it and put the McLaren alongside Prost – not level, alongside. The McLaren's front wheel was at the Ferrari's rear wheel.

As Prost reached the racing line he squeezed Senna. The two cars struck each other hard and interlocked. The impact pitched Senna on to the red and white kerbing, pieces of bodywork cascaded away behind them. Deep into the sand trap the McLaren swivelled before it sank. Senna kept the engine running and kept the wheels turning but they churned going nowhere. The McLaren did not move.

The Ferrari had sunk nearby. Prost levered himself out and stalked off in one direction, Senna levered himself out and stalked off in the other.

Prost said that what Senna had done was 'disgusting. I am not prepared to fight against irresponsible people who are not afraid to die. In Islam for someone who is about to die death is a game. The problem today was we have seen Senna take all the risks to win the championship. I am not ready to play this game.'

'I was coming faster than him,' Senna said, 'because I had more acceleration. In the first corner when you are with cold tyres, low pressure, the car heavy, you normally brake earlier and if you try hard you can overtake. It's difficult, it's risky but in my position I had to that. I think he made a big mistake to close the door because he took a chance that went wrong. In his position it was the wrong tactic in the first corner, just ignoring that I was coming tight on the inside. If he hadn't shut the door nothing would have happened because we would have been through the corner. I cannot be responsible for his actions. He is always trying to destroy people. He tried to destroy me in the past on different occasions and he hasn't managed and he will not manage because I know who I am and where I want to go.'

The world of Formula 1 raked over the wreckage and conducted its own inquest. There were many, many points of view, some around the notion that the crash of 1990 was a direct result of the crash of 1989 at the chicane, others claiming that the modern car had become so strong and safe that a driver's first consideration was no longer preserving his life. Cynics added *funny, wasn't it, that taking Prost out gave Senna the championship. Suppose it had been the other way round...*

Ron Dennis was interviewed on British television and explained patiently that the door had been opened. A slo-mo replay captured that: the instant when Prost's Ferrari lurched and straightened a second time. If you freeze-frame it, you do have a door – not ajar and not closed, either. The opening existed for one frame, perhaps two, a desperately short space of time and distance.

Some murmured about ethics because this was, after all, a sporting contest. Wasn't it? The ground rules of Formula 1 said that an overtaking car had to be level with the car it was taking. At no stage, even frame-by-frame, had Senna been that.

Prost had done a most normal thing, made a better start, taken the lead, helped himself as he was surely entitled to do to the best route to the racing line. A sense of profound mystery remained that he had not taken the most direct route to it, which was – Senna behind him, remember – getting across fast to the inside and leaving Senna only three choices:

> To run into the back of him.
> To back off and follow him through.
> To try and take him on the outside.

Perhaps Watson holds the key. Prost was so far mentally into getting to fifth gear and going through flat that he weighed it more than anything Senna might do once he was ahead of Senna.

Senna's anger remained undiluted a year later when he said: 'I don't care if I upset Balestre. I think once and for all we must say what we feel. That's how it should be. There have been [expletive] rules which say you cannot speak what you are thinking, you are not allowed to say someone made a mistake. We are in a modern world. We are racing professionals. There is a lot of money involved, a lot of image and we cannot say what we feel. If you say what you feel you get banned, you get penalties, you pay money, you get disqualified, you lose your licence. Is that a fair way of working? I said what I thought and what took place afterwards was pure theatre.

'If you get [expletive] every single time when you're trying to do your job cleanly and properly, by the system, by other people taking advantage of it, what should you do? Stand behind and say "Thank you, yes, thank you"? No, you should fight for what you think is right. And I really felt I was fighting for something that was correct because I was [expletive] in the winter and I was [expletive] when I got pole. I tell you: if pole had been on the good side nothing would have happened. I would have got a better start. It was the result of a bad decision. And we all know why, and the result was the first corner accident. I did contribute to it, yes, but it was not my responsibility.'

1991

FINAL BRAKEDOWN

Japanese Grand Prix, Suzuka

The deceptive season reached a deceptive climax and all of it improbable, fateful and at times stretching credulity.

Senna took his McLaren Honda to victory in the first four races, a feat never achieved before. It proved to be the initial deception. Senna knew a huge amount of work was needed on the car, engine, even the fuel, but as he subsequently confessed, convincing people of that is extremely difficult when you've just won Phoenix, Interlagos, Imola and Monte Carlo and already lead your nearest challenger, Prost in the Ferrari, by 29 points.

There had been a moment, almost a private moment, when Senna knew. He'd had Patrese (Williams Renault) tucked in behind him, Senna had stolen past a backmarker and accelerated. *That's taken care of Patrese for a while*, he thought, and the next instant he glanced in his mirrors and Patrese was there again. *The Williams is quite a car*, Senna concluded, *and the Renault is giving it a lot of power*. Mansell had that Williams car, too, and began to make full use of both.

He'd been outdriven by Patrese early on but bestrode the mid and late season, mature now but still combative. There were ifs, notably at the Canadian Grand Prix in June. Mansell led every lap and within sight of the finishing line changed down. The semi-automatic box snapped into neutral and he hadn't enough revs to keep the engine running. He was classified sixth, worth a single point – 9 points gone because a win was now worth 10.

In Belgium, the race before the Italian, West German Michael Schumacher made his debut in a Jordan and astonished the Grand Prix community by his composure, intelligence and speed.

By Monza, which Mansell won, he had 59 points against Senna's 77. The next race was Portugal.

At the end of lap 30 Mansell angled the Williams into the pits for a routine tyre stop. He had a nice lead over Patrese and both had a nice lead over Senna, running third. By definition an unhurried pit stop does not exist in a Grand Prix race with the World Championship in play. Mansell's car was stationary for 7.75 seconds, nicely safeguarding the race for him. Peter Windsor, the man in charge, stood directly in front of the car and when he saw four hands raised from the four wheels he stepped quickly aside and that was the signal for Mansell to go back out and win.

He accelerated down the pits and had travelled thirty yards, perhaps a little more, when the right rear wheel came off and bounded violently into the Tyrrell pit nearly knocking two mechanics over like skittles.

Mansell beat his fists in frustration.

There had been a misunderstanding. The nut on the right-rear cross-threaded but, as the man on the hammer worked, the mechanic next to him – with no way of knowing what was happening – raised an arm, Windsor saw it and made the only assumption: wheel on, ready to go.

Now Mansell sat beached in the pit lane, a very dangerous place to be. The team reacted fast, worked on the car there to get the right-rear on and Mansell did rejoin, seventeenth. The disqualification was inevitable. The team had worked on the car outside their pit area. Mansell, coming up through the field, was black flagged and returned to the pits close to tears.

Senna 83, Mansell 59 and all sixteen rounds counted. Spain, Japan and Australia remained. Mansell won Spain, Senna fifth so that Senna led 85–69. Mansell went to Japan knowing that he had to win and Senna finish no higher than third for the championship to go to Adelaide.

Mansell, Williams and Renault were eminently capable of winning the Japanese Grand Prix but what they could not do was exercise any control over Senna. In one sense that made Suzuka easier. Mansell could concentrate on his own performance and leave the rest to fate.

Berger went quickest in both qualifying sessions. 'The first lap was a good one but the front right tyre went off even as early as the hairpin so I was over-cautious for the second part of the lap. On my second run my tyres were better but I had a slight clutch problem which stopped me getting out of sixth and fifth gears. I'm still not sure about the race set-up.'

Behind these predictable words lay a plan because Senna would line up alongside him on the front row, Mansell on the second.

'I am a little bit disappointed we didn't go quicker,' Mansell would say, 'but overall I am comfortable with today. In race conditions we are going to be in good shape.'

Confirmation came in the Sunday warm up, Senna quickest but Mansell only a fraction behind:

Senna	1m 41.4s
Mansell	1m 41.9s

The strategy was revealed from the start, Berger setting off into the distance and Senna holding Mansell who, of course, had to win. Mansell faced no immediate crisis because the race was over 53 laps (192.9 miles/ 310.5km) but he couldn't afford to let Berger get too far out of reach when he got past Senna. Berger covered the opening lap in 1m 46.6s – fast – but Mansell knew that in a superior car you can haul enormous chunks of time back. Around lap 2 he radioed the pits and said no panic but he'd drop back a bit to review the situation.

'The biggest problem I had was giving the tyres too hard a time in the beginning,' Berger said. 'I wanted to get as far away as possible because I was worried that Riccardo might overtake Ayrton.' Patrese was poised behind Mansell to lend whatever assistance he could and, if he and Mansell took Senna, the whole current of the race and the championship might be altered: Mansell moving on Berger and drawing Patrese with him, Senna fourth when he needed to be third – but Mansell had not taken Senna...

Senna knew Mansell 'was having a hell of a time in the turbulence behind me'.

Berger took his lap times down through 1m 45.1s and 1m 44.9s to

1m 44.5s successively. From lap 5, Mansell matched Senna move for move. As Frank Williams would say, Mansell and Senna 'shake hands in public but they can't stand each other. I don't know if Nigel is the only driver Senna hasn't psyched out but he's certainly one of them'.

	Senna	Mansell
Lap 6	1m 46.1s	1m 46.1s
Lap 7	1m 45.9s	1m 46.1s
Lap 8	1m 46.2s	1m 45.7s
Lap 9	1m 46.0s	1m 45.9s

Mansell radioed to his pit that he was ready to mount a proper assault on Senna. He could wait no longer. They came down the start-finish straight to Turn 1 nose-to-tail. Senna took the racing line but at the corner Mansell's car seemed to skip momentarily. Was that the turbulence? As Mansell braked the pedal went soft and the impetus of the car carried it across to the outside on to the kerbing. The tyres scrabbled for grip but the impetus was too strong and the car bored deep into the run-off area, swivelling and churning a dust storm.

Frank Williams, watching on the TV in the pit, accepted the instant philosophically.

When Senna 'saw Mansell go off I cannot say I was sorry.'

As soon as Berger 'heard Mansell was out I slowed down to take care of the engine'.

Mansell semi-skipped across the track when he'd clambered out of the car – he still had the lingering after-effects of an injury playing football a month before – and walked back. 'I was just relieved to be able to walk away from a 200mph shunt. In that gravel trap sideways I was worried the car might flip. I had no de-acceleration at all from the brakes by the time I was running off the circuit. I mean, that worried me a lot. It was a relief to be out of the car and in one piece and all my body still working.' He waited in the pits to congratulate Senna.

'After Mansell was gone it was almost an instant reaction for me to think, "right, we've got to go for it and we can have some fun",' Senna said. His radio crackled. The team reminded 'me that I should think of the Constructors' Championship'. Williams led that 117–116 going into Suzuka.

'Ayrton was pushing and I thought maybe he wanted to make a nice race,' Berger said. 'Then he got past...'

For seven laps Senna gained until he and Berger were together. Senna went by in a tight and potentially risky move almost demanding Berger's consent. However ... 'I was leading and having to drive 99.9 per cent and we had agreed earlier that whoever led for the opening stages would be allowed to win,' Senna said. He radioed Ron Dennis in the pits asking for instructions, but 'I couldn't hear the messages clearly over it and I knew nobody would believe I hadn't heard them if I didn't give way. I backed right off to cut the noise from the engine and asked again. Ron said yes, he wanted us to change positions. It hurt to do it but the pain was nothing compared with the feeling I had from my third World Championship.'

Two postscripts.

Senna joined Brabham, Stewart, Lauda, Piquet and Prost as three-times champions. On the evening of Sunday 20 October 1991, only Fangio was ahead with five and, as it seemed, Senna had plenty of time for even that. He was thirty, Fangio had been forty-four when he won the fifth.

Before the 1992 season, Frank Williams hosted a lunch for some British journalists at the factory. He said in his own candid way: 'Was it a mistake in Japan or was it the car? I don't know.' He repeated 'I don't know.'

Have you tried to analyse it or look at your data?

'The data doesn't say the driver's made a mistake, got too much oversteer, spun getting the oversteer back. The data doesn't tell you that.'

1992

MANSELL'S RHAPSODY

Hungarian Grand Prix, Budapest

He smoothed his white flame-proof Balaclava, hoisted his helmet and adjusted it to his head, moved from the shade of the umbrella held over him and slipped into the cockpit. He sat and composed himself.

The clocks moved towards 2.0 on the hot, dusty afternoon of 16 August.

If Mansell glanced left he saw the Williams Renault of team-mate Patrese fractionally ahead because Patrese had pole. The stagger of the grid gave him a small advantage but it might expand on the run to the first corner. Whoever reached that first would almost certainly win the race, and for the most infuriating of reasons to every driver behind: all the Hungaroring except this start-finish straight prohibited overtaking, and to pass on the straight you needed decisively more power than the man in front. In that, Mansell and Patrese were evenly matched.

A whole conjunction of factors brought Mansell to this moment. Prost was commentating not driving in 1992 and Senna's McLaren Honda couldn't live with the Williams. Mansell and Patrese enjoyed enormously the best car and Mansell had reached the point in his career where he could exploit it enormously. He seized the season and held it tight: stormed South Africa, murdered Mexico, blitzed Brazil, stunned rainy Spain, savaged San Marino, and even a puncture at Monaco couldn't stop him coming a strong second behind Senna. He crashed in Canada going for the lead, flew in the wet in France, made Silverstone surrender to him, and ground out his eighth win in Germany. In terms of victories Mansell was now the most successful British driver since our story began on 13 May 1950 at a much more restrained Silverstone than the one we'd just had.

In the end, the simplicity was all beguiling. Sitting on the grid he nursed 86 points and the only man able to overhaul him, Patrese, had 40. If Mansell reached the first corner first, and controlled the rest of the race from there, he was World Champion whatever Patrese did. After thirteen years, after the nightmare of Adelaide in 1986, the pain of Suzuka in 1987 and 1991, Mansell would achieve the championship with five rounds to spare.

They moved into the parade lap and came at a measured pace round the final right-hander to the start-finish straight, feeling for their positions on the grid, Patrese to the left and Mansell to the right, Senna behind Patrese, the young Schumacher (Benetton) behind Mansell, Berger behind Senna.

Patrese knew all about the importance of the first corner, and so did Mansell and so did Senna. As the cars settled for the red light Senna sensed that if he got there first he could win the race: the Williams might be more nimble, the Renault engine might deliver more power but none of that would be decisive with Senna setting his own pace and keeping all the other cars behind him for the seventy-seven laps.

Mansell started so furiously that his wheels laid heavy rubber on the track but now Patrese's power arrived and he moved to mid-track forcing his car half a length clear of Mansell. Within fifty yards Patrese was completely clear and on the inside leaving the rest of the track a vacuum. Senna filled it, Berger in the other McLaren behind him.

As Patrese followed the rim of the corner to lead the race Senna flicked the McLaren in front of Mansell and Berger, in a sort of swoop. Order:

Patrese, Senna, Berger, Mansell.

Senna's McLaren couldn't stay anywhere near Patrese although he tried throughout the first lap. He told himself the truth – even you can't do this – and contested the lead no more. Patrese moved off alone, Senna keeping Berger and Mansell in his wake. As each moment passed Patrese extended his lead so that by the third lap it was three and a half seconds – and growing. If Mansell could not find a way past Berger and Senna, soon Patrese would be too far away.

After four laps Senna was more than six seconds behind Patrese and Mansell almost two seconds behind Senna with Berger in between. Mansell had been staying in touch with Berger but not close enough to attack. He might advance on or retreat from Berger but Senna dictated the pace of both of them. The timing devices showed an academic gap of 8.36 seconds from Patrese to Mansell.

Curious, too, that the choice of tyre compounds seemed to be playing no significant part. Senna had chosen a softer compound than either Patrese or Mansell and that ought to have given him an advantage about now. It didn't.

Mansell struck decisively at Berger on the start-finish straight, ducking to the inside and staying there, leaving Berger the outside and no chance to loop round him this time. That made Mansell third. He moved on Senna and drew up to him but Patrese had a twelve-second lead, and after only eight laps. Patrese would stroke his Williams into the distance for maybe another twenty laps, drop his pace and canter it. A clear track inviting him forward, Patrese set fastest lap so far. His lead went out to 14.9 seconds and was growing.

A fencing match developed between Senna and Mansell. Through the dips and rises, Mansell probed and they darted through the little snap-snap-snap of corners to the curve which brought them on to the start-finish straight.

Patrese cranked up the pace with another fastest lap while Mansell made another lunge to the inside approaching the first corner but Senna blocked that, Mansell had a look on the outside – no – slotted in behind Senna again and the fencing match resumed. Senna remained unmoved.

Patrese stretched the lead to seventeen seconds, and after twelve laps to 18.4 – 19.1 seconds over Mansell. The fractions lacked great significance in themselves but as they multiplied they demonstrated Patrese's complete command of the race.

Traffic might have helped Mansell by creating a gap from nowhere but Senna dealt with every slower car absolute clarity of purpose. He made the McLaren into a knife. Pierluigi Martini (Dallara) watched Senna cut past him but, on a twisty section, followed the racing line keeping Mansell behind. Mansell shook a fist at him but Martini was still ahead, Senna pulling away. Mansell had to wait until the end of the straight to go by himself.

Mansell could now demonstrate what he could do on a clear track and caught Senna very, very quickly, although of course that only brought him to the fencing match again.

Patrese stretched the gap to 21.2 seconds, set fastest lap again and soon he started the canter – although not yet, the gap increasing to twenty-three seconds.

Mansell dropped away from Senna and, using the empty space in between, set fastest lap. Senna responded by setting fastest lap himself but Patrese's lead was out to 25.4 seconds then 26.5, the fractions still multiplying. Mansell made a sudden probe to Senna's left but ran just wide in a corner. Berger stole through.

Mansell was fourth and it had all gone. He needed to re-take Berger just to return to Senna's wake. He swarmed Berger, took a breather, swarmed again. By then Patrese led by 30.9 seconds. On the straight Mansell went inside and Berger – in a frightening instant – moved over on him, wheel-to-wheel. Berger twitched the McLaren away and Mansell seized the corner – third. Berger responded in the snake-twist of a left after the first corner by chancing it outside but was never close enough.

Mansell set a new fastest lap as he chased Senna, shedding Berger in the process. Mansell caught Senna, Patrese as it would seem starting the canter by allowing the lead to narrow to 25.8 seconds.

Senna, accelerating, held Mansell. Then the whole race broke up and the championship opened. In the snake-twist of a left after the first corner Patrese ran on to oil or dust. The kerbing had been removed for the 500cc motorcycle World Championship race the month before and cars had been digging dust here. Patrese held his usual line and the car veered off left, left, spun backwards towards a gravel trap and came to rest half on the track and half off it. He churned the rear wheels searching for adhesion but they just spun. Marshals sprinted up and as they tried to push it Senna went by. As a marshal heaved, Mansell went by, followed by Berger.

With a push, and flinging up a shower of gravel, Patrese set off needing to be fourth to keep the championship alive. Would he be disqualified for the push? Could he get away with that because the car had been in a dangerous position? Where was he in the race? Mansell set a new fastest lap and the immense crowd on the hillsides ticked the cars off as they came through: Senna, a short gap to Mansell, a five-second gap to Berger, then the Benettons of Brundle and Schumacher, then Finn Mika Häkkinen, then a long gap to Patrese.

It was lap 39, leaving Patrese thirty-eight more to reach fourth. The exact scale of that:

Senna	54m 26.7s
Mansell	@ 1.7s
Berger	@ 6.9s
Brundle	@ 8.2s
Schumacher	@ 8.8s
Häkkinen	@ 14.9s

Mansell continued his advance on Senna and into lap 41 was on him but Patrese had a car which might cut mightily past Häkkinen, Schumacher and Brundle. The gap from Senna to Patrese was 22.8 seconds so that Patrese wasn't hopelessly out of touch with Häkkinen, was only twelve seconds from him and would be a great deal closer in a few laps. When he reached and took Häkkinen, the Benettons would only be six seconds further on.

Mansell drifted back again.

Subsequently it would be easy to forget Senna's race, the great scope of it against this parched and arid landscape, easy to forget the seeming ease and certainty of it. As the race moved towards its final third he'd conserved his tyres well enough to be able to increase his tempo. At 44 laps he'd taken the lead out to 3.2 seconds.

Patrese was nine seconds behind Häkkinen but reeling him in, closing. As Senna moved from Mansell, Patrese moved to Häkkinen, seven seconds away now and setting his fastest lap.

From nowhere Mansell eclipsed that by setting fastest lap of the race. Senna bettered it and Mansell bettered that …

Patrese was within three seconds of Häkkinen. At lap 50:

Senna	1hr 9m 15.8s
Mansell	@ 6.2s
Berger	@ 13.5s
Schumacher	@ 13.9s
Brundle	@ 16.0s
Häkkinen	@ 25.6s

Senna set another new fastest lap, forcing the gap out to eight seconds, Patrese went even faster but, on lap 56, Patrese was suddenly bringing his Williams into the curved entrance to the pit lane. He moved slowly, smoke from the engine rising and dispersing. He reached the Williams pit and he raised a hand above the lip of the cockpit. *It's all over.* The engine hadn't sounded right virtually from the start, he would say, and 'I didn't think I'd be able to finish the race'.

At this moment all Mansell needed was the second place he was in, or even third – which would increase his points to 90, and if Patrese won all the final five rounds and Mansell didn't get a single point more, they'd both be on 90 but Mansell champion on the most wins tie-breaker 8-5. At lap 55:

Senna	1h 15m 57.9s
Mansell	@ 9.5s
Berger	@ 23.1s

Mansell let the gap go out, no hurry now. With twenty laps to go, the pressure of the race and the pressures of a lifetime were ebbing by the instant. Mansell had time. He wielded the car like a friend and ally, soothed it like a trusty and trusted accomplice. Those laps were laps for purists as well as the many thousands of British supporters who'd travelled to the Hungaroring with their flags and banners and pennants.

On lap 59 Mansell let the gap out to twenty one seconds, then twenty-three. He was still thirteen seconds in front of Berger – and the championship broke open again. Mansell approached the corner for the start-finish straight but slowing, angling into the pit lane as Patrese had done. A mechanic hung a board over the pit lane wall, black with a Union Jack on top and the single word PUNCTURE? on it in phosphorescent yellow, but Mansell already knew via the radio: a monitoring device on the car warned of a puncture. The mechanic, hearing Mansell approach behind him, turned away from the pit lane wall.

The car was stationary for 8.7 seconds although of course he'd had to leave the track, slow into the pit lane and would have to accelerate from it. That represented a long time. At lap 62:

Senna	lh 25m 21.3s
Berger	@ 42.2s
Schumacher	@ 42.5s
Brundle	@ 42.9s
Häkkinen	@ 44.9s
Mansell	@ 58.0s

With fourteen laps to go, and Mansell making the Williams go very, very fast, Schumacher's rear wing failed on the main straight, flew up and away as if an angry god wrenched it from the car. Schumacher described two complete rotations with so much smoke from all four wheels that the car was almost obscured and went deep into the run-off area.

Mansell was fifth.

Within a couple of laps he was close to Häkkinen, now at the tail end of Berger-Brundle. Onto the straight Mansell squeezed up to the Lotus, got a 'tow' and went inside He was through, and fourth.

He did the same thing to Brundle, and third would be enough. He tracked Berger while Senna came in for a precautionary tyre stop, was stationary for 6.33 seconds and emerged still in the lead. Mansell followed Berger down the straight, came out for a feel of that first corner, wasn't quite there to take it and moved nicely in behind Berger again. Next lap hc was closer and almost elbowed Berger away from him. Mansell was second.

On a circuit where overtaking was damnably difficult Mansell had overtaken Berger three times. He had eight laps to run. Senna won by a distance, Mansell quite alone back there, isolated in a kind of splendour. He crossed the line but didn't seem intoxicated, as if he had wrung so much out of himself that emotion would be something to be explored later.

The podium was a happy place. Senna and Mansell and Berger embraced, Senna insisting they join him on the top rung, and when Senna and Berger had gone Mansell remained, punched and stabbed the air while below, those thousands of British supporters roared and cheered.

A few moments after that they all sat in the little interview room. Mansell wiped his face with a towel, let his body go slack. His eyes glazed over.

Senna once said, at just such a moment: 'well, I think to all of us different feelings come and go but one thing that perhaps we all have in common – apart from our differences – is that we are all racers, we love our activity, we take chances, we take risks, we go through pain, we sacrifice lots of things in life just to be in Position 1...'

Giuseppe Farina would have understood perfectly, and Ascari, and Fangio himself. Clark and Hill and Stewart, they'd known this and so had Lauda and Piquet and Prost, so had they all.

Now Nigel Mansell understood, too.

1993

PROST, FOUR AND FAREWELL

Portuguese Grand Prix, Estoril

'Life's like a race, you know. Sometimes you win and sometimes you lose when you don't deserve it.' Alain Prost remained philosophical to the end.

At Estoril on Friday, 24 September, Senna announced his intention to leave McLaren, an announcement in the nature of confirmation. It had long been rumoured and few at the circuit evinced even mild surprise. He'll go to Williams Renault in 1994 now, every whisper said, and maybe he's already signed. Yes, but to partner Prost? It was a genuinely staggering thought after 1989 and 1990.

An hour later the small man with the shaggy hair faced a familiar thicket of microphones and announced his intention to retire from Formula 1 as of the finishing line at Adelaide, 7 November, an announcement anticipated by some and a genuine surprise to others. Prost had retired before of course, at the end of 1991, taken a sabbatical and returned, with Williams. No, he'd say, this second retirement is not about Senna coming to the team.

'It is a difficult decision but it has been growing all year. I made it about a month ago. I wanted to announce it after winning the championship but the way circumstances have developed it is better for me and the team to do it now and concentrate on the title. There is not one reason. I've had one of my happiest years, maybe the happiest. The ambience has been very good. It is not often you are happy when your team-mate [Damon Hill] wins but it is like that here. After thirteen years I know it is the right decision. I will finish driving. There won't be another comeback.'

It had been an immense career spanning generations. On his debut in Argentina, 1980, he'd driven against Scheckter and

Villeneuve. In this Portuguese Grand Prix, 1993, he'd drive against Christian Fittipaldi who was nine in 1980 and Karl Wendlinger who was eleven.

A fourth championship remained to be secured, placing him above everyone except Fangio. Prost ought to have been poised to do it. Williams was the best car, Renault the best engine and Hill trusty in a supporting role. Hill made his debut at Silverstone in 1992 in a Brabham and finished sixteenth, four laps from the winner, Mansell. The Brabham was uncompetitive and the distance between Hill's position and Mansell's was a chasm.

Even Senna couldn't really expect to beat Prost. He'd do whatever he could with his McLaren and its Ford engine – as he had done at the start of the season – but overall the Williams Renault would be too strong.

There'd been stutters for Prost along the way: rain in Sao Paulo when he spun off, rain at Donington for the European Grand Prix when nobody could circumnavigate Senna, a stop-go penalty at Monaco, an engine blow-out at Monza but none of these disturbed the essential balance. Prost reached the Portuguese Grand Prix with 81 points, Hill 58, Senna 53 and Schumacher 42.

Senna still had a chance but that involved winning Portugal, Japan and Australia, and Prost had to take no more than two points from any of them. Hill found himself in a much stronger position but if Prost finished in front of him and Senna in Portugal he had the fourth championship.

After an unhappy season with McLaren, the American Michael Andretti departed and his replacement, Mika Häkkinen, outqualified Senna in Portugal. That set a tone of uncertainty about the race, compounded when Hill took pole from Prost.

The geography of Estoril made it a difficult circuit for overtaking except the long straight, meaning if Hill took the lead Prost might well have to remain behind for the whole race. What would Hill do? Did the fact that Prost intended to retire remove any moral responsibility from Hill to help him? Hill had not been confirmed with Williams for 1994 and so he was driving to protect his career.

Shortly before the race, Hill was asked what he would do. In that quizzical way that he had he replied that he'd been thinking about it, of course, and hadn't made up his mind yet. The uncertainty spread further. Would the Williams team order Hill to let Prost go? Frank Williams did not like doing that. He liked to hire racers and give them the equipment to race, then watch in delight. Almost certainly Prost would be in that familiar place for racing drivers: on his own.

On a beautiful early afternoon in Estoril the sky was so blue it seemed like a heavenly canopy. When the ONE MINUTE sign was hoisted Hill nodded briefly to some final instruction, touched the side of his helmet and prepared himself. An official stood on the start-finish line holding two yellow flags which billowed in a light breeze. The THIRTY SECONDS sign was hoisted and the mechanics melted from the grid. As one of them passed the snout of Prost's Williams he patted it, part affection, part good luck.

The official with the yellow flags began to wave them and the cars moved off into the parade lap except Hill. 'The starter device jumped out – in fact I think it did it more than once, to the point where other cars were beginning to leave the grid around me. Finally it did fire up, whereupon I promptly stalled it, so that ended any question of my taking up pole position.' He'd have to start from the back, the track now opened to Prost.

	Vacant	
		Prost
Häkkinen		
		Senna
Alesi		
		Schumacher

The red light blinked to green. Even as Prost cleared his grid bay Häkkinen had drawn almost level, Senna had begun foraging for an opening directly behind, Jean Alesi (Ferrari) staying full left and coming fearsomely fast. Prost moved to centre track, the classical positioning to line the car up for the first corner, a right. Häkkinen, alongside now, moved over on him. For a handful of instants it defied belief.

Prost had to fling the Williams towards the white rim of the track. Level with the pit lane exit, well on the way to the corner, Häkkinen moved further over and now Prost's wheels were on the white line, briefly over it. Four cars were essentially abreast: Prost on the extreme inside, Häkkinen, Senna and Alesi.

'I got away quite well,' Prost would say, 'although perhaps with a touch too much wheelspin. Häkkinen was alongside me but I was on the inside and thought I had no problem leading into the first corner. If I had done one-tenth of what Häkkinen did, for sure I'd have been given a penalty.'

Round the corner Alesi still came and led, Häkkinen close, Senna close on Häkkinen, Prost a distance back with Schumacher close to him but that first lap he demonstrated the purity of his thought-processes. Alesi stretched the lead, but so what? You couldn't imagine a Ferrari lasting the full seventy-one laps. Häkkinen and Senna rode in tandem, but so what? You couldn't imagine Häkkinen going the full seventy-one laps like that. Schumacher swarmed, but so what? Prost had him behind. It left Senna, who didn't have Renault power and at some stage would be vulnerable.

Prost permitted the race to unfold without materially trying to disturb the process because it was a vast distance to go.

Senna went past Hakkinen into second place and this order – Alesi, Senna, Häkkinen, Prost, Schumacher – endured to lap 19, just before the pit stops for tyres, when Senna's engine let go. Hill, coming through the field at extraordinary pace, was seventh but so what? Alesi, Häkkinen and Schumacher pitted. Prost stayed out and set fastest lap so that at lap 23:

Prost	30m 26.8s
Hill	@ 15.1s
Schumacher	@ 19.9s
Alesi	@ 24.5s
Häkkinen	@ 24.8s

Soon Schumacher would catch Hill but Hill had the power of Renault and that might keep Schumacher behind while Prost drew far enough away to pit and resume in the lead. The balance of the race became delicate because Prost led by twenty seconds but needed more and didn't get it. When he pitted it was 20.5. He was stationary for 6.6 seconds, coming out behind Schumacher in the lead. Hill pitted next lap and that put him back to fifth.

Häkkinen ran wide on the loop to the start-finish straight, the McLaren clipping the Armco and battering against it. It was one car less for Prost to weigh in the equation. Schumacher accelerated and a gap to Prost came up, 5.2 seconds. Prost responded with a new fastest lap. 'For a long time I thought Michael would be stopping for another set of tyres because he had made his first stop so early. When I realized he wasn't going to I pushed hard.'

Alesi needed a further stop on lap 44 and that was another car less to weigh in the equation. Prost and Hill traded more fastest laps, altering the balance of the race again. Could Hill catch Prost? He was twenty-three seconds away but 'I kept pressing on and I was really enjoying myself.'

Schumacher, normally so aggressive in traffic, wasn't and Prost drew up to less than a couple of seconds. 'I knew Senna,' Prost would say, 'was out and Damon was behind me. Overtaking is not easy at this circuit and if I'd gone off while I was trying to take the lead I can imagine what everyone would have said. Still, I went for it sometimes but Michael weaved a little bit and I said OK. I understood.'

Hill set fastest lap again. At 53 laps:

Schumacher	1hr 09m 46.0s
Prost	@ 0.9s
Hill	@ 10.7s

Prost clung to Schumacher, sometimes close, sometimes allowing a small gap, taking minimal risk but allowing Schumacher no room for error. Le Professeur was doing what he had always done, balancing all the factors logically. Five laps remained and although Hill did another hot lap he ran eight seconds behind Prost. It was too late now.

Into the last lap Prost made his final gesture, tried at a right-hander but Schumacher didn't deviate. Crossing the line 0.9 seconds behind Schumacher, Prost had lifted himself above Brabham, Stewart, Lauda, Piquet and Senna. Only Fangio remained in front, as he always would.

Prost stopped on the slowing down lap and someone pressed a tricolore into his hand.

As he and Schumacher walked towards the podium Schumacher, bottle of mineral water in hand, hesitated so Prost could catch him up. Prost patted him on the back and they made a joke. About overtaking? The rest dissolved into the waterfall of champagne on the podium, the endless interviews and lovely chewing of the English vowels we had heard so often and liked so much.

After Adelaide, it would be no more.

1994

SCHUMACHER CRASHES IN

Australian Grand Prix, Adelaide

It was the same as any road crash. If he'd been a little quicker or a little slower he'd have missed it. On a warm, dry, sunny afternoon in the genteel city of Adelaide, Damon Hill didn't. He arrived right in the middle and saw, like a terrible vision, the underbelly of the car he'd been chasing as it went past him in the air, landed and skewed headlong into a barrier.

Of all the crashes in Showdown races this surely was the most spectacular.

Senna duly joined Williams to partner Hill and was expected to romp the season but in Brazil he spun off and at Aida, Japan, crashed at the start. Yes, if he'd been a little quicker or a little slower he'd have missed it – but he didn't. Schumacher won both. They came to Imola for the San Marino Grand Prix, the pressure on Senna. On the Saturday a newcomer called Roland Ratzenberger (Simtek) crashed fatally. That seemed to set a murderous feel to the weekend. During the race Senna, leading, went into the wall at Tamburello and for a whole generation motor racing would never be the same again.

Certain shadows will always lie across Grand Prix racing, Rindt and Clark, Bruce McLaren and Gilles Villeneuve, but this one was as deep as any and deeper than most.

This book is no place to examine Senna's immense legacy, no place to dissect how the other drivers reacted to his death, or their self-questioning, or how the season limped forward from Imola, regrouping. Suffice it to say that Schumacher and Benetton endured a variety of setbacks, Schumacher banned for his driving, Benetton punished for alleged illegalities while Hill became the Williams Number 1, obliged to assume Senna's role and obliged to take

Schumacher on. Hill achieved this well enough and they came to Adelaide separated by one point – Schumacher 92, Hill 91.

The build-up was bizarre. Schumacher had already verbally criticised Hill by saying he wasn't really a Number 1 driver and 'he has not been very helpful when I was in big trouble.' Schumacher even suggested he did not respect Hill. To this, Hill responded with dignity, saying he didn't want to 'drag the championship down' and for too long drivers going for championships 'seemed to hate each other's guts.'

Meanwhile Hill was still negotiating with the Williams team over his retainer for 1995 – rumours implied Hill wasn't well paid – and mentioned this to a journalist, who wrote the story. Patrick Head, the Williams designer, said that Hill was 'having a whine and a whinge' and if he – Head – had $100,000 he'd put it on Schumacher to win. He insisted this was not meant to 'undermine' Hill but it seemed an odd thing to say in the circumstances.

After Japan – a wet race which Hill had won from Schumacher – Hill flew to Brisbane and spent time with former World Champion bike rider Barry Sheene at Sheene's home at Surfers' Paradise. Arriving in Adelaide, Hill found that a Press Conference had been organised at the airport. During it he made 'few pointed remarks' about the financial negotiations and proceeded to the circuit, where he found Frank Williams 'pretty unhappy' that all this had been made public. Hill felt pretty unhappy himself.

He might have felt unhappy about another aspect. After Senna's death Renault evidently felt they needed a proven race winner to take on Schumacher and the Benetton's Ford engine. They reached for Mansell to 'guest' for Williams in races which didn't clash with his IndyCar programme – so far France, the European Grand Prix at Jerez and Japan. Schumacher had regularly outdriven Hill and only the fact that he'd been disqualified twice and missed two races because of suspension kept the championship alive. What would Mansell do at Adelaide? Prove he could still beat them all or help Hill? Mansell told Hill quietly that he would be helping him, an aspect which assumed even more importance because Mansell took pole from Schumacher, Hill on the second row.

How would Mansell handle this? He could scarcely help Hill by leading the Australian Grand Prix if Schumacher was behind him and Hill behind Schumacher, and anyway Mansell's room for manoeuvre would have to be limited by the constrictions of a street circuit.

The Williams team decided on a three-stop strategy – mandatory refuelling during races had been introduced at the start of the season – and believed Benetton would be doing that, too.

Hill felt so relaxed it began to worry him. Between the Sunday morning warm-up and the race he spent twenty minutes in a quiet corner of the pit. He lay and, eyes closed, kept the relaxation. Then he had a massage. Once in the car he felt the adrenaline begin to flow but curiously not as much as he'd felt it on other, less important occasions. Grid:

Mansell	Schumacher
Hill	Häkkinen

The shape of the race was settled in the instants after the green light. Mansell had wheelspin allowing Schumacher past on the right and Hill on the left. Hill had constructed a 'mental picture' of outgunning Schumacher from the green light and angling right to the racing line for the chicane at the end of the start-finish straight because he knew Mansell wouldn't move over on him. Now Hill found himself trapped far to the left, Mansell mid-track, and Hill had to back off at the mouth of the chicane to avoid Schumacher, who had a clear track and maximized that.

Crossing the line to complete lap 1 he'd opened a two second lead and increased it for half a lap more. Then Hill found his proper running pace and set fastest lap so that, crossing the line, 3/10ths separated them. Schumacher forced the gap to two seconds again and Hill reduced it again. This was the shape. Hill glanced in his mirrors and couldn't see Mansell. He was alone against Schumacher. They were among back-markers by lap 11, Schumacher famed for his ruthlessness with them. Hill determined to be as ruthless: he dare not let Schumacher get away. Once Hill locked brakes and thought instantly *if I hit the rear of the Benetton I must try and hit it with my nosecone, I mustn't damage my wings*. He missed.

They both pitted on lap 18 and Hill has described the desperate frustration of having to go down the pit lane at the mandatory 50mph (80kmh), how long the stop felt and how he nursed a hope of getting out ahead. He didn't. They circled again and Hill faced the same problem: finding a place to make a move, getting close enough to make it. Neither was ever easy at Adelaide.

He matched Schumacher for pace and felt the pressure was reaching Schumacher. On lap 23 he pushed so hard he was (briefly) off the track, brakes locked again. He told himself *calm it, drive smoothly* and got to work bringing the gap down.

On lap 36 they travelled along Westfield Road towards a sequence of three corners: a 90-degree right, a tiny straight, a 90-degree left, a tiny straight, a 90-degree right. Hill was two seconds behind Schumacher. Schumacher went through the first right but – Hill too far away to see – lost control in the left. The Benetton crossed a wedge of grass and battered the wall. A bump on the track caused it, Schumacher said.

Hill did see Schumacher returning towards the track across the grass. He could have no idea what had happened or if the Benetton might be damaged, certainly no way of knowing that its steering had been damaged. If he'd known he'd have braked, waited, kept good and clear, let Schumacher retire.

The Benetton regained the track diagonally. Instantaneously Hill thought Schumacher would go to the right to have the racing line for the next 90-degree right-hander, so Hill went left to go round him but Schumacher came left. Hill ploughed the brakes, saw the gap to the right and flicked the car out towards it. He thought Schumacher was too wide to be able to turn onto the racing line himself and anyway Hill had to try it. This might be the only chance he'd get. He'd write in his book *Grand Prix Year* (Macmillan) that Schumacher came across 'very acutely' and 'I was pretty sure he knew where I was.'

Schumacher would say 'I went to turn into the corner and suddenly I saw Damon next to me.'

Hill even put wheels onto the kerb in a final attempt to create more space for Schumacher. They crashed. 'I drove over his front wheel,' Schumacher said, 'and I went up in the air. I was afraid because I thought I was going to roll over but the car came back.' It pumped the barrier and Schumacher watched Hill drive on. 'That was the worst moment.' Hill drove to the pits. He'd noticed damage to his suspension and could feel how awkward the car now handled. The mechanics confirmed it was all over. Schumacher, watching from behind the barrier, waited in great suspense for Hill to come round again and continue to the championship. Schumacher saw a Williams – Mansell. He heard the track commentator saying over the loudspeakers that Hill had a problem. He watched Mansell pass again and only then thought that's it. He was World Champion.

At the televised Press Conference Schumacher apologized for what he'd said about Hill and did so again more privately the next morning. Excited newspaper reporters tried to insinuate that Schumacher knew his Benetton was crippled and took Hill out. Experts raked over replays, drawing many differing conclusions. If you watch again, you see that Schumacher could mount the perfect defence. There wasn't room enough for two cars in Turn 4 and two cars reached it at the same time – in the revered phrase, a motor racing accident.

Was it?

Only Michael Schumacher knows and he's not saying.

1995

TWO ANGRY MEN

Pacific Grand Prix, Aida

They'd argued on the track and they'd argued off it. People wondered what they really thought about each other and the mystery gave the rivalry a real edge. The truth only emerged much later. They barely knew each other, had barely ever exchanged a word except about what the rivalry produced day after day, week after week all season long.

Early, the season resolved itself into comparative simplicity, Schumacher clear favourite to retain the championship and Hill the only man to prevent him. Johnny Herbert, partnering Schumacher, couldn't get on the pace and initially David Coulthard, partnering Hill, couldn't either. Alesi and Berger in the Ferraris were nearing the pace but rarely on it.

So Schumacher and Hill replayed 1994. They'd crash – at Silverstone, at Monza – and that increased the edge but by the fourteenth round, the European at the new Nürburgring, Schumacher had won six times. Instead of playing safe for second place behind Alesi and six more points (Hill had spun off) he stabbed past Alesi, risking all – and won.

Three rounds remained and he needed only three points whatever Hill did. A formality? You never know.

Hill faced a problem of his own. Coulthard, by now competitive and building his own career, was leaving to join McLaren and, as we have seen, Frank Williams actively disliked giving team orders, anyway. Hill meanwhile publicly conceded the championship and said he would be working towards 1996. Coulthard said, equally publicly, that he found such an attitude hard to understand.

Aida was a very curious place, a typically modern track lost in the middle of mountainous Japan and neutered (or 'technical' in the modern jargon). Very likely Giuseppe Farina wouldn't have realized it was a Grand Prix track unless someone told him... Aida was remote enough for there to be nothing to do except drive racing cars and the hours hung heavy. Drivers were so bored they wanted to give interviews, something rarely witnessed before or since.

With the season's incidents and crashes fresh in memory, Hill reasonably asked the governing body for clarification of the rules on overtaking but the best the FIA could do was 'drivers are free to drive as they wish, provided they do not deliberately endanger another driver or repeatedly obstruct him on the straight.' Hill would remember the wording exactly.

In qualifying the Williamses proved quicker than Schumacher, as they had so often, and they filled the front row, Schumacher and Alesi on the second. Hill knew exactly what he had to do: win, and win at the Japanese Grand Prix, Suzuka, and win in Adelaide.

At the green light Coulthard, pole, led into the first corner, a right. Hill and Schumacher were abreast but Hill on the inside. Schumacher tried to go round him on the little spurt to the next corner, another right. Hill moved over to block him: muscular, perhaps previously unethical but scarcely dangerous. Hill believed he was acting within the FIA ruling. It created, however, enough space on the inside for Alesi to steal past Hill and Berger to steal past Schumacher.

Schumacher insisted Hill was 'so concerned about looking for me that we lost two places to the Ferraris. I didn't have a particular problem but if he had got on the throttle a little earlier we would have kept our positions and I still wouldn't have been able to overtake him.'

Hill insisted 'I tried to make sure it was difficult for him to overtake. A Ferrari [Alesi] slipped up the inside.'

The order – Coulthard, Alesi, Hill, Berger, Schumacher – produced an immediate thought: on such a track even Schumacher cannot win from fifth, especially not with Coulthard already pulling strongly away and the quartet of pursuers running in a train, any overtaking problematical. Naturally Hill harried Alesi and naturally Schumacher harried Berger but the train continued. On lap 5, however, Schumacher solved the overtaking problem. He thrust out into a right and passed Berger, taking fourth place and the championship if he stayed there. At that moment Hill was in a vice. Alesi was holding him up, Coulthard kept on pulling strongly away – making the necessary victory more and more remote – and Schumacher was arriving behind. Crossing the line into lap 6, the gaps to Coulthard:

Alesi	@ 8.4s
Hill	@ 9.1s
Schumacher	@ 10.9s

Schumacher arrived quickly but the problem of overtaking Hill might be more difficult to solve because Hill had a championship to try and win, however improbable.

Travelling along the back straight on lap 11 Hill moved to mid-track to block Schumacher, locked wheels as he went into the right-hander at the end of the straight and forced Schumacher aside.

'It's a personal thing between him and me,' Schumacher said.

'You're allowed to change lines more than once on the straight,' Hill said, 'so he had to go to the left and he was upset that, somehow or other, when we went into the braking area I did something wrong but I can't see how I did anything wrong. It's like one rule for him and another rule for everyone else sometimes. I just think that either you allow that sort of thing and there should be no complaints or you have rules and stick to them.'

Once through the corner, Schumacher radioed the pits 'Hill is trying to drive me off the road.' The pits reportedly responded 'what do you expect, Michael?'

At lap 18 the train pulled into the pits for the initial tyre and fuel stops. Coulthard stayed out, following his new strategy of two stops, not three. The Benetton team, famed for precision and speed, sent Schumacher on his way in 6.3 seconds and Ferrari took slightly longer for Alesi but Hill was stationary for 12.2 – a problem with the refuelling rig. Schumacher regained the track ahead of Alesi, Hill eighth. The odds against Hill lengthened towards infinity.

Schumacher didn't need to show the slightest interest in catching Coulthard with the vice holding Hill so tight. Hill had some overtaking to do just to reach Alesi. So a safe, unhurried second place? Schumacher did not think like that. Coulthard led by thirty-seven seconds but hadn't stopped yet. Schumacher set fastest lap and cut the gap to thirty-three. Coulthard pitted on lap 25 and under the logistics of the two-stop strategy he had to be stationary for 11.3 seconds to take on enough fuel. Although he kept the lead, Schumacher lurked (the gap 7.5 seconds), Alesi third, Hill now up to fourth but virtually half a minute down. Worse, Hill tapped Eddie Irvine (Jordan) in a corner and the Williams sustained light damage.

Schumacher caught Coulthard 'but he was going too quickly for me to pass him. However, I knew that I was going to make another stop soon. Before the race we hadn't made a firm decision about two stops or three. We wanted to see how it developed.' The decision: three. Schumacher pitted on lap 38 – stationary for 9.1 – and retained second place. The team fitted used tyres, keeping his final set of fresh ones for the third stop and the final assault. At 40 laps Schumacher circled 18.1 seconds behind Coulthard but he set a new fastest lap and picked up a second a lap. The race was ebbing from Coulthard who, inescapably, would have to stop sooner than Schumacher for fuel. The two-stop logistics demanded it. Equally inevitably, that would pass the lead to Schumacher, who would maximize the advantage by going faster and faster to protect his own third stop.

With forty laps to go Coulthard led by almost sixteen seconds. Schumacher cut the gap to 14.5 seconds, cut it again on lap 46 to 13.7 and set another new fastest lap. On lap 50 Coulthard reached the struggle for sixth place between Herbert, Irvine and Frentzen, the gap 11.98. He lost more and more time waiting to overtake, and shook his fist at Frentzen. As the Williams crew prepared for Coulthard's stop, the gap was 8.7 seconds. Coulthard pitted and emerged fourteen seconds behind Schumacher.

Coulthard had to gain on Schumacher before Schumacher's final stop but he found himself in traffic again and by lap 55 the gap extended to 20.3 seconds. Schumacher needed more than that to retain the lead, increased his pace and when he peeled into the pit lane had it out to nearly twenty-two seconds.

It was enough.

He crossed the line to become the youngest double-champion in history. When it was done Hill went to Schumacher in the parc fermé to congratulate him but Schumacher took issue over the incident at the hairpin. They proceeded to the unilateral television interviews. Schumacher spoke predictably enough, discussing the incident at the start and pointing out that Hill had destroyed his (Hill's) own race by letting Alesi through.

The television interviews over, Schumacher exchanged strong words with Hill in the corner of the room. Fuji TV was still filming but were asked to erase it. Schumacher and Hill proceeded to the written media Press Conference at which Hill asked 'why don't you tell them what you just told me upstairs?' and added 'Michael has told me he is unhappy with my driving. Well, I drove in the style we have just been advised [we can] and he didn't like it. Michael didn't complain publicly so perhaps it's wrong for me to raise the matter, but I don't see how he could possibly object to anything I did on the circuit considering what has passed between us this season. I find it incredible. It seems total hypocrisy to me.'

Later Schumacher said he intended to have a talk with Hill 'when everything has settled down.'

The problem of course is that if everything ever did settle down we wouldn't have Grand Prix racing.

One postscript.

Schumacher had become the youngest double champion at the age of 26, specifically: Ascari 35, Graham Hill 39, Clark 29 and Fittipaldi 27 when they'd done it. The ages of those who went on to a third title were, at their second: Brabham 34, Stewart 32, Lauda 28, Piquet 31, Senna 30 while Prost was 31 and Fangio 43. On the evening of 22 October 1995 nobody knew if Schumacher would win another title, of course, not least because each is so precious and often so difficult. Twelve drivers had only one and if Ascari, Hill, Clark and Fittipaldi couldn't get past two what chance had Schumacher? More than that he was leaving Benetton for the dangerous, darkened waters of Ferrari – and Ferrari hadn't had a champion since Scheckter in 1979. There seemed no compelling reason why they should ever have a champion again.

For Schumacher, championships might just be a memory now and probably were.

1996

THE SON IN HIS OWN RIGHT

Japanese Grand Prix, Suzuka

At one level the similarities were so precise that they had a haunting, haunted feel to them.

Jim Clark, greatest driver of his generation, died when his Lotus left the Hockenheim track and hit a tree with terrible force in a Formula 2 race. His team-mate Graham Hill became, amid the grief, the main weight-carrier at the Spanish Grand Prix five days later.

Ayrton Senna, greatest driver of his generation, died when his Williams left the Imola track and hit the wall. His team-mate Damon Hill became, amid the grief, the main weight-carrier at Monaco fourteen days later.

At another level the similarities were not precise. In the spring of 1968, when Clark crashed, Graham Hill was of course a former World Champion (1962) and pillar of the whole sport. In the spring of 1994, when Senna crashed, Damon Hill was thirty-four and had driven a mere twenty-one races. He'd come to it late after long struggles – when Graham himself died in a plane crash in 1975 he left the family in straitened circumstances. Damon test drove for Williams while he raced a desperately uncompetitive Brabham, obediently partnered Prost at Williams in 1993 and – as 1994 began to unfold – iconic, immense Senna was suddenly gone.

Hill was very much alone and only he truly knows how much the weight weighed. He carried the eternal comparison with his father and now he had to replace Senna. That he emerged from this by taking Schumacher to the final race of the season in the 1994 championship, and became the only man who could seriously challenge him in 1995, remains a feat of considerable courage, resource and fast learning. The Williams was a superb car and in a strange way people attributed his success to that, without adding that almost without exception since 1950 the winners had had the best cars. This may be because Hill was no extrovert – and carried that eternal comparison with his father – but, rather, presented himself as a diffident Englishman who, one suspected, was highly uncomfortable with Formula 1's daily diet of politics, accusations, crashes and controversies.

In 1996 he might even be able to avoid them because, as we have just seen, Schumacher had gone to Ferrari and would need time, perhaps a lot of it, to make an impact there.

There was, however, a further haunting if that word isn't being stretched a bit. Coulthard had gone to partner Häkkinen at McLaren, bringing Jacques Villeneuve, the reigning IndyCar champion, to partner Hill.

Villeneuve carried his own burden because his father Gilles, the fastest driver of his generation and in his time as iconic as Senna, crashed and died during qualifying at Zolder in 1982. Jacques had had to live with the same comparison as Hill and in a more acute form because, when he'd been racing Formula 3 in Italy, people wanted him to be his father reincarnated. At least nobody had demanded that of Hill.

The tone of the season was set at Melbourne in March when Hill won from Villeneuve, adding Brazil and Argentina. By Canada, the mid-point, he had 53 points, Villeneuve 32 and Schumacher 26. Villeneuve, fast-learning himself, was getting stronger and stronger but, into the final race at Suzuka, all Hill needed was sixth place.

There was a curious background. In the autumn Williams had told Hill they would not be re-signing him and were taking Heinz-Harald Frentzen instead. All Frank Williams revealed was that it wasn't about money. Hill signed with the Arrows team for 1997.

At Suzuka, Villeneuve took pole from Hill, who expressed satisfaction. 'I had to wait for a clear lap [just before the end]. I did what I wanted to do, which was to get the car on the front row. Everything's going very well and now I've got a very good opportunity to beat Jacques into the first corner. The best form of defence is attack.'

That might have suggested a re-run of the Senna-Prost debacle in 1990 but Hill wasn't like that. Nor had he any need to be. Coulthard couldn't move from the grid and the start was aborted. The re-start spread the championship before Hill: away really fast, Villeneuve – wheels spinning, the car lurching sideways – swamped by Berger in the Benetton, then it was Häkkinen in the McLaren, Schumacher and Irvine in the Ferraris. Completing the lap Villeneuve, sixth, was already 3.9 seconds slower than Hill.

'I said I wanted to get ahead,' Hill would explain, 'and that was the best way to the championship. Once I was in front I was determined to stay there.'

Villeneuve had another fifty-one laps.

On lap 4 Berger, who bent the front of his car attacking Hill, drifted back – Villeneuve fifth but Hill feasting on a clear track. That fourth lap Villeneuve was 5.8 seconds away with, of course, Häkkinen, Schumacher and Irvine in between.

On lap 12 Villeneuve, who'd caught Irvine and was pressuring him, outbraked him into the chicane but he was now 8.9 seconds from Hill. More immediately, Villeneuve had Schumacher 1.6 seconds ahead – and Villeneuve had just set fastest lap. Villeneuve couldn't get closer by the first pit stops. Order when they resumed:

Hill, Schumacher, Häkkinen, Villeneuve.

They ran there to the second pit stops, Villeneuve stationary longer than the others because his front wing required adjustment. That let Berger by so that they resumed:

Hill, Schumacher, Häkkinen, Berger, Villeneuve.

Villeneuve would not cede it. He set a new fastest lap on lap 34 but a couple of laps later the Williams began to feel unstable. He imagined he might have a puncture. He hadn't. The right rear wheel was working loose and he radioed that to the pits. The on-board camera caught how delicately Villeneuve was manipulating the car into Turn 1 and then, from nowehere, the wheel bounded past the car deep into the run-off area. Villeneuve did not think *the championship is lost*, he thought *that wheel is going into the crowd and might kill somebody.*

Whatever, Damon Hill was World Champion.

Villeneuve waved to the crowd and, clutching his helmet, marched off at military speed.

Hill was told by radio and 'it was almost too much to take in while I was driving. It was quite hard to concentrate when I heard Jacques was out but then I told myself to get on with it, win the race for Williams on my last drive for the team. I wanted to win the race.'

That is what he did. On his second last lap he flung the Williams over towards the pit lane wall and the mechanics the way winners in the modern era invariably did. Had he miscounted the laps? No, he was just rehearsing, just warming the mechanics up for the big finish.

As the mechanics scaled the wall, Hill's wife Georgie was there at the front, peeking over onto the track and grinning from ear to ear. Hill gave her and everybody else the fly past and, almost unnoticed, Schumacher drew alongside, waved his congratulations, accelerated away. By then Hill had both his hands out of the cockpit punching the air, waving, punching the air, waving. Georgie held up a white board

DAMON
WORLD
CHAMPION
1996

No father and son had won the championship before.

Georgie made her way to the parc fermé and when Hill was out of the car he went to her. They embraced for a long, long moment – so intense that anybody watching felt a voyeur – and then he went off for the weigh-in. On the podium Häkkinen enthusiastically applauded Hill who breathed deeply and seemed, for a moment, to be seeing something far away.

Georgie said 'everything we have been working for over the last fifteen years has come together today.'

Hill described the championship and all its demands over seven months as an 'agonising thing.' The agony was over and he never went through it again: the season with Arrows and a couple of seasons with Jordan represented decline towards retirement.

Two postscripts, however.

Graham Hill drove 176 Grands Prix for thirteen pole positions and fourteen wins. Damon Hill drove 115 Grands Prix for twenty pole positions and twenty-two wins. Which was the better driver?

In 2006, Hill – once a despatch rider and unregarded driver in lesser formulae, career going nowhere at all – became President of the British Racing Drivers' Club.

The son had risen.

1997

THE OTHER SON ALSO RISES

European Grand Prix, Jerez

Seventeen rounds and completing the sixteenth of them, Suzuka, Jacques Villeneuve had 79 points and Schumacher 78. Since all results counted, whoever finished in front of the other at the final race, the European at Jerez, became champion. Easy? You know it isn't like that...

Villeneuve had been given a one-race ban suspended for nine races – itself not easy to understand – at Monza, round thirteen, when he had failed to slow under yellow flags in the race warm-up. Villeneuve responded by winning in Austria and Luxembourg so that he had 77 points and Schumacher 68.

Schumacher responded to that by winning Suzuka, Villeneuve fifth but he'd been excluded from the race for ignoring yellow flags again, this time in Saturday free practice. Williams appealed, getting Villeneuve into the race but the FIA's Court of Appeal would give a final ruling some time afterwards. They did. They stripped Villeneuve of his 2 points so that he went to Jerez with 77. That tilted the situation because, now, all Schumacher had to do was finish anywhere in front of him and, if neither finished, Schumacher had it anyway. Easy? You know it really isn't like that...

Actually, if Villeneuve was third, fourth or fifth and Schumacher a place behind, they finished equal on points but Villeneuve took the championship on the most wins tie-break.

Jacques Villeneuve was a most interesting man. He had a wide range of interests from music to technology, he was very international (Canadian by birth, Monaco by upbringing, Swiss by education) and long ago had come to terms with being the son of Gilles in much the same way that Damon had come to terms with being the son of

Graham. There was nothing you could do except to live your life as yourself and, whenever questioned, make polite responses. Jacques Villeneuve was a racer with a bit of devilment and a bit of daring about him who was not afraid to speak his mind, either.

After the Saturday morning practice session at Jerez, Irvine discovered this. Villeneuve journeyed from his Williams to where Irvine sat in his Ferrari and, theatrically as well as verbally, accused him of deliberately blocking. *You're behaving like an idiot*, Villeneuve said, adding: 'We all know he is a clown.'

Irvine, a most interesting man in his own right – Senna once tried to physically attack him, which Irvine thought amusing – had said he would help Schumacher in any legal way he could. Now, Irvine murmured that Villeneuve was always talking like that and so what?

Nobody had ever seen a qualifying session like Jerez. These days the word 'unbelievable' is attached to almost anything, including a huge number of things which are eminently believable, but round the parched circuit in Andalucia the word became entirely authentic. We need this to three decimal points.

After a quarter of an hour Villeneuve went out and attacked. He did a lap of 1m 21.072s, which maybe would survive the coming onslaught to be pole.

Schumacher waited a quarter of an hour and launched his counter-attack, faster through sections one and two, dropping a fraction thereafter. He did a lap of 1m 21.072s and the odds against were so long it produced consternation.

Some ten minutes remained when Frentzen, Villeneuve's team-mate, attacked, too. It was a strong, hard lap of … 1m 21.072s. The odds against this thrice were beyond computing (if anything these days is truly beyond computing) and the grid had to be decided chronologically: the order in which the laps had been driven. Villeneuve's time had survived to be pole, then Schumacher, then Frentzen – Irvine seventh.

On race day shadows fell across the track and when the mechanics migrated in their herds from the grid and the cars came round from the parade lap Villeneuve moved towards mid-track but Schumacher was on the power faster. As they moved towards the right-hander

Curva Expo he led. Frentzen even flirted with a move on Villeneuve – who seemed to let him through. Schumacher stroked the Ferrari away from the Williamses and completed the opening lap 1.9 seconds before Frentzen, 3.2 before Villeneuve.

It was stunning.

The gaps became 2.2 and 3.2 at the end of the second lap. At least Villeneuve was holding Schumacher's pace. It went like that until lap 8 when Frentzen gracefully let Villeneuve by, Schumacher 4.3 seconds ahead, and they traded fastest laps as they moved towards the pit stops. It settled again after them with Schumacher still leading, Villeneuve still pursuing. They ran to the second stops, Villeneuve forcing the Williams so hard that at lap 39 he'd cut the gap to 1.04 seconds. Schumacher was stationary for 9.4 seconds, meaning he had taken on enough fuel to reach the end of the race. One lap after that Villeneuve came in, was stationary for 8.3 seconds – he'd enough fuel, too.

By purest ill-luck Villeneuve emerged from the pits just as Coulthard's McLaren was passing. Villeneuve had to follow for a whole lap until Coulthard pitted and the gap widened to 2.5 seconds.

Villeneuve went for it – 'hard after Michael,' as he'd say. His tyres determined the tactics because they should be good enough to sustain an attack and overtaking move for maybe three laps before they'd go off. Villeneuve had very little time to make himself champion.

Into lap 48 of the 69 he'd forced the gap down to 0.3 seconds and was on Schumacher. The crucial moment was at hand. He harried Schumacher through Curva Expo, clung through a right and a left, drew up squeezing through the next right. They were on the long, descending straight to the right-hander called Dry Sack. They were both over on the left as the mouth of the corner opened to them. Villeneuve estimated he was some ten to fifteen yards behind the Ferrari and 'I just went for it. I think the move surprised him.' Villeneuve concluded *I caught him out*.

He angled the Williams to mid-track. Schumacher's head turned to his wing mirror and he saw where Villeneuve was coming. Villeneuve saw Schumacher look in the mirror 'and I was way behind him and suddenly I was ahead of him.'

Under braking, both cars trembled, no doubt because the surface doesn't seem to have been perfectly level. By then Villeneuve was almost abreast and had reached mid-track. Still the cars trembled.

Villeneuve led by half the length of the Ferrari as he reached the very beginning of the corner, Schumacher holding the Ferrari at the same angle but three feet away. Villeneuve was hemmed so tight that fleetingly he put two wheels on the grass beyond the white line marking the corner. 'I couldn't go any more to the inside: I was already on the grass.' Suddenly Schumacher turned into the Williams.

The Ferrari's right front wheel hoofed the Williams just where Villeneuve was sitting. Laconically, Villeneuve would recount that – however shocking the instant seemed to millions watching on television all round the world – it 'wasn't really a surprise. Actually I was surprised that he left the door open but once I was inside him it was just a matter of time before he decided to turn in on me. I expected he'd do that so I knew I was taking a big risk. We banged wheels and I really thought I'd broken the car. I knew he was out right away.'

Schumacher was on the brakes, digging smoke, but the Ferrari ebbed onto the rim of a great gravel trap and sank there, wheels spinning furiously but going nowhere.

Villeneuve kept on.

Schumacher got out, walked to a low wall, climbed it and spectated. It made for a strange, haunting image: a man alone with the track to his left, an arid, stone-strewn slope to his right and what appeared to be a metal drum in front of him, seemingly being used for litter and painted day-glo blue. Eventually he got a lift back to the pits on a scooter, and still Villeneuve kept on. He had no interest in holding up Häkkinen and gave him the lead, no interest in holding up Coulthard and gave him second place. Third, fourth, fifth or even sixth would have been enough. Sixth would have brought him equal on points, 78 each, but Villeneuve getting it 7-5 on the wins.

Schumacher seems to have suffered as much introspection as he ever did in all his career. He started with a robust self-defence, claiming that what Villeneuve had done was 'optimistic,' adding: 'I was very surprised by what he did.' Later the self-defence became defensive. 'I made an error. I'm a human, not a machine.'

The FIA's World Motorsports Council stripped him of his second place in the championship although Max Mosley, president of the FIA, said they judged Schumacher's move instinctive, not pre-meditated.

Schumacher himself insisted it had been instinctive and said for three nights after the race the matter had preyed upon him so heavily that he couldn't sleep.

Villeneuve, of course, had no such problems. 'The championship feels great.'

1998

JUST MIKA

Japanese Grand Prix, Suzuka

Mika Häkkinen was so softly spoken and so properly behaved that you'd have missed him in a bus queue. He had a perceptive, naughty sense of humour but unless you were a selected victim you'd have missed that, too. Of his generation he was the only driver able to go head-to-head with Schumacher without leaving a trail of arguments, accusations and physical debris behind them. As a consequence of the quietness you could define the 1998 championship – and 1999 – as the ones Schumacher lost rather than the ones Häkkinen won.

It's high time to correct that.

The season was a balance, in fact, between the strength of the McLaren, Häkkinen's ability to summon speed from it without making mistakes, and Schumacher's gathering power as he moved into his third Ferrari season.

They traded race wins in a great, intense struggle – so intense, so all-enveloping that only Häkkinen's team-mate Coulthard (San Marino) and Hill in the Jordan (Belgium) were able to break in and win a race for themselves. After the Luxembourg Grand Prix at the Nürburgring in late September, Häkkinen had 90 points and Schumacher 86. Since the sixteen rounds counted, all Häkkinen had to do was finish anywhere in front of Schumacher at Suzuka in the last race. There were other combinations, naturally, but they all loaded the pressure from Häkkinen to Schumacher.

Häkkinen was intuitively fast, always had been. As he said in his own cryptic way 'I don't take stress out of situations,' meaning he didn't let things worry him. If you allay this great mental strength with the speed, it was never going to be easy to beat.

His relaxed attitude could perplex and provoke team managers because other drivers had to work so hard to find it within themselves and he could just do it. Once upon a time West Surrey Racing, running him in British Formula 3, ventured to Hockenheim for a round of the German Championship (good publicity) and there encountered the same Schumacher. Häkkinen had not seen the circuit before and the car had an elusive misfire. He was not remotely concerned. He knew they'd cure the misfire and when they did he'd put it on pole, whatever the circuit was or wasn't.

| Häkkinen | 2m 08.3s |
| Schumacher | 2m 09.3s |

If a World Championship involves psychology, mind games and stress, anybody trying to apply them to Häkkinen was going to have a difficult time. He didn't respond.

Qualifying at Suzuka followed the season's tempo and character. Häkkinen struck early – after only five minutes – with a lap of 1m 37.0s, which was a full second and a half quicker than anybody else and 1.6 seconds faster than he'd done himself in the morning untimed session.

Schumacher murmured that he'd expected Mika to produce something like it and wasn't surprised. Towards the session's mid-point he angled the red Ferrari out and fashioned his response: a lap danced on the limit of the possible. 1m 36.7s. It looked impregnable.

Häkkinen wasn't heard to murmur anything before he fashioned his response to that: at the second split, 0.002 up before the fleeting seconds ebbed away. 1m 36.8s, a deficit of 0.086 over Suzuka's 3.6 miles.

Schumacher came out and danced again, the Ferrari engine propelling him through one speed trap at more than 196 miles an hour. 1m 36.2s. Someone described the lap as genuinely sensational. Schumacher had forced the gap out to 0.562 which, in the context of the 3.6 miles, is very difficult for ordinary people to imagine at all.

Häkkinen fashioned his reponse to that: 1m 36.4s and, in a final bid, adjusted the front of the car to reduce downforce and generate more speed. It was the intuitive speed he understood so well, the familiar place to be. He had more of it along the straight, he was slightly up through the sweeps behind the pits but, emerging from the Degner Curve, he went wide. His impetus carried him on to the grass.

Schumacher had pole, Häkkinen alongside.

On the grid Häkkinen quite naturally walked to Schumacher and shook his hand, and that caught the mood of the men. There really had been no trail of arguments, accusations and physical debris behind them and there wouldn't be now, either.

On a dry Suzuka afternoon – warm and sunny, as the description invariably goes – they came from the parade lap to the grid but, on the gantry above them, three yellow lights began flashing: start aborted. Jarno Trulli on the seventh row had stalled his Prost.

Schumacher led them into the second parade lap and they came from it to the grid again, Trulli now at the back. Schumacher settled, Häkkinen settled but pointing his McLaren towards mid-track. A klaxon sounded, shrill and echoing. On the pit lane wall a yellow flag fluttered urgently. Schumacher sat immobile, his right arm raised, the index finger pointing towards the sky. The engine was dead – second start aborted.

'The engine stalled because the clutch didn't free itself and I don't know why,' he'd say. Now he'd have to join Trulli at the back, the championship which had seemed so close a moment before now virtually dead.

Häkkinen led them into the third parade lap, Schumacher – static on the dummy grid while all the others flew by – eventually following. He had a single tactic now: full attack. If it failed, it failed. If it worked…

As the red lights released them Häkkinen led while Schumacher launched the full attack. Down the long, sloping start-finish he rammed the Ferrari between Trulli and Esteban Tuero's Minardi, Shinji Nakano's Minardi and Herbert's Sauber. He hammered it round Toranosuke Takagi's Tyrrell, hammered round Turn 1 at the end of the straight and went deep into the opening lap. He finished it twelfth but already 9.6 seconds from Häkkinen, no matter how many cars lay in between. That was the balance that would always be moving against Schumacher. He'd slice through the slower cars but then meet the faster one and that would take longer. Each moment

Häkkinen would be moving away, in his own time, knowing that Schumacher had to catch and overtake him.

On lap 2, Schumacher dealt bluntly with Olivier Panis in the Prost and Alesi in the Sauber, making him tenth. On lap 3 he outpowered Giancarlo Fisichella (Benetton), on lap 4 he sling-shot past Alexander Wurz in the other Benetton. On lap 5, he moved past his brother, who did not scamper out of the way. That made Schumacher seventh. He was now among the mid-field runners and, because of what he'd been making the Ferrari do, there would be an inevitable cost in tyre wear – under the imperative of the full attack he hadn't been able to worry about that. Any attempt to conserve tyres would take him further back from Häkkinen, who was sailing stately round unmolested by Irvine in second place.

Schumacher spent a frustrating period behind Hill (who had no incentive whatever to be civil) and Villeneuve, which meant the gap stretched to 18.6s. On lap 14 Hill pitted and Schumacher took Villeneuve on a power play at the hairpin but, as he caught Coulthard, he pitted. He emerged sixth and as others pitted rose to third by lap 22 – but twenty-six seconds from Häkkinen. Schumacher was going so fast he went clean across the chicane, grinding dust and stones, and kept on. He was locking wheels, churning smoke. The Ferrari looked right on the edge of control and still he maintained full attack.

Takagi and Tuero crashed on lap 29. It seems Schumacher picked up debris because down the start-finish straight the right rear tyre exploded at some 170 miles an hour. He guided the car on three wheels through the corner at the end and parked it on the grassy verge. He got out and levered himself onto a white wall, loosened the neck of his overalls, looked down.

Häkkinen was told on the radio by Ron Dennis that he was now World Champion and he did feel 'stress' for a moment or two. 'It was quite something to take in.' Dennis, pragmatic to the end, said that there was still a race to be won and there were still Constructors' Championship points to be garnered. Häkkinen responded like a professional, telling himself to calm down and not think about the championship. He won the race by 6.4 seconds from Irvine.

When Häkkinen brought the McLaren into the parc fermé Schumacher, now changed into jeans, was the first to reach him. He held his hand out and Häkkinen clasped it. Then, sensing who the moment really belonged to, Schumacher went quietly away.

Irvine congratulated him, Coulthard bear-hugged him, he bear-hugged Ron Dennis: no trail of debris but – just this once – a valley of smiles all the way through Formula 1. A lot of the old-timers would have appreciated that, and no doubt some did.

1999

JUST MIKA – AGAIN

Japanese Grand Prix, Suzuka

On the opening lap of the British Grand Prix at Silverstone, Schumacher's brakes failed and he went off into a tyre barrier carrying enough speed to break his leg. It was, in modern context, a severe crash – drivers habitually walked away from ravaged cars – but it was much, much more. Since 1996 Ferrari had of course concentrated their great effort, and a king's ransom, on Schumacher.

When he hit the tyre barrier the championship had been Häkkinen (McLaren) 40 points, Schumacher 32, team-mate Irvine 26 and Frentzen (Jordan) 23. Coulthard, partnering Häkkinen, won the race – Häkkinen had a wheel problem – from Irvine, Frentzen fourth.

What would Ferrari do? Schumacher was going to need some time for the leg to mend and in fact did not return until round fifteen of the sixteen in Malaysia. Häkkinen took 62 points to Malaysia, Irvine 60 and Frentzen 50.

Ferrari confronted the uncomfortable dilemma of trying to make Schumacher – one of the greatest of drivers and easily the best paid – offer Irvine obedient support to achieve the culmination of their great effort, and that on the back of three valiant seasons trying to get there himself. How would Schumacher react? Would he react? Would – fantastically – Ferrari prefer to risk waiting another year and have Schumacher do it rather than Irvine now because, if Irvine did it, what had they been paying the king's ransom to Schumacher for?

The man himself seemed ambivalent. At an early Suzuka Press Conference he used these words: 'I have said right from the start that I won't have to be a support to Eddie, but I will have to win the race to ensure the Constructors' Championship and in doing that I will be helping Eddie as much as possible.'

Irvine had 70 points, Häkkinen 66 and all results counting. It meant if Häkkinen won he went to 76 and the best Irvine could total would also be 76 – a dead heat, but Häkkinen taking it 5-4 on wins. If Irvine finished anywhere in front of Häkkinen, Ferrari had their champion at last. If Schumacher won from Häkkinen, Irvine third, Ferrari still had it (Häkkinen 72, Irvine 74).

Häkkinen did not need Schumacher to storm Suzuka.

In Friday free practice Häkkinen went quickest (1m 41.7s) from Coulthard (1m 41.8s), then Schumacher (1m 42.2s), Irvine tenth (1m 43.3s). Schumacher (1m 39.0s) reversed that in the Saturday free, Häkkinen next (1m 39.5s), Irvine twelfth (1m 40.6s).

It brought them to qualifying where Schumacher created an imperious lap of 1m 37.4s, ample for pole (Häkkinen 1m 37.8s to be on the front row next to him) but the story was Irvine, fifth (1m 38.9s), bumped there by Frentzen's 1m 38.6s.

Schumacher said again: 'I don't think my tactics will change. It is very clear that the best thing which can happen for us is if I win the race. I will give the most help I can for Eddie and the team. That will be the strategy.' He confirmed that he'd be helping Irvine with his car. 'We are a team and we will be working with each other very deeply in terms of set-up. Whatever information he wants he will have available. Obviously he has the Number 1 package, which is normal. All number one parts go to him and I am driving the second class ... if you can call it that, because to be honest we only have number one parts.'

Quietly, Schumacher did say that when you're 'fighting for the title' – as Irvine was – it changes everything. 'He is not getting into the circuit and a rhythm, for whatever reason.'

This was not exactly a resounding endorsement of Irvine's chances.

Häkkinen judged that the start was 'the key' – overtaking was surprisingly difficult at this circuit, despite its open appearance – and, because the start-finish straight sloped, the fact that he wasn't on pole didn't trouble him.

As the red lights went off Häkkinen moved away faster than Schumacher, who tried to get to mid-track to hold him but by then Häkkinen had gone. He scampered the McLaren into the curves behind the pits, Schumacher in his wake, Olivier Panis (Prost) inspired, then Irvine. They completed the lap:

Schumacher	@ 0.9s
Panis	@ 3.3s
Irvine	@ 4.2s
Coulthard	@ 4.5s

Irvine tried to attack Panis on lap 2 but couldn't and the gap went out to 6.0 seconds. In fact the first four remained in the same positions until the first pit stops, which began on lap 16 when Panis came in, and Häkkinen had been forcing the gap. Panis's stop lifted Irvine to third.

Nor could Schumacher do anything about Häkkinen except follow. Häkkinen pitted (stationary for 8.8 seconds), Schumacher three laps later (6.3). Coulthard's stop (7.1) was fast enough to relegate Irvine (7.1) to fourth. That was lap 23 of the 53, Irvine into a nightmare or, as Coulthard put it, 'I held up Eddie and I didn't like doing it.' This was the middle part of the race, Häkkinen and Schumacher trading fastest laps.

Irvine pitted a second time and now Coulthard went off, reshaping the nosecone. That liberated Irvine on lap 35 but it trapped Schumacher because after Coulthard's stop for a new nosecone he found Schumacher behind him and held him there for as long as legally possible under waved blue flags.

Häkkinen and Schumacher made second pit stops and, after them, fourteen laps remained. Häkkinen led by 9.6 seconds, Schumacher catching him meant, if he won, Irvine's third place would be enough for the championship.

Häkkinen brought everything down to a phrase – 'it was just a matter of not making any mistakes' – which reflected the man himself and keeping stress so firmly under control.

And when it was done, Irvine a lifetime away from the pace and the championship, there it was almost exactly a calendar year later – the valley of smiles all the way through Formula 1.

Two postscripts.

Ferrari won the Constructors' Championship, their first title for an astonishing 16 years. Who noticed? Well, Ferrari did. They had still not had a World Champion since Scheckter, Monza, 1979? Who noticed? Everybody ...

Only six drivers had won back-to-back championships: Ascari, Fangio, Brabham, Prost, Senna and Schumacher. Häkkinen was, as Schumacher said, a good man and a great champion. He was now in very, very good company.

2000

LOOKING BLOODY GOOD

Japanese Grand Prix, Suzuka

This was the fifth Schumacher season at Ferrari and, although a graph wouldn't show it conclusively, he had been moving towards giving them what they yearned for: a championship for the first time since 1979. In 1996 he'd been third, in 1997 second (and disqualified), in 1998 second, in 1999 fifth (the broken leg) and now here he was in 2000. He won the first three rounds but Häkkinen in the McLaren put together a strong mid season so that after Belgium, round thirteen, Häkkinen led 74-68 with team-mate Coulthard still in it on 61.

Schumacher won Monza from Häkkinen and won the United States Grand Prix at Indianapolis, Häkkinen halted by an engine problem. That gave Schumacher 88, Häkkinen 80 and Coulthard 63.

Two rounds remained, Japan and Malaysia.

If Schumacher won Japan he'd total 98 points. If Häkkinen finished second and won Malaysia he could only total 96.

Schumacher and Coulthard had had problems at Indianapolis where they rubbed wheels, which made Schumacher angry because he said Coulthard, with no chance in the championship, shouldn't have been doing that. Coulthard replied: 'I have a lot of respect for Michael. He has earned that because he is hard, aggressive and hungry in every condition, wet or dry. There are, however, enough indications that when Michael is desperate he is prepared to do something that people are likely to question as unsporting. He should push it to the limit but not beyond. I will do what I can to help the team, but I will do so within the rules and they would not ask me to go beyond that.'

An earthquake shook Japan on the Friday although its epicentre was a hundred miles away. It disturbed some buildings at Suzuka bad enough to make the people run outside although Schumacher, on the track at the time, didn't feel a thing.

They had preliminary skirmishes in the Friday free practice (Schumacher quickest, then Häkkinen, Barrichello and Coulthard) and the Saturday free (Häkkinen quickest from Schumacher and Barrichello, Coulthard sixth). Schumacher forecast the qualifying session would be tight. He was not wrong. 'We feel optimistic because we know that we have a very good car and if we get the maximum we know we can do it, but then that's the point: do we always get the maximum or not? And what about the other side?'

That other side – McLaren – sent Coulthard out early. Schumacher judged 'the circuit wasn't in good condition' yet and preferred to wait, watching Coulthard do a 1m 36.6s.

After twenty-five minutes Schumacher felt the track was coming to him and moved out into Suzuka's curves warming the tyres, composing himself, getting ready. As he went, Häkkinen brought the McLaren out...

Schumacher pitched the Ferrari into the fast lap and, when he reached the third timed sector, was decisively faster than Coulthard had been in it. At that instant Häkkinen was travelling through the first timed sector faster than Schumacher had gone. You need three decimal places to appreciate what was going on.

Schumacher   1m 36.094

The crowd waited and didn't have to wait long.

Häkkinen   1m 36.168

Advantage Schumacher, by 0.074 of a second. This was to be a duel of extraordinary intensity and ambition, mental as well as physical, and like great drama it built upon itself. Some twenty-one minutes of the session remained when Häkkinen came out again and, in the second timed sector, found 0.098 of a second.

Häkkinen   1m 36.017.

Advantage Häkkinen, by 0.077 of a second. Four minutes later Schumacher made his response.

Schumacher   1m 35.908.

Advantage Schumacher, by 0.109 of a second. Häkkinen sat in the McLaren studying a television monitor and when he saw what Schumacher had done he gesticulated. Six minutes later he went out and Schumacher sat watching a monitor. Häkkinen was fractionally slower in the first timed sector (0.043) and slower again in the second (0.025) but somehow somewhere in the third found a little more speed.

Häkkinen   1m 35.834.

Advantage Häkkinen, by 0.074 of a second. With some three and a half minutes left, tactician Ross Brawn had found a gap in the traffic and pitched Schumacher out into it. In the first sector he was 0.039 slower, in the second 0.012 quicker. He forced the Ferrari into the third and as he did that the prehensile snout of the McLaren was coming down the pit lane...

Schumacher   1m 35.825.

Advantage Schumacher, by 0.009 of a second. Häkkinen of the intuitive speed found 0.002 in the first timed sector but crucially lost 0.088 in the second.

Häkkinen   1m 36.018.

Schumacher had pole by the 0.009 over 3.6 miles, which is 5.8 kilometres. He seemed quieter than usual and somebody asked if that was true, adding: 'How much pressure are you under?'

'Naturally this is not a race like any other,' he answered. 'We can finish the championship here, but there is no point in celebrating this pole position big time. It's nice, but it isn't the end result. We will have to fight for that very hard tomorrow. We are ready.'

The weather forecast said rain might fall during the race.

From the lights Schumacher veered across towards Häkkinen who swerved towards the pit lane wall but kept accelerating and repaid the move by placing the McLaren directly in front. Häkkinen swept imperiously through Turn 1 and into the sweepers, Schumacher following.

The gap at the end of the opening lap was 0.8 of a second. They circled towards the distant pit stops – starting on lap 22 – with Coulthard third, Ralf Schumacher (Williams) fourth, Irvine (Jaguar) fifth and Barrichello sixth. He, it seemed, would be in no position to help Schumacher.

When Häkkinen pitted he was stationary for 6.8 seconds and took on enough fuel for thirteen laps. Schumacher came in next lap and was stationary for 7.4 seconds, taking on enough for fifteen. Those two extra laps would allow him to go so fast that when he pitted himself he'd emerge in front of Häkkinen. It was a classical way for Schumacher and Ferrari to turn the running order of a race upside down.

After some thirty laps the weather forecasters were vindicated because light rain began to fall. Ricardo Zonta (BAR) almost tapped Schumacher into the chicane – a moment from a nightmare – and the rain died away. Schumacher tracked Häkkinen, keeping him to a lead of around 1.0 second. That was setting Häkkinen up for the two-lap blitz, compounded by the fact that the rain began again and the Ferrari liked that enough to draw up. On lap 37, Häkkinen made his second stop (stationary 7.4 seconds) but the rain hardened and Schumacher had both Jaguars ahead. He needed a lap to clear them, which he did in 1m 42.3s. A gap flicked up, 25.6s to Häkkinen.

Schumacher stayed out that other lap, Häkkinen 1.2 seconds slower. Alex Wurz (Benetton) spun and Schumacher just missed him…

Schumacher pitted and was convinced he hadn't 'done enough. It was spitting with rain and I thought I hadn't gone as fast as I should have done.' He was stationary for 6.0 seconds and drove down the pit lane held by the speed limit there while Brawn scanned the horizon for when Häkkinen was coming. Schumacher could see nothing.

Brawn said into the radio: 'It's looking good.'

Schumacher wondered.

Brawn repeated 'it's looking good.'

Schumacher still wondered.

Brawn said: 'It's looking bloody good!'

Häkkinen had just appeared round the curve onto the start-finish straight as Schumacher reached towards the track, accelerating and the two-decade Ferrari journey through the deserts and jungles of Formula 1 was almost over.

It lasted a further thirteen laps, Schumacher leading by 4.0 seconds, then 4.7, 4.8, 5.0, 4.6, 4.3, 3.9, 4.2 until at the end it was 1.8. He'd never been threatened and even in heavier rain appeared absolutely assured. The Ferrari didn't look fast but, rather, as if the whole circuit had been moulded to it. He wobbled, just once, and didn't wobble again.

The celebrations in the Ferrari pit, in the parc fermé, on the podium and all over Italy were deeply emotional, as if a nation had found self respect again through this. Ferrari, the team of Formula 1 since 1950 – and a great team across the 1920s and 1930s before that – had become the team again. No more championships for Schumacher after Benetton? He'd just joined the triple champions and you could paraphrase an American President, Ronald Reagan, who seeking re-election said:

You ain't seen nothin' yet.

We hadn't.

2001

NO PRESSURE, NO HURRY

Hungarian Grand Prix, Hungaroring

He came to the Hungaroring able to win the championship with four rounds to spare. Time works in two dimensions in motor sport. The first – precious seconds during a Grand Prix – is easy to appreciate. The second – the seasons which tumble into decades – is more elusive. How long ago was it that Italy despaired of Ferrari ever having another champion? How long ago that Ferrari were themselves difficult to appreciate because they spent so much for so little? Sometimes it felt like yesterday, despite what Schumacher did in 2000.

To put what was happening into context, since Mansell plundered the whole of 1992, five championships had been decided at the final race of the season, one (Schumacher, 2000) with a race to spare, the remainder with two rounds to spare.

Now Schumacher was preparing to do something not seen since Mansell won at this same Hungaroring. By the seventh round he had 52 points, Coulthard 40 and he put together a sprint: second in Canada to Ralf (Williams), then taking the European at the Nürburgring and giving Ralf anxious moments by squeezing him at the start. Ralf did not exhibit brotherly love afterwards but the sprint went on unabated. Schumacher won France and was second to Häkkinen at Silverstone, making his points total a monument of a thing at 84, Coulthard 47. Nor did the German Grand Prix disturb this. Neither finished.

When Schumacher arrived at the Hungaroring he explained that he felt very relaxed and hastened to add that this was not some psychological ploy to deflect pressure. 'It was just like that, not deliberate at all.'

Ordinarily you win the championship at the earliest moment

because, as we have seen, motor racing can be a fearfully fragile thing but the 84 points and the remaining four rounds meant that, if he had been putting pressure on himself, it would have been entirely wrong psychologically because it would have been artificial. Schumacher confirmed his mood when he said, bluntly, to Jean Todt, running the team: 'You know, I haven't got a very good feeling, I'm not sure that this is the weekend we'll do it'.

Brawn demurred. First he judged Schumacher to be in 'great shape' – a phrase loaded with significance even to anyone following Schumacher's career casually – and then explored the overall psychology. Schumacher's monument, Brawn concluded, had transferred the pressure directly to the others. That meant Coulthard on the 47, Ralf on 41 and Barrichello in the other Ferrari on 40. Häkkinen was totally out of it on 19. 'The fact that he won the championship last year has made this season less stressful for him,' Brawn said. 'I have seen no signs of pressure.'

Schumacher was, whether he cared to be or not, viewed in an historical context. Alain Prost was running his own team – Alesi had finished sixth at Hockenheim for him – and, at the Hungaroring, Prost and Schumacher fell into conversation. Prost held the all-comers record of fifty-one wins and complained that people went on and on to him about that. Schumacher complained that now he had fifty people went on and on to him about that. They seem to have reached a concensus. The moment Schumacher had fifty-one too they could both proceed comparatively unmolested.

Mind you, McLaren team co-ordinator Jo Ramirez assured Prost – who'd won thirty races with the team – that they'd be doing everything they could to prevent Schumacher drawing level. Presumably Schumacher and Prost both had ambivalent feelings about that.

Schumacher went fastest in Friday free practice (1m 16.6s) from Barrichello (1m 16.7s), Häkkinen third (1m 16.7s), Ralf fourth (1m 17.3s). Coulthard thumped a kerb and damaged the chassis, restricting him to tenth.

In Saturday free practice Coulthard went fastest (1m 15.2s) from Schumacher (1m 15.4s).

He romped qualifying. He made just two runs, the first after some thirty minutes (1m 14.4s) to take provisional pole from Häkkinen (1m 15.4s), the second ten minutes later to settle the whole thing (1m 14.0s). It was a lap of great certainty and great balance. Coulthard produced an outstanding lap of his own (1m 14.8s – that's 0.801 seconds slower, a huge gap) to join Schumacher on the front row.

'It's the result of a perfect lap and a car that was already 100% in the morning.' Schumacher explained the two runs by saying it was 'not to save tyres. I just felt I had got the maximum out of myself and the car so it was better to sit rather than waste effort.' (Brawn called it 'exceptional'.)

In fact there was only one discordant moment, when Schumacher went through a gravel trap on the warm-up lap before the race, provoking the Ferrari mechanics to swarm the car checking it.

A Finn, Kimi Räikkönen, qualified his Sauber ninth and a Spaniard, Fernando Alonso, his Minardi eighteenth. Both had made their debut in the first race, Australia, and within the Grand Prix world both were attracting attention as very, very promising.

The nature of the Hungaroring favoured the driver reaching the first corner first. From the lights Schumacher was on the power while Barrichello veered across, protecting him from Coulthard. Schumacher was free as a bird, not seeking prey but soaring. He led Barrichello by 1.3 seconds, Coulthard third. He understood – as Fangio had done, Stewart had done and more particularly Prost had done – that a race is a long time and if you don't have to hurry, don't. He was content to keep the gap successively at 1.3, 1.3, 1.2, 1.4. Coulthard produced a couple of fastest laps but they didn't take him past Barrichello, who closed the gap to Schumacher to 0.9.

Schumacher was preserving his tyres because he judged that that would be important later. He didn't make a move until he was ready, lap 11 when he set fastest lap and forced the gap to 2.7 – Coulthard was 3.4. On lap 12 he set fastest lap again and increased the gap 4.1, 4.4 and 5.3 – another fastest lap. On lap 16 he broke Mansell's track record, which had astonishingly lasted since 1992.

He led every lap except four during his first pit stop and two during his second. There were concerns – Barrichello was pressuring him, oil on the track – and he didn't tell himself he'd done it until three laps remained.

Afterwards he said all the right things.

Until now, only Alberto Ascari had won consecutive championships with Ferrari and Schumacher, uninterested in the sport's history, might never even have heard of him. It didn't matter. Schumacher was poised to leave Ascari in his wake, and Prost's fifty-one wins, and Prost's four championships.

It bears repeating.

We hadn't seen nothin' yet.

2002

ALONE WITH FANGIO

French Grand Prix, Magny-Cours

To repeat, the context of 2001 had been that, since Nigel Mansell plundered the whole of 1992, five championships had been decided at the final race, one championship (Schumacher, 2000) with a race to spare and the remainder with two rounds to spare. What context can you give to 2002? Here were the four most recent early winners:

Clark	Germany, 1 August 1965	3 rounds to spare
Stewart	Austria, 15 August 1971	3 rounds to spare
Mansell	Hungary, 16 August 1992	5 rounds to spare
Schumacher	Hungary, 19 August 2001	4 rounds to spare

Hosting a decisive race was dictated by the overall calendar, which – amazingly – had been relatively stable since 1950 in its overall shape. Imola and Monaco came early, Canada, France and Britain in mid-season. They were unlikely ever to see a decisive race. Germany, just after Britain, hadn't seen one since Clark (above) in 1965: still too early except for that. The rounds at season's end – particularly Monza, the USA at Watkins Glen and Las Vegas, Japan and Australia – by definition hosted decisive races regularly.

In the early days, motor racing was conscious of the fact that the championship needed to remain alive for as long as possible each season to sustain interest. Hence, as we have seen (and suffered), the ingenious yet artificial imposition of restricting the number of rounds a driver could count: 4 out of 7 in 1950, and then all manner of combinations until 1991 when, for the first time, all the rounds counted.

Mansell proved so dominant in 1992 that no scoring system would have made any sensible difference. Michael Schumacher found himself in exactly this position in 2001 but 2002 was beyond even that. The French Grand Prix was the eleventh of seventeen and Schumacher journeyed to it having won seven, been second twice and third once. He had 86 points, team-mate Barrichello 32, Juan Pablo Montoya (Williams) 31, brother Ralf (Williams) 30. Barrichello's contract restricted him to supporting Schumacher so that his deficit – 54 points – had to be academic. It might as well have been 1,154. Montoya and Ralf had essentially to think of strong finishes here but if Schumacher won and Montoya was lower than second, Schumacher took the championship. Same if Ralf was third.

Putting this more starkly, after Magny-Cours the season had a very long way still to go, across to Hockenheim, south to Hungary, further south to Italy, over the Atlantic to Indianapolis and then what ought to have been the big finish at Suzuka on 13 October. Schumacher could neuter these races round the strange contours of Magny-Cours on 21 *July*.

Four days before, Ferrari test driver Luca Badoer drove the spare and both race cars at the team's Fiorano track, including 'some practice starts.' All seemed in perfect working order.

Schumacher confessed at Magny-Cours that it really was too early to be talking of championships and in any case such a thing was not in his thoughts. The next race, Hockenheim – itself impossibly early – would surely by a better place to talk and think of it, making one of the great German sporting occasions.

The McLarens were stong on the Friday, Coulthard taking his McLaren round in 1m 14.0s, then Räikkönen in the other McLaren 1m 14.0s, Schumacher third on 1m 14.2s, Barrichello fourth on 1m 14.7s.

'As usual here when it gets hot,' Schumacher said, 'unlike at other circuits the surface gets more slippery and you end up sliding around a lot. The other tyre company [Michelin] seems to be showing strongly, but we have often been in this situation at the start of the weekend only to find it changes for the race. We planned to do a long run to see what the tyre performance was like.'

And that's what they did.

Montoya took pole from him after what Schumacher described as an enjoyable battle. 'On my first run I missed the apex at the last chicane, hit the kerb and ran wide, so my time did not count. I thought it was so slow that they would allow it, but it did not matter. Then on my third run the car stepped out at the fast chicane and I had to go in a straight line. Quite rightly, they took that time away also. Then on my final run I lost a bit of time in the final sector. The heat was not a problem this afternoon but at the last corner you are just sliding, not driving. As for tomorrow, I think it will be a much closer race then the last ones, but we don't really have a full picture of what to expect. Starting on the "dirty" side of the track does not make a big difference at this circuit.'

At the start of the parade lap Barrichello's car was still on its jacks with an electrical problem which couldn't be found. His race was over, leaving only Montoya and Ralf. Montoya led Schumacher, Räikkönen third, Ralf fourth a little distance away.

The order lasted to the first pit stops between laps 24 and 28 but Schumacher led after them – briefly. The Stewards decided he'd crossed the white line exiting the pit lane and must serve a drive through penalty. He did that on lap 35, creating a new order:

Montoya, Räikkönen, Schumacher, Ralf.

On lap 43, Montoya made his second stop – slow – and Räikkönen led from Schumacher. When they'd pitted a second time Montoya was drifting back with tyre wear. And Ralf was given a drive through penalty...

Räikkönen felt pressure from Schumacher but resisted until lap 68 when, approaching the Adelaide hairpin and smoke rising from his tyres under braking, he overshot: the McLaren was on oil dropped almost immediately before by the Toyota of Allan McNish. As Räikkönen twisted the McLaren back towards the track Schumacher was through and not to be caught.

'As I took the flag I felt an outburst of emotion and realized how much it means and how I love the sport. All the titles have felt special in a different way [...] you never get used to it.' You could see that by the way he wiggled the car at frenetic speed at the line, how he punched the air with his clenched fist.

The fifth championship wasn't confirmed for two hours, however. Had Schumacher overtaken Räikkönen under waved yellow flags? The FIS said no.

'I don't want to get into comparisons,' Schumacher said. He couldn't escape it, because now he had five titles, just like Fangio. Schumacher did however say that 'what he achieved in his time is more than I can ever achieve.'

Of more significance, Schumacher said he intended to continue his career, treating each race as the next great challenge. It meant he might go far beyond Fangio, go to where no man had been before. As if to give that statement great strength, rather than regard the remainder of 2002 as a milk run he won Germany, was second in Hungary, won Belgium and was second in Italy, was second in the USA and won Japan.

2003

SCHUMACHER, SIX

Japanese Grand Prix, Suzuka

It seemed a formality and even though that is a dangerous thing to say about motor sport – where, as we have seen, any one of dozens of cheap components can bring very expensive failure – you couldn't escape the fact that to take the championship Kimi Räikkönen had to win the Japanese Grand Prix and Schumacher to get no points. The scoring had been revised, or rather extended, to the first eight – 10 points, 8, 6, 5, 4, 3, 2, 1 – so that even if Räikkönen won and totalled 93 points, Schumacher's 1 for eighth would give him 93, too, and he'd get the title very comfortably on the most wins tie-break.

Räikkönen had tracked Schumacher all season long and at moments forced tremendous speed from his McLaren but, more than that, he was an old-fashioned racer. He looked like the next generation and might, after Suzuka, be this generation.

He wasn't about to surrender at Suzuka whatever the facts and formalities, and then the rain came, rewarding some, punishing others. The Saturday running order was governed by the Friday times, removing discretion, tactics and judgement. You went when you had to go. That was: Räikkönen fifth last, Schumacher third last.

Barrichello put his Ferrari on pole ('definitely my best ever qualifying lap at Suzuka') – he went seventh from the end – just as the rain began. Räikkönen could do no more than eighth and Schumacher, the rain much harder, fourteenth. At the first split, he'd been 1.008 seconds off Barrichello and 2.034 at the second split. He hadn't been this far down a grid since Spa, 1995. He'd describe it as an 'interesting session' and expressed satisfaction that Barrichello did have the pole. 'Having one car in that position is ideal for us. The session could have been much worse for me and I think that Kimi was also affected a bit by the rain.'

Räikkönen, speaking so softly it was hard to hear him, talked about winning the race, his 'only chance.'

They jostled down the incline to Turn 1 when the red lights went off, jostled into Turn 1 and through it, Barrichello leading ... Räikkönen seventh ... Schumacher twelfth. Different imperatives: Räikkönen somehow had to get through the field and take the lead, Schumacher somehow had to get through the field to eighth.

Montoya, who'd put his Williams on the front row, hounded Barrichello on this opening lap and went past and Räikkönen went past Panis (Toyota) so that completing the lap Montoya led, Barrichello at 1.3 seconds. Räikkönen sixth at 3.4, Schumacher still twelfth at 6.1. Ahead, in the order he would reach them, were: Takuma Sato (BAR), Justin Wilson (Jaguar), Mark Webber (Jaguar) and Jenson Button (BAR) – only 1.4 seconds from Button to Schumacher.

Montoya shed Barrichello while, intriguingly, Trulli brought his Renault up to Schumacher, who responded by overtaking Wilson (Sato had already gone past the Jaguar).

At lap 4 Räikkönen ran fifth but 10.1 seconds from Montoya and 5.7 from Barrichello. On lap 7 Schumacher tried to take Sato at the chicane – a move without conviction – and the BAR damaged the Ferrari's nosecone. He pitted and resumed twentieth...

Montoya's hydraulics failed and after the first pit stops the order had become: Barrichello, Coulthard, Räikkönen – Schumacher into a long recovery from the back which would take him to tenth on lap 23, including a fastest lap. On lap 24 he made his second stop (stationary 6.8), back to twelfth. He set off again.

After Coulthard's second stop Räikkönen ran second to Barrichello. Others pitted – a profusion of them – and suddenly Schumacher was sixth. At lap 35, Barrichello leading:

Coulthard	@ 23.7
Räikkönen	@ 39.0
Da Matta	@ 46.7
R Schumacher	@ 47.2
Schumacher	@ 48.5

Schumacher's third pit stop put him back to tenth s
into his third recovery. Cristiano Da Matta (Toyota) and b
pitted and, emerging, Schumacher placed the Ferrari betw
da Matta ahead, Ralf behind. Ralf raced him and so vehem
on the start-finish straight Schumacher had to veer and bloc

Coulthard pitted, Räikkönen up to second.

On lap 41 of the 53 da Matta braked for the chica
Schumacher, wheels locked, lurched to the other side of the tra
Ralf's path. Da Matta threaded through the chicane, Schum
bumped over the grass and Ralf travelled backwards down the
road. That made Schumacher eighth. He pressed on although
vibration from the tyres was so intense 'I had vision problems d
the straight. I was also worried about a puncture and I was just try
to get the car to the flag.'

Barrichello led Räikkönen by 16.4 seconds.

Schumacher backed away from da Matta and ran to the end b
himself, although that produced a paradox. When Barrichello crossed
the line to win it – Räikkönen 11.0 seconds further back – he
simultaneously took the championship for Schumacher, almost a full
minute away on the other side of the track.

Afterwards, catching the mood of the moment, he'd explain that 'I
find it difficult to say what I am feeling at this moment because,
honestly, this has been a tough year, a tough last part of the season
and today was one of the toughest races.' It was a strange feeling
'because usually I have won the championship with a victory but now
I am here in eighth place, so there are some mixed emotions.'

He was of course past Fangio although he still wouldn't allow a
comparison. 'I have a lot of respect for what Fangio achieved but for
me it's the team that is important.'

2004

SCHUMACHER, SEVEN

Belgian Grand Prix, Spa

You can arrange and rearrange it as much as you want. You can approach it from any direction you want. You can try and rationalize it this way and that. It is all useless.

Schumacher won the Australian Grand Prix on 7 March from his team-mate Barrichello. From pole he led all 58 laps.

He won the Malaysian Grand Prix from Montoya (Williams) on 21 March. From pole he led 52 of the 56 laps.

He won the Bahrain Grand Prix from Barrichello on 4 April. From pole he led 50 of the 57 laps.

He won the San Marino Grand Prix from Button (BAR) on 25 April. From the front row he led 54 of the 62 laps.

He won the Spanish Grand Prix from Barrichello on 9 May. From pole he led 51 of the 66 laps.

At this point it seemed entirely possible he would win all eighteen rounds. Only that one pole had eluded him (Button took it) and of the 299 laps he had led 265, but it was even more overwhelming than that. Apart from Button leading the first eight laps at Imola, and Trulli the first eight in Spain, Schumacher had only lost the lead – and unavoidably – through pit stops.

The sequence was broken, rudely, at Monaco where he qualified on the second row and, leading, was struck from behind by Montoya in the tunnel under the Safety Car. This was a great controversy at the time, of course, but exercised no bearing whatsoever on the rest of the season as Schumacher proceeded on his regal way.

He won the European Grand Prix from Barrichello at the Nürburgring on 30 May. From pole he led 53 of the 60 laps.

He won the Canadian Grand Prix from brother Ralf on 13 June.

From the third row he led 39 of the 70 laps.

He won the United States Grand Prix from Barrichello on 20 June. From the front row he led 59 of the 73 laps.

He won the French Grand Prix from young Fernando Alonso (Renault) on 4 July. From the front row he led 34 of the 70 laps.

He won the British Grand Prix from Räikkönen (McLaren) on 11 July. From the second row he led 49 of the 60 laps. The scale of it all was hard to fit into a context: this win at Silverstone was his tenth of the season, beating his own record of nine he'd shared with Mansell.

He won the German Grand Prix from Button on 25 July. From pole he led 53 of the 66 laps.

He won the Hungarian Grand Prix from Barrichello on 15 August. From pole he led every lap. This made the championship a curiosity and little more. He took 120 points to the next race, Belgium, Barrichello 82, Button 65. Barrichello, of course, was contracted to support Schumacher, not beat him, and if Button won all the five remaining rounds he could still only total 115.

Even if Ferrari tore up the contracts and unleashed Barrichello, Schumacher need only finish two points ahead of him at Spa and the thing was done. It had only ever been done nine times as early as August (Ascari 1952 and 1953, Fangio 1954, Brabham in 1960, Clark 1965, Stewart in 1971, Mansell in 1992 and Schumacher himself in 2001). The fact that there were eighteen rounds protected Schumacher's 2002 feat of doing it in July: the more the races, the longer it would have to take to reach statistical certainty. That was mathmatics, not motor racing.

So he came to Spa and generating any sort of championship excitement was not easy. What he said on the Friday (2nd and 3rd in the free practices) reflected that. 'It was productive and we seemed to have plenty of time to work through our planned programme without having to hurry. I am quite happy with the balance of the car.'

He qualified on the front row in a wet session (Trulli, Renault, pole) and spoke of slight mistakes but 'I have no complaints.'

He made a slightly hesitant start, Trulli gone immediately but several crashes developed and the Safety Car came out. Barrichello felt his Ferrari weaving – he had a puncture as well as a damaged nosecone after contact with Webber – and was brought into the pits immediately to change tyres (not the nosecone yet). Order:

Trulli, Alonso, Coulthard, Schumacher, Räikkönen, Montoya.

They raced again, Räikkönen overtaking into Eau Rouge and bringing Montoya up to attack. Barrichello, meanwhile, pitted again to have the nosecone replaced. Sixteen cars remained and he was the last of them.

Into the Bus Stop chicane Montoya went round the outside, crowded Schumacher, risked elbowing him – and was through. Schumacher struggled 'to get my tyres up to the right temperature and pressure.' Now he was sixth.

Räikkönen moved past Coulthard.

At lap 7, Schumacher was 8.4 seconds behind Trulli, still leading. The first pit stops spread from laps 10 to 17, giving:

Räikkönen, Button (who hadn't stopped), Schumacher, Trulli.

Barrichello had recovered to tenth. When Button did stop, on lap 21, Schumacher moved up to second but some 13 seconds behind Räikkönen. Barrichello charged on, pitted – back to tenth – and charged again.

Button's rear tyre exploded, the Safety Car came out and Schumacher pitted immediately. He slotted in behind Räikkönen as they waited for the Safety Car to pull in – Barrichello fourth...

Räikkönen led Schumacher by 1.3 seconds and Montoya had a suspension problem and a puncture. Barrichello cut past him into third. The Safety Car was out again and, when it pulled off, Räikkönen put together a lap half a second better than Schumacher would do in the race. With a lap to go Schumacher was 3.3 seconds behind but that didn't matter. Barrichello was 2.0 seconds behind him and they ran to the end like that.

Schumacher explained that 'every title has felt different and has given me different emotions. This one is very special coming here in Spa, which means so much to me, and to do it for the seventh time at Ferrari's seven hundredth Grand Prix is also something special.'

Ross Brawn distilled everything. 'It has been a pretty straightforward year, I must say.'

This seventh championship, itself straightforward in its execution, would need time to be appreciated because the Belgian Grand Prix was, truth to tell, pretty straightforward, too. The true appreciation would come when the next generation, perhaps years later, gazed at the champions' list and saw

M Schumacher	7
JM Fangio	5
A Prost	4

They wouldn't need to see much more.

2005

SWEETNESS OF YOUTH

Brazilian Grand Prix, Interlagos

Fernando Alonso's father worked in an explosives factory. That tells you a great deal about what you need to know.

Alonso was good early. Mike Wilson runs a karting business in Italy and he remembers 'Fernando started here at twelve and practically all his karting career was with me. He drove until 1999 and by then he was already doing cars in Formula Nissan in Spain. One of the main ways you can tell the difference in drivers is when there is a little problem, because you cannot always set the kart up 100% as you would like. He would change driving style and make the kart work regardless. He could drive round the problem.

'Understeer? He'd throw the kart so he'd get round the corner anyway. A normal kid with the same understeer wouldn't try to change his driving to get the kart round that corner. Fernando was doing that at the age of twelve, thirteen. It's instinctive, something that nobody can tell you. You've either got it or you haven't and he had it. He proved that in every category that he moved up to.

'The last race we did together was in Belgium. I said "listen, Fernando, I don't know if you'll get into Formula 1 because unfortunately there are a lot of doors to be opened and you need luck and so on, but listen, if you do, when I come to watch the Italian Grand Prix at Monza, and I'm standing at the fence gazing into the paddock, and I shout out "hello, Fernando" do NOT dare to put your head down and fail to recognise me. Don't play the superstar." He said "no, no, I will never behave like that. You're joking, you're joking saying that to me" – and he hugged me and he was crying. One of the things that perhaps makes people think he is arrogant is his shyness. People say "he never says hello" but he is just a shy guy.'

Alonso's Formula 1 career detonated early – he made his debut in a Minardi in 2001 at 19 years seven months and three days, the third youngest of all.

He was impressive enough to attract the interest of Flavio Briatore, running Benetton, who gave him a testing contract for 2002. It was a good investment both ways because in 2003 – Benetton had become Renault – he took a pole (Malaysia), the youngest to do that, and won a race (Hungary), the youngest to do that, too.

He finished 2004 in fourth place on 59 points behind Schumacher 148, Barrichello 114 and Button 85. These four and the McLaren pairing of Montoya and Räikkönen, suggested a toxic and perhaps epic season in 2005 with one proviso: that Schumacher didn't massacre it.

Fisichella, partnering Alonso, won Australia and Alonso won the next three, Malaysia, Bahrain and San Marino. The massacre had been avoided already - the Ferrari was suffering tyre and aerodynamic problems - and by mid-season only Räikkönen could realistically hold Alonso. Räikkönen won Turkey and Belgium but Alonso kept finishing second so that, approaching Brazil, Alonso had 111 points and Räikkönen 86. There were still three rounds to go but if Alonso scored 6 points – or indeed finished on the podium – he'd become the youngest World Champion at 24 years one month and 27 days. In 1972, Fittipaldi had been 25 years 8 months and 29 days.

In qualifying Alonso went nineteenth and did a 1m 11.9s. Räikkönen, next, locked wheels into the Senna S and that cost him so much time he lined up on the third row. Montoya joined Alonso on the front row. Of more possible significance, Fisichella qualified third and Renault could deploy him as a spoiler, holding Räikkönen back while Alonso escaped.

Alonso made a lovely start, Montoya second, Fisichella defending and – inevitably – Räikkönen attacking. Fisichella ran wide in the left-handed curve after the Senna S and Räikkönen was through on the inside, neat as a thief. The Safety Car came out – a start line crash – and when they raced again Alonso was slightly ragged through the Senna S, allowing Montoya to draw up and go past. That delivered Alonso to Räikkönen, directly behind...

They ran in this order, however, to the first pit stops, starting with Alonso on lap 22 – early. He rejoined sixth and had a alarming moment when one of the Minardis braked so heavily that he had to veer to miss it. Montoya went to lap 28 before he stopped and Räikkönen to lap 31. He led Montoya by 22.0 seconds, Alonso by 34.5. Montoya went by in the lead, Alonso 9.8 seconds from Räikkönen.

Like so many races, it was a mosaic of move and counter-move.

Alonso made his second stop at lap 48, again early, letting Schumacher past into third place. Montoya and Schumacher pitted on lap 54 so that Räikkönen led, Montoya holding second and Alonso third. Räikkönen pitted, passing the lead back to Montoya: there was no sense in McLaren playing around with the running order because Alonso's third made whatever they did irrelevant to the championship.

Alonso stroked it home, as the saying goes, although for the last five or six laps 'I heard noises from everywhere on the car – gearbox, everything – so I was a little bit worried.'

He stood on his Renault and used his arms so theatrically he might have been waging warfare on the air around him. He blew kisses, raised both arms and, with index finger splayed, made the figure

1

Alonso paid tribute to Räikkönen who, he said, had fought so hard that it made the championship taste sweeter. He pointed out that, as the first man to beat Schumacher since Häkkinen in 1999, it tasted sweeter still. Alonso did feel that the first season after Schumacher finally retired might make for a hollow championship but at Interlagos Schumacher had been lively and, at moments, threatened Alonso's third place. In the parc fermé Schumacher came across and they embraced lightly, as if something precious was being passed on.

There'd been nothing hollow about how Alonso became the youngest World Champion of all.

2006

THREE STORY AFTERNOON

Brazilian Grand Prix, Interlagos

That warm, dry October afternoon became a beginning, a middle and an end. It ought perhaps to have been the single story of the champion and the championship he'd just won but it was more. When the shadows of early evening crept across Interlagos it became heavy with many, many emotions.

Ferrari recovered from what, to them, was a debacle in 2005 – third in the Constructors' Championship, which they'd won every year since 1999. Barrichello went to Honda, replaced by Felipe Massa from Sauber, although he'd done testing for Ferrari in the past.

The season quickly devolved to Alonso and Schumacher. By Germany, round twelve, they'd won every race between them except Malaysia, which fell to Alonso's team-mate at Renault, Fisichella.

Leaving Germany, Alonso had 100 points, Schumacher 89, the season tightening so that when Schumacher won Italy and China they were both on 116. Crucially, however, Schumacher's engine failed as he led the Japanese Grand Prix and Alonso won it. Only Brazil remained.

Schumacher had announced his retirement so that, whatever happened, the race would mark physically as well as psychologically the end of something unlike anything which had gone before in Formula 1. A glance at the monumental statistics told that and perhaps one will suffice. Since 1996, when Schumacher had gone to rescue Ferrari, they scored 1,709 points in the Constructors' Championship. In the ten years before, that was 572. Schumacher always spoke of the team effort and here it was. Many gifted people had created this team, managed it and maintained it but at the crucial moments all their efforts had been, quite literally, in Schumacher's gloved hands.

As a driver he had shaped it in his own image, a compound of technical mastery, supreme physical fitness, relentless mental application and all of it allied to a rare tactical awareness as well as great reservoirs of speed. He understood the imperatives of corporate identity, too. As Alonso said the year before, his leaving would create a hollowness which would take time to fill.

All that wouldn't begin until after the 71 laps of the Brazilian Grand Prix when he would have his eighth championship or Alonso his second, although the engine failure at Suzuka made the latter little short of inevitable. Schumacher had to win and Alonso get no point, giving them both 126 but Schumacher taking it on the most wins tie-break 8-7.

Qualifying belonged to Massa, a Paulista, whose pole created the sort of jubilation and abandon at Interlagos so familiar to Monza. Alonso was safely fourth quickest.

Schumacher had always seemed lucky but now, after Japan, it was running out very quickly. He did a 1m 10.3s lap in the second of the three runs – this would have meant pole easily if he had been able to carry it forward to the third run. Instead as he emerged for that third run he slowed with a fuel pressure problem. 'All I could do was cruise round slowly back to the pits.' He'd be on the fifth row, courtesy of the 1m 10.3s, and that smoothed any permutations away. He had to go for the win, something which accorded precisely with his notion of what he'd been doing at every race of his life, anyway.

Alonso could wait, look, work it out and take no risks.

Massa made a glorious start, clearly and cleanly ahead through the Senna S, Alonso a prudent fourth – keeping away from any jostling cars which might bring doom to him – while Schumacher sliced through to eighth. The Safety Car came out after Nico Rosberg crashed his Williams and when it was gone Massa resumed control.

Schumacher ran sixth behind Fisichella, Alonso just ahead of Fisichella. Into the Senna S, Schumacher executed a power play and was through although, travelling so fast, the Ferrari flicked sideways as if the move was too much for its balance. He caught that. The imbalance was a puncture, probably picked up from debris. It happened at exactly the wrong place, just beyond the pit lane exit, making him travel over two miles all the way back. The tyre chewed as he went, car after car passing him.

That was lap 9, Massa still leading from Räikkönen, Alonso third.

After the first pit stops Massa had Alonso behind him, Schumacher coming up through the field. Inevitably the world watched Schumacher: Massa circling like clockwork, Alonso circling like clockwork and Schumacher attacking so savagely he'd reached seventh. Schumacher was the race. He made a second stop on lap 47 – the last pit stop of his career, barring the unforeseen – and set a new fastest lap despite hauling the fuel he'd just put in. That provoked consternation that it could be done. He cut past Barrichello, sixth, while Massa made his second stop and didn't sacrifice the lead. Alonso pitted, emerged second again.

Still Massa circled like clockwork, Alonso like clockwork.

On lap 69 of the 71, flowing towards the mouth of the Senna S, Schumacher positioned the Ferrari inside Räikkönen who tried to defend the position by moving over so far that he gave Schumacher the width of the Ferrari and barely a centimetre more. They went through side-by-side, wheel-to-wheel in a moment crackling with electricity. The camber took Schumacher to mid-track and, avoiding him, Räikkönen slithered wider. Schumacher was through and the mechanics in the Ferrari pit were on their feet cheering and waving clenched fists.

It had been the move of a young man, immortal and exuberant, mixing ambition, nerve and reflex – but Schumacher was thirty six, a father of two and about to retire...

He ran fourth, Button a mere 0.4 of a second behind Alonso. Could Schumacher catch Button? He was six seconds away and, suddenly, this is the way it might have gone: Button attacking Alonso and they tangled. Massa would then lead from Schumacher and if necessary slow so much he could walk beside it while Schumacher went by as World Champion.

The world isn't like that.

Schumacher set fastest lap.

The immense crowd saluted Massa as he went into his final lap – charged moments because no Brazilian had won their own Grand Prix since that other Paulista, Senna.

Schumacher took the Ferrari to its limit on his own final lap as if he wanted to beat the fastest lap he had just set, leaving Grand Prix racing with one ultimate, immortal gesture.

Alonso came home second, no drama and no histrionics, just a proper professional doing what he does. At 25 he was the youngest double champion, of course, and yet consolidating the middle of his career. Flavio Briatore, running Renault, was on the radio during the slowing down lap, distilling it. 'A fantastic job. Thank you for this year. It has been a pleasure for me.'

Alonso underlined how tight it had been through the season 'and to win the championship at the last race is even more emotional.' It had been, he added, a long Grand Prix. What looks so inevitable from the grandstand or Media Centre might – and usually does – look very different from the cockpit.

Massa won and said 'this for sure is the best memory of my life.' He wore the biggest grin you've ever seen until you saw Alonso.

Schumacher finished fourth. 'I am very happy for Felipe, who drove an amazing race,' he said looking serene and, amazingly, a father figure to the whole thing after all these turbulent years. 'It is great for him to be the first Brazilian to win at Interlagos since Ayrton Senna. It would have been nice if I could at least have made it to the podium alongside him. I would also like to congratulate Fernando. Today, my race was compromised after the puncture I picked up on lap nine when I had just passed Fisichella. I was unaware of it until the team told me about it on the radio. I had a good climb back up the order, thanks partly to an amazing car and exceptional Bridgestone tyres.' The arrangement of the words were as they had always been, and would be no more. From this moment he would be an ex-racer.

He had devastated every important record since the championship began: the seven championships, the 91 wins (next Prost 51, Senna 41), the 154 podiums (next Prost 106, Senna 80), the 68 pole positions (next Senna 65, Clark and Prost 33), the 76 fastest laps (next Prost 41, Mansell 30), the 1,369 points (next Prost 798.50, Senna 614), the 141 Grands Prix led (next Senna 86, Prost 84), the 5,091 laps led (next Senna 2,931, Prost 2,683), the thirteen wins in a season (next himself with eleven, 2002), the 17 out of 17 podiums in 2002, the 148 points in a season (next himself, 144 in 2002).

You can argue forever (and some do) about relative merits and where these records really leave Schumacher. If you look at them with a careful eye, however, nobody from Giuseppe Farina all the way to here had ever constructed anything like it.

Anyway that was it, the beginning, the middle and the end all on the same warm, dry afternoon. You might think that the world watching Schumacher was something of a shame for Alonso but however emotional you care to be about the last ride of the Prancing Horse, however magnificent it was in execution, the record books will always say, and only say, this:

World Champion, 2006:   F Alonso (Spain)

2007

THE ICE MAN COMETH

Brazilian Grand Prix, Interlagos

Kimi Räikkönen was like Mika Häkkinen in at least one sense, so softly spoken that you'd have missed him in a bus queue, too. But Räikkönen wasn't always properly behaved in night clubs, as if racing drivers ever should be.

Again like Häkkinen he had a perceptive, naughty sense of humour but you could miss that, too, because in public he never showed it or anything like it. He had been able, too, to go head-to-head with Schumacher without leaving a trail of arguments, accusations and physical debris behind them. You wondered what would happen when Schumacher left the stage because Räikkönen was as fast a driver as any man on the planet, maybe faster: he'd been in Grand Prix racing since 2001 and poignantly he was now with Ferrari. Would it be The Räikkönen Era? That's always a dangerous thing to postulate but, by 2007, it seemed an entirely fair question.

All seasons are intriguing but few more than this. Alonso, himself softly spoken, joined McLaren to partner their debutant Lewis Hamilton – and he, too, was softly spoken.

Hamilton made an astonishingly mature debut in Australia, where Räikkönen won from Alonso, Massa sixth. Alonso won Malaysia, Massa won Bahrain and Spain but Hamilton and Räikkönen were scoring points, too. By Silverstone, just after half distance, Hamilton had 70 points, Alonso 58, Räikkönen 52 and Massa 51. With eight rounds left the championship was wide open: Alonso won the European at the Nürburgring, Hamilton won Hungary, Massa won Turkey, Alonso won Italy, Räikkönen won Belgium, Hamilton won Japan, Räikkönen won China. The openness was breathtaking and was becoming more and more intriguing.

The Schumacher Era seemed much further away than 2006 and the season didn't feel hollow at all.

Leaving China for Brazil and round 17, Hamilton had 107 points, Alonso 103 and Räikkönen 100 but Massa, 86, was out of it. He took pole, which stirred the crowd ('it's fantastic feeling their affection and seeing them celebrate in the stands'). This pole might have profound tactical importance. Massa, clearly, would help Räikkönen while by now the relationship between Hamilton and Alonso had completely broken down, Alonso displaying petulance and saying unfortunate things. It didn't help that he was twice World Champion and Hamilton in his first season but, at pressure moments, outdriving him. Nobody had come to Formula 1 and handled it with such maturity.

Hamilton joined Massa on the front row, Räikkönen and Alonso on the second.

Räikkönen said: 'Of course it would have been better to be on pole position but third place is certainly no bad thing and leaves me in a good position in light of the strategy we have chosen and the performance of the car. On my final flying lap I lost precious time at Turn 4 because of Hamilton: it is a real shame but there is no point in recriminations. I am confident I will be able to keep my chances alive right to the end.'

Hamilton said he was quite happy with his own qualifying and 'it was good fun.'

Alonso said 'it's getting tough for me.'

If Hamilton finished first or second he had the championship.

If Alonso won and Hamilton wasn't second, Alonso had the championship.

If Räikkönen won, and Alonso was no better than third, Hamilton no better than sixth, Räikkönen had the championship.

Yes, Massa might be pivotal to all this.

Massa led from Räikkönen through the Senna S, Alonso and Hamilton side-by-side. Alonso elbowed past. Into the left-handed Reta Oposta, taken at 90 miles an hour, Hamilton locked wheel and ran off the track, ran back on. Massa led completing the opening lap, then Räikkönen, then Alonso – Hamilton eighth. He made that seventh, going inside Trulli's Toyota, but was already 4.7 seconds from Massa.

On lap 7 Hamilton took Nick Heidfeld (BMW) but the gearbox failed. 'I was down-shifting into Turn 4 and the car just selected neutral. After a year without problems it's just unfortunate we had that little one today.' Eventually, as he cruised, the gearbox 'clicked back in and I was able to get going again' – but eighteenth. He had lost thirty seconds. He responded by doing a personal best time and the third quickest of all so far. It wasn't over, not with more than sixty laps to go. At lap 12, Massa leading

Räikkönen	@ 1.6s
Alonso	@ 9.4s
Hamilton (16th)	@ 41.0s

After the first pit stops the leaders resumed in the same order but by lap 29 Hamilton was running twelfth after a stunning, audacious thrust down the inside at the Senna S – Barrichello wise enough to leave him just enough room. Robert Kubica, the young Pole in the BMW, wasn't afraid of Alonso who was falling back towards him and executed a classical overtaking move into the Senna S. The race was tilting towards Räikkönen…

By lap 33 Hamilton ran ninth, knowing fifth would be enough. He was some 15.0 seconds behind Heidfeld. Hamilton made a second pit stop on lap 36 and didn't lose ninth place. A gap flashed up, Räikkönen to Alonso: 27.7 seconds so that the championship was simplifying itself. Assuming Massa allowed Räikkönen through to win, Räikkönen would have 110 points. If Alonso stayed third – Kubica had pitted and lost the place – he would have 109 points. If Hamilton did get to fifth place he would have 111. In order to disturb this, Alonso had to start travelling much more quickly and, it seemed, he couldn't.

On lap 42 Coulthard (Red Bull) pitted, making Hamilton eighth but at some point he'd have to make a third stop. He hadn't taken on enough fuel at the second stop to run to the end. Of more significance he wasn't lapping fast enough to catch the drivers in front – Trulli, Kubica and Rosberg, in the order he would reach them – to be fifth.

The gap from Räikkönen to Alonso was 35.4 seconds, Alonso to Hamilton 47.7.

Massa made his second stop and Räikkönen stayed out another three laps, allowing him to deploy the Schumacher tactic. You go so fast you gain enough time to pit yourself and hold the lead. Nobody ever doubted that Räikkönen had speed and now he proved he still had it. He emerged just in front of Massa, sparing Ferrari the necessity of instructing him to allow Räikkönen past, something which was against the rules but unenforceable.

Seventeen laps remained.

A provocative thought: if McLaren needed Alonso to defer to Hamilton to gain a place what would Alonso, leaving the team bearing scars, do? Hamilton pitted – the only driver so far to make three stops – and that removed the possibility of any request to Alonso. Hamilton, however, set fastest lap so far but was still 21.8 seconds behind Trulli.

Räikkönen looked neat, contained and at his ease. He had long taken the measure of the circuit and now, with the laps ebbing away, bestrode it. He stayed on the racing line, he stayed away from the kerbs but – on lap 63 of the 72 – Trulli pitted, making Hamilton seventh. More to the point, Rosberg, Heidfeld and Kubica were having a lively scrap and might easily take each other out in any combination.

McLaren would then be making a telephone call to Señor Alonso, who might give his command of English full vent.

Hamilton was still 17.0 seconds behind Heidfeld and needing something to happen up there. The statistics were suggestive of great heroics but it was too late:

	Heidfeld	Hamilton
Lap 64	1m 14.5s	1m 13.3s
Lap 65	1m 14.4s	1m 13.3s
Lap 66	1m 14.6s	1m 13.4s

That brought the gap down to 15.8 seconds. Yes, too late.

Almost as if to amuse himself Räikkönen set a new fastest lap and it would endure to the end. Hamilton had cut the gap to Heidfeld to

9.6 seconds but suddenly this was the final lap. Räikkönen crossed the line and there was a last irony for Hamilton, not the seventh place but the fact that he was a lap down so that even if the earth opened and swallowed Alonso and the BMWs and Rosberg it was no good. Under the rules Hamilton could not unlap himself once Räikkönen did cross the line.

They called him The Ice Man and he did some fist shaking from the cockpit but nothing approaching emotional abandon. He toured very slowly and did some more fist shaking when he'd parked the car. He embraced Massa but didn't milk the moments. The Schumacher Era really did seem a long way away.

The Ice Man said: 'Even when we went through some difficult times and it looked as if there was no way to fight back we never gave up and this work produced its reward. In Ferrari I have found a great family and I am proud to have won the title with them.'

Alonso felt Räikkönen deserved it.

At the Press Conference, Räikkönen said he was going to enjoy himself tonight and for about a month, and smiled his most captivated, boyish grin. 'I am very happy.'

He'd melted.

2008

HAMILTON'S LAP OF THE GODS

Brazilian Grand Prix, Interlagos

The long season – eighteen rounds on five continents from March to November – reflected, at the very end, so many seasons before it. Two men from utterly different backgrounds driving two utterly different cars would confront each other for slightly over an hour and a half. One would join the list which was already twenty-nine names long, the other would go away through the teeming, chaotic streets of Sao Paulo to the team hotel defeated.

It had always been like that, a single winner, but this carried more profound dimensions. Hamilton was of mixed race, which inevitably came to mean that whatever his own feelings he represented a huge proportion of the world's population who had not seen motor racing as anything to do with them. Tiger Woods, another man of mixed race, had already done this with golf. Woods had begun to change the perception of that sport and Hamilton could continue it, or perhaps consolidate it, by opening Formula 1 to vast new audiences. Woods and Hamilton actually resembled each other because they were both clean cut and instinctively polite even under extreme pressure. Woods was rich beyond avarice and Hamilton about to become so.

The Hamilton story has been told exhaustively, the penury and the karting, the early approach to Ron Dennis, the career path to Formula 1 which was almost inevitable, the unequalled debut the season before. Hamilton was impeccably groomed, word-perfect and, more surprisingly, a driver in attitude from the 1950s: *I will take risks, big risks, whenever I feel I need to.*

He'd put together a solid foundation in the seventeen rounds to Brazil, winning five, adding a couple of second places and three thirds.

He had 94 points and fifth place would do it. Sixth would, too, provided Massa didn't win the race. If Massa did, they both finished on 97 points but Massa was champion on the most wins tie-break, 6-5.

Felipe Massa matured during the season after a hesitant start and simply outdrove Räikkönen. He came to Brazil with 87 points, and he didn't just come to Brazil: he came to his home town with all that that involved in local pride – his and everybody else's – and although Brazil had had three World Champions none won it in Brazil: specifically, Fittipaldi in Monza and Watkins Glen, Piquet in Las Vegas, Kyalami and Suzuka, Senna in Suzuka.

'Racing at home, with the crowd on your side, is a great motivation for me. It's a fantastic feeling but difficult to put into words,' Massa said. He put it into action instead during qualifying.

	First Run	Second Run	Third Run
Massa	1m 11.830s	1m 11.875s	1m 12.368s
Trulli	1m 12.226s	1m 12.107s	1m 12.737s
Räikkönen	1m 12.083s	1m 11.950s	1m 12.825s
Hamilton	1m 12.213s	1m 11.856s	1m 12.830s

Massa's pole lap, his third in a row at the circuit, was a beautiful construction of power, poise and precision brought together so comprehensively that good judges thought he must have been fuelled light – meaning Ferrari were planning to stop three times. 'I got a great lap on my first run [in the Third sector] and I could have even not bothered to finish the second lap, but you never know what might happen. I will try and win: that is my aim. I'm not thinking about the rest, because it doesn't just depend on me or even the team. I feel calm. There is so much expectation around me but all this attention gives me a very positive energy which I will try and exploit. When your story started here' – in karting – 'you remember everything and you really want to do the best for the crowd.'

Hamilton, interviewed on television, said: 'Pole position is always a little bit easier because you have a clean sweep down to Turn 1 but although I have three people in front of me I can still get a good start. These guys in front can do whatever they want.' He seemed impossibly composed, deflecting gently any suggestion that there were other drivers who might act as spoilers – Alonso (now back at Renault) was open about wanting Massa to win, but Alonso hadn't been able to get higher than the third row. Trulli (Toyota) might be a player, too.

The weather forecast said a 50% chance of rain.

Massa came late from his pit to bring the Ferrari round to the grid and, as he moved through the curves and undulations of the circuit, the vast, noisy crowd saluted him in a great cascade of noise and waving. Massa threaded through the cars already on the grid to his place at the front.

Rain fell and stopped, facing the teams with risking dry tyres and hoping the track dried completely, or intermediates (in reality wets). Great darkened folds of cloud gathered round the circuit. The weather forecast said no more rain for thirty or forty minutes and there were seven minutes to the start.

The Safety Car did a reconnaissance lap.

McLaren put Hamilton onto intermediates just as Ferrari did for Massa, and they moved into the parade lap. The five lights came on, went out. Massa fed in the power carefully, Trulli behind, then Räikkönen, then Hamilton, then Sebastian Vettel (Toro Rosso) – a feisty, lively ambitious young man who'd won the Italian Grand Prix – then Alonso. Coulthard was tapped in the Senna S and halted, bringing the Safety Car out. It circled for four laps and released them. This is how they covered lap 5:

Massa	1m 19.9s
Trulli	1m 20.1s
Räikkönen	1m 20.3s
Hamilton	1m 20.6s
Vettel	1m 20.3s
Alonso	1m 20.4s

It meant fractions covered the first six. Vettel had been drawing towards Hamilton who responded.

	Hamilton	Vettel
Lap 6	1m 19.6s	1m 19.9s
Lap 7	1m 20.4s	1m 20.7s
Lap 8	1m 20.5s	1m 20.6s

That translated to a gap of 0.1 of a second which in turn translated to something near striking distance. Hamilton, however, eased away. 'Straight from the beginning of the race I sat back and just kept my position,' Hamilton would say. 'I didn't attack anyone and was looking after my car. It was great not to have to push and try to come second or something like that.'

Räikkönen kept probing at Trulli, the track was drying and on lap 9 Alonso and Vettel pitted for dry tyres.

Fisichella (Force India) had pitted as early as the second lap for them and now the track was coming to him. On this lap 9 he went fastest of all in the middle sector and completed the lap in 1m 21.4s, close to the 1m 20s which the leaders were doing. On lap 10 Massa and Hamilton's team mate Heikki Kovalainen pitted but Trulli, Hamilton and Räikkönen stayed out another lap. It was costly because Massa still led at lap 12 but

Vettel	@ 0.9s
Alonso	@ 2.0s
Räikkönen	@ 5.5s
Fisichella	@ 6.2s
Trulli	@ 7.5s
Hamilton	@ 8.1s

Trulli suddenly slewed, almost sideways, and Hamilton went smoothly past. Räikkönen meanwhile was either slow or backing Fisichella towards Hamilton, allowing Massa to stretch further and further away. Massa set a new fastest lap, the first driver into the 1m 16s – Hamilton in the high 1m 17s. Räikkönen accelerated and Hamilton needed to deal with Fisichella to have the coveted fifth place. It was not an idea which appealed to Fisichella…

	Fisichella	Hamilton
Lap 15	1m 17.4s	1m 17.4s
Lap 16	1m 17.1s	1m 17.1s
Lap 17	1m 16.9s	1m 16.7s

Hamilton's McLaren looked twitchy on a track still wet-dry but he set up Fisichella perfectly towards the Senna S: inside – a risk, getting off the dry line – and then threading through side-by-side although, with exquisite judgement, he was able to keep two wheels just on the dry. It was a move from the 1950s – *I will take risks, big risks, whenever I feel I need to* – and it unified Hamilton with those who had gone before him. The move was such a risk that it carried within it an historical continuity. Farina would have understood and applauded, and Ascari, and Fangio, and …

That was lap 18, that was fifth place and Räikkönen was 4.5 seconds up the road.

The weather forecast said no more rain expected.

Hamilton was lapping a second slower than the leaders and another young, hungry driver – Timo Glock in the other Toyota – was coming up behind.

	Massa	Hamilton	Glock
Lap 19	1m 14.7s	1m 15.8s	1m 15.7s
Lap 20	1m 15.0s	1m 15.7s	1m 15.4s
Lap 21	1m 14.7s	1m 15.3s	1m 15.0s

That gave a gap of 1.5 seconds from Hamilton to Glock but Vettel was catching Massa and on that lap 21 set a new fastest lap. That gave a gap of 0.6 of a second. Massa accelerated, pushed the gap to 0.8, 0.9, 0.9, 0.8, set a new fastest lap. Hamilton accelerated, too.

Vettel made his second pit stop on lap 27, some ten laps and more before the others, and it left him sixth – Hamilton up to fourth, of course. Massa led Alonso by 4.2 seconds. Hamilton advanced towards Räikkönen, Vettel starting his recovery.

At lap 34, Massa leading:

Alonso	@ 5.0s
Räikkönen	@ 15.1s
Hamilton	@ 20.2s
Glock	@ 21.7s
Vettel	@ 31.4 s

Massa dipped into the 1m 13s, forcing the gap to Alonso out to 7.1. That was a prelude to the second pit stops: Glock on 36 – but a fuel nozzle problem dropped him to fourteenth, taking pressure off Hamilton – Massa on lap 38, Alonso and Hamilton on 40. It resettled, Massa leading then

Vettel	@ 4.2s
Alonso	@ 6.6s
Räikkönen	@ 18.0s
Hamilton	@ 20.8s

Glock was some 19.0 seconds from Hamilton with thirty of the 71 laps to run. At lap 48 Vettel was 2.4 seconds from Massa, Alonso 8.4, Räikkönen 18.6 and Hamilton 21.3. There was no immediate threat from behind Hamilton. He could remain serene and drive serenely, too, Massa a prisoner of the mathmatics: he could only win the race, not the championship unless something happened to Hamilton. Vettel pitted on lap 51 – out of sequence again, of course – and emerged with Hamilton already gone into fourth place. He could be even more serene. Massa was bombing round in the 1m 14s, Alonso in the 1m 15s, Hamilton in the 1m 15s, too. He looked serene – but Vettel was coming and he was in the 1m 14s.

Hamilton responded and ran at the same pace as Vettel.

The weather forecast changed from no more rain to rain in ten minutes. If that was accurate it would begin when the race had around six laps left and scatter every calculation. Dare you stop for wet tyres? Dare you not? When do you make those decisions and how? A shiver went down the pit lane, compounded by memories of – it did seem a long time ago – the shower before the start, which left some parts of the circuit properly wet and some parts completely dry.

What would that do to the decision making if it happened again? Dark clouds, banks of them, were gathering.

At lap 57 Massa led Alonso by 11.1 seconds, Räikkönen by 15.7, Hamilton by 25.2 and Vettel by 26.2. Räikkönen was catching Alonso although that wouldn't disturb anything either way.

Hamilton was alone.

The Williams drivers were told that when you felt rain on your visors you pit for tyres and just then, with eight laps to run, rain fell in the paddock. It was light. Hamilton's brother Nick emerged from the McLaren garage and craned his head up towards the cloud. Alonso was told on the radio that spots of rain were falling on the main straight.

Seven laps to run. Vettel was with Hamilton, Glock 20.0 seconds further away but a pit stop was taking some 26.0 seconds – slowing, stopping, accelerating – which meant that if Hamilton made one, even as a precaution, he'd be sixth, the championship gone.

Six laps to run. The rain was heavier but Glock in the Toyota stayed out. 'We were running seventh and we'd have probably finished there if it had been totally dry. We saw we had the opportunity to make up some places because of the rain. It started to rain lightly on parts of the circuit with around six laps to go and at that stage everyone was on dry tyres. We took the decision to stay out even though the intensity of the rain was increasing. We were sure we could make up positions when the other cars pitted for wet weather tyres.'

Heidfeld pitted for intermediates from tenth place. It was a rotation of a roulette wheel, all to gain and little to lose. A television camera positioned between two Williams mechanics in the pit lane caught plump raindrops stabbing into what was already a puddle.

Vettel attacked Hamilton, who defended.

The Ferrari mechanics were bringing out intermediate tyres and the finest judgement was at hand: if you went past the pits into another lap and the heavens opened you had to cover the 2.6 miles back, every instant full of danger. If you went into the pits and the heavens closed...

Alonso pitted, total duration 26.6s
Räikkönen pitted, 26.4s.

Hamilton pitted, 26.4s.
Vettel pitted, 26.8s.

On lap 67 – four more to run – Massa pitted, 27.2s, and as he did that the skies darkened but the rain eased. Glock's risk was offering rich rewards as well as potentially dealing a fatal blow to Hamilton's championship. Hamilton now had Vettel poised to swarm all over him, Vettel with his own race to run and his own great truths to prove, Vettel wanting Hamilton's fifth place. McLaren were saying to Hamilton *don't race Vettel, let Vettel through, don't tangle with Vettel, his tyres are in better shape than yours.* McLaren had become convinced that Glock, on dry tyres in the wet, would be vulnerable by the last lap.

Crossing the line to complete lap 68 – three more to run – Massa led then

Alonso	@ 12.4s
Räikkönen	@ 14.2s
Glock	@ 25.3s
Hamilton	@ 35.0s
Vettel	@ 35.9s

Into lap 69 – two more to run – everything tightened around Hamilton who was travelling more slowly than Vettel but doing everything to keep him at bay rather than let him through. Lapping a Force India, Hamilton went wide and Vettel thrust the Toro Rosso towards a gap, couldn't get into it.

Hamilton and Vettel suddenly had Kubica up to them and fully intending to unlap himself. Vettel let him by and then Hamilton let him by into Junção, a 130 mile an hour left. Hamilton drifted towards the rim of the track and Vettel found himself looking at a vast gap. He went cleanly through it, and Hamilton was sixth. His immediate reaction was *I have to retake Vettel and I have two laps to do it.* 'You don't have time to lose focus or think "Oh, God, it's gone."'

Vettel's immediate reaction was that it had cost Hamilton the championship.

Father Anthony Hamilton said 'to be honest, I thought it was over. They were absolutely the worst few moments of my life.'

Brother Nicolas said 'it was terrible for me. As the rain came I started to get really, really scared.'

The rain was falling again but could Glock on dry tyres survive and could he maintain enough pace to stay fourth, holding Hamilton to sixth? Glock felt that the conditions 'were not too bad' and he was exploiting that fully. They completed lap 69:

Massa	1m 19.8s
Alonso	1m 21.7s
Räikkönen	1m 20.3s
Glock	1m 18.6s
Vettel	1m 23.3s
Hamilton	1m 24.6s

Into lap 70 – this lap and one more to run – Vettel and Hamilton lapped a Honda without any drama but Vettel was stretching the gap and Trulli was coming at Hamilton: only 3.4 seconds away. The crucial times and positions completing lap 70, Massa already in to the last lap, Trulli falling away:

		Gap to Hamilton
Glock	1m 28.0s	13.2s
Vettel	1m 25.2s	0.8s
Hamilton	1m 25.5s	
Trulli	1m 33.5s	10.8s

The rain was falling a lot harder, Trulli out of it now but Hamilton faced a great imperative: overtake Vettel. 'I was pushing to get close to Sebastian, who was very quick,' Hamilton said. 'It just got harder and harder. I couldn't get close enough. I didn't know where Glock was and Vettel was the guy to beat. I couldn't catch him so at that point I was going to finish sixth. My heart was in my mouth. I don't know how I kept my cool.'

Massa rounded the great imperious, uphill curve and crossed the line to win the race. It had taken him 1h 34m 11.4s and now everything depended on Hamilton. Massa's race engineer, Rob Smedley, said over the radio that the championship was still alive 'but just wait.'

Glock's risk had suddenly left him exposed and very, very vulnerable as he passed onto the equivalent of ice. 'It was just impossible – so difficult to keep the car on the track. The car was basically undriveable in those conditions. I was sliding everywhere with absolutely no grip at all. I was fighting as hard as I could.'

McLaren told Hamilton *Glock is slowing, you have got to get past him*.

Hamilton could still find nothing to bring him up to Vettel through the curves and undulations as they reached towards Junçäo, the last corner on the circuit. A back marker loomed up ahead then Glock on the right of the track as he struggled with the Toyota. He had no idea Hamilton was so close although Toyota had been constantly updating him about Vettel's position – Vettel closing so fast and poised to take the fourth place. Glock did the only thing he could and concentrated on 'keeping the car on the track.'

Vettel went by just where the track dipped.

Hamilton positioned the McLaren as if he was tucking in behind Glock but, in a fluid movement, angled it towards mid-track and then hugged the left. As they turned through this left at the end of Junçäo and began the climb to the start-finish straight Hamilton was already a car's length ahead. Glock, lost in his concentration, had no idea it was Hamilton. Cars had been passing on the lap – Glock estimated three or four – 'and it was not easy to keep track of what was going on.' Glock certainly didn't know he had settled the World Championship.

The Ferrari pit miscounted it and, after a riot of jubilation, subsided into a wake of stunned faces.

Hamilton crossed the line and was imploring 'do I have it? Do I have it?'

Smedley told Massa, now deep into his slowing down lap, that Hamilton was champion by single point.

'Sport is like this and you have to accept it,' Massa would say. He would though – his own words – leave Interlagos with his head held high, adding: in life you learn when you win and you learn when you lose.

The Hamilton clan, including girlfriend Nicole Scherzinger, were making the pit lane a carnival of emotions. Anthony couldn't speak and sounded breathless even not speaking. Eventually, in a reverberating murmur, he did say 'absolutely great, absolutely great.'

On the slowing down lap Hamilton lifted his visor and dabbed his eyes. He said on the radio 'I am speechless.' Eventually he said the team deserved it and his family deserved it, so the championship was for all of them.

In all this, it was easy to forget he'd become the youngest man to win it.

The statistics of the final lap explained how. He'd done 1m 26.1s, poor Glock 1m 44.7s and that gave Hamilton a margin of 5.4 seconds over him.

In the parc fermé Massa lifted his visor and put a gloved hand to his eyes. Then he clambered out, stood and faced the crowd. Gently he tapped his heart three or four times, bowed, and raised both hands with the index fingers making the figure 1. At least I won the race, at least I did all I could.

Vettel, grinning broadly, said 'dramatic finish!'

When Hamilton reached the parc fermé everybody wanted to embrace him and he wanted to embrace everybody. A few minutes before, that had been Massa's father in the Ferrari pit. The championship had been won and lost very, very quickly.

Massa led the Champagne fight on the podium although, of course, Hamilton wasn't there because fifth places might get you a championship but never a podium place by right. Below Massa, Hamilton sprinted the pit lane as if he'd explode if he didn't get the release of movement. His father embraced him.

Somewhere, someone explained quietly to Timo Glock that it was indeed Hamilton who'd gone past.

Hamilton summed up the mood of the moment, and summed up the whole of his life, when he said in his own soft-spoken way: 'You just have to keep believing.'

He might have been speaking for all the twenty-nine champions before.

APPENDIX 1:
THE DRIVERS

In chronological order of first winning it. Winning year or years in brackets. Career statistics complete to the end of 2008.

Giuseppe Farina (1950), born Turin, Italy, 30 October 1906, died in a road accident 30 June 1966. Thirty-three races for Alfa Romeo and Ferrari between 1950 and 1955, 5 poles, 5 wins, 6 fastest laps.

Juan Manuel Fangio (1951, '54, '55, '56, '57), born Balcarce, Argentina, 24 June 1911, died 17 July 1995. Fifty-one races for Alfa Romeo, Maserati, Mercedes and Ferrari between 1950 and 1958, 28 poles, 24 wins, 23 fastest laps.

Alberto Ascari (1952, '53), born Milan, Italy, 13 July 1918, died 26 May 1955 testing at Monza. Thirty-two races for Ferrari, Maserati and Lancia between 1950 and 1955, 14 poles, 13 wins, 11 fastest laps.

Mike Hawthorn (1958), born Mexborough, Yorkshire, England, 10 April 1929, died 22 January 1959 in a road accident. Forty-five races for Cooper, Ferrari, Vanwall, Maserati and BRM between 1952 and 1958, 4 poles, 3 wins, 6 fastest laps.

Sir Jack Brabham (1959, '60, '66), born Hurstville, Australia, 2 April 1926. One hundred and twenty-six races for Cooper, Maserati, Lotus and Brabham between 1955 and 1970, 13 poles, 14 wins, 10 fastest laps.

Phil Hill (1961), born Santa Monica, California, 20 April 1927, died 28 August 2008. Forty-eight races for Maserati, Ferrari, Cooper, ATS and Lotus between 1958 and 1966, 6 poles, 3 wins, 6 fastest laps.

Graham Hill (1962, '68), born London, England, 17 February 1929, died 29 November 1975 in a plane crash. One hundred and seventy-six races for Lotus, BRM, Brabham, Shadow and Lola between 1958 and 1975, 13 poles, 14 wins, 10 fastest laps.

Jim Clark (1963, '65), born Kilmany, Fife, Scotland, 14 March 1936, died 7 April 1968 in a Formula 2 race, Hockenheim. Seventy-two races for Lotus between 1960 and 1968, 33 poles, 25 wins, 28 fastest laps.

John Surtees (1964), born Surrey, England, 11 February 1934. One hundred and eleven races for Lotus, Cooper, Lola, Ferrari, Honda, BRM, McLaren and Surtees between 1960 and 1972, 8 poles, 6 wins, 11 fastest laps.

Denis Hulme (1967), born Motueka, New Zealand, 18 June 1936, died 4 October 1992. One hundred and twelve races for Brabham and McLaren between 1965 and 1974, 1 pole, 8 wins, 9 fastest laps.

Jackie Stewart (1969, '71, '73), born Milton, Dumbarton, Scotland, 11 June 1939. Ninety-nine races for BRM, Matra and Tyrrell between 1965 and 1973, 17 poles, 27 wins, 15 fastest laps.

Jochen Rindt (1970), born Mainz, Frankfurt, 18 April 1942 but evacuated to Austria and took Austrian citizenship, died 5 September 1970 qualifying for the Italian Grand Prix, Monza. Sixty races for Brabham, Cooper and Lotus between 1964 and 1970, 10 poles, 6 wins, 3 fastest laps.

Emerson Fittipaldi (1972, '74), born Sao Paulo, Brazil, 12 December 1946. One hundred and forty-four races for Lotus, McLaren, Copersucar and Fittipaldi between 1970 and 1980, 6 poles, 14 wins, 6 fastest laps.

Niki Lauda (1975, '77, '84), born Vienna, Austria, 22 February 1949. One hundred and seventy-one races for March, BRM, Ferrari, Brabham and McLaren between 1971 and 1985, 24 poles, 25 wins, 25 fastest laps.

James Hunt (1976), born Sutton, Surrey, England, 29 August 1947, died 15 June 1993. Ninety-two races for Hesketh, McLaren and Wolf between 1973 and 1979, 14 poles, 10 wins, 8 fastest laps.

Mario Andretti (1978), born Montona, Trieste, Italy, 28 February 1940, emigrated to the United States in 1955, became a naturalized American. One hundred and twenty-eight races for Lotus, March, Ferrari, Parnelli, Alfa Romeo and Williams between 1968 and 1982, 18 poles, 12 wins, 10 fastest laps.

Jody Scheckter (1979), born East London, South Africa, 29 January 1950. One hundred and twelve races for McLaren, Tyrrell, Wolf and Ferrari between 1972 and 1980, 3 poles, 10 wins, 6 fastest laps.

Alan Jones (1980), born Melbourne, Australia, 2 November 1946. One hundred and sixteen races for Hesketh, Lola, Surtees, Shadow, Williams, Arrows and Lola between 1975 and 1986, 6 poles, 12 wins, 13 fastest laps.

Nelson Piquet (1981, '83, '87), born Rio, Brazil, 17 August 1952. Two hundred and four races for Ensign, McLaren, Brabham, Williams, Lotus and Benetton between 1978 and 1991, 24 poles, 23 wins, 23 fastest laps.

Keke Rosberg (1982), born Stockholm, Sweden, 6 December 1948 but of Finnish parents and Finnish nationality. One hundred and fourteen races for Theodore, ATS, Wolf, Fittipaldi, Williams, McLaren between 1978 and 1986, 5 poles 5 wins, 3 fastest laps.

Alain Prost (1985, '86, '89, '93), born St-Chamond, France, 24 February 1955. One hundred and ninety-nine races for McLaren, Renault, Ferrari and Williams between 1980 and 1993, 33 poles 51 wins, 41 fastest laps.

Ayrton Senna (1988, '90, '91), born Sao Paulo, Brazil, 21 March 1960, died 1 May 1994 in a crash at the San Marino Grand Prix. One hundred and sixty-one races for Toleman, Lotus, McLaren and Williams between 1984 and 1994, 65 poles, 41 wins, 19 fastest laps.

Nigel Mansell (1992), born Upton-on-Severn, England, 8 August 1953. One hundred and eighty-seven races for Lotus, Williams, Ferrari and Mclaren between 1980 and 1995, 32 poles, 31 wins, 30 fastest laps.

Michael Schumacher (1994, '95, 2000, '01, '02. '03, '04), born Hürth-Hermülheim, Germany, 3 January 1969. Two hundred and fifty races for Jordan, Benetton and Ferrari between 1991 and 2006, 68 poles, 91 wins, 76 fastest laps.

Damon Hill (1996), born Hampstead, London, 17 September 1960. One hundred and twenty two races for Brabham, Williams, Arrows and Jordan between 1992 and 1999, 20 poles, 22 wins, 19 fastest laps.

Jacques Villeneuve (1997), born Saint-Jean-sur-Richelieu, Quebec, 9 April, 1971. One hundred and sixty five races for Williams, BAR, Renault and Sauber between 1996 and 2006, 13 poles, 11 wins, 9 fastest laps.

Mika Häkkinen (1998, '99), born Vantaa, Finland, 28 September, 1968. One hundred and sixty five races for Lotus and McLaren between 1991 and 2001, 26 poles, 20 wins, 25 fastest laps.

Fernando Alonso (2005, '06), born Oviedo, Spain, 29 July, 1981. One hundred and twenty three races for Minardi, Renault and McLaren between 2001 and 2008, 17 poles, 21 wins, 11 fastest laps.

Kimi Räikkönen (2007), born Espoo, Finland, 17 October, 1979. One hundred and forty races for Sauber, McLaren and Ferrari between 2001 and 2008, 16 poles, 17 wins, 35 fastest laps.

Lewis Hamilton (2008), born Stevenage, Hertfordshire, 7 January 1985. Thirty-five races for McLaren between 2007 and 2008, 9 wins, 13 pole positions, 3 fastest laps.

APPENDIX 2:
THE RACES

Note: World Champion in italic type.

Championship points: between 1950 and 1991 a driver could only count a certain number of finishes (it varied from season to season). The points he could count are given, followed by his grand total in brackets.

The half points (expressed as .5) are where drivers shared a car and divided the points or a race was stopped before the end.

1950 Italian Grand Prix, Monza, 80 laps (312m/502km)
1 *G. Farina* (Alfa Romeo) 2h 51m 17.4s (109.7mph/176.5kmh)
2 D. Serafini/A Ascari (Ferrari) at 1m 18.6s
3 L. Fagiolo (Alfa Romeo) at 1m 35.6s
4 L. Rosier (Talbot) at five laps
5 P. Etancelin (Talbot) at five laps
6 E. de Graffenried (Maserati) at eight laps
Championship: Farina 30, Fangio 27, Fagioli 24 (28)

1951 Spanish Grand Prix, Barcelona, 70 laps (274.4m/441.5km)
1 *J. M. Fangio* (Alfa Romeo) 2h 46m 54.1s (98.7mph/158.9kmh)
2 F. Gonzalez (Ferrari) at 54.3s
3 G. Farina (Alfa Romeo) at 1m 45.6s
4 A. Ascari (Ferrari) at two laps
5 F. Bonetto (Alfa Romeo) at two laps
6 E. de Graffenried (Alfa Romeo) at four laps
Championship: Fangio 31 (37), Ascari 25 (28), Gonzalez 24 (27)

1952 German Grand Prix, Nürburgring, 18 laps (254.7m/409.9km)
1 *A. Ascari* (Ferrari) 3h 6m 13.2s (82.2mph/132.2kmh)
2 G. Farina (Ferrari) at 14.1s
3 R. Fischer (Ferrari) at 7m 10.1s
4 P. Taruffi (Ferrari) at one lap
5 J. Behra (Gordini) at one lap
6 R. Laurent (Ferrari) at two laps
Championship: Ascari 36 (52.5), Farina 24 (28), Taruffi 22

1953 Swiss Grand Prix, Bremgarten, 65 laps (294.0m/473.1km)
1 *A. Ascari* (Ferrari) 3h 1m 34.4s (97.1mph/156.3kmh)
2 G. Farina (Ferrari) at 13.2s
3 M. Hawthorn (Ferrari) at 1m 36.3s
4 F. Bonetto/J. M. Fangio (Maserati) at one lap
5 H. Lang (Maserati) at three laps
6 L. Villoresi (Ferrari) at three laps
Championship: Ascari 34.5 (46.5), Fangio 28 (29.5), Farina 26 (32)

1954 Swiss Grand Prix, Bremgartcn, 66 laps (280.5m/451.4km)
1 *J. M. Fangio* (Mercedes) 3h 0m 34.5s (99.2mph/159.6kmh)
2 F. Gonzalez (Ferrari) at 58.0s
3 H. Herrmann (Mercedes) at one lap
4 R. Mieres (Maserati) at two laps
5 S. Mantovani (Maserati) at two laps
6 K. Wharton (Maserati) at two laps
Championship: Fangio 42 (57), Gonzalez 25 (26.5), Hawthorn 24.5

1955 Italian Grand Prix, Monza, 50 laps (310.6m/500.0km)
1 *J. M. Fangio* (Mercedes) 2h 25m 4.4s (128.4mph/206.7kmh)
2 P. Taruffi (Mercedes) at 0.7s
3 E. Castellotti (Ferrari) at 46.0s
4 J. Behra (Maserati) at one lap
5 C. Mendiléguy (Maserati) at one lap
6 U. Magiolo (Ferrari) at one lap
Championship: Fangio 40 (41), Moss 23, Castellotti 12

1956 Italian Grand Prix, Monza, 50 laps (310.6m/500.0km)
1 S. Moss (Maserati) 2h 23m 41.3s (129.7mph/208.7kmh)
2 P. Collins/*J. M. Fangio* (Ferrari) at 5.7s
3 R. Flockhart (Connaught) at one lap
4 F. Godia (Maserati) at one lap
5 J. Fairman (Connaught) at three laps
6 L. Piotti (Maserati) at three laps
Championship: Fangio 30 (33), Moss 27 (28), Collins 25

1957 German Grand Prix, Nürburgring, 22 laps (311.3m/500.9km)
1 *J. M. Fangio* (Maserati) 3h 30m 38.3s (88.8mph/142.9kmh)
2 M. Hawthorn Ferrari) at 3.6s
3 P. Collins (Ferrari) at 34.6s
4 L. Musso (Ferrari) at 3m 27.6s
5 S. Moss (Vanwall) at 4m 27.5s
6 J. Behra (Maserati) at 4m 28.5s
Championship: Fangio 40 (46), Moss 25, Musso 16

1958 Moroccan Grand Prix, Casablanca, 53 laps (250.3m/402.8km)
1 S. Moss (Vanwall) 2h 9m 15.ls (116.4mph/195.0kmh)
2 *M. Hawthorn* (Ferrari) at 1m 24.7s
3 P. Hill (Ferrari) at 1m 25.5s
4 J. Bonnier (BRM) at 1m 46.7s
5 H. Schell (BRM) at 2m 33.7s
6 M. Gregory (Maserati) at one lap
Championship: Hawthorn 42 (49), Moss 41, Brooks 24

1959 United States Grand Prix, Sebring, 42 laps (217.3m/349.7km)
1 B. McLaren (Cooper) 2h l2m 35.7s (98.8mph/159.0kmh)
2 M. Trintignant (Cooper) at 0.4s
3 T. Brooks (Ferrari) at 3m 00.9s
4 *J. Brabham* (Cooper) at 4m 57.3s
5 I. Ireland (Lotus) at three laps
6 W. von Trips (Ferrari) at four laps
Championship: Brabham 31 (34), Brooks 27, Moss 25.5.

1960 Portuguese Grand Prix, Oporto, 55 laps (256.3m/412.4km)
1 *J. Brabham* (Cooper) 2h 19m 0.0s (109.2mph/175.8kmh)
2 B. McLaren (Cooper) at 57.9s
3 J. Clark (Lotus) at 1m 53.2s
4 W. von Trips (Ferrari) at 1m 58.8s
5 T. Brooks (Cooper) at six laps
6 I. Ireland (Lotus) at seven laps
Championship: Brabham 43, McLaren 34 (37), Moss 19

1961 Italian Grand Prix, Monza, 43 laps (268.3m/431.7km)
1 *P. Hill* (Ferrari) 2h 3m 13.0s (130.1mph/209.3kmh)
2 D. Gurney (Porsche) at 31.2s
3 B. McLaren (Cooper) at 2m 28.4s
4 J. Lewis (Cooper) at 2m 40.4s
5 T. Brooks (Cooper) at 2m 40.5s
6 R. Salvadori (Cooper) at one lap
Championship: P. Hill 34 (38), von Trips 33, Moss and Gurney 21

1962 South African Grand Prix, East London, 82 laps
(199.9m/321.7km)
1 *G. Hill* (BRM) 2h 8m 3.3s (93.5mph/150.6kmh)
2 B. McLaren (Cooper) at 49.8s
3 T. Maggs (Cooper) at 50.3s
4 J. Brabham, (Brabham) at 53.8s
5 I. Ireland (Lotus) at one lap
6 N. Lederle (Lotus) at four laps
Championship: G Hill 42 (52), Clark 30, McLaren 27 (32)

1963 Italian Grand Prix, Monza, 86 laps (307.2m/494.4km)
1 *J. Clark* (Lotus) 2h 24m 19.6s (127.7mph/205.5kmh)
2 R. Ginther (BRM) at 1m 35.0s
3 B. McLaren (Cooper) at one lap
4 I. Ireland (BRM) at two laps
5 J. Brabham (Brabham) at two laps
6 T. Maggs (Cooper) at two laps
Championship: Clark 54 (73), G Hill 29, Ginther 29 (34)

1964 Mexican Grand Prix, Mexico City, 65 laps (201.9m/324.9km)
1 D. Gurney (Brabham) 2h 9m 50.3s (93.3mph/150.1kmh)
2 *J. Surtees* (Ferrari) at 1m 08.9s
3 L. Bandini (Ferrari) at 1m 09.6s
4 M. Spence (Lotus) at 1m 21.8s
5 J. Clark (Lotus) at one lap
6 P. Rodriguez (Ferrari) at one lap
Championship: Surtees 40, G. Hill 39 (41), Clark 32

1965 German Grand Prix, Nürburgring, 15 laps (212.2m/341.5km)
1 *J. Clark* (Lotus) 2h 7m 52.4s (99.7mph/160.5kmh)
2 G. Hill (BRM) at 15.9s
3 D. Gurney (Brabham) at 21.4s
4 J. Rindt (Cooper) at 3m 29.6s
5 J. Brabham (Brabham) at 4m 41.2s
6 L. Bandini (Ferrari) at 5m 08.6s
Championship: Clark 54, G. Hill 40 (47), Stewart 33 (34)

1966 Italian Grand Prix, Monza, 68 laps (242.9m/390.9km)
1 L. Scarfiotti (Ferrari) 1h 47m 14.8s (135.9mph/218.7kmh)
2 M. Parkes (Ferrari) at 5.8s
3 D. Hulme (Brabham) at 6.1s
4 J. Rindt (Cooper) at one lap
5 M. Spence (Lotus) at one lap
6 B. Anderson (Brabham) at two laps
J.Brabham (Brabham) did not finish
Championship: Brabham 42 (45), Surtees 28, Rindt 22 (24)

1967 Mexican Grand Prix, Mexico City, 65 laps (201.9m/324.9km)
1 J. Clark (Lotus) 1h 59m 28.7s (101.4mph/163.2kmh)
2 J. Brabham (Brabham) at 1m 25.5s
3 *D. Hulme* (Brabham) at one lap
4 J. Surtees (Honda) at one lap
5 M. Spence (BRM) at two laps
6 P. Rodriguez (Cooper) at two laps
Championship: Hulme 51, Brabham 46 (48), Clark 41

1968 Mexican Grand Prix, Mexico City, 65 laps (201.9m/324.9km)
1 *G. Hill* (Lotus) 1h 56m 43.95s (103.8mph/167.0kmh)
2 B. McLaren (McLaren) at 1m 19.3s
3 J. Oliver (Lotus) at 1m 40.1s
4 P. Rodriguez (BRM) at 1m 41.0s
5 J. Bonnier (Honda) at one lap
6 J. Siffert (Lotus) at one lap
Championship: G. Hill 48, Stewart 36, Hulme 33

1969 Italian Grand Prix, Monza, 68 laps (242.9m/390.9km)
1 *J. Stewart* (Matra) 1h 39m 11.2s (146.9mph/236.5kmh)
2 J. Rindt (Lotus) at 0.08s
3 J. P. Beltoise (Matra) at 0.1s
4 B. McLaren (McLaren) at 0.1s
5 P. Courage (Brabham) at 33.4s
6 P. Rodriguez (Ferrari) at two laps
Championship: Stewart 63, Ickx 37, McLaren 26

1970 United States Grand Prix, Watkins Glen, 108 laps
(248.2m/399.5km)
1 E. Fittipaldi (Lotus) 1h 57m 32.7s (126.7mph/204.0kmh)
2 P. Rodriguez (BRM) at 36.3s
3 R. Wisell (Lotus) at 45.1s
4 J. Ickx (Ferrari) at one lap
5 C. Amon (March) at one lap
6 D. Bell (Surtees) at one lap.
J. Rindt (Lotus) killed in qualifying for the Italian Grand Prix.
Championship: Rindt 45, Ickx 40, Regazzoni 33

1971 Austrian Grand Prix, Österreichring, 54 laps (198.3m/319.1km)
1 J. Siffert (BRM) 1h 30m 23.9s (131.6mph/211.8kmh)
2 E. Fittipaldi (Lotus) at 4.1s
3 T. Schenken (Brabham) at 19.7s
4 R. Wisell (Lotus) at 31.8s
5 G. Hill (Brabham) at 48.4s
6 H. Pescarolo (March) at 1m 24.5s
J. Stewart (Tyrrell) did not finish
Championship: Stewart 62, Peterson 33, Cevert 26

1972 Italian Grand Prix, Monza, 55 laps (197.3m/317.5km)
1 *E. Fittipaldi* (Lotus) 1h 29m 58.4s (131.6mph/211.8kmh)
2 M. Hailwood (Surtees) at 14.5s
3 D. Hulme (McLaren) at 23.8s
4 P. Revson (McLaren) at 35.7s
5 G. Hill (Brabham) at 1m 05.6s
6 P. Gethin (BRM) at 1m 21.9s
Championship: Fittipaldi 61, Stewart 45, Hulme 39

1973 Italian Grand Prix, Monza, 55 laps (197.3m/317.5km)
1 R. Peterson (Lotus) 1h 29m 17.0s (132.6mph/213.4kmh)
2 E. Fittipaldi (Lotus) at 0.8s
3 P. Revson (McLaren) at 28.8s
4 *J. Stewart* (Tyrrell) at 33.2s
5 F. Cevert (Tyrrell) at 46.2s
6 C. Reutemann (Brabham) at 59.8s
Championship: Stewart 71, Fittipaldi 55, Peterson 52

1974 United States Grand Prix, Watkins Glen, 59 laps (199.1m/320.4km)
1 C. Reutemann (Brabham) 1h 40m 21.4s (119.1mph/191.7kmh)
2 C. Pace (Brabham) at 10.7s
3 J. Hunt (Hesketh) at 1m 10.3s
4 *E. Fittipaldi* (McLaren) at 1m 17.7s
5 J. Watson (Brabham) at 1m 25.8s
6 P. Depailler (Tyrrell) at 1m 27.5s
Championship: Fittipaldi 55, Regazzoni 52, Scheckter 45

1975 Italian Grand Prix, Monza, 52 laps (186.7m/300.5km)
1 C. Regazzoni (Ferrari) 1h 22m 42.6s (135.4mph/218.0kmh)
2 E. Fittipaldi (McLaren) at 16.6s
3 *N. Lauda* (Ferrari) at 23.2s
4 C. Reutemann (Brabham) at 55.1s
5 J. Hunt (Hesketh) at 57.1s
6 T. Pryce (Shadow) at 1m 15.9s
Championship: Lauda 64.5, Fittipaldi 45, Reutemann 37

1976 Japanese Grand Prix, Mount Fuji, 73 laps (197.7m/318.1km)
1 M. Andretti (Lotus) 1h 43m 58.8s (114.0mph/183.6kmh)
2 P. Depailler (Tyrrell) at one lap
3 *J. Hunt* (McLaren) at one lap
4 A. Jones (Surtees) at one lap
5 C. Regazzoni (Ferrari) one lap
6 G. Nilsson (Lotus) at one lap
Championship: Hunt 69, Lauda 68, Scheckter 49

1977 United States East, Watkins Glen 59 laps (199.2m/320.5km)
1 J. Hunt (McLaren) 1h 58m 23.2s (100.9mph/162.5kmh)
2 M. Andretti (Lotus) at 2.0s
3 J. Scheckter (Wolf) at 1m 18.8s
4 *N. Lauda* (Ferrari) at 1m 40.6s
5 C. Regazzoni (Ensign) at 1m 48.1s
6 C. Reutemann (Ferrari) at one lap
Championship: Lauda 72, Scheckter 55, Andretti 47

1978 Italian Grand Prix, Monza, 40 laps (144.1m/231.9km)
1 N. Lauda (Brabham) 1h 7m 4.5s (128.9mph/207.5kmh)
2 J. Watson (Brabham) at 1.4s
3 C. Reutemann (Ferrari) at 20.4s
4 J. Laffite (Ligier) at 37.5s
5 P. Tambay (McLaren) at 40.3s
6 *M. Andretti* (Lotus) at 46.3s
(Andretti penalised a minute for jumping the start)
Championship: Andretti 64, Peterson 51, Reutemann 48

1979 Italian Grand Prix, Monza, 50 laps (180.2m/289.9km)
1 *J. Scheckter* (Ferrari) 1h 22m 0.2s (131.8mph/212.1kmh)
2 G. Villeneuve (Ferrari) at 0.4s
3 C. Regazzoni (Williams) at 4.7s
4 N. Lauda (Brabham) at 54.4s
5 M. Andretti (Lotus) at 59.7s
6 J. P. Jarier (Tyrrell) at 1m 01.5s
Championship: Scheckter 51 (60), Villeneuve 47 (53), Jones 40 (43)

1980 Canadian Grand Prix, Montreal, 70 laps (191.8m/308.6km)
1 *A. Jones* (Williams) 1h 46m 45.5s (107.8mph/173.4kmh)
2 C. Reutemann (Williams) at 15.5s
3 D. Pironi (Ligier) at 19.8s
4 J. Watson (McLaren) at 30.9s
5 G. Villeneuve (Ferrari) at 55.2s
6 H. Rebaque (Brabham) at one lap
Championship: Jones 67 (71), Piquet 54, Reutemann 42 (49)

1981 United States Grand Prix, Las Vegas, 75 laps (170.1m/273.6km)
1 A. Jones (Williams) 1h 44m 9.0s (97.9mph/157.7kmh)
2 A. Prost (Renault) at 20.0s
3 B. Giacomelli (Alfa Romeo) at 20.4s
4 N. Mansell (Lotus) at 47.4s
5 *N. Piquet* (Brabham) at 1m 16.4s
6 J. Laffite (Ligier) at 1m 18.1s
Championship: Piquet 50, Reutemann 49, Jones 46

1982 United States Grand Prix, Las Vegas, 75 laps (170.1m/273.6km)
1 M. Alboreto (Tyrrell) 1h 41m 56.8s (100.1mph/161.1kmh)
2 J. Watson (McLaren) at 27.2s
3 E. Cheever (Ligier) at 56.4s
4 A. Prost (Renault) at 1m 08.6s
5 *K. Rosberg* (Williams) at 1m 11.3s
6 D. Daly (Williams) at one lap
Championship: Rosberg 44, Pironi and Watson 39, Prost 34

1983 South African Grand Prix, Kyalami, 77 laps (196.3m/315.9km)
1 R. Patrese (Brabham) 1h 33m 25.7s (126.1mph/202.9kmh)
2 A. de Cesaris (Alfa Romeo) at 9.3s
3 *N. Piquet* (Brabham) at 21.9s
4 D. Warwick (Toleman) at one lap
5 K. Rosberg (Williams) at one lap
6 E. Cheever (Renault) at one lap
Championship: Piquet 59, Prost 57, Arnoux 49

1984 Portuguese Grand Prix, Estoril, 70 laps (189.2m/304.4km)
1 A. Prost (McLaren) 1h 41m 11.7s (112.1mph/180.5kmh)
2 *N. Lauda* (McLaren) at 13.4s
3 A. Senna (Toleman) at 20.0s
4 M. Alboreto (Ferrari) at 20.3s
5 E. de Angelis (Lotus) at 1m 32.1s
6 N. Piquet (Brabham) at one lap
Championship: Lauda 72, Prost 71.5, de Angelis 34

1985 European Grand Prix, Brands Hatch, 75 laps (196.0m/315.4km)
1 N. Mansell (Williams) 1h 32m 58s (126.5mph/203.6kmh)
2 A. Senna (Lotus) at 21.3s
3 K. Rosberg (Williams) at 58.5s
4 *A. Prost* (McLaren) at 1m 06.1s
5 E. de Angelis (Lotus) at one lap
6 T. Boutsen (Arrows) at two laps
Championship: Prost 73 (76), Alboreto 53, Rosberg 40

1986 Australian Grand Prix, Adelaide, 82 laps (192.6m/309.9km)
1 *A. Prost* (McLaren) 1h 54m 20.3s (101.0mph/162.6kmh)
2 N. Piquet (Williams) at 4.2s
3 S. Johansson (Ferrari) at one lap
4 M. Brundle (Tyrrell) at one lap
5 P. Streiff (Tyrrell) at two laps
6 J. Dumfries (Lotus) at two laps
Championship: Prost 72 (74), Mansell 70 (72), Piquet 69

1987 Japanese Grand Prix, Suzuka, 51 laps (185.6m/298.7km)
1 G. Berger (Ferrari) 1h 32m 58.0s (119.8mph/192.8kmh)
2 A. Senna (Lotus) at 17.3s
3 S. Johansson (McLaren) at 17.6s
4 M. Alboreto (Ferrari) at 1m 20.4s
5 T. Boutsen (Benetton) at 1m 25.5s
6 S. Nakajima (Lotus) at 1m 36.4s
N. Piquet (Williams) did not finish
Championship: Piquet 73 (76), Mansell 61, Senna 57

1988 Japanese Grand Prix, Suzuka, 51 laps (185.6m/298.7km)
1 *A. Senna* (McLaren) 1h 33m 26.1s (119.2mph/191.8kmh)
2 A. Prost (McLaren) at 13.3s
3 T. Boutsen (Benetton) at 36.1s
4 G. Berger (Ferrari) at 1m 26.7s
5 A. Nannini (Benetton) at 1m 30.6s
6 R. Patrese (Williams) at 1m 37.6s
Championship: Senna 90 (94), Prost 87 (105), Berger 41

1989 Japanese Grand Prix, Suzuka, 53 laps (192.9m/310.4km)
1 A. Nannini (Benetton) 1h 35m 06.2s (121.7mph/195.9kmh)
2 R. Patrese (Williams) at 11.9s
3 T. Boutsen (Williams) at 13.4s
4 N. Piquet (Lotus) at 1m 44.2s
5 M. Brundle (Brabham) at one lap
6 D. Warwick (Arrows) at one lap
A. Prost (McLaren) did not finish
Championship: Prost 76 (81), Senna 60, Patrese 40

1990 Japanese Grand Prix, Suzuka, 53 laps (192.9m/310.4km)
1 N. Piquet (Benetton) 1h 34m 36.8s (122.3mph/196.9kmh)
2 R. Moreno (Benetton) at 7.2s
3 A. Suzuki (Lola) at 22.4s
4 R. Patrese (Williams) at 36.2s
5 T. Boutsen (Williams) at 46.8s
6 S. Nakajima (Tyrrell) at 1m 12.3s
A. Senna (McLaren) did not finish
Championship: Senna 78, Prost 71 (73), Piquet 43 (44)

1991 Japanese Grand Prix, Suzuka, 53 laps (192.9m/310.4km)
1 G. Berger (McLaren) 1h 32m 10.6s (125.7mph/202.2kmh)
2 *A. Senna* (McLaren) at 0.3s
3 R. Patrese (Williams) at 56.7s
4 A. Prost (Ferrari) at 1m 20.7s
5 M. Brundle (Brabham) at one lap
6 S. Modena (Tyrrell) at one lap
Championship: Senna 96, Mansell 72, Patrese 53

1992 Hungarian Grand Prix, Budapest, 77 laps (191.5m/308.3km)
1 A. Senna (McLaren) 1h 46m 19.2s (107.1mph/172.4kmh)
2 *N. Mansell* (Williams) at 40.1s
3 G. Berger (McLaren) at 50.7s
4 M. Häkkinen (Lotus) at 54.3s
5 M. Brundle (Benetton) at 57.4s
6 I. Capelli (Ferrari) at one lap
Championship: Mansell 108, Patrese 56, Schumacher 53

1993 Portuguese Grand Prix, Estoril, 71 laps (191.9m/308.8km)
1 M. Schumacher (Benetton) 1h 32m 46.3s (124.1mph/199.7kmh)
2 *A. Prost* (Williams) at 0.9s
3 D. Hill (Williams) at 8.2s
4 J. Alesi (Ferrari) at 1m 07.6s
5 K. Wendlinger (Sauber) at one lap
6 M. Brundle (Ligier) at one lap
Championship: Prost 99, Senna 73, D. Hill 69

1994 Australian Grand Prix, Adelaide, 81 laps (190.2m/306.1km)
1 N. Mansell (Williams) 1h 47m 51.4s (105.8mph/170.3kmh)
2 G. Berger (Ferrari) at 2.5s
3 M. Brundle (McLaren) at 52.4s
4 R. Barrichello (Jordan) at 1m 10.5s
5 O. Panis (Ligier) at one lap
6 J. Alesi (Ferrari) at one lap
M. Schumacher (Benetton) did not finish
Championship: Schumacher 92, D. Hill 91, Berger 41

1995 Pacific Grand Prix, Aida, 83 laps (129.6m/208.6km)
1 *M. Schumacher* (Benetton) 1h 48m 49.9s (105.2mph/169.4kmh)
2 D. Coulthard (Williams) at 14.9s
3 D. Hill (Williams) at 48.3s
4 G. Berger (Ferrari) at one lap
5 J. Alesi (Ferrari) at one lap
6 J. Herbert (Benetton) at one lap
Championship: Schumacher 102, D. Hill 69, Coulthard 49

1996 Japanese Grand Prix, Suzuka, 52 laps (189.3m/304.7km)
1 *D. Hill* (Williams) 1h 32m 33.7s (122.7mph/197.5kmh)
2 M. Schumacher (Ferrari) at 1.8s
3 M. Häkkinen (McLaren) at 3.2s
4 G. Berger (Benetton) at 26.5s
5 M. Brundle (Jordan) at 1m 07.1s
6 H.H. Frentzen (Sauber) at 1m 21.1s
Championship: D. Hill 97, Villeneuve 78, Schumacher 59

1997 European Grand Prix, Jerez, 69 laps (189.8m/305.5km)
1 M. Häkkinen (McLaren) 1h 38m 57.7s (115.1mph/185.2kmh)
2 D. Coulthard (McLaren) at 1.6s
3 *J. Villeneuve* (Williams) at 1.8s
4 G. Berger (Benetton) at 1.9s
5 E. Irvine (Ferrari) at 3.7s
6 H.H. Frentzen (Williams) at 4.5s
Championship: Villeneuve 81, Frentzen 42, Coulthard and Alesi 36
Note: Schumacher (78 points) excluded from the championship

1998 Japanese Grand Prix, Suzuka, 51 laps (185.7m/298.8km)
1 *M. Häkkinen* (McLaren) 1h 27m 22.5s (127.5mph/205.2kmh)
2 E. Irvine (Ferrari) at 6.4s
3 D. Coulthard (McLaren) at 27.6s
4 D. Hill (Jordan) at 1m 13.4s
5 H.H. Frentzen (Williams) at 1m 13.8s
6 J. Villeneuve (Williams) at 1m 15.8s
Championship: Häkkinen 100, Schumacher 86, Coulthard 56

1999 Japanese Grand Prix, Suzuka, 53 laps (192.9m/310.5km)
1 *M. Häkkinen* (McLaren) 1h 31m 18.7s (126.8mph/204.0kmh)
2 M. Schumacher (Ferrari) at 5.0s
3 E. Irvine (Ferrari) at 1m 35.6s
4 H.H. Frentzen (Jordan) at 1m 38.6s
5 R. Schumacher (Williams) at 1m 39.4s
6 J. Alesi (Sauber) at one lap
Championship: Häkkinen 76, Irvine 74, Frentzen 55

2000 Japanese Grand Prix, Suzuka, 53 laps (192.9m/310.5km)
1 *M. Schumacher* (Ferrari) 1h 29m 53.4s (128.8mph/207.3kmh)
2 M. Häkkinen (McLaren) at 1.8s
3 D. Coulthard (McLaren) at 1m 09.9s
4 R. Barrichello (Ferrari) at 1m 19.1s
5 J. Button (Williams) at 1m 25.6s
6 J. Villeneuve (BAR) at one lap
Championship: Schumacher 108, Häkkinen 89, Coulthard 73

2001 Hungarian Grand Prix, Hungaroring, 77 laps (190.1m/306.0km)
1. *M. Schumacher* (Ferrari) 1h 41m 49.6s (112.0mph/180.3kmh)
2. R. Barrichello (Ferrari) at 3.3s
3. D. Coulthard (McLaren) at 3.9s
4. R. Schumacher (Williams) at 49.6s
5. M. Häkkinen (McLaren) at 1m 10.2s
6. N. Heidfeld (Sauber) at one lap
Championship: Schumacher 123, Coulthard 65, Barrichello 56

2002 French Grand Prix, Magny-Cours,72 laps (190.0m/305.8km)
1 *M. Schumacher* (Ferrari) 1h 32m 09.8s (123.7mph/199.1kmh)
2 K. Räikkönen (McLaren) at 1.1s
3 D. Coulthard (McLaren) at 31.9s
4 J. P. Montoya (Williams) at 40.6s
5 R. Schumacher (Williams) at 41.7s
6 J. Button (Renault) at one lap
Championship: Schumacher 144, Barrichello 77, Montoya 50

2003 Japanese Grand Prix, Suzuka, 53 laps (191.1m/307.5km)
1 R. Barrichello (Ferrari) 1h 25m 11.7s (134.5mph/216.6kmh)
2 K. Räikkönen (McLaren) at 11.0s
3 D. Coulthard (McLaren) at 11.6s
4 J. Button (BAR) at 33.1s
5 J. Trulli (Renault) at 34.2s
6 T. Sato (BAR) at 51.6s
8 *M. Schumacher* (Ferrari)
Championship: Schumacher 93, Räikkönen 91, Montoya 82

2004 Belgian Grand Prix, Spa, 44 laps (190.7m/306.9km)
1 K. Räikkönen (McLaren) 1h 32m 35.2s (123.5mph/198.8kmh)
2 *M. Schumacher* (Ferrari) at 3.1s
3 R. Barrichello (Ferrari) at 4.3s
4 F. Massa (Sauber) at 12.5s
5 G. Fisichella (Sauber) at 14.1s
6 C. Klein (Jaguar) at 14.6s
Championship: Schumacher 148, Barrichello 114, Button 85

2005 Brazilian Grand Prix, Sao Paulo, 71 laps (190.0m/305.9km)
1 J. P. Montoya (McLaren) 1h 29m 20.5s (127.6mph/205.4kmh)
2 K. Räikkönen (McLaren) at 2.5s
3 *F. Alonso* (Renault) at 24.8s
4 M. Schumacher (Ferrari) at 35.6s
5 G. Fisichella (Renault) at 40.2s
6 R. Barrichello (Ferrari) at 1m 09.1s
Championship: Alonso 133, Räikkönen 112, Schumacher 62

2006 Brazilian Grand Prix, Sao Paulo, 71 laps (190.0m/305.9km)
1 F. Massa (Ferrari) 1h 31m 53.7s (124.1mph/199.7kmh)
2 *F. Alonso* (Renault) at 18.6s
3 J. Button (Honda) at 19.3s
4 M. Schumacher (Ferrari) at 24.0s
5 K. Räikkönen (McLaren) at 28.5s
6 G. Fisichella (Renault) at 30.2s
Championship: Alonso 134, Schumacher 121, Massa 80

2007 Brazilian Grand Prix, Sao Paulo, 71 laps (190.0m/305.9km)
1 *K. Räikkönen* (Ferrari) 1h 28m 15.2s (129.2mph/207.9kmh)
2 F. Massa (Ferrari) at 1.4s
3 F. Alonso (McLaren) at 57.0s
4 N. Rosberg (Williams) at 1m 02.8s
5 R. Kubica (Sauber) at 1m 10.9s
6 N. Heidfeld (Sauber) at 1m 11.3s
Championship: Räikkönen 110, Hamilton and Alonso 109

2008 Brazilian Grand Prix, Sao Paulo, 71 laps (190.0m/305.9km)
1 F. Massa (Ferrari) 1h 34m 11.4s (121.0mph/194.8kmh)
2 F. Alonso (Renault) at 13.2s
3 K. Räikkönen (Ferrari) at 16.2s
4 S. Vettel (Toro Rosso) at 38.0s
5 *L. Hamilton* (McLaren) at 38.9s
6 T. Glock (Toyota) at 44.3s
Championship: Hamilton 98, Massa 97, Räikkönen and Kubica 75

INDEX